Dirty Words & Filthy Pictures

Dirty Words & Filthy Pictures

FILM AND THE FIRST AMENDMENT

—

Jeremy Geltzer

FOREWORD BY ALEX KOZINSKI,
Chief Judge of the U.S. Court of Appeals
for the Ninth Circuit

UNIVERSITY OF TEXAS PRESS
AUSTIN

Requests for permission to reproduce material
from this work should be sent to:
Permissions
University of Texas Press
P.O. Box 7819
Austin, TX 78713-7819
http://utpress.utexas.edu/index.php/rp-form

The paper used in this book meets the minimum requirements
of ANSI/NISO Z39.48-1992 (R1997) (Permanence of Paper). ∞

Library of Congress Cataloging-in-Publication Data
Geltzer, Jeremy, 1969– author.
Dirty words & filthy pictures : film and the First Amendment /
Jeremy Geltzer. — First edition.
Pages   cm
Includes bibliographical references and index.
ISBN 978-1-4773-0740-3 (cloth : alk. paper) — ISBN 978-1-4773-0743-4 (pbk. : alk. paper) —
ISBN 978-1-4773-0741-0 (library e-book) — ISBN 978-1-4773-0742-7 (nonlibrary e-book)
1. Motion pictures—Censorship—United States. 2. Motion pictures—Law and legisla-
tion—United States. 3. Motion picture industry—Law and legislation—United States.
4. Motion pictures—History. 5. Freedom of speech—United States.
I. Title. II. Title: Dirty words and filthy pictures.
PN1995.62.G45 2015
363.310973—dc23
2015010217

doi:10.7560/307403

The censor's sword pierces deeply into
the heart of free expression.

CHIEF JUSTICE EARL WARREN,
Times Film Corp. v. City of Chicago,
1961

CONTENTS

———

ACKNOWLEDGMENTS

———

Dirty Words & Filthy Pictures is the result of a lifelong passion for film. My first memory of seeing a movie was slipping through the red-curtained entrance of the Regency Theater as Chaplin's *Modern Times* lit up the screen. During the great NYC blizzard of 1978, my family traipsed over snowdrifts to *The Man Who Would Be King* at the Thalia. We saw great films at historic theaters.

I'd like to express gratitude to the people who made this work possible. I could not have written the book without the encouragement and support of my wife, Heather, and son, Jackson. My family loves films and great writing— I received helpful opinions, advice, and reviews from Mom and Dad and Gabe.

Many thanks to Judge Alex Kozinski for penning the foreword and hosting excellent screenings at his Pasadena courthouse—he too is a true film lover. I have much appreciation for my editor, Jim Burr, as well as Abby Webber, Sarah Rosen, and Angie Lopez at University of Texas Press.

The book would not be as much fun without photos courtesy of Faye Thompson and Sue Gulden at the Margaret Herrick Library, Ed Frank and Christopher Ratcliff at the University of Memphis Library, Holly Wilson at the Temple University Library, Adam Grayson and Chris Gentile of Evil Angel Productions, John Schoenknecht and Elizabeth Engle of the Waukesha County Museum in Wisconsin, Rosemary Morrow at the *New York Times/ Redux Pictures*, and Angela Troisi at the *New York Daily News*.

FOREWORD

—

THE HONORABLE ALEX KOZINSKI

CHIEF JUDGE OF THE U.S. COURT OF APPEALS
FOR THE NINTH CIRCUIT

American democracy introduced a social experiment that permitted people—all people—to speak, criticize, complain, comment, raise new ideas, and persuade others. This broad freedom covers ideas wise and witless, protecting valuable insights along with notions that many find foolish or offensive. The freedom of speech is one of America's great contributions, and over the course of the twentieth century we can see that motion pictures track the development of First Amendment rights.

Arriving in America from Communist Romania at the age of twelve, I logged in hours of movies and media—more than the recommended dosage. Hollywood films were a primer on Americanism. As my tastes matured I discovered that movies could offer more. *Cabaret* brought vivid scenes of decadent Berlin to light. *Easy Rider* captured youth culture chafing against "the system." Even *Mad Max Beyond Thunderdome* could be seen to comment on judicial process. There was abundant schlock as well as movies with deeper meanings and worthwhile messages.

Jeremy Geltzer's *Dirty Words & Filthy Pictures* begins in an era when the country was more insular, at a time when state-run civic authorities held greater control over the intellectual lives of citizens. In the 1910s short films featuring dancing girls were seen as threats to the social order. Legal decisions of the time generally deferred to the moral custodians. Decades later a new generation of culture police attempted to banish European art films and exploitation B movies from the screen. But by the 1950s a broader construction of First Amendment rights had developed. The range of protected speech expanded, growing alongside technology. Over a century this development charted a course toward greater freedoms, and everyone is ultimately better off when the marketplace of ideas teems with new and innovative voices.

But there are limits, and this is where the courts become instrumental. In determining the constitutionality of a government restriction on speech, the state's interest in regulation is weighed against the value of the speech. It is reasonable to accord greater protection to a nude performer in *Hair* than to a topless dancer in a bar. Drawing legal and cultural lines, digging into the essence of a matter, and reinforcing or redirecting legal precedent are part of the elegance of the law.

Dirty Words & Filthy Pictures introduces a new perspective to film-legal history. That Geltzer is a lover of film is evident. His personal relationships with Golden Age movie icons helped inform behind-the-scenes descriptions. As a studio attorney he witnessed the guts of the dream machine. Together these insights generate a new kind of film history: instead of focusing on great films, directors, or stars, Geltzer chronicles what films *could* be made at certain points in history and shows us what was outside the realm that the authorities and courts were willing to accept.

Freedom of speech leads a precarious existence in the best of times. Most Americans consider themselves fortunate to live in a land of liberty where robust speech is allowed and encouraged even if it disturbs others. The freedoms contained in the First Amendment have paid extraordinary dividends for American society even beyond the role of shoring up democratic principles. The First Amendment and freedom of expression may be America's greatest contribution to the arts, and the movies may be the greatest American art form.

When I watch the early Edison-made films once pronounced controversial or offensive, I am amazed to see how much times have changed, for the better and perhaps not so better. Geltzer's entertaining history of American entertainment helps to track changing principles. What the state once banned as abhorrent may be embraced by a future generation as nostalgic. In the end, it is essential that current filmmakers and their legal counterparts continue to push the envelope to raise the free speech challenges of tomorrow.

Dirty Words & Filthy Pictures

INTRODUCTION

━━━

Can ogling a forbidden image sow the seeds of rebellion? Can a curse word be an act of defiance? Should there be *any* limit to creative expression on film? Audiences accustomed to horrific splatter violence, explicit sexual acrobatics, CGI explosions, or streams of profanity might not realize that not long ago a naughty word or risqué picture was thought to threaten the moral fabric of America. Rising from its roots as a nickelodeon attraction and sideshow amusement to its emergence as an art form and multibillion-dollar business, the American film industry has an alternative history. Court decisions and censorship codes influenced *what* movies could be financed and filmed and *which* pictures state censors, regional regulators, and municipal moral guardians had the power to suppress.

Dirty Words & Filthy Pictures: Film and the First Amendment is the story of the movies that entertained America, but it also presents the history of the motion pictures that expanded fundamental freedoms. In the beginning forbidden films focused on lewd dancers, boxers, and outlaws. By the 1920s the movies brought images of sex, drugs, and VD to neighborhood screens. The cinema could unspool shocking, scandalous, salacious, and often socially relevant stories. These controversial movies challenged a society still anchored in Victorian values, Christian morals, and "proper" modesty.

While movies provided cost-effective entertainment for the masses and a massive economic boom for well-positioned investors, the projected image came under fire almost immediately. As nickelodeon parlors opened their doors, censors sprang into action. Within a decade regulatory boards criss-crossed the country.

After Chicago enacted a film ordinance in 1907 and New York City threatened to shutter theaters in 1908, other cities fell in line. Beginning in 1915 film commissions opened in Atlantic City, Boston, Chattanooga, Dallas, Detroit, Duluth, Fort Worth, Indianapolis, Kansas City, Los Angeles, Memphis, Milwaukee, Nebraska City, Pasadena, Pittsburgh, Portland, Providence, San Francisco, Seattle, Spokane, St. Louis, Topeka, and Wichita. States added another layer of review: after the first laws were put in place in Pennsylvania and New York, codes were enacted in Alabama, Connecticut, Georgia, Indiana, Illinois, Iowa, Kansas, Maryland, Massachusetts, Minnesota, Missouri, Ohio, Oklahoma, Tennessee, Virginia, West Virginia, and Wisconsin. Some regions set up their own film czars; others relied on neighboring censors. Sacramento's film commission looked to Chicago; the state of Florida relied on the New York board of regents.[1] Additionally, in over fifty cities and townships censor boards operated sporadically, triggered when a picture aroused controversy elsewhere. Filmmakers in the young industry were faced with multiple layers of government approval as well as outspoken temperance unions and evangelical activists who also had strong ideas on what was to be permitted and prohibited.

The censors could be random and unpredictable. From topical newsreels to Revolutionary War stories, local laws threatened a national distribution network. Even family-friendly Walt Disney was not immune. *The Vanishing Prairie* (1954) was halted in New York for a scene depicting the birth of a buffalo. The state's film division issued a special exemption, and the Academy Award–winning documentary played on.[2]

For filmmakers, financiers, audiences, and moral authorities the key question was, where is the line that divides free speech from forbidden films? After watching Shirley Temple in *Honeymoon* (1947), Baltimore censor Helen Tingley commented, "We can reject pictures that are sacrilegious, obscene, indecent, immoral or inhuman. Too bad we can't bar this little gem for inhumanity . . . to the audience."[3] Could a censor ban a film simply because she didn't like it? "'I'd like to scream after [watching] a whole day of B-pictures,' Mrs. Tingley continued, 'and I frequently do.'" Another censor, when asked about his method of review, merely replied, "It's just our own opinion."[4] Personal preference seemed to be the guiding force for the most powerful censors during Hollywood's Golden Age.

Just as *The Birth of a Nation*, *The Jazz Singer*, and *Citizen Kane* define eras in American cinema, film-legal history has its own benchmarks. In 1915 the *Mutual* decision excluded motion pictures from constitutional protection, allowing censors to trim, edit, cut, and ban as they saw fit. The *Miracle* decision shifted the balance of power in 1948. But freedom of the screen was a hard fought battle. A series of cases won a bit more ground for free expression; these decisions stand as important but overlooked markers: *Superior*, *Excelsior*, *Kingsley*, and *Freeman*.

In addition to the pictures and the cases, the history of cinema and censorship also shines a spotlight on the colorful, controversial, and often forgotten characters who changed the course of American film. From the tragic Robert Goldstein, whose *Spirit of '76* was branded treasonous propaganda, to the triumphant Ephraim London, an attorney who tirelessly crusaded for free speech. From the firebrand censors, such as Major M. L. C. Funkhouser and Lloyd T. Binford, to the uncompromising filmmakers who pushed the envelope, such as Howard Hughes and Otto Preminger.

Hollywood studios opted for self-censoring solutions that minimized risk, so the battle for creative freedom was mostly left to independent filmmakers. Highbrow European art films and low-budget grindhouse exploitation flicks occupy key positions in the story of film and the First Amendment. *The Miracle*, *Mom and Dad*, and *Garden of Eden* may not be as familiar as the canon of classic movies, but these were the films that furthered the medium. As the limits of the permissible gained ground, many of the fights were not glamorous. Roger Diamond, an attorney who represented a fetish pornographer, commented that his client's films "were so disgusting I couldn't even watch them. . . . But that doesn't mean they're not free speech."[5]

What began with the hand-cranked images of a kissing couple, striptease shows, and boxing bouts grew into outrageous displays of sexual acrobatics, eye-popping violence, and animal cruelty. Through much of the century state regulations held motion pictures to strict standards that forced filmmakers to find creative solutions. Without these limitations Golden Age Hollywood could not have developed; however, filmmakers also pushed legal authorities to reevaluate and reconsider what should be deemed constitutionally protected speech. The underlying question remains relevant: in what situations should the state use its power to limit the freedom of expression? *Dirty Words & Filthy Pictures* is the story of the movies that expanded personal rights and furthered free expression.

PART I

Censoring the Cinema

The John C. Rice–May Irwin Kiss (1896).

1

BOXING, PORN, AND THE BEGINNINGS
OF MOVIE CENSORSHIP

—

Where many stories end is where film and the First Amendment begins: with a kiss. Produced by the Edison Manufacturing Co., *The Kiss* was one of the first motion pictures commercially available in America.

Edison's forty-seven-second featurette, formally entitled *The John C. Rice–May Irwin Kiss* (1896), captured a pivotal moment in cinema history and American culture. The short film depicted a climactic scene from a popular stage play featuring Rice and Irwin entitled *The Widow Jones*. While the promotional picture was notable as the first on-screen lip-lock, *The Kiss* also had far-reaching consequences.

Since the mid-1880s May Irwin (1862–1938) had been a well-regarded performer on the vaudeville circuit. In 1893 she began working with playwright John J. McNally. Two years later *The Widow Jones* was their breakthrough, premiering at the Bijou Theatre on Broadway. The play centered on a woman who avoided romantic relationships by pretending to be in mourning. In a key scene Irwin belted out a ragtime song, "I'm Looking for de Bully," and finished by lingering on the puckered lips of John Rice. This kiss punctuated the show-stopping number and brought down the house.[1]

A sensation in its day, *The Kiss* does not survive as titillating material. There would have been little controversy surrounding the tableaux had Thomas Edison's Kinetograph not focused on the scene. It was one thing to view a kiss on the stage from a distance, but audiences were shocked by the intimacy of seeing a lip-lock in close-up, flickering through a peephole projector. One contemporary reviewer noted, "The spectacle of the prolonged pasturing on each other's lips was hard to bear. When only life size it was pronouncedly beastly. Magnified to Gargantuan proportions and repeated three times over, it is absolutely disgusting."[2]

The film presented the actors in close-up, which was a technical innovation for early filmmaking. The scene was repeated to fill out the running time and provide a solid nickel's worth of entertainment. Anticipation built in the opening seconds. The actors giggled, cooed, and flirted. Then Rice pulled away, nervously twirled his mustache, and moved in to plant one on Irwin. The effect was more amusing than amorous; yet the film represented a watershed moment because *The Kiss* broke the cultural code of acceptable public behavior shaped by Christian values and Victorian mores.

For fifty years prior to *The Kiss* proper manners and conduct had been based on Victorian morality. Privacy was valued, and sexual restraint was the rule. Motion pictures became a target in an ideological battle for the minds and morals of cinema spectators for several reasons. First, film threatened the private sphere valued by Victorians. *The Kiss* shattered that prudish etiquette. The magnification of intimate details and the projection of personal moments replaced traditionally accepted behavior with mass media voyeurism. A second issue was the new environment: movie theaters and nickelodeon parlors mixed male and female audiences, immigrant and native born, young and old, bourgeois and blue collar. The picture shows assimilated classes in close proximity, mingling the diverse groups unsupervised in a darkened theater. Third, the plots and themes of many movies mocked traditional values and figures of authority—silly policemen, bathing beauties, and daring criminals were staples on-screen. The scene was set for a culture war pitting the old ways against the new cinema-shaped society.

The cinema of the 1890s was produced, or rather manufactured, under a different division of labor. Before the compartmentalization of writers, directors, and cinematographers, the first filmmakers had been technicians. Thomas Edison claimed credit for inventing motion pictures in America, but the Wizard of Menlo Park employed a stable of research and development engineers to fine-tune the details of his devices. Edison housed the project managers for his film venture in a workshop in West Orange, New Jersey.

This first movie studio was a windowless workspace with a retractable roof that allowed sunlight for filming. It was called the Black Maria. The Edison production facility, a literal film *factory*, was operational by 1893. Without overstating the authorship of early one-shot films, it is interesting to note that a single technician was behind the camera for several controversial reels. William Heise (1847–1910) was a machinist-engineer-technician-filmmaker with Edison's motion picture unit from its earliest days in 1890.[3] In one of the first test films, *The Dickson Greeting* (1891), Heise rolled film on the more generally acknowledged motion picture pioneer W. K. L. Dickson (1860–1935). It is Heise who serves as the connective tissue between three early controversial pictures. Heise was credited as the director and cinematographer for *The Kiss* as well as two other provocative pictures: *Fatima's Coochie-Coochie Dance* and *Dolorita's Passion Dance*.

At the 1893 Chicago World's Fair a dancer on the "Streets of Cairo" stage named Farida Mazar Spyropoulos introduced American audiences to Egyptian belly dancing. Her gyrating performance competed with Buffalo Bill's Wild West Show for the most popular attraction at the expo, and Edison's camera rolled on both. While audiences raved about *Fatima's Coochie-Coochie Dance* (1896), Farida's show also provoked condemnation and complaint: one observer fumed that her performance was "immodest to the point of indecency." Another wrote, "This dance shows strange skill in the manipulation in all the muscles of the body, but its description does not come within the bounds of propriety."[4] What distinguished *Coochie-Coochie Dance* from other Edison-produced dance films of the period, such as *Annabelle's Butterfly Dance* (1894), *Carmencita's Dance* (1894), and *Lola Yberri's Fan Dance* (1895), is that *Coochie-Coochie Dance* was censored by Edison. In this first instance of self-censorship, the picture was offered to exhibitors in an explicit or clean version in which the dancer's gyrating pelvis was covered up by a grid-like white picket fence of hatching.

Released the following year, Edison's film of a dancer named Dolorita took the erotic display one step too far for a society still entrenched in Victorian manners. Even though she remained clothed, the dancer's movements overpowered the limits of cultural acceptability. *Dolorita's Passion Dance* (1897) was a racy spectacle that attracted nickel-plugging customers. The long lines and enthusiastic word of mouth came to the attention of New Jersey authorities. Police raided an Atlantic City parlor, and mayor Franklin Pierce Stoy prohibited *Passion Dance*, assuring the little film a place in history as the first motion picture to be banned in the United States. Still, by the time the mayor's order was issued, *Passion Dance* had become the most viewed Kinetograph picture the parlor had ever hosted.[5]

Annabelle's Butterfly Dance (1894).

William Heise's risqué one-reelers proved to be popular at the growing number of neighborhood nickelodeons. As these cinematic public displays of affection and female bodies in motion challenged the code of Victorian values, a hidden history was simultaneously occurring. *The Kiss*, *Passion Dance*, and *Coochie-Coochie Dance* may have raised eyebrows at mainstream parlors, but in the back rooms a far steamier event was unspooling. Imported from Europe, the pornographic pictures of a forgotten film pioneer further eroded the division between the public and the private spheres.

Based in France, Eugène Pirou (1841–1909) built his reputation as a portrait photographer during the 1870s. In the shadow of the newly constructed Eiffel Tower at the Paris Exposition of 1889, Pirou watched as Étienne-Jules Marey displayed his chronophotography device. He was intrigued by the new motion picture technology. When the Lumière brothers debuted their *cinématographe* on December 28, 1896, Pirou was not far behind. Within four months Pirou introduced his own motion picture apparatus, becoming one of the earliest rivals to the frères Lumière.[6]

As a still photographer, Pirou shot notorious and celebrity subjects. He was known for his gruesome images of slain Communards on the Paris streets after the "Bloody Week" of 1871 as well as his portraits of Gustave Eiffel, Buffalo Bill, and the early flamboyant days of Czar Nicholas II. A precursor to the paparazzi, Pirou was the self-styled *photographe des rois*. He also had a penchant for risqué *cartes postales*, or "French postcards." It is through trading these images that Pirou met Albert Kirchner and engaged Kirchner for technical support on a motion picture. Under the alias "Léar," Kirchner directed the pioneering porno film *Le coucher de la mariée* (*Bedtime for the Bride*, 1896).

Le coucher de la mariée captured Louise Willy's burlesque act, a titillating routine she performed in a long-running stage show. In one popular sketch Willy stripped out of her gown and corset—showing bare shoulder and ankle—pulled on a nightgown, and got into bed. The act was a must-see because Willy did not wear a *maillot de corps* (body stocking).[7] The picture's Paris premiere was such a success that it led to the creation of a new genre, the "risqué film," and inspired other pioneering picture makers to film women taking off their clothes.

There is an ironic postscript to the tale of the first truly erotic motion picture. The following year Léar was commissioned by a cinema-savvy priest named Father Bazile and the Catholic publishing company Maison de la Bonne Presse to produce a twelve-scene version of the *Passion du Christ* (1897). The association between priest and pornographer appears to be a bizarre alliance; however, Léar was an early freelancer, a technical hand hired to produce films for his employers, whether they were interested in sacred subjects or profane pictures. By the turn of the century, Pirou and Léar's erotic pictures disappeared altogether from history—or more likely went underground.

Eager to cash in on the lucrative genre, other filmmaking pioneers put out risqué films. Before his *Trip to the Moon*, Georges Méliès contributed *Après le bal* (1897). Several of Pathé's early erotic pictures followed a mischievous man in hotels and apartment corridors as he peered through keyholes to reveal private moments. In Ferdinand Zecca's *Ce que l'on voit de mon sixième* (1901) a man on a balcony focused his telescope to reveal iris-masked images of a couple kissing and a woman undressing. Early cinema subjects thrived on prying open private spaces to expose once-forbidden moments on-screen.

While risqué films were popular among nickel-holding patrons of film parlors, the cinematic assault on Christian principles and Victorian values was not welcomed in all quarters. Protectors of mainstream morality fought back.

In 1897 a play staged in New York entitled *Orange Blossoms* triggered legal response. *People v. Doris* held that "the public exhibition of a pantomime representing the retiring of a husband and wife on their wedding night, [was] indictable as outraging public decency and injurious to public morals."[8] *Orange Blossoms* was not a motion picture, but the holding would affect the limits of permissible display.

Georges Méliès's risqué film *Après le bal* (1897).

Violent content came simultaneously with sex films. To civic authorities, battling boxers were just as offensive as risqué films and posed yet another challenge to morality. While Edison's film factory manufactured hundreds of shorts between 1894 and 1899, some of the most financially successful subjects were prizefighting pictures. Interest in boxing was evident from the earliest days of motion picture making. Dickson and Heise produced a test shot of *Men Boxing* in 1891. The film showed two amateur pugilists in puffy boxing gloves squaring off in a makeshift ring. On the right side of the frame Dickson is seen on the defensive against his sparring partner, Heise.

The prizefighting genre began in earnest with Edison's *Leonard-Cushing Fight* (1894). This motion picture captured a six-round bout between light-weight boxers Michael Leonard (the "Fashion Plate" of pugilism) and Jack Cushing. Rather than filming the actual fight, Dickson hired the professional pugilists to reenact the match before a studio audience. The fistic sport squared perfectly with technological limitations: the static camera captured action unfolding in a fixed space during a two-minute round; also, the multiple rounds kept viewers feeding their coins into the peephole viewing devices.

When *The Leonard-Cushing Fight* opened at the Kinetoscope Exhibiting Company's New York parlor in August 1894 the picture drew enough patrons that police were called to keep order.[9] *Leonard-Cushing* was not a main event, but the fight between two second-rate boxers proved popular. Edison's company hit a box office bonanza with its next boxing title. *Corbett and Courtney Before the Kinetograph* (1894) featured heavyweight champion James J. "Gentleman Jim" Corbett sparring against Peter Courtney. Corbett toyed with his opponent for five rounds—long enough for a feature presentation—before he KO'd the challenger in the sixth.[10] *The Leonard-Cushing Fight* and *Corbett and Courtney* were among the most profitable films released by Edison's motion picture unit, the latter earning Corbett up to $20,000 in royalties.[11]

But there were signs of trouble. The day after Corbett and Courtney's performance a grand jury was convened. Judge David A. Depue of the circuit court of New Jersey announced that "prize fighting of all kinds, even gloved contests and stage exhibitions" would be banned in the state.[12]

Edison's boxing films established a lucrative market, but the Kinetoscope was still a peephole device. To watch the rounds audiences had to queue up and peer into the device's viewfinder. It was up to one of Edison's licensed distributors to focus on the next issues critical to motion picture exhibition: longer films and projection of the image.

As the Edison Company prepared to bring its first Kinetograph films to market in 1894, the film manufacturer licensed several entities to distribute and exhibit moving pictures. The Latham brothers, Grey (1867–1907) and

Film-pioneering pugilists W. K. L. Dickson (right) and
William Heise (left) in *Men Boxing* (1891).

Corbett and Courtney before the Kinetograph (1894).

Otway (1868–1906), were among these first distributors. Along with their father, Major Woodville Latham (1837–1911), a former ordinance officer in the Confederate army, the brothers formed the Lambda Company. Adding to their staff were ex-Edison personnel poached from the Black Maria, including chief engineer Dickson.[13]

From the start Lambda was interested in more than the distribution of motion picture product. Lambda focused on maximizing profits with several innovations. First, the Lathams reduced and standardized film speed to thirty frames per second, which increased the running time of a reel. Woodville arrived at a second solution for manufacturing longer-running films: the Latham loop. The Latham loop was a slackened section in the camera and projector that isolated the filmstrip from vibration and tension as it moved through the apparatus. This simple innovation allowed for longer scenes without compromising the filmstrip. A third innovation to emerge from Lambda's labs focused on the problem of projection. Projecting the moving image would ease the issue of long lines at the peephole as well as serve as a cost-effective method of delivering entertainment to growing audiences. A by-product of this new approach would change the nature of spectatorship, creating a communal atmosphere in the nickelodeons and introducing the "filmgoing experience."

Lambda's films boasted longer running times and a unique experience. Within a year of distributing Edison's Kinetograph peepshows, the Lathams premiered their own production: *Young Griffo v. "Battling" Charles Barnett* (1895). Albert "Young Griffo" Griffiths was the Australian world feather-weight champion. On May 4, 1895, he faced "Battling" Barnett at Madison Square Garden for four rounds before knocking Barnett out. The two pugilists reconvened several weeks later to reenact the fight in front of the Lathams' camera.[14] The circle was squared: the Lathams found the winning formula when they presented celebrity boxers in multiple rounds projected on a screen to a paying audience. Of course, this newly created popular pastime did not escape the attention of Christian moralists, arbiters of Victorian values, and the champions of the status quo.

The success of prizefighting films reached new heights with *The Corbett-Fitzsimmons Fight* (1897). For this battle the Veriscope Company developed a proprietary widescreen motion picture technology for an epic eleven-reel feature. Heavyweight champion "Gentleman Jim" was paired with Robert "Lanky Bob" Fitzsimmons. The prefight drama was tense. Two years before the fighters faced off, Fitzsimmons had pummeled Cornelius "Con" Riordan to death in the ring.[15] A grand jury indicted Fitzsimmons, but the pugilist was found not guilty.[16] Cleared of charges, Fitzsimmons was eager to fight Corbett. Corbett, who would be defending his championship belt, was less keen. Increasing the drama, Corbett delayed the bout by voicing his concerns about the technology. After the ruse had been resolved, the fight was set to proceed.[17]

But there was another obstacle: the antiprizefighting laws in place across the country. Anticipation of the Corbett-Fitzsimmons fight had led many states, including Arkansas, Georgia, Massachusetts, New York, and Texas, to enact prizefighting laws. The *New York Times* lamented, "Not likely that Fitzsimmons and Corbett will meet anywhere."[18] The fight was in jeopardy; Veriscope even considered taking the bout to Mexico until promoter Dan Stuart lobbied Nevada to repeal its prizefighting ordinance.[19] Stuart convinced officials the Corbett-Fitzsimmons fight would boost the state's economy; the state representatives agreed to host the bout "provided that the revenue to be derived by the state was sufficient and a price was fixed."[20] In a decision that left many civic and religious leaders agog, prizefighting was legalized in Nevada on January 16, 1897.[21]

On March 17, 1897, Corbett and Fitzsimmons met in Carson City, Nevada. Veriscope cameras were rolling. Fourteen thrilling rounds later Fitz KO'd Gentleman Jim.

The fight was only seen live by a select group. Around the nation audiences eagerly awaited scenes of the fistic ballet.[22] While many states prohibited prizefighting, the laws did not forbid exhibition of prizefighting pictures—Veriscope planned to turn a profit not from the fight itself but from distribution of the films. In 1896 President Grover Cleveland signed the Catron Anti-Prizefighting Bill, which banned pugilistic encounters in the District of Columbia and Indian Territories, but the legislation excluded fight films.[23] Within days of the Corbett-Fitzsimmons event, new federal antiprizefighting legislation was proposed. In addition to prohibiting the actual battles, the new bill would censure fight films, prohibiting exhibition "by kinetoscope or kindred devices."[24] The revised bill did not pass the Senate committee.

Prohibition of fight films would be addressed on the state level. By March 1897 Maine blocked pugilistic pictures: "Any Person exhibiting publicly any photographic or other reproduction of prize fights shall be punished by a fine

The Corbett-Fitzsimmons Fight (1897).

Stadium under construction for the Corbett-Fitzsimmons fight (1897).

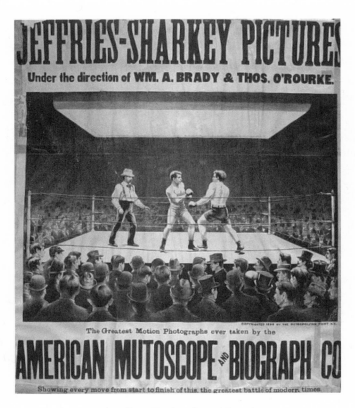

The Jeffries-Sharkey Contest (1899).

not exceeding five hundred dollars."[25] Maine's statute was the first legislative act of movie censorship in the United States. Within months Illinois, Minnesota, Massachusetts, New Jersey, New York, and Pennsylvania enacted similar ordinances.[26]

Despite municipal regulations on the books, *The Corbett-Fitzsimmons Fight* premiered on May 22, 1897, to a packed house at the Academy of Music in New York.[27] While laws prohibited prizefighting films, the regulations seem to have rarely been effectively enforced. In the absence of enforcement the genre grew rapidly.

Fledgling film producers were drawn to fight films. Philadelphia-based Siegmund Lubin (1851–1923) established himself as the "Duping King," pioneering film piracy. Shortly after *Corbett-Fitzsimmons* proved to be a draw, Lubin issued the duped *Reproduction of the Corbett and Fitzsimmons Fight* (1897). Vitagraph filmed the next heavyweight championship bout, *The Fitzsimmons-Jeffries Fight* (1899), only to compete with Lubin's lavishly titled *Reproduction of the Fitzsimmons-Jeffries Fight in Eleven Rounds Showing the Knockout* (1899). Lubin soon churned out original titles from his Lubinville studio, including *Reproduction of the Jeffries and Sharkey Fight* (1899), *Reproduction of the Sharkey and Fitzsimmons Fight* (1900), and *Reproduction of the Jeffries-Corbett Fight* (1903).

Lubin wasn't the only producer of fistic ballets. American Mutoscope and Biograph entered the game with original titles such as *Jeffries-Sharkey Contest* (1899) and *Jeffries Boxing with Tommy Ryan* (1899) and with dupes such as *Reproduction of Corbett-McGovern Fight* (1903). Selig Polyscope Company issued *The Gans-McGovern Fight* (1901) and *The Gans-Nelson Fight* (1903). Clearly the laws on the books had little effect on billings at the box office. The need to control content intensified, and tougher enforcement was on the horizon.

2

THE RISE OF SALACIOUS CINEMA

—

By 1899 conservative-minded folk felt threatened by the popularity of penny arcade presentations, believing the new technology violated decorum. This moral majority exercised considerable force, pressuring elected officials to establish and enforce mechanisms of film regulation. But by the first decade of the twentieth century the film industry was already difficult to control. Besides fistic films, off-color comedies and risqué pictures continued to pack storefront nickelodeons despite content regulations. New York authorities led by antivice crusader Anthony Comstock raided picture parlors as early as 1900, but the situation had already progressed beyond their control.[1] By 1904 it was common to see glimpses of ankles, prolonged embraces, kissing, and women disrobing on-screen. In Biograph's *A Busy Day for the Corset Models*, Pathé's *Ladies of the Court Bathing*, and Lubin's *Beauty Bathing*, all from 1904, women were seen in their bloomers, undergarments, and less. Pressure was building for censors to assert a greater role, but it would take a triggering event to galvanize the regulators.

That triggering event was the first modern celebrity scandal: the Thaw-White affair. The event was a perfect storm: a sordid sex scandal involving a deranged socialite, a decadent and extravagantly wealthy two-timing letch, a beautiful underage victim, a cold-blooded murder, and a high-profile trial. With a single sensational event, Thaw-White set off a media frenzy that inaugurated the modern era of tabloid journalism.

Harry K. Thaw (1871–1947) was a fixture on New York's high-society party scene. He lived off a trust fund left by his father, a captain of industry who had helped build the infrastructure of America in banking and railroads. In 1905 Harry married twenty-one-year-old Evelyn Nesbit (1884–1967). Nesbit had gained a measure of notoriety for her nude modeling before joining the chorus of the *Florodora* show on Broadway. On the evening of June 25, 1906, Harry took Evelyn to a show playing at Madison Square Garden's rooftop restaurant. A few rows separated them from celebrity architect Stanford White. During the final musical number Thaw stood up, walked over to White, and shot him dead at point-blank range. Adding to the surreal moment, eyewitnesses reported that the stage manager leapt on a table, directing the show to continue and shouting, "Go on playing! Bring on that chorus."[2]

White had designed such New York landmarks as Penn Station, the arch in Washington Square Park, and Madison Square Garden, which would be the scene of his murder. A married family man, White also kept a secret sex den. Six years prior to the fatal encounter, he had spent an illicit evening with Evelyn, then an unmarried sixteen-year-old showgirl. The details of their debauched night were outrageous. White had brought the girl to his playpen gilded with mirrored ceilings, upholstered walls, and a red velvet swing where the lovers frolicked. After a bottle of wine, White allegedly raped the teen.[3] Years later, as Harry Thaw shot the lothario, he shouted, "He ruined my wife!"[4]

The press devoured the story and its most salacious elements. Broadway promoters the Mittenthal brothers staged *A Millionaire's Revenge* with amazing speed. The show premiered in November 1906, just four months after the incident.[5] Biograph capitalized on the motion picture market, releasing two dramas within months of the crime: *The Thaw-White Tragedy* (1906) and its sequel, *In the Tombs* (1906).

Thaw's trial played out in the courtroom and in the press. Alienists debated the socialite's sanity. The case reached a fevered pitch as defense attorney Delphin M. Delmas introduced a novel legal theory he called "dementia Americana." "It is a species of insanity," Delmas argued, "which makes every American believe that his home is sacred . . . that the honor of his wife is sacred."[6] Under this argument Thaw had acted within his rights because the God-given, unwritten law protected the purity of homes. Delmas urged for his client to be cleared of all charges. With the jury unable to reach a verdict, a mistrial was declared on April 13, 1907.[7] Lubin anticipated the result, timing the release of *The Unwritten Law: A Thrilling Drama Based on the Thaw-White Case* (1907) nearly simultaneously with the breaking story.[8]

Lubin's *Unwritten Law* showed Evelyn visiting White's lavish apartment, drinking wine, swooning, and disappearing behind a Chinese screen for the ultimate scene. The decadence, the perverse lifestyle of the rich and famous, and the suggestion of sex and violence fascinated audiences and scandalized authorities.

Despite the salacious material—or because of it—Lubin's picture was a hit, selling over one thousand units at the premium price of $104 per reel.[9] A police inspector stopped the show at a Minneapolis screening, calling the picture "mind poisoning."[10] In Houston an audience of several hundred spectators watched as authorities intervened; even after the theater offered to cut the mirrored bedroom scene, the film was not permitted.[11] A Wisconsin theater was packed with an audience "two thirds women, and as the first pictures were thrown upon the screen depicting an artist's studio the interest was intense. The exhibition got no further, however, for at this point the chief of police walked upon the stage and dramatically stopped the show."[12] In New York an exhibitor was charged with impairing the morals of children and fined one hundred dollars.[13] Lubin's film succeeded too well: *The Unwritten Law* became a lightning rod for developing regulatory concerns surrounding moving pictures.

A flashback sequence in Lubin's *The Unwritten Law: A Thrilling Drama Based on the Thaw-White Tragedy* (1907) in which the prisoner lying on his cot recalls the fatal shot.

Evelyn Nesbit (1884–1967). From the collections of the Margaret Herrick
Library, Academy of Motion Picture Arts and Sciences.

The Unwritten Law was singled out by censors and gave momentum to the growing campaign against the detrimental effects of nickelodeons. The *Chicago Tribune* was one of the strongest voices advocating that "the city has a right to exercise its police power in censoring immoral pictures."[14] Within months of *The Unwritten Law*'s Chicago premiere, Chicago's aldermen passed a film censorship ordinance. On November 4, 1907, the Second City became the country's first to systematically censor motion pictures.[15]

Like many celebrity scandals, Thaw-White remained in the news. In 1908 Thaw was found not guilty by reason of insanity and committed to an asylum. He made headlines again when he escaped in 1913.[16] The tabloids screamed, "Thaw's Escape Last of Series of Sensations" and "With the escape of Thaw the scandal is complete. The public needs no more proof that the murderer with money is safe."[17] The new incident became fodder for more films: IMP's *Escaped from the Asylum* (1913) and Canadian-American Feature Film Company's *Harry K. Thaw's Fight for Freedom* (1913).

Evelyn Nesbit parlayed her own sudden celebrity into a fifteen-year film career prefiguring reality TV stardom by a century. Nesbit appeared in several pictures, often with her son, Russell, that capitalized on the family's notoriety, including *Threads of Destiny* (1914) for Lubin and *Thou Shalt Not* (1919) for Fox. Her career ran its course. In 1918 the *New York Times* reviewed her film *I Want to Forget*, writing, "So do we."[18] From supermodel to star witness to movie starlet, Evelyn Nesbit had been a pop culture phenomenon. By the roaring twenties she was a footnote.

A celebrity scandal teeming with salacious details and a cold-blooded murder helped elevate the Thaw-White affair into a media firestorm. Frenzied coverage of the event, its aftermath, and the continuing popularity of its key figures played an important role that roused the machinery of censorship into action. In order to maintain the status quo anchored by Christian morality and Victorian values, civic activists recognized that popular culture's fascination with crime and decadence had to be controlled.

3

STATE REGULATIONS EMERGE

—

Within six months of Lubin's film adaptation of the Thaw-White scandal in *The Unwritten Law*, municipal authorities stepped up their efforts to censor motion pictures. Responding to moral reformers and the local press, Chicago's city council ratified regulations that Mayor Fred A. Busse quickly signed into law. On November 19, 1907, Chicago's "Ordinance Prohibiting the Exhibition of Obscene and Immoral Pictures and Regulating the Exhibition of Pictures of the Classes and Kinds Commonly Shown in Mutoscopes, Kinetoscopes, Cinematographs and Penny Arcades" became effective.[1] Ellis Oberholtzer, a contemporary activist based in Pennsylvania, commended the Windy City in his book *The Morals of the Movie*.[2]

The effect of Chicago's ordinance resonated. This law was not a repetition of the laissez-faire approach of the antiboxing statutes but a move toward strict enforcement. With a name to fit the role of a modern praetorian, Major Metellus Lucullus Cicero Funkhouser (1864–1926) emerged as Chicago's appointed "guardian of public morals" in March 1913.[3]

Funkhouser was an eager and enthusiastic censor. The *Moving Picture World* reported that Funkhouser "says his hands are full trying to live up to his principles of forbidding all plays exploiting crime, showing degradation of women, making a hero of a criminal, or ridiculing authority."[4] Within a year his style proved too ambitious. The trade journal commented that the major "has got himself into hot water recently because he has presumed to cut films based on the stories of Dickens, Hawthorne, etc. . . . On Oct. 14 [1914] a part of the film showing Martin Chuzzlewit was cut out. . . . [U]p until [now] nobody ever ventured an opinion that Charles Dickens was a corrupter of morals."[5] Funkhouser was lampooned in Nestor Films' *Pruning the Movies* (1915), in which a character named Major Bughouser was portrayed as an excitable official who demanded ridiculous cuts to the film within the film: "The scenes are shown as originally produced [and] as they appear when the Bughouser Board is through with them. . . . The last scene shows the gallant Major filling up on his usual favorite food—a large dish of prunes."[6] The pun may not seem as fresh a century later (pruning the pictures, eating prunes), but the film's satirical intent to lampoon authority remains clear.

The following year *Photoplay* magazine published an article entitled "Censorship vs. Regulation." The story recognized that Funkhouser had "become nationally known as the extreme type of police censor." The article presented two perspectives on the issue. Speaking against regulation was Lucien Cary, editor of the liberal-leaning magazine *The Dial*. Giving voice to the other side was Funkhouser himself. Funkhouser's op-ed lectured on the historical importance of censorship in maintaining societal norms. He also confided, "When I became censor in Chicago I found very little to guide me in the laws of Illinois and the ordinances of Chicago; the office was too new." Funkhouser's methodology was based on personal taste—the very essence of arbitrary censorship. "We have cut a good many miles of films—scenes obscene, scenes of the nude, scenes of ugly violence, scenes reflecting on constituted authority—because we thought they were unsuitable to present before audiences, 80 per cent of whom are women and children."[7]

Since Chicago was the nation's second largest market, film industry executives and financiers took notice when Funkhouser suppressed material. Indeed, by banning films that demonstrated dances such as the turkey trot and the tango,[8] Funkhouser embodied a capricious censor. With regard to the dance moves, he commented, "The objection is not based so much upon these pictures in themselves, but upon the effect they would have on thousands of young people. . . . [T]hat is where the danger is."[9] By 1917 civic authorities began to question Funkhouser's aggressive censoring.[10]

Funkhouser's unpredictable bans would be his downfall. In April 1918 the major brought his family to the Art Institute of Chicago. As they arrived Funkhouser espied a seven-foot bronze of a nude male that stood at the museum's entrance. Within moments he ordered the statue removed. When the

Chicago censor Maj. M. L. C. Funkhouser, in the
Chicago Daily News, July 5, 1916.

massive figure could not be budged, the censor had it draped.[11] Two months later Funkhouser was removed from his post. *Variety* reported, "The firing of Funkhouser brings great joy to the men of the picture business. For his absurd censorship of pictures, Funkhouser had achieved national notoriety. His name had become synonymous with narrow-minded, carping criticism and deletion."[12]

Funkhouser had been an influential figure in the story of film and the First Amendment, holding his post as Chicago's movie censor from 1913 until 1918. The sculpture, *The Sower*, was draped in storage for eighty years until its rediscovery in June 2005.

The next scene in the drama of cinema and censorship was New York City. The New York–New Jersey area had been the birthplace of American cinema. The Edison Company outgrew its first film factory, the Black Maria, in 1901 and moved to a glass-enclosed rooftop facility at Oliver Place and Decatur Avenue in the Bronx, also operating a second stage at 41 East Twenty-First Street in Manhattan. Several competitors were located in and around New York, including Biograph on Fourteenth Street in Manhattan and Vitagraph on Avenue M in Brooklyn. Slightly farther afield, Thanhouser built a production house in New Rochelle, Éclair in Fort Lee, Pathé in Jersey City, and Nestor in Bayonne. In addition to production facilities, exhibition also grew quickly in the region. Storefront screening rooms, nickelodeons, and penny arcades radiated from the central hub of Times Square. By 1907 the *New York Times* estimated that five hundred nickelodeons and moving picture emporiums were operating in the city.[13] Civic authorities were wary. In March 1907 at least forty parlors were cited and shuttered for noncompliance with electricity permits.[14] Despite the city's efforts, film was becoming a cultural force, generating substantial revenues and exerting significant influence over a growing audience.

Less than a month after Chicago passed its film ordinance, New York increased film regulation. Enforcing blue laws, police commissioner Theodore Bingham ordered all theaters to be shuttered on Sundays.[15] Vaudeville and legitimate stages were subject to the regulation, but nickelodeon owner William Fox petitioned for an injunction for picture parlors. Fox prevailed— the fifty-year-old blue law that regulated "public entertainment on a stage" would not be applied to movie houses.[16] Within months vaudeville stages across the city converted to motion picture theaters. It was a simple business decision: by switching to filmed entertainment the venues could remain open for business on Sunday. As the movie boom accelerated in New York—in part due to the city's own actions—the desire to inspect and regulate motion pictures intensified.

Like Chicago, with its Maj. Funkhouser, New York had its own version of an enthusiastic municipal enforcer: Mayor George McClellan Jr. The son of a Civil War major general, McClellan is perhaps best remembered for opening the IRT subway lines. He is notable in the history of cinema and censorship for his attempt to shut down all New York nickelodeons.

In 1908 McClellan received a report from Commissioner Bingham that condemned several hastily built movie houses and noted the questionable content of exhibitions. On Christmas Eve 1908 McClellan revoked licenses to over five hundred movie houses. On the night before Christmas, all through the town, motion picture parlors were served with notices to quit. The reason given was poor safety conditions. "I am informed that the inspections in regard to the fire exits have been inadequate," read the mayor's statement. "As these licenses for moving-picture shows are issued by me, I feel personally responsible for the safety and lives of the patrons, and take this action on personal knowledge of existing conditions and the firm conviction that I am averting a public calamity."[17] The statement was a ploy; while safety was an issue, the underlying concern was over both the darkened auditoriums that could breed moral corruption and the unapproved content of films.

Mayor George B. McClellan Jr. (1865–1940), from
World's Work, December 1903.

Leading the opposition once again was pugnacious independent exhibitor William Fox. Fox appealed to judge William Jay Gaynor (1849–1913) to enjoin the mayor's order.[18] In a decision that no doubt brought him popular support among the moviegoing public, Gaynor issued the injunction.[19] New York's nickelodeons stayed open that Christmas.[20] With the endorsement of the city's Moving Picture Exhibitors' Association, the following year Gaynor won the mayoral seat and replaced McClellan.[21]

Aside from the short-term victory that kept the doors open and the reels unspooling that Christmas, producers, distributors, and exhibitors began to develop a strategy to address censorship in the longer term. To oppose state censorship industry leaders opted for a system of self-regulation. The Motion Picture Patents Company (MPPC), known informally as the Edison Trust, was the most powerful organization in the American film industry. It formed an alliance with the People's Institute, a division of the Cooper Union for the Advancement of Science and Art. The Institute was a socially progressive think tank guided by visionary reformer Charles Sprague Smith. Together, the alliance of filmmakers and academics formed a panel to assess motion picture content. Within three months of McClellan's threat to shutter cinemas the National Board of Censorship began reviewing movies.[22]

Despite its name, the National Board of Censorship's objective was not to ban pictures but rather to uplift the medium toward lofty educational and artistic goals. While the Institute's intentions may have been noble, the film community made no secret of its purpose to contain governmental regulation, announcing a "nation-wide campaign against all forms of official or legalized censorship."[23] The scheme initially worked. The *Moving Picture World* reported that many jurisdictions requiring preapproval of motion pictures "have stated that they will recognize the censorship of the National Board of Censors."[24] Under the MPPC's direction the board members publicized their censoring skills, boasting that within two years they had destroyed two million feet of objectionable film.[25] By 1910 a contentious relationship had arisen between the MPPC and independent filmmakers, but one thing both Edison Trust members and indies could agree on was that the board was preferable to social reformers and state censors.

To fit exhibitors' needs the board's guidelines were left broad, vague, and flexible: "No iron rules can be laid down for the judging of motion pictures . . . [but] scenes depicting crime and vice and those depending on immorality or suggestiveness are frowned upon."[26] The board was a quick fix to fend off state censorship, but the uneasy alliance of industry and academia quickly began to unwind. When Smith died in 1910, so did the Institute's passion for advocating on behalf of uplifting educational pictures. The censorship board's new leadership was more willing to compromise core values and come to terms with the film industry's emphasis of profits over moral value. The Institute's mission shifted from the encouragement of quality to the mere oversight of pictures. Within five years the group changed its name to the National Board of Review. Although not true to its founding principles, the board's new mission offered financial incentives. A fee was charged for each film reviewed. The partnership was mutually beneficial: the film community gained arm's-length, nongovernmental oversight, and the board filled its coffers with license fees.

By 1914 Mutual Film Corporation claimed that 96 percent of its catalog had been inspected and approved by the board.[27] Still, religious leaders, women's groups, and civic-minded moralists were unhappy over the board's failure to censor more vigorously. After Smith's death a letter came to light in which Smith promised not to deal too harshly with the films submitted.[28] Outrage followed this exposure of the relationship between the board and the MPPC. The *Brooklyn Eagle* wrote, "If the National Board of Censorship receives money from the film manufacturers, then it is an institution which relies for its very life on the manufacturers and it would be suicide for the

National Board to censor too strictly."[29] Once it was clear the board was in the pocket of film producers, the tide shifted; communities began to make their own cuts.

In New York oversight of motion pictures and theaters had been divided among several agencies, including the Health Department, the Bureau of Buildings, and the Bureau of Licenses. In 1911 the city consolidated control, appointing a dedicated board of censorship empowered to review and permit pictures in the city.[30]

There were new developments on the national stage as well. Reverend Wilbur Crafts was a longtime lobbyist for temperance and the prohibition of alcohol. In 1914 he turned his attention to the movies. His message: federal film oversight was needed to ensure clean and decent pictures. For Crafts, local boards were still necessary, but a federal agency could provide enforcement.[31] Crafts lobbied Senator M. Hoke Smith (D-GA) and Representative Dudley M. Hughes (D-GA) to establish a Federal Motion Picture Commission.[32] The Smith-Hughes bill came before the House Committee on Education in July 1914, again in October 1915, and was debated for a third and final time in May 1916.[33] The bill failed. On the other side of the issue a group of congressmen filed a counter report,[34] and the *Moving Picture World* offered anticensorship slides for exhibitors to rally their audiences—"The fight against censorship is your fight. Show these slides on your screen . . . and help create a strong public sentiment against this unnecessary and un-American form of legislation. Four slides 50¢."[35] The trade paper saw no resolution in sight on the issue of censorship: "Whatever action may be taken by the Congressional Committee this hearing is practically but the opening gun of a strenuous fight that will follow."[36]

As audiences continued to grow so did civic concerns over who controlled production and exhibition. One factor that influenced this concern was the shifting demographic of ownership in the industry. Before 1910 film production had been in the hands of white Protestants—from executives such as Edison, the Latham brothers, J. Stuart Blackton, and William Selig to technicians such as Dickson, Heise, and Edwin S. Porter. The Lubin company provided a notable exception. Essanay's director-star Broncho Billy Anderson concealed his own Jewish heritage. The nickelodeon boom provided opportunities for risky venture capitalists, and by 1911 a new breed of entrepreneurs—mostly Jewish immigrants—was beginning to join the industry. With this minority group gaining control of the increasingly popular pastime, the perceived need for regulation increased.

Even before Chicago's film ordinance took effect, the city was actively monitoring motion pictures. In October 1907 the *Moving Picture World* reported, "Our Chicago correspondent sends us the following: Lieutenant Alexander McDonald, Chief [of Police George M.] Shippey's five-cent theater and dance hall censor, stopped the display of fourteen pictures this week. . . . The titles of the pictures which were stopped are: *Easy Money . . . Kidnapping a Child* . . . [and] *Clara Got His Money.* . . . The pictures according to Lieutenant McDonald were unfit for exhibition and would easily lead some child or man with a weak mind into an evil path."[37] Soon after the city's censorship ordinance was ratified one exhibitor challenged the law, and on February 19, 1909, the Supreme Court of Illinois rendered its decision in *Block v. City of Chicago. Block* is a landmark—the first film censorship case to be tried in U.S. courts.

Jake Block owned a chain of nickelodeons in Chicago. He challenged the city's interference with the exhibition of two films: *The James Boys in Missouri* and *Night Riders*. Block argued that the city's film regulation was vague and ambiguous and that the terms "obscene" and "immoral" were so broad that delegation of censorship power to the chief of police violated the Constitution. The films at the center of the controversy provide color and detail to Block's claim.

Gilbert M. "Broncho Billy" Anderson (1880–1971) directed *The James Boys in Missouri* (1908). Even in 1908 Broncho Billy was a seasoned professional in the young industry. Anderson had made his screen debut as the telegraph operator in *The Great Train Robbery* (1903). He moved to Selig Polyscope, where he wrote, directed, and appeared in films until partnering with George K. Spoor in 1907 to form Essanay Studios (from *S* and *A* for Spoor and Anderson). *The James Boys* was Essanay's first Western. The one-reeler ran eighteen minutes and covered high points in the life of Jesse James—joining Quantrill's Raiders, leading his gang in a railroad robbery, and getting shot down by Robert Ford.[38] Like the bandit brothers Jesse and Frank, the film was a magnet for trouble; it was banned in Dallas as late as 1911.[39]

The second film was *Night Riders* (1908), produced by the Kalem Company. Kalem was formed in 1907 by the partnership of film pioneers George Kleine, Samuel Long, and Frank J. Marion (*K, L, M* for Kleine, Long, and Marion). The studio's star director, Sidney Olcott, earned his own place in film-legal history when his unauthorized, unlicensed adaptation of *Ben-Hur* (1907) became the first motion picture to come before the U.S. Supreme Court, in *Kalem Co. v. Harper Bros.* (1911). *Night Riders* was a violent thriller to be sure;

the film focused on a true-life vigilante group known as the masked riders, active in Kentucky and Tennessee since 1906. The riders notoriously burned tobacco factories to protest unfair pricing. The self-proclaimed freedom fighters had been making headlines with skirmishes that culminated in a climatic battle with the Kentucky National Guard the very month that Kalem's film was released.[40] *Night Riders* was an actioner ripped from the newspapers.

There was no doubt that both films depicted controversial subject matter; however, crime and criminals had been popular subjects on the screen for years without formal censorship. Edison had issued a steady stream of pulpy crime dramas, including *The Great Train Robbery* (1903), *Kit Carson* (1903), *Capture of the "Yegg" Bank Burglars* (1904), and *Life of an American Policeman* (1906). What was different with *The James Boys* and *Night Riders* was that for the first time the courts stepped in.

Regulators saw the need to protect vulnerable audiences, particularly children, women, and uneducated viewers, from the threat of morally questionable motion pictures. Chicago's 1907 municipal ordinance required permits for Mutoscope, Kinetoscope, and cinematograph parlors and prohibited public exhibition of obscene and immoral pictures.[41] Block prayed for an injunction against the law, complaining it unfairly burdened his business. The state countered that the purpose of the law was "to secure decency and morality in the moving picture business, and that purpose falls within the police power."[42]

In the court's brief reasoning it seemed at first that Block's argument was persuasive. There was no discussion regarding any specific objectionable element in either of the pictures. "It is true," wrote the court, "that pictures representing the career of the James Boys illustrate experiences connected with the history of the country, but it does not follow that they are not immoral."[43] Block had argued that depictions of true events, acceptable if reported or recorded in other media, from newspapers to adventure magazines, should not be deemed inappropriate when conveyed through the medium of motion pictures. The court rejected this reasoning. Abruptly changing direction in the final sentences of the opinion, the court found both films immoral, asserting that "their exhibition would necessarily be attended with evil effects on youthful spectators. If the other pictures for which permits were refused were of similar character, the chief of police should be commended for the refusal."[44]

Illinois saw the need to protect audiences "whose age, education, and situation in life specially entitle them to protection against the evil influence of obscene and immoral representations. The welfare of society demands every effort of municipal authorities afford such protection."[45] With little discussion as to the actual offensive elements in the pictures, the municipal regulation of film content was upheld.

After a decade of explosive growth for the film medium a line was drawn. The court saw little value in the cinema as a developing art or industry. The law was clear: in 1909 Chicago's nickelodeons had little power to challenge municipal regulations.

The following year Delaware regulators challenged the Hyrup Amusement Company in *State v. Morris*. The name of the censored film was not recorded. Regulators relied on chapter 117, section 1 of Delaware's revised code of 1893: "Every building, tent, space or area where feats of horsemanship, or acrobatic sports or theatrical performances are exhibited, shall be deemed a circus within the meaning of this act."[46] Since the cinema embodied a "theatrical performance," it could be regulated. *Morris* found film exhibition could be controlled under an ordinance aimed at circuses.

Interestingly, neither the *Block* nor the *Morris* decision contemplated First Amendment rights. These cases came down in 1909–1910, prior to the incorporation of the Bill of Rights to the states. Although there were indications of change prior to 1925, at that time the Bill of Rights only applied to the federal government. Illinois and Delaware could readily censor film exhibitors by relying on their police powers; constitutional protections were not necessarily relevant to a counter argument. The topic of constitutional guarantees would simmer in the background for six more years before the courts would recognize the issue.

New York, the hub of production, distribution, and film financing had resisted regulating the cinema since Mayor McClellan's attempted Christmas Eve closures. In December 1912 Mayor Gaynor, the former judge and proven ally of the motion picture community, vetoed a bill for more stringent movie censorship.[47] Gaynor commented, "Our forefathers abolished censorship and declared for freedom of speech and a free press. Now apparently, you want all these things and yet you are arguing for a specific censorship. . . . For all I know, this ordinance might deprive us of a personal liberty.[48] Gaynor's endorsement of First Amendment rights fell on deaf ears. In the end it was the inherent danger of the film medium itself—not the thematic content of film—that tipped New York in favor of film regulation. More rigorous laws were passed in 1913 after flammable nitrate film stock was identified as the cause of several fires.[49] The city could rely on its authority to protect the safety of its citizens—the ability to reign in controversial content was an added perk.

Mayor William Jay Gaynor (1849–1913). Photo taken c. 1910,
the year he survived an assassination attempt.

Chicago, Delaware, and New York were not the only communities to regulate motion pictures. On June 19, 1911, Governor John Kinley Tener signed P.L. 1067 into law, creating a board of censors. Pennsylvania became the first to regulate motion pictures on a statewide level. The Keystone State's ordinance stipulated that "no film can be sold, leased, lent, or exhibited until it has been submitted to and approved by this Board of Censors."[50] J. Louis Breitinger (1877–?) and Ellis Paxson Oberholtzer (1868–1936) were named as the state's morality czars.[51] Dr. Oberholtzer was a more thoughtful and academic censor than Funkhouser. He considered his role as follows:

I have often been told, when I protested against a particular scene in a film, that this is but a transcript of what is described in a newspaper or magazine. Conditions are very different; the analogy is false. . . . [A motion picture] can be understood by persons of the lowest degree of intelligence and by children. They can sit in cushioned seats and look, to the accompaniment of music, at the vivid and seductive representation of scenes upon the screen for hours. . . . [T]here must be special agents whose duty it shall be to watch the movie. . . . Such film as no changes can disinfect and purify must be entirely barred from exhibition.[52]

To Oberholtzer, the censor's value was in protecting impressionable audiences from the evil influences of the moving image.

State legislatures took varying approaches to motion picture regulation. Pennsylvania's statute empowered censors to "investigate and . . . approve

34

such moving-picture films, or reels, or stereopticon views, as shall be moral and proper, and disapprove . . . [films] which are sacrilegious, obscene, indecent, or immoral, or such as tend to corrupt morals."[53] Ohio, enacting its stricter film ordinance in 1913, stated, "Only such films as are, in the judgment and direction of the board of censors, of a moral, educational, or amusing and harmless character shall be passed and approved by such board."[54] That same year Kansas "made [it] the duty of [the censor] to examine the films or reels intended for exhibition, and approve such as he shall find to be moral and instructive, and to withhold his approval from such as tend to debase or corrupt the morals."[55] None of these statutes defined moral or immoral; the state censors reviewed pictures based on vague, arbitrary, and often personal standards.

The landscape of the film industry had changed drastically from the freewheeling pioneering days only a decade earlier. The once-powerful Edison Trust came under fire, first in *MPPC v. Independent Moving Pictures Co.* (1912) and then in *United States v. MPPC* (1915). The Trust was finally busted by the

Pennsylvania censor Ellis Oberholtzer (1868–1936) (center), April 28, 1931.
Courtesy Special Collections Research Center, Temple University
Libraries, Philadelphia, Pennsylvania.

Supreme Court in 1917.[56] For a decade the MPPC had reigned as a restrictive cartel, but it had also been an aggressive proponent of industry self-regulation. The MPPC's monopoly had squeezed independent competition but kept civic censors at bay. Into this power vacuum stepped state actors, who increased their strength in the largest urban markets—New York and Chicago—as well as statewide in Pennsylvania, Ohio, and Kansas.

Topics considered content-permissible were changing as well. Boxing films, once box office gold—local bans notwithstanding—evaporated after Vitagraph's *Jeffries-Johnson World's Championship Boxing Contest, Held at Reno, Nevada, July 4, 1910* (1910). This bout pitted the heavyweight champion James Jeffries against Jack "The Galveston Giant" Johnson. With a historic punch, African American Johnson became the first fighter to knock Jeffries down and in the process stir up racial animosities. Two years later Johnson was involved in another controversy when "Fireman" Jim Flynn was disqualified for head butting him in their July 4, 1912, bout, released on film as *Jack Johnson vs. Jim Flynn* (1912). These racially charged matchups factored into the federal government's decision to act. Congress banned distribution of prizefighting pictures on July 31, 1912, less than a month after the Johnson-Flynn film was released. The Simmons bill made it unlawful "to bring or to cause to be brought into the United States from abroad, any film or other pictorial representation of any prize fight or encounter of pugilists, under whatever name, which is designed to be used or may be used for purposes of public exhibition."[57] The federal law criminalized importing and exploiting fight films with a $1,000 fine and prison time.[58]

The Supreme Court upheld the ban on boxing pictures. In 1915 L. Lawrence Weber, a New Jersey film distributor, imported a "photographic film of a pugilistic encounter" shot in Havana, only to have his picture impounded by U.S. Customs. Weber brought suit, claiming the state exceeded its powers under the Commerce Clause. The Supreme Court disagreed. Writing for the unanimous bench in *Weber v. Freed*, Chief Justice Edward Douglass White declared that Congress had the power to prohibit importation of fight films.[59] The following year local censors also cracked down on fistic photoplays, banning imports and exhibition.[60] The genre of prizefighting pictures had come to an end, or at least went underground for stag party viewings.

As government regulations were enforced, a black market motion picture trade arose. Like the boxing films, a shadow industry of sex loops emerged. Back in 1897 even the most audacious striptease films, such as *Fatima's Coochie-*

Unidentified stag loops produced in Austria by Johann Schwarzer (1880–1914)
for Saturn Film, c. 1906–1908.

Early American porn, *A Free Ride* (c. 1915).

___

Coochie Dance and *Dolorita's Passion Dance*, could play to mainstream audiences in most public parlors. However, once these films went underground the aesthetics turned hardcore, giving rise to "modern" pornography. Many early stag films were foreign imports. From France came *A l'ecu d'or ou la bonne auberge* (c. 1908), which explicitly depicted a soldier's tryst with girls at an inn. Another French loop entitled *A les culs d'or* (*The Golden Bottom* or *Mousquetaire au restaurant, Musketeers at the Restaurant*, c. 1908) featured two men, one portly and the other a studly musketeer, entering a tavern to sample the hostess. Imported from Argentina came *El satario* (c. 1908), possibly the earliest surviving pornographic film.[61] In this film three women bathing in a river encounter a devil or satyr who tempts them with forbidden pleasures. Notable for its pioneering use of the extreme close-up, *El satario* moves through a series of scenes that would become standard in the genre. Film aesthetics had certainly progressed—or degenerated—in the decade since the close-up of *The Rice-Irwin Kiss* rankled the petticoats and starched collars of Victorian standard-bearers. From Germany came *Am Abend* (c. 1910). Based in Vienna, Johann Schwarzer's prolific Saturn Film Company mass-produced stag loops such as *A Modern Eve*, *Diana Bathing*, and *Games of Youth* (all films c. 1906–1911). Blue movies were not all imported; *A Free Ride* (c. 1915) is thought to be the oldest American stag film in existence. Typical of American filmmaking as compared to foreign films, *A Free Ride* presented greater narrative structure. The film depicts a man driving his Model T through the country-side with two female passengers, culminating in a pastoral pleasuring in flagrante delicto.

Government regulations intended to promote morals and sanitize screen content played an important role in the development of this shadow industry. While motion picture theaters were unspooling censor-approved reels in Chicago, New York, and the states of Pennsylvania, Ohio, and Kansas, the underground trade in boxing films and porno loops developed into a secret cinema. By 1913 state regulatory mechanisms unwittingly contributed to the rise of a cinematic subculture.

Beginning with the motion picture adaptations of the Thaw-White scandal, the waning days of an older era became apparent. Pugilistic photoplays, shocking stripteases, and thrilling outlaws roiled Victorian sensibilities and galvanized social reformers. The crowd-pleasing formula of sex and violence became the catalyst that encouraged film censorship laws. The 1909 *Block* decision demonstrated the power of state censors over filmmakers and exhibitors. But *Block* avoided discussing the issue of whether film censors chilled free speech. Such constitutional issues would be definitive in determining the balance of power between state regulators and creative filmmakers, between social reformers and champions of the motion picture industry. The parties were not left waiting long: the matter would be decided in the landmark *Mutual* decisions of 1915.

4

MUTUAL AND THE CAPACITY FOR EVIL

—

The increasing popularity and intensifying outrage over violence and nudity in films served as a backdrop for the landmark *Mutual* decisions. After 1915 the *Mutual* precedent would empower censors throughout the Golden Age of American film.

The Mutual Film Corporation was one of the most important production and distribution entities of the second wave of motion picture pioneers. The first wave of American filmmakers—from roughly 1896 to 1914—was composed of members of the Edison Trust and independent filmmakers who opposed the monopoly. Edison Trust members included Edison Manufacturing Company, American Mutoscope and Biograph, Vitagraph Studios, Lubin Manufacturing Company, Selig Polyscope, Essanay Film, Kalem Company, and European distributors Star Film Company (Méliès) and American Pathé. The most vocal independents opposing the Edison Trust were led by William Fox of Fox Film Corporation and Carl Laemmle's IMP (Independent Moving Pictures). This first wave of filmmaking met its formal end as the courts enforced antitrust laws, ultimately disbanding the MPPC's monopoly.[1]

The second wave of industrial development emerged in the mid-1910s. The new power players were Universal, Paramount Pictures, and Mutual Film Corporation.

The beginnings of Mutual can be dated to 1906, when Harry (1877–1956) and Roy Aitken (1882–1976) established the Western Film Exchange in Milwaukee, Wisconsin. A film exchange was a distribution hub. In the Supreme Court's words, "Film exchanges such as the Mutual Film Corporation are like clearing houses or circulating libraries, in that they purchase the film and rent it out to different exhibitors."[2] After an exchange purchased a title from a motion picture manufacturer, the exchange rented out the reels, usually on a states' rights basis. The holder of distribution rights for a particular territory could sublease pictures to individual theaters.

In 1910 Western Film Exchange partnered with the American Film Manufacturing Company, a Chicago-based film studio run by S. S. Hutchinson and staffed with former Essanay employees. Two years later Western-American acquired Thanhouser Studios and renamed the new company Mutual Film Corporation.

By combining these units, Mutual emerged as a powerhouse of production and distribution. The distribution and exchange hub was supplied with a steady stream of content from Thanhauser and American. Thanhauser delivered prestige productions such as *Joseph in the Land of Egypt* (1914), starring

Harry Aitken (1877–1956) at Mutual Film Corp., c. 1912. Courtesy of the
Waukesha County Museum, Waukesha, Wisconsin.

James Cruze; *Thirty Leagues under the Sea* (1914), made in conjunction with Williamson Submarine Film Corporation; and the self-reflexive *When the Studio Burned* (1913), with footage of a fire that destroyed the Florida stages in January 1913. American Film Manufacturing (a.k.a. Flying A) was known for potboilers such as *Another Man's Wife* (1913), directed by Allan Dwan; *The Tattooed Arm* (1913), with heartthrob Wallace Reid; and the early exploitation film *Damaged Goods* (1914).

In addition to these in-house productions, the Aitkens negotiated deals with the industry's three most promising talents. In 1913 Mutual picked up distribution for Mack Sennett's Keystone Studios comedies. Sennett delivered *The Bangville Police* (1913), introducing the Keystone Cops to wider audiences (the Cops had made their screen debut a year earlier in *Hoffmeyer's Legacy*). Other Keystone comedy classics distributed by Mutual included *Mabel's Awful Mistake* (1913), *Fatty's Day Off* (1913), and the feature-length *Tillie's Punctured Romance* (1914). The following year Mutual picked up distribution for Majestic Motion Picture Company, which included D. W. Griffith's proto-features (approximately fifty minutes long). Griffith's Mutual films included the expressionistic *The Avenging Conscience* (1914) and domestic drama *The Battle of the Sexes* (1914). To the Mutual slate, Thomas Ince's Kay Bee Pictures added *The Law of the West* (1912) and William S. Hart sagebrush soaps such as *Scourge of the Desert* (1915). Together Sennett, Griffith, and Ince were the most vital filmmakers of the period, and Mutual was their exclusive distributor in 1915.

Beyond these comedies and dramas Mutual also distributed newsreels. Beginning in 1912 *Mutual Weekly* was offered to exhibitors to supplement their marquee titles.[3] *Mutual Weekly*'s one and two-reel actualities included news ripped from the headlines as well as human interest stories such as *Winter Sports in Norway* (1912), *Tashkent, Asiatic Russia* (1912), *Mosques and Tombs of Caliphs and Mamelukes* (1912), *Village Customs in Ceylon, India* (1912), *Microscopic Animalcules Found in Stagnant Water* (1913), and *Los Angeles Parade* (1913). In one of the more daring deals in film history, Harry Aitken blurred the line between fact and fiction when he negotiated with the charismatic Mexican rebel Pancho Villa for exclusive movie rights. Aitken assigned Griffith to produce the docudrama. Griffith picked a promising talent from his stable, and Raoul Walsh was sent south of the border to codirect with Griffith's trusted colleague Christy Cabanne. Together they photographed actual battles between rebels and *federales* as well as recreated and staged scenes for *The Life of General Villa* (1914).

The Life of General Villa (1914).

With a strong lineup of talent, a steady stream of popular films, and the threat of the Edison Trust contained, Mutual Film Corporation was poised to be a dominant force in the U.S. film industry. Then in 1915 Mutual suffered a series of setbacks. Coming under pressure for cost overruns on Griffith's Civil War epic, which Mutual had begun financing, Harry Aitken was squeezed out of the company. Griffith remained loyal to Aitken, leaving Mutual with him; Sennett and Ince joined them. Majestic, Keystone, and Kay Bee were shuttered, and together Griffith, Sennett, Ince, and Aitken formed the Triangle Film Corporation.[4] Following the directors' exodus came their loyal stars, including Mary Pickford, Lillian Gish, Mabel Normand, Fatty Arbuckle, and William S. Hart. Not only did Mutual find itself bereft of its top talent, but the company also found itself challenging state censorship laws on several fronts: in Pennsylvania, Ohio, Kansas, and the city of Chicago.

The resulting *Mutual* decisions were significant because for the first time courts applied concepts of First Amendment rights to motion pictures. The results were a major victory for censors. Although the film industry was twenty years old, the courts were not yet ready to consider motion pictures as speech worthy of constitutional protection.

Mutual Film Corp. v. Industrial Commission of Ohio came down on February 23, 1915. At issue was the Ohio film regulation ordinance and the permitting of Mutual's newsreels. The statute vaguely directed state censors to approve films of a moral, educational, or amusing and harmless character.[5] Mutual claimed the approval process slowed distribution, creating a bottleneck before the reels could reach theaters. Each film was required to obtain a permit from the board of censors; so the regulation impacted Mutual's ability to create an efficient distribution network.

The substance of the law was quickly dispensed with. The censorship board conceded that in the *Mutual Weekly* releases "nothing is depicted of a harmful or immoral character."[6] The court then concentrated its analysis on the procedural aspect of Ohio's statute. "The Board has demanded of complainant that it submit its films to censorship, and threatens . . . to arrest any and all persons who seek to place on exhibition any film not so censored or approved by the censor congress on or after November 4, 1913." Mutual countered that, for the distribution of weekly newsreels, "it is physically impossible to comply with such demand and physically impossible for the board to censor the films with such rapidity as to enable complainant to proceed with its business, and the delay consequent upon such examination would cause great and irreparable harm to such business."[7] Mutual's argument was that submission of newsreels was impracticable given the timely information in the films and the speed with which the films were produced.

Three significant issues were presented: first, whether Ohio's statute imposed an unlawful burden on interstate commerce with its requirement of submission for each film; second, whether the statute violated the state's constitution by depriving Mutual of due process by allowing the board to both set rules and judge permissible films; third—and perhaps most critical—was whether the statute violated the First Amendment by chilling the free expression of ideas.[8]

The federal government's power to regulate interstate commerce derives from article I, section 8, of the U.S. Constitution, granting Congress the power and authority "to regulate Commerce with foreign Nations, and among the several States." The Supreme Court further defined the balance of power in *Gibbons v. Ogden* (1824), asserting that the federal government overrides state law in all aspects of interstate commerce.[9]

The interstate commerce issue in *Mutual v. Ohio* hinged on motion pictures imported by the film exchange. Mutual argued that their business of selling and leasing films from offices outside Ohio to purchasers and exhibitors within the state constituted interstate commerce. Such interstate commerce should be subject to federal regulation on the one hand and could not be burdened by state laws on the other hand. The Court disagreed: "The censorship . . . is only of films intended for exhibition in Ohio, and we can immediately put to one side the contention that it imposes a burden on interstate commerce. It is true that . . . some of the films of complainant are shipped from Detroit, Michigan, but they are distributed to exhibitors, purchasers, renters, and lessors in Ohio, for exhibition in Ohio. . . . In other words, it is only the films which are to be publicly exhibited and displayed in the state of Ohio which are required to be examined and censored."[10]

On the first issue, the state prevailed. Mutual's imported films would be subject to the state's regulation.

The Court next considered Mutual's complaint that Ohio's statute deprived the distributor of a remedy by due process of law. Rather than discuss deprivation of constitutional protections, the Court framed the issue as an exercise of police power for the social welfare of the community. Writing for the unanimous Court, Justice Joseph McKenna observed that motion pictures

> may be used for evil, and against that possibility the statute was enacted. . . . They take their attraction from the general interest, eager and wholesome it may be, in their subjects, but a prurient interest may be excited and appealed to. Besides, there are some things which should not have pictorial representation in public places and to all audiences.[11]

Seeking guidance from the common law test for obscenity and sidestepping the issue of due process, the Court deferred to the state's power, authority, and, furthermore, duty to protect vulnerable members of society.

Finally, the Court opined on First Amendment protections available to Mutual. It was a critical moment in film-legal history. This would be the first time the High Court considered whether constitutional protections would apply to motion pictures.

Unfortunately for the film industry, the issue was summarily dismissed: "We need not pause to dilate upon the freedom of opinion and its expression, and whether by speech, writing or printing."[12] The Court reasoned that motion pictures indeed may be mediums of thought, but so are many things. So is the theater, the circus, and all other shows and spectacles, and their performances may be thus brought by the like reasoning under the same immunity from repression or supervision as the public press. . . . Counsel have not shrunk from this extension of their contention [that films should be protected by the First Amendment]. . . . The *first impulse* of the mind is to reject the contention. We immediately feel that that argument is wrong or strained which extends the guarantees of free opinion and speech to the multitudinous shows which are advertised on the billboards of our cities and towns.[13]

While the *first impulse* may have been to reject the contention, further thought may have led to an understanding of the cinema's power and potential to disseminate ideas, comment, and criticism. But in 1915 legal culture was not yet ready to consider entertainment as speech worthy of constitutional protections, instead comparing the medium to a circus sideshow, long subject to restrictions on exhibition.

The *Mutual* holding was another victory for regulators and another setback for the film community. Dismissing the notion that motion pictures could be an art form, a mode of communication, or a medium of public discourse, the Court positioned film as a mere diversion. "It cannot be put out of view that the exhibition of moving pictures is a business, pure and simple, originated and conducted for profit, like other spectacles, not to be regarded, nor intended to be regarded by the Ohio Constitution, we think, as part of the press of the country, or as organs of public opinion."[14]

The Supreme Court reduced motion pictures to "a business, pure and simple." This is inconsistent with First Amendment protections for newspapers. Constitutional protections for the press lie at the heart, the very essence of the First Amendment. The fact that newspapers could be businesses for profit does not and should not detract from the medium's free speech guarantees. Similarly, the fact that motion pictures were necessarily a commercial enterprise should not have factored into an analysis of whether constitutional rights extend to the medium.

Nevertheless, in a 9–0 decision the Court declared motion pictures to be "a business, pure and simple," unworthy of protection under the First Amendment. Not only *could* the cinema be regulated under the law but its "capacity for evil" *should* be regulated to protect the health, safety, welfare, and morality of citizens. With the benefit of hindsight we can see that the Court's reasoning was flawed—that commercial aspects should not negate constitutional protections, that capacity for evil should not demand state control. Still, *Mutual* would stand as a defining precedent for over three decades.

Simultaneous with *Mutual v. Ohio*, the Supreme Court also ruled on a related case originating from Kansas: *Mutual Film Corp. v. Hodges*. The same *Mutual Weekly* newsreels were at issue, and the Court pragmatically dispensed with any overlap. Justice McKenna, again speaking for a unanimous majority wrote, "It is here contended that the Kansas statute has the same invalidity and for the same reasons as it was contended that the statute of Ohio had. We need not, therefore repeat the reasoning. It establishes that both statutes are valid exercises of police power of the states . . . [and] do not interfere with interstate commerce nor abridge the liberty of opinion; nor are they delegations of legislative power to administrative officers."[15]

The key issue in *Mutual v. Hodges* rested on standing to bring suit. Legal standing refers to the proper party eligible to bring a claim. The Kansas statute, "An Act Regulating the Exhibiting or Using of Moving Picture Films or Reels,"[16] had been enacted in 1913. The ordinance regulated exhibition; therefore, film exhibitors would be the party affected—exhibitors alone had standing to challenge the law. On behalf of Governor George Hodges the state argued that per the letter of the law, Mutual should be barred from bringing suit because the distributor lacked requisite standing to sue under the statute: "It will be observed that the law makes only exhibitors or those permitting exhibitions of unapproved films liable to the penalties of the act. . . . [I]t is alleged by the defendants that, as complainant is in neither class, it has no standing to attack the statute."[17] Mutual claimed its business was vulnerable to local legislation; since the exchange handled wide distribution, it was better suited than exhibitors to challenge the law. The Court rejected this argument, refusing to allow Mutual to "enlarge the character of the statute, or give to it an operation which it does not have."[18] Under the letter of the law Mutual lacked legal standing; Kansas exhibitors alone could challenge the regulator's ban within the state. The effect of this decision would be to drive local exhibitors away from controversial fare.

A third Mutual decision came down in Pennsylvania four months after *Mutual v. Ohio* and *Mutual v. Hodges*. In *Buffalo Branch, Mutual Film Corp. v. Breitinger*, the distributor threw everything it had at state regulators. The Film exchange alleged a panoply of legal theories before the Pennsylvania Supreme Court with hopes that one would stick. Mutual claimed that the [state censorship] act is in violation of section 1, art. 14 of the Constitution of the United States, in that it abridges plaintiffs' right in the transaction of business with citizens of states other than Pennsylvania; that it is arbitrary and inflicts a tax and burden on plaintiffs which is unlawful and contrary to the provisions of the Constitution of Pennsylvania; that the fees provided in it are exorbitant; that it is in contravention of the Constitution of the United States and of the Constitution of the commonwealth of Pennsylvania in that the plaintiffs are subject to the arbitrary action of defendants, from which there is no provision for appeal, and that the act is an unwarranted interference with plaintiffs' right to carry on lawful business, make contracts, or use and enjoy their property; that it is unconstitutional because it imposes a legal duty beyond the police powers of the General Assembly as a condition precedent to the right to rent films of obtaining approval of defendants, and which approval may be withheld in their discretion without hearing and without right of appeal, if, in their judgment, the films are sacrilegious, obscene, indecent, immoral, or such as tend to corrupt morals, and that plaintiffs are deprived of the right to pursue a lawful business and the freedom to contract, and of their property without due process of law or the equal protection of the laws; that the extreme penalties imposed evidences an intent to limit or prevent judicial inquiry as to the validity of the act, and that fear of fines will prevent exhibitors from renting films; that the act attempts to give defendants legislative power, and delegates to them power to determine judicial questions without right of appeal to any court; and that it restrains the right of plaintiffs to freely write and publish their sentiments, guaranteed by the Constitution.[19]

In *Mutual v. Breitinger* a strange alliance emerged between the MPPC and state censors. By 1915 the Edison Trust was in its final throes as an industry leader. Interestingly, Trust members aligned themselves with the board of censorship in an effort to freeze out Mutual. The General Film Company— the Trust's distribution arm—testified that it submitted its own films, which were approved and permitted in a timely manner, and that the fee was not burdensome.[20] Pennsylvania's board of censorship and General Film together overpowered Mutual. Drawing on the state's police powers to preserve the health, safety, welfare, manners, and morals of its citizens, the *Mutual v. Breitinger* court dismissed Mutual's claim.

The court's lengthy opinion made many references to the useful and necessary regulations on public utilities in place. The decision cited railroad regulations as well as statutory restrictions on tobacco, liquor, building inspections, agriculture, roadways, milk production, coal mining, and oil drilling. After running through an exhaustive list of police power properly and legitimately put into action, the court turned to the few precedental cases of film regulation available:

> In *Laurelle v. Bush* 17 Cal. App. 409 [1911], an ordinance requiring moving picture shows to be licensed by the board of police commissioners and limiting the places where such licenses should be granted was held valid. In *Higgins v. Lacroix* 199 Minn. 145 [1912], an act imposing a license fee on moving picture shows was held to be constitutional, and in *Dreyfus v. Montgomery* 4 Ala. App. 270 [1911], where an ordinance restricted the location of moving picture shows to a prescribed district, it was decided to be valid.

The opinion then went on to quote the *Dreyfus* case at length:

> Moving picture shows are of comparatively recent origin, but of rapid growth, springing up everywhere in the large cities and invading even villages and towns of modest size. While as generally conducted, some educational value may be conceded to exist in these shows, it is never less than true that the chief aim is to furnish the sort of entertainment that will draw the most dimes. To furnish the people with innocent and cheap amusement is laudable, but experience teaches that, where amusements are furnished for pecuniary profit, the tendency is to furnish that which will attract the greatest number, rather than that which instructs or elevates. . . . [Motion pictures] must therefore be classed among those pursuits which are liable to degenerate and menace the good order and minds of the people, and may therefore not only be licensed and regulated but also prevented by a village council.[21]

To the *Mutual v. Breitinger* court, the movies' capacity for evil once again cried out for state regulation. The court commended Mutual's effort but ruled in favor of the state board: "Neither the eloquent argument nor the able and exhaustive brief by the counsel for the plaintiffs have convinced the court that the act of June 19, 1911 (P.L. 1067) is unconstitutional."[22]

Mutual next challenged film regulations in Chicago. In *Mutual Film Corp. v. City of Chicago*, the court held that the municipal ordinance for motion picture censorship did not violate the Constitution.[23]

Despite Mutual's tireless attempts to challenge motion picture regulations in Ohio, Kansas, Pennsylvania, and Chicago, the film distributor was unable to convince any court that motion pictures were speech or expression that should be protected under the provisions of the First Amendment. The *Mutual* cases of 1915 established five significant precedents that would stand for years and impact the development of the motion picture industry. First, motion pictures were outside the constitutional guarantees of freedom of speech. Because cinema was seen as "a business, pure and simple," not meriting First Amendment protections, there was an increased drive toward regulation of content. Second, the Commerce Clause would not be triggered by state regulations despite films in the stream of commerce moving through various jurisdictions. Third, states could regulate, license, and censor motion pictures as an exercise of police power to protect the social welfare of a community. Fourth, film exchanges, the mechanisms of film distribution, would have standing to challenge state regulations. Finally, *Mutual* changed the strategy of future legal actions concerning motion picture regulation. For three decades after *Mutual* the film industry ceased invoking First Amendment rights in favor of more practical arguments. The approach changed from the ideological stance that *all* movie censorship is wrong to the more narrowly focused position that censorship of *this* movie is wrong.

Despite its losses Mutual quickly rebounded. After the upsets of 1915, the exodus of top talent, and the adverse decisions, Mutual signed Charlie Chaplin and became the Little Tramp's exclusive distributor. Producing comedy shorts through Lone Star Studios, Chaplin delivered some of his most memorable films to Mutual, including *The Vagabond* (1916), *The Pawnshop* (1916), *The Rink* (1916), and *The Immigrant* (1917).

Mutual was a major player in the American film industry's second phase that followed the demise of the Edison Trust. But times were changing as a new series of studios were coalescing, giving rise to Hollywood's classic era. By 1919 Mutual was acquired and absorbed into Film Booking Offices of America (FBO). In 1926 Joseph Kennedy purchased FBO, transforming it into the foundation for RKO Pictures. The new studio would be a key player in the industry's transition to sound film. By then—just over a decade after the *Mutual* decisions of 1915—the film exchange had become a distant memory.

Of any film genre, the newsreel would have the greatest potential to come under the First Amendment because of its connection with the press. The founding fathers explicitly enumerated freedom of the press as a core guarantee, thereby conferring an exalted status to news media in terms of constitutional protections. Still, seven years after *Mutual*, the Pathé News Corporation was also denied the protection granted to the printed press.

Pathé Frères was incorporated in France in 1896 and quickly became a dominant force in worldwide filmmaking. Acquiring the Lumière brothers' motion picture operation by the turn of the century, Pathé rapidly expanded from its Paris headquarters. The company opened offices in Moscow in February 1904, New York in August 1904, Brussels in October 1904, Berlin in March 1905, Vienna in July 1905, Chicago in August 1905, St. Petersburg in December 1905, Amsterdam in January 1906, Barcelona in February 1906, Milan in May 1906, London in July 1906, and Odessa in July 1906. Pathé's outposts expanded through Central Europe, India, Southeast Asia, Central and South America, and Africa.[24] In 1908 Pathé became the first producer of newsreels, able to gather footage from its far-flung offices and distribute it through a centralized hub. Representative titles include *The Funeral of Count Tolstoi* (1910), *Danses cambodgiennes* (1910), *À l'école de samouraïs* (1911), and *Elephant Hunting in Victoria Nyanza* (1911). British Pathé, a subsidiary entity that was later spun off, captured images from the front lines of World War I. Although Pathé did not operate like a contemporary news-gathering organization, with an assignment desk that coordinated individual units, the production and distribution company's extensive reach made it an unparalleled resource at the time and for many years to come.

By any measure, Pathé's early and elaborate contribution to modern news media was an amazing achievement. Before the advent of synchronized sound pictures, the purely pictorial world of actualities could truly create a global village connecting diverse communities. While we can appreciate Pathé as an amazing news-gathering organization from a modern perspective, this may not have been so obvious in 1922, as demonstrated in *Pathé Exchange v. Cobb*.

Following Chicago's ordinance of 1907 and the triumph of Ohio's censorship statute in the 1915 *Mutual* decision, New York State enacted a comparable regulation in 1921. The statute was almost immediately invoked to challenge Pathé's newsreels. In *Pathé v. Cobb* the New York court framed the issue as follows:

Unless the biweekly motion picture news reel is in the same legal category as a newspaper, and the liberty of the press would protect newspapers from such restraint as is here sought to be exercised, there would be no denial of equal protection of the laws. The main question before us, therefore, is whether the biweekly motion picture news reel is in the same legal category as a newspaper, and whether the restraint caused by this act is of such a character as to be a violation of that provision of our state Constitution relating to the liberty of the press.[25]

By 1922 Pathé's newsreel operation had been an industry leader for nearly fifteen years; still, the court seemed wary of the visual news source:

We cannot say that the moving picture is not a medium of thought, but it is clearly something more than a newspaper, periodical, or book, and clearly distinguishable in character. It is a spectacle or show, rather than a medium of opinion, and the latter quality is a mere incident to the former quality. It creates and purveys a mental atmosphere, which is absorbed by the viewer without conscious mental effort. It requires neither literacy nor interpreter to understand it. Those who witness the spectacle are taken out of bondage to the letter, and the spoken word.[26]

Again, the decision turned on the state's perceived need to protect the innocence of children and shield illiterates from the cinema's capacity for evil: "The newspaper offers no particular attraction to the child. . . . But the moving picture attracts the attention so lacking with books, or even newspapers, particularly so far as children and the illiterate are concerned. . . . Its value as an educator for good is only equaled by its danger as an instructor in evil."[27]

The cinema was too seductive, too immediate, too real, and this verisimilitude was the medium's liability. The court concluded, "We do not think that the biweekly motion picture news reel, so far as it becomes a part of such show or spectacle in such a public place of amusement, is a part of the press of the country. It is therefore subject to the regulation of the act in question."[28]

The *Mutual* precedent was clear: motion pictures fell outside the realm of the First Amendment protections and were subject to regulation, censorship, and even prior restraint. *Pathé* elaborated on *Mutual*, finding that newsreels were separate and apart from the traditional news-gathering function of the traditional press. These holdings were grim portents indeed for the future of filmmaking.

This question of whether newsreels were legitimate news media resonated for nearly five years. Finally the New York State Motion Picture Censorship Regulation was amended in 1927 to provide that "current events film,
or newsreels, may be exhibited without a permit or a license, at the risk of the
exhibitor that they are fit to be seen."[29] This was a victory for newsreel producers. Although the genre was still not nestled within the protections of the
First Amendment's freedom of the press, and exhibitors could still be exposed
by the content of their pictures, the procedural element of regulation—which
Mutual had initially protested because of the logistical impracticability—was
finally waived for newsreels in the influential jurisdiction of New York.

Pathé Exchange, the American arm of the French motion picture behe-
moth, was spun off in 1927 and like Mutual sold to Joseph Kennedy. Its infrastructure was folded into RKO. Meanwhile, the home office of Pathé Frères
independently maintained its operation, producing and distributing motion
pictures worldwide. The first maker of newsreels was also the last man standing; Pathé News continued production of its newsreels until the mid-1970s,
when television cannibalized the market.[30]

In 1915 the movie business had exploded to become the fifth largest industry in the nation, with capital investments topping $500 million.[31] With such
achievement came the notice of authorities. After Chicago and New York
City passed film regulations in 1907 and 1909, the floodgates opened. Pennsylvania enacted statewide censorship in 1911. Ohio and Kansas implemented
their own ordinances in 1913. Federal regulation was debated in 1914. The
federal bill did not pass, but the authority of the *Mutual* decisions in 1915
cleared the way for local censors. The Maryland State Board of Censors was
created in 1916 and "approved only those films that they deemed 'moral and
proper.'"[32]

New York State's motion picture regulation passed in May 1921 and proved
to be influential.[33] The bill created a film commission charged with examining and permitting pictures "unless such film or a part thereof is obscene,
indecent, immoral, inhuman, sacrilegious, or is of such a character that its
exhibition would tend to corrupt morals or incite to crime."[34] The following
year Florida enacted a law requiring all films intended for exhibition in the
state to be approved by either the National Board of Review or the New York
State Film Commission. Florida's censorship mechanism vested authority in
two agencies—one private, the other governmental, both in other states.[35]
On March 17, 1922, Virginia enacted a regulation that cribbed from New
York's statute.[36]

Similar statutes were considered in Connecticut, Georgia, Iowa, Kentucky, Louisiana, Michigan, Mississippi, Missouri, Nebraska, New Jersey, North Carolina, Rhode Island, South Carolina, and West Virginia. Popular support for state censorship was at its highest level. In several states, including Massachusetts, Minnesota, Nevada, and New Mexico, film regulation bills were vetoed.[37] They were the exceptions.

Censorship also thrived on a local level. In addition to Chicago and New York, other metropolitan areas set up their own review boards, including Atlanta, Dallas, Detroit, Indianapolis, Joplin, Kansas City, Los Angeles, Memphis, Milwaukee, New Haven, New Orleans, Oklahoma City, Omaha, Portland, San Francisco, Salt Lake City, Seattle, and Tacoma.[38] Arkansas City, Kansas, passed a censorship bill that was later modified to specifically allow for images of alcohol consumption in Westerns. The *Arkansas City Daily Traveler* reported that "drinking scenes are inevitable in frontier pictures or pictures showing western life in the cow country."[39] The reach of the censor's stamp was felt far beyond each city's limits. Approximately thirty film exchanges serviced the nation; thus a film edited for one locale would be distributed in its abridged version throughout the region. When larger cities created review boards, they became the de facto censors for smaller towns. In the less populated western territories there was no need for states to become involved so long as the urban centers enacted censorship regulations.

In addition to the moral uplift, the logistics of film regulation were attractive. Regulation was a revenue generator; boards charged distributors for examination and approval and charged theaters for permitted exhibitions. By placating community activists, authorities could fill their coffers. But the decentralized system of overlapping regulations imposed vague and often arbitrary standards of morality and decency. These complexities burdened the film industry at a time when producers and distributors were consolidating into integrated studios. Although the industry's early experiment with self-regulation had been a failure, the time was right for a second attempt. The film factories of Hollywood were on the horizon, but before they could strengthen, the crazy quilt of interstate standards had to be contained.

In July 1916 major filmmakers and industry executives, including D. W. Griffith and Adolph Zukor, banded together to create a trade association: the National Association of the Motion Picture Industry (NAMPI). Griffith was one of the fiercest opponents of censorship, predicting a "calamity if [a] Federal Bill was passed."[40] Other organizations, such as the National Independent Motion Picture Board of Trade and the Motion Pictures Producers

Association, were also developing. While these groups were short lived, they encouraged filmmakers to maintain a vigilant and proactive policy toward censorship.

In 1922 the major studios founded the Motion Picture Producers and Distributors of America (MPPDA). With NAMPI and MPPDA, the industry was once again taking steps toward creating a code that would defuse governmental regulations.

5

WAR, NUDITY, AND BIRTH CONTROL

—

Under the *Mutual* decisions, the courts ruled that film censorship laws did not necessarily conflict with the First Amendment. Motion picture producers, distributors, and exhibitors were left vulnerable to a patchwork of state regulations. Film exhibition was seen as mere entertainment, not speech worthy of protection. In the aftermath of the 1915 rulings, state censorship boards sharpened their scissors when they saw three film subjects in particular enter their jurisdictions: political content in the popular genre of war films, art films that revealed female nudity, and pictures by reform-minded filmmakers using the medium as a platform to discuss progressive social issues. To the state censors, these three subjects—war, art, and social reform—were threats to the status quo that needed to be regulated.

From the beginning, war films with striking images of explosive modern, mechanized combat and clearly drawn good and bad guys were a natural fit for the medium of motion pictures. The Spanish-American War offered a perfect testing ground for cameramen. As conflict broke out in Cuba, film studios deployed their photographers. Edison's crew was on location for *Burial of the Maine Victims* (1898) and *United States Troops Landing at Daiquirí, Cuba* (1898), followed by real-time executions in *Shooting Captured Insurgents* (1898). Biograph offered audiences *Wounded Soldiers Embarking in Row Boats* (1898) and *Wreck of the Vizcaya* (1898).[1] Vitagraph re-created the drama of combat in *The Battle of Santiago Bay* (1898), the first war film to offer visual effects. The special effects were primitive to be sure—miniature ships in a tub of water with puffs of cigar smoke to simulate explosions.[2] Still, it was popular enough that Lubin pirated the film to release his own *Battle of Santiago* (1899).

Combat films returned solid box office receipts. To record the revolution in the Philippines, Vitagraph enlisted its effects team to recreate the *Battle in Manila* (1898). Turning their lenses on the Second Boer War, Edison's cameramen captured *Charge of the Boer Calvary* (1900) and *Boers Bringing in British Prisoners* (1900). Biograph charged to the front lines for *A Reconnoitre in Force* (1899), *Naval Guns Firing at Colenso* (1899), and *Off for the Boer War* (1900).[3]

It was natural that as Europe prepared for World War I, motion picture cameras would be rolling. Only months after the assassination of Archduke Franz Ferdinand, director Will S. Davis released *The War of Wars; Or, The Franco-German Invasion* (1914). He ratcheted up the violence for his next picture, *The Ordeal* (1914). *The Ordeal* pictured a young man as he dreamt of marching off to glorious battle, leaving his family and sweetheart. His fantasy is shattered when he's taken prisoner and tortured. His mother, sister, and sweetheart are executed before his eyes. And then "at the end, when the young man awakes, the whole family has come to life again and appear in a happy group."[4] After witnessing the horrors of war, audiences were comforted by the "it was all just a dream" ending.

Due to *The Ordeal*'s vivid portrayal of a sadistic German officer, New York film commissioner George H. Bell denied the picture a license. It was not immorality, indecency, or obscenity that angered the city's German-American audiences but rather the film's unfair characterization of the Kaiser's army. Judge E. E. Whitaker observed in *Life Photo Film Corp. v. Bell* that "there is no claim made by the defendant that the picture is immoral, indecent, or in any way unfit to be exhibited. . . . [However, the board of censors ruled that] it would be inadvisable to exhibit the picture because it might occasion racial differences at this particular time."[5] The court disagreed with the commissioner: "The only possible objection that could be made is that possibly some supersensitive Teuton might consider [the picture] . . . an unfair characterization and misrepresentation of the German army. . . . This, in my opinion, would not form a proper basis for preventing the exhibition. . . . [P]laintiff should not, therefore be interfered with in the transaction of its legitimate business because of the supersensitiveness of alien residents."[6]

Just three months after the Supreme Court cleared the way for censors in *Mutual*, New York pushed back to establish some limits. The *Ordeal* decision was significant because it demonstrated that the courts would scrutinize arbitrary and capricious censorship.

A similar scene played out in Chicago. In 1917 Fox Film released a World War I thriller entitled *The Spy*. Matinee star Dustin Farnum (*The Squaw Man*, 1914; *Davy Crockett*, 1916) played a secret service agent operating undercover in Germany. He is caught and tortured by Baron von Bergen (Howard Gaye) and put through the paces of torment in scenes of graphic violence. Funkhouser banned the film, and Fox challenged his ruling. In *Fox Film Corp. v. City of Chicago* the court found that the violent scenes did not rise to the level of prohibited conduct: "The mere fact that scenes of torture . . . may be terrifying and horrifying does not bring the film within the purview of section 1627, which authorizes a permit to be refused only under the enumerated conditions of the section."[7] Once again, in the shadow of *Mutual*, a court favored the filmmaker, finding that denial of a permit was an abuse of discretion. Judge Samuel Alschuler found "there is nothing that [the licensing commissioner] stated there which, under the ordinance, would be considered immoral, obscene, or unlawful, or otherwise objectionable, but that objection consists wholly in the horrifying nature of the tortures which are portrayed as inflicted upon the hero of the play and his ultimate shooting by a firing squad."[8] He enjoined the board's ban and permitted exhibition of *The Spy*.

The *Spy* decision held up on appeal. The Seventh Circuit ruled that "there is nothing obscene or immoral; no portrayal of any riotous, disorderly, or other unlawful . . . scene; nothing tending to disturb the public peace; but the action of the play, where great drops of sweat stand out on the face and chest of the hero as he endures torture and faces death, is too harrowing, in the honest judgment of the city's administrators, for the sensibilities of minors; and for this reason, and that alone, the permit under [section] 1627 was refused."[9] The court declined to reverse the decision unless there was an abuse of discretion, a misunderstanding of the facts, or a misapplication of the law. In the absence of these factors Judge Francis E. Baker declared, "If the glycerine tears and beads of sweat of the moving picture art are too horrifying for children, it was not for the administrator of these ordinances to say so; it must first be declared by a lawmaking body."[10]

With decisions for *The Ordeal* and *The Spy* upheld, World War I films became staples on the marquee. Vitagraph attempted a big budget pacifistic epic, *The Battle Cry of Peace* (1915), but it was the wrong film for an audience ready to root for war, bloodshed, and patriotism. Riding on the success of *The Birth of a Nation* (1915), author Thomas F. Dixon Jr. sharpened his pen once more for *The Fall of a Nation* (1916), which portrayed an unprepared United States conquered by invading European armies. William de Mille had German agents undermining American democracy in *The Secret Game* (1917).

The Kaiser, the Beast of Berlin (1918) was considered one of the most notorious films of the time, but it packed the house—selling seventy-five thousand tickets in a two-day booking at the Kansas City Convention Center.[11] Rupert Julian starred as the maniac Prussian leader who reveled in cold-blooded murder and outrageous affronts. *The Claws of the Hun* (1918) and *To Hell with the Kaiser!* (1918) added fuel to the fire. In Thomas Ince's *Behind the Door* (1920) a U-boat crew ravaged a woman, afterward dispatching her through a torpedo hatch.[12]

The violence of World War I was popular with audiences and palatable by censors; but *The Birth of a Nation*'s Civil War and *The Spirit of '76*'s Revolutionary War ran into trouble for incendiary content injected into historical conflicts. Regulators permitted violent scenes, but pictures depicting racism or unpopular political views crossed the line.

Few films have been critiqued, celebrated, or reviled as *The Birth of a Nation* (1915). Despite the film's racist elements, it remains a cornerstone of American motion picture development because of its epic staging, expert editing, and remarkable dramatic tension. Even at the time of its release, *Birth* was controversial. A month prior to the film's opening the NAACP voiced objections.[13] The film premiered in Los Angeles on February 8, 1915, and was banned shortly thereafter. Chicago, Denver, Des Moines, Newark, Pittsburgh, and St. Louis also banned *Birth*, as did the states of Ohio and Kansas.[14] Back in New York the NAACP continued to campaign against the film, but the organization's effect was minimal. *Birth* opened in New York with minor cuts.[15] In Boston a mob of five hundred stormed the Tremont Theater. One hundred policemen responded; they cleared the area, and the show proceeded.[16] Pickets and protests were of little effect. Fervor in favor of the film gained momentum, and regional censors stood down as *Birth* marched across the country's screens.

The city of Minneapolis was willing to challenge Griffith's blockbuster. A. G. Bainbridge Jr. licensed distribution rights for the region. He first booked *Birth* in St. Paul.[17] The next showing would be across the river at Minneapolis's Shubert Theater. Once Bainbridge advertised the event, Mayor W. G. Nye served notice he would revoke the venue's license if the film played.[18]

According to *Bainbridge v. City of Minneapolis* (1915), the municipal censors objected to Griffith's bigoted portrayal of African Americans. The film, they claimed, "characteriz[ed] the Southern Negro as lustful, brutal, inhuman, and treacherous, as a humiliating caricature of the colored race, as calculated to engender race hatred and animosity."[19] The Minnesota court declined to weigh merits of the film's artistic and technical innovation against its racist

The Birth of a Nation (1915).

elements: "It is useless to spend time arguing the question whether reasonable people might differ as to the advisability of permitting the exhibition of
this play. The showing is conclusive that they differ on this point. . . . There is
no reason to doubt that the mayor, in proposing to revoke plaintiff's license
if he persists in presenting this play, is acting in the honest belief that such
course is in the interest of public welfare and the peace and good order of
the city." The court deferred to municipal regulators: "We cannot substitute
the discretion of the court for that of our mayor, to whom the Legislature
has specially confided its exercise. If it were otherwise, the city would be governed by the courts, and not by the city officials in whom the law vests the
governmental power."[20] And so *Birth* was banned in Minneapolis. The opinion was affirmed without opinion by the Supreme Court in *Bainbridge v. City
of Minneapolis* (1916).[21]

Despite the legal victory for regulators, the power of the people demanded
the historic film. By the end of October 1915 *Birth* unspooled at the Shubert
and returned for a second engagement in St. Paul.[22]

The Birth of a Nation was rereleased in 1924, 1930, and 1938. Each time, the
film met with opposition, but the picture proved to be unstoppable. Not so
for *The Spirit of '76* (1917), which was wiped from existence and remains a lost
film to this day.

Robert Goldstein (1883–?) was a German-Jewish immigrant. Trained as
a tailor, he opened a costume shop in Los Angeles in the 1910s. One day a
director came in to discuss outfits needed for a film. Like many independent
producers, this filmmaker had a limited budget. They negotiated a deal: in
exchange for points on the film (a percentage of the box office), Goldstein
would supply the costumes and defer payment. This was a typical negotiation
to leverage production costs against expected future profits. In exchange for
risk, Goldstein became an income participant. The director was D. W. Griffith,
the film *The Birth of a Nation*, and Goldstein's risk paid off. Actor Joseph Henabery, who played President Lincoln in Griffith's picture, recounted the story
in his memoir: "The costumes for the picture were supplied by a Los Angeles
costumer, I believe, Robert Goldstein. I was told this man was given an interest in 'The Clansman' as his payment. Goldstein got a tremendous reward for
taking a chance."[23]

Inspired by Griffith's historic success and massive profits, Goldstein
decided to produce his own movie. *Birth*'s cinematic depiction of the Civil
War was a hit, so Goldstein figured he would focus on an equally epic subject:
the Revolutionary War.

Relying on the template of *Birth*'s family melodrama set against the War Between the States, Goldstein crafted a similar scenario. *The Spirit of '76* unfolded against the backdrop of the American Revolution. The film told the story of a half Native American girl (Adda Gleason) who aspired to become the queen of America. She falls in love with a treasonous colonial soldier (Howard Gaye)—who turns out to be her brother. The dramatic revelation occurs on their wedding day. Into this lurid tale of forbidden love Goldstein inserted historical reenactments, a technique aped from *Birth*.

While *Birth* presented historical moments with somber realism, *The Spirit of '76* opted for extravagant excess and eye-popping violence. In *United States v. Motion Picture Film The Spirit of '76* the court observed, "*The Spirit of '76* attempts to portray some of the more important phases of the American War for Independence and special scenes like Paul Revere's Ride, the signing of the Declaration of Independence, and the like, are given particular mention and prominence. In addition—and these are the parts of the film inveighed against—scenes purporting to illustrate the Wyoming Valley Massacre are shown. A British soldier is pictured impaling on a bayonet a baby lying in its cradle and then whirling it around his head so impaled. Other unspeakable atrocities committed by British soldiers, including the shooting of harmless women . . . are exhibited."[24] In another scene Goldstein showed "King George III crashing his fist in the face of kindly old Benjamin Franklin."[25]

In a quirk of poor timing, *Spirit* premiered in Chicago on May 15, 1917—one month after the United States' entry into World War I. The crux of *Spirit*'s problem was its adamant patriotism: Goldstein's film demonized the British. Moving into World War I, America's former enemy was now her greatest ally. The film's affront to the British was tantamount to treason.

On May 12, 1917, the film was granted a provisional permit.[26] The Windy City's watchdog, Maj. Funkhouser, sprang into action. By May 26 Chicago's board of censors released a report that positioned *Spirit* as dangerous propaganda intended to incite hatred of England.[27] Funkhouser rescinded the permit and demanded changes. Goldstein complied. At a screening for the board, the objectionable scenes were deleted. But then the censors discovered that "immediately following this preliminary presentation . . . [Goldstein] inserted [back] into the film in appropriate places the scenes of the Wyoming Massacre. . . . [T]his he did, he says, to excite the audience and attract greater attention to his production."[28]

This time Goldstein's gamble did not pay off. Authorities went after both the film and its producer.

Going further than *Mutual*, which denied motion pictures First Amendment protections, the *Spirit* decision took the next step. The court held that "the constitutional guaranty of free speech carries with it no right to subvert the purposes and destiny of the nation."[29] The film's portrayal of the British was viewed as beyond the pale of ordinary expression, entering into the realm of subversive propaganda.

Judge Benjamin Franklin Bledsoe gave great weight to the fact that the United States was at war and now supported a historical rival. He opined:

> History is history, and fact is fact. There is no doubt about that. At the present time, however, the United States is confronted with what I conceive to be the greatest emergency we have ever been confronted with at any time in our history. . . . We are engaged in a war in which Great Britain is an ally of the United States. It is a fact that we were at war with Great Britain during the Revolutionary times, and whatever occurred there is written upon the page of history and will have to stand, whomsoever may be injured or hurt by the recital or recollection of it. But this is no time, in my judgment (this is the thought that controls me in this matter) . . . for the exploitation of those things that may have the tendency or effect of sowing dissention among our people, and of creating animosity or want of confidence, between us and our allies, because so to do weakens our efforts, weakens the chances of our success, impairs our solidarity, and renders less useful the lives we are giving.[30]

Even though elements of *Spirit* were factual, the court determined that wartime was an inopportune moment to resurrect sordid history:

> Ordinarily the exploitation of such harmless, in one sense, highly inspiring in another sense, scenes such as Paul Revere's ride, which is one of the most beautiful things in history could not be detrimental or distasteful to anybody. . . . There are interspersed in this play those things which tend to appeal to the passions of our nature, which tend to arouse our revenge and to question the good faith of our ally, Great Britain, and to make us a little bit slack in our loyalty to Great Britain in this great catastrophe or emergency. Therefore, I say, this is no time or place for the exploitation of that which, at another time or place, or under different circumstances, might be harmless and innocuous in every aspect.[31]

Spirit's timing was wrong, the court determined: "There may come a time and place where this play, devoid of some of its horror, which never ought to be in it at any time, and devoid of its immorality, which is and ought to be shocking to any man who possesses a respectable quantum of decency in his makeup, devoid of those things, the time may come when it could be put on, and put on entertainingly and refreshingly before an audience of American people."[32]

Most notable about the *Spirit of '76* case was that the state did not stop with merely suppressing the film; authorities went after the filmmaker as well. In California Goldstein was arrested under the Espionage Act of 1917 for promoting insubordination and interference with military recruitment. He was convicted.[33] The filmmaker appealed to the Ninth Circuit, to no avail. He was sentenced to ten years imprisonment and fined $5,000 dollars—no filmmaker in the United States had ever been sentenced to jail time for the content of a

Robert Goldstein gives direction on the set of his ill-fated film, *The Spirit of '76* (1917). The picture was deemed to be treasonous propaganda under the Espionage Act of 1917. From the collections of the Margaret Herrick Library, Academy of Motion Picture Arts and Sciences.

motion picture. After the armistice President Wilson commuted his sentence to three years. Although Goldstein regained his freedom by 1921, he had lost his film and his fortune.

Coinciding with Goldstein's release, *The Spirit of '76* was revived for a screening. The *New York Times* covered the event on July 14, 1921. The footage that remained riled audiences but underwhelmed critics: "The photography is amazingly poor, and the acting, if it may be called that, generally below the level of the poorest movies commonly shown in the cheaper houses."[34] Goldstein did not see the show. Discouraged and destitute, he retired from filmmaking and returned to Germany, where he found himself once again in the wrong place at the wrong time. According to Anthony Slide, who published an expert reconstruction of *Spirit*, the last known communication from Goldstein was a letter postmarked 1935 from Germany to the Academy of Motion Picture Arts and Sciences. In the letter Goldstein requested a loan: "Because I can't pay $9 to have my American passport renewed I have been fined 75 Marks—and as I consequently can't pay that either—two weeks in jail."[35] Without any money to flee the country as the Nazis gained control, Goldstein almost certainly died in the Holocaust.

War films were able to pass censors as long as political alliances were properly coordinated. Films permitted by municipal censors proved that violence—even grisly, over-the-top scenes of torment—could be tolerated as long as the Germans were on the receiving end. But pictures whose politics ran afoul of the censor boards became vulnerable. *The Birth of a Nation* found its unreformed racism challenged, but box office success granted a certain immunity. *The Spirit of '76* was not as fortunate. Politically unwelcome because of its provocative portrayal of the redcoats, *Spirit* became an example of censorship at its worst. Both film and filmmaker suffered. To date, *The Spirit of '76* remains a lost picture and Robert Goldstein a tragic example of wartime legal fervor.

While the political speech of war themes galled regulators, various censorship boards were uncharacteristically permissive of artistic nudity during the 1915–1920 period.

Audrey Munson (1891–1986) bared all in two films distributed by Mutual: *Inspiration* (1915) and *Purity* (1916). Prior to her unabashed appearances on film, Munson, called the "Venus of America," served as a muse for several notable artists. In 1912, when Alexander Calder was appointed to chair the sculpture program at San Francisco's Panama–Pacific International Exposition, he turned to the lithe twenty-one-year-old beauty. Munson modeled for

Ad for *Purity* (1916) featuring Audrey Munson, from
the *El Paso Herald*, October 5, 1916.

Calder's *Star Maiden* (1913–1915) as well as for several other sculptors at the
exhibition. By the conclusion of the world's fair her film career had begun.

Munson's film appearances did not stray far from her role as an artist's
model. In *Inspiration*, Munson embodied the ideal of feminine perfection,
which provided fitting grounds for her to undress on-screen. *Purity* added a
bit more plot; this time the girl posed nude in order to raise money to publish
her boyfriend's poetry. While briefly held up by New York's review board,
Purity passed the censors and was often praised.[36] The *Moving Picture World*'s
reviewer commented, "Audrey Munson represents the perfection of womanly
form."[37] In many theaters art lovers queued up and "patiently waited for seats
to view the classic posings of the most celebrated art model in the world."[38]
The film was banned in certain regions, such as Ohio, Kansas, and Dallas, but
the prohibition never rose to the level of warranting a legal decision.[39]

Audrey Munson was not the only celebrity to appear nude on-screen.
Swimming star Annette Kellerman (1886–1975) also displayed the full fron-
tal with little legal consequence. Kellerman shot to fame in 1905 when she
attempted to swim the English Channel, but it was her public appearances
wearing a one-piece swimsuit that made her a star. She appeared in several
films that capitalized on her sleek shape, including *The Mermaid* (1911), *Siren
of the Sea* (1911), and *Neptune's Daughter* (1914). These were but a prelude to
her nautical epic, *A Daughter of the Gods* (1916). Shot on location in Jamaica on

a reported $1 million budget, *Daughter* was most notable for what Kellerman did *not* wear. Like Audrey Munson's unclothed display, there is no record of outrage or censorship.

It wasn't only art cinema that got away with female nudity: studio films also promised hints of forbidden flesh. IMP, the seedling that would become Universal, released *Traffic in Souls* (1913), the story of a prostitution ring shot in faux documentary style. The nascent Warner Bros. also drew on exploitation-type fare with *Open Your Eyes* (1919), an exposé on venereal disease. Paramount and Fox were most adept at peddling the flesh parade—and getting their pictures past the censors. In *The Cheat* (1915) Cecil B. DeMille told the story of a socialite who becomes indebted to an Asian ivory trader (Sessue Hayakawa) and is unable to repay the loan. Taking his recompense,

Ad for *A Daughter of the Gods* (1916) featuring Annette Kellerman, from the *New York Tribune*, December 26, 1916.

Inspiration (1915), featuring Audrey Munson.

Annette Kellerman (1886–1975) in *A Daughter of the Gods* (1916).

Hayakawa passionately seizes the girl and literally possesses her—branding her with a red-hot iron on her bare shoulder. The scene remains outrageous one hundred years after the film was released, for DeMille's direction delights in explicit sadism.

The undisputed champion of titillating audiences and overriding the censorship boards was Fox Film. Fox released *A Daughter of the Gods* with Annette Kellerman, but the studio built a veritable franchise upon the ample bosom of Theda Bara, the screen's first true sex symbol. Bara (1885–1955) burst onto the scene in *A Fool There Was* (1915). She was a femme fatale, a dangerously voracious woman, a man-eating temptress. Bara's character introduced audiences to the "vamp," a type of woman as far removed from Mary Pickford and Lillian Gish as humanly possible. A predatory home wrecker, Bara was adored by audiences for her memorable lines such as, "You have ruined me, you devil, and now you discard me!" and the immortal "Kiss me, my fool!"

William Fox realized he had a voluptuous gold mine. The studio followed *A Fool* with films promising even more unbridled nymphomania. The curvaceous bombshell appeared in *Siren of Hell* (1915), *Sin* (1915), and *The Vixen* (1916). She personified historical temptresses with *Cleopatra* (1917), *Salome* (1917), and *DuBarry* (1917).

Successful at the box office, Bara's films were anathema to censorship boards. She was "every young man's dream and every maiden's despair."[40] Bara's siren was exactly the type of woman that censors did not want to see on-screen. While outraged women's groups and social reformers followed Bara's films across the country, Kansas actively took steps to censor her films. *The Devil's Daughter* (1915) and *The Eternal Sappho* (1916) were cited by the board. The *Topeka Daily Capital* announced *The Serpent* (1916) with a proviso: "From advance reports, it is indicated the censorship scissors may descend."[41] Several other municipalities attacked Bara, but these rejections did not rise to the level of lawsuits or published opinions. The *Moving Picture World* commented, "The Seattle Board had almost barred *A Fool There Was* . . . but passed it after quite a little trimming."[42] Bara's films were successful enough that Fox simply avoided the burden of bringing suits in prudish regions.

Theda Bara (1885–1955) in *Cleopatra* (1917). From the collections of the Margaret Herrick Library, Academy of Motion Picture Arts and Sciences.

Munson and Kellerman appeared nude with little legal consequence. Bara tempted audiences with transparent costumes and insatiable vixens but escaped censure in many cases. But one film, which offered neither explicit nudity nor sexual temptation, was the subject of condemnation and prohibition. *The Sex Lure* (1916) was banned for provocative advertising.

After building his reputation on the Yiddish stage, Ivan Abramson (1886–1934) specialized in titillating motion pictures.[43] He wrote and directed *Forbidden Fruit* (1915), *The Faded Flower* (1916), and *Her Surrender* (1916), films that promised salacious showings. *The Sex Lure* (1916) had a spicy title, but the melodrama was mostly humdrum. The scenario centered on a wealthy man whose adopted daughter attempts to seduce him and break up his marriage. The New York board of censors found no issue with the story or the images but rather with the title. In *Ivan Film Productions v. Bell* the court wrote, "The title of the play, *The Sex Lure*, and the method of advertising, are in offense against morality, decency, and public welfare, and . . . the title of the photoplay and the method of advertising are purely for the purpose of holding out to the public that the photoplay is of an indecent character, thus creating an immoral curiosity as to the nature of the same."[44]

At trial, the issue did not rest on whether the film was obscene or immoral. Rather, "the question . . . is whether the commissioner of licenses has the power to revoke the license of a theater simply upon the ground that the name of the play and the methods of advertising on billboards and elsewhere are objectionable."[45] Could a motion picture be banned because its advertisements were too sexy?

The court weighed the film's sensational marketing against its more modest handling of the content. "The method of advertising a play may be disgusting, [and] offensively sensational . . . either on billboards or in the newspapers or elsewhere; but this has nothing to do with the character of the exhibition itself, and is obviously not an offense committed in the exhibition."[46] Judge Clarence Shearn's opinion at first seemed to oppose the prohibition. But then the winds changed:

That the name and the method of advertising invite the public to a prurient and disgusting performance is only too obvious. The performance itself, however, is said to be a clean one . . . so it is established that the plaintiff is inviting the public to the theater upon false pretenses, and seeking to capitalize whatever the degenerate interest there may be created by the use of this name and the posters that go with it. Furthermore, the name, and the posters taken together are indecent, nasty, and offensive. Such practices result, too, in bringing odium unjustly upon the many respectable members of the important motion pictures industry. The plaintiffs do not come into court with clean hands, and upon this ground the motion for injunction is denied.[47]

New York banned *The Sex Lure* based on salacious advertising. Actual nudity could be permitted as long as it was "artistic." But a marketing campaign that pandered to prurient interests was unacceptable.

Sex and violence were both obvious magnets for film censorship. But films featuring both of these subjects were able to bypass the state regulators in many instances. Perhaps less obvious were the threats from social reformers advocating birth control.

One of the prime movers of progressive social reform was Margaret Sanger (1879–1966). Working as a nurse on the Lower East Side of Manhattan, Sanger was an eyewitness to the damage caused by back alley abortions and frequent childbirth among the working classes. By 1914 she wrote and distributed a newsletter advocating birth control and family planning as part of the solution to ease economic burdens. Sanger's educational articles ran

Ad for Ivan Abramson's naughty-titled melodrama *The Sex Lure* (1916),
Moving Picture World, November 11, 1916.

afoul of the Comstock Law, which criminalized not only obscene and lewd materials but also dissemination of information on birth control. By 1916 she opened the first birth control clinic in the United States and was arrested for distributing contraception. To further her cause Sanger directed and appeared in a film with the straightforward title of *Birth Control* (1917).

Birth Control was a brazenly propagandistic picture. In *Message Photoplay Co. v. Bell*, Judge Nathan Bijur noted:

> The scenario of the play may be summarized as follows: it presents a number of pictures showing the poverty and misery frequently associated with the presence of large families of children among the poor. It illustrates the sufferings of one or more women to whom childbirth means serious danger to life. It then presents picture[s] of comfort among the rich where smaller families are supposed to obtain. Intermingled with these are pictures of Mrs. Sanger acting as a nurse. She is strongly tempted to advise some of the poor suffering women on the subject of birth control, but refrains from giving such information because it is forbidden by law, Penal Law [section] 1142. . . . [N]o suggestion or hint of the methods or means looking to a violation of the law or facilitating birth control is anywhere contained in the proposed exhibition. It may perhaps be inferred from the picture that the rich violate the law by employing contraceptive methods of which the poor are ignorant.[48]

While New York's film censors objected to the subject matter of *Birth Control*, Judge Bijur framed the issue differently. He inquired "whether there is any valid or reasonable basis for the Commissioner's opinion that the play is against morality, decency or public welfare."[49]

Bijur did not bow to social pressures in his opinion:

> The objections to the exhibition . . . may . . . be summed up as follows: First, that it deals with a subject which is in itself immorally suggestive; second, that it advertises the existence of contraceptive methods or means . . . third, a subject of this kind is not fit treatment in a public moving picture theater; fourth, that the performance encourages a violation of the law. Taking up the last objection first, I can find no sound basis for it. The result of the exhibition is to show Mrs. Sanger punished for a violation of the law. There is no encouragement for others to follow the same course. . . . The objection that the matter is not of a character fit for

treatment at a public moving picture exhibition seems to me to lie rather to the good taste of the promoters of the picture rather than to any legal impropriety in the play itself."[50]

Bijur was sympathetic to Sanger's progressive platform, writing that "viewed as other than an ordinary dramatic entertainment, the exhibition is merely a pictured argument against an existing law. As such it deals with undoubtedly great problem[s] of life, in which our citizenship as a whole has the right to take an active interest. . . . The picture suggests nothing erotic or obscene; neither the subject of birth control nor the course of its advocates or opponents is presented in 'high colors' nor with undue exaggeration, but rather in a measured and dispassionate tone."[51] In a coup for free speech advocates, Bijur held in the film's favor: "It is a measured and decent exercise of the right of free speech guaranteed by our constitutions, essential to our national well being, and, as such, beyond the power of the commissioner to forbid."[52]

The success was short lived. One month later the decision was reversed on appeal. Judge Frank C. Laughlin set aside Bijur's ruling and deferred to the board of censors. Once again *Birth Control* was found to be injurious to public morality, decency, and welfare. Wrote Laughlin: "I am of opinion that the action of the commissioner is justified both in the interests of public decency and public welfare. . . . [B]y virtue of the statute conferring upon the commissioner authority to grant and to revoke licenses, he necessarily has a broad discretion in the interests of public welfare."[53]

Sanger may have lost the battle over *Birth Control*, but in the long run she greatly impacted the American cultural landscape. Going on to found Planned Parenthood, Sanger also contributed her efforts to the landmark *Griswold v. Connecticut* case, which legalized contraception.[54] Almost fifty years after her film was banned, Sanger's message was accepted on a nationwide scale.

Sanger was not the only feminist using the cinema to reach the masses. Unlike Sanger, who was a nurse and social reformer, Lois Weber (1881–1939) began her career as an urban missionary. In the spirit of evangelism, she turned to the cinema to spread the message of social change.[55] Many of her more than 125 films touched on social themes, including religious tolerance, abortion, alcoholism, birth control, drug addiction, prostitution, and the inadequacy of teacher's salaries.[56]

In 1914 Weber wrote, directed, and produced her first feature, a faith-infused allegorical tale entitled *Hypocrites* (1914). The semitransparent figure of a nude actress, "Naked Truth" personified, flitted through the film's segments. Although the nudity was "artistic," the National Board of Review called a special session. The film was passed with positive comments.[57] Several markets, including Ohio, Boston, Portland (Maine), Lexington, and Minneapolis banned the picture; nevertheless, *Hypocrites* was seen as a critical and commercial success. In Jacksonville *Hypocrites* played to capacity crowds. Return and extended engagements were booked in Pittsburgh, Nashville, Louisville, Montgomery, Dallas, San Francisco, San Jose, and Los Angeles, among other markets.[58]

Lois Weber's films were not restricted to art houses, and they were not all educational films with limited releases. Rather she was one of the top directors at Universal. Backed by Carl Laemmle, Weber had surprisingly little interference from censors, despite her choice of provocative subject matter. That is, until she returned to a certain topic.

Where Are My Children? (1916) and *The Hand That Rocks the Cradle* (1917) sermonized on the subjects of abortion and birth control. Brooklyn's district attorney, Harry Lewis, seemed to have a personal vendetta against Weber's films: "If I never do anything else in my life, I will see to it that the morals of youths and young girls are afforded every protection the law allows. I am bitterly opposed to . . . films that portray the sex relations, and also exhibit the hidden crimes of society for the curious mind of the young."[59] Lewis aimed to silence Weber's social issues films. The same month that Bijur ruled in favor of Sanger's *Birth Control*, Judge Samuel Greenbaum ruled against Weber's *Hand That Rocks the Cradle*.

The similarities between the two films were not coincidental. Weber's *Cradle* was based on Sanger's 1916 trial for distributing contraception. In the film, Weber starred as a woman who discovers the importance of family planning after observing the plight of sickly and impoverished mothers. Attempting to help, she is arrested for supplying birth control. After much hand-wringing drama the governor pardons the woman, creating a Hollywood ending for the urban nightmare.[60]

Notwithstanding the *Mutual* precedent, which denied motion pictures First Amendment protections, Weber's defense positioned *Cradle* as political speech. The court took note in its analysis, "We have here . . . an exhibition, which, it is claimed, is produced for the purpose of accomplishing the repeal of an objectionable law."[61] But Judge Greenbaum's court did not treat Weber with the same deference that Bijur afforded Sanger.

The court interpreted *Cradle* as sympathetic to the criminal actions. Weber's character acted "with full knowledge that what she was doing was

Director Lois Weber (1879–1939). From the collections of the Margaret Herrick
Library, Academy of Motion Picture Arts and Sciences.

contrary to existing law . . . expounding methods of contraconception [*sic*] to
miscellaneous audiences of women."[62] Despite acknowledging that Weber's
platform was intended to challenge existing law, the court avoided any discussion of political speech, oddly focusing on icons of outlaw culture: "It is true
that plays have been produced and exhibited in which great criminals are the
principal figures. Instances may be cited in which the lives of such notorious historical and fictional bandits as Robin Hood, Captain Kidd, and men
of the type of Dick Turpin have been staged; but such productions are not
presented for the purpose of accomplishing the repeal of the laws forbidding

murder, robbery or piracy."[63] The argument—that *The Hand That Rocks the Cradle* was political speech and should be protected because it approached core constitutional values—was simply ignored.

Once again, film was seen as a business, pure and simple. For *The Hand That Rocks the Cradle*, the court opined, "We are dealing with a place of amusement . . . whose right to exhibit plays is not an absolute one, but in the nature of a privilege granted by the state."[64] Judge Greenbaum deferred to the censors and declined to intervene so long as their decision was not arbitrary or capricious: "It is wholly immaterial what the court's opinion may be as to the wisdom of the commissioner's action as long as he acted in good faith. The court cannot act as a commissioner of licenses. The commissioner did not act arbitrarily or capriciously. . . . [T]he discretion honestly exercised by the commissioner in the discharge of his duties may not be overthrown by the court, excepting only where it may be shown that his actions were influenced by corrupt or dishonest considerations, the burden of which rests upon the moving party."[65] While Sanger's birth control film prevailed in the lower court and was overturned on appeal, Weber's birth control film could not surmount the first challenge despite her argument that political speech should be closely protected.

The 1910s ended with the removal of the most ardent advocate of film regulation. Maj. Funkhouser had been the driving force behind film censorship in Chicago. Ultimately, his obsessive control proved to be his undoing, and by the end of the decade Chicago reined in its watchdog as his decisions grew increasingly capricious and his manner increasingly ornery. A storm of protest erupted when he cut two anti-German scenes from Griffith's *Hearts of the World* (1918). The *Exhibitor's Trade Review* commented that Funkhouser was discriminating in favor of the Germans.[66] Funkhouser filed a libel suit, but the periodical only expanded its attacks to his treatment of the Mary Pickford and Cecil B. DeMille production *The Little American* (1917), Theda Bara's *The Rose of Blood* (1917), and *My Four Years in Germany* (1918). Based on his erratic behavior and controversial rulings, Funkhouser was removed in June 1918 as the city revamped its censorship policy. Chicago's city council voted to abolish a single censor in favor of a panel.[67] In the coming years, instead of concentrating power in an individual, motion picture regulation would be handled in a more systematic manner by multimember state agencies, as well as by the MPPDA, presided over by the diplomatic and even-tempered Will Hays.

6

SELF-REGULATION REEMERGES

—

In the 1910s evangelical groups protested what they saw as evil influences unspooling in motion picture parlors. A decade later a new wave of filmmakers turned to the religious right as allies against state-sponsored censorship. Enter Will H. Hays.

William Harrison Hays (1879–1954) was a paragon of conservative values. Elected chairman of the Republican National Committee in 1918, Hays rode Warren Harding's coattails to the White House in 1920. For his service, Harding appointed Hays to the cabinet-level position of postmaster general. The president's conservatism was a public persona; in private Harding was known to stock bootlegged liquor and carry on extramarital affairs. Harding's executive term would be marked by scandal. Not so for Hays—his record was immaculate.[1]

By the early 1920s film industry executives stood by as states enacted film censorship laws. Following Pennsylvania's law, Maryland, New York, Florida, and Virginia ratified motion picture regulations. Equally troubling were the municipal censors. As the industry coalesced into vertically integrated studio-powerhouses, localized regulations increased the difficulty of establishing a nationwide distribution network. And then there were the scandals. America's innocent sweetheart, Mary Pickford, divorced her first husband (on March 3,

1920) and married screen stud Douglas Fairbanks (on March 20, 1920). It was a bad year for the powerful Pickfords: in September 1920 Mary's brother, Jack, was implicated in his wife's death. Jack's wife, Olive Thomas, had been a pinup model and Ziegfeld Girl before marrying into Hollywood royalty. On holiday in Paris Thomas died of an overdose. Only increasing the scandalous nature of the incident, the autopsy revealed that Thomas had ingested her husband's topical syphilis medication. Divorce, death, and VD were only the beginning—the Fatty Arbuckle scandal (1921), William Desmond Taylor's unsolved murder (1922), Wallace Reid's drug-related death (1923), charges of bigamy against Rudolph Valentino (1923), and Thomas Ince's mysterious murder (1924) loomed in the near future. To the rest of America, Hollywood looked like a moral cesspool.

Self-regulation took on renewed importance. In response to the *Mutual* decisions and increasing regulatory pressure, film executives formed the National Association of the Motion Picture Industry (NAMPI).[2] By February 1921 NAMPI issued standards, which became known as the Thirteen Points. This list enumerated cinematic taboos, such as (1) exploiting interest in sex in an improper or suggestive manner; (2) white slavery; (3) illicit love that tends to make virtue odious and vice attractive; (4) nakedness and bedroom or bathroom scenes; (5) prolonged demonstrations of passionate love; (6) the underworld and vice; (7) drunkenness and gambling; (8) stories or scenes that may instruct the morally feeble in methods of committing crime; (9) depreciation of law officers; (10) offense to religious beliefs; (11) bloodshed and violence; (12) vulgar and improper gestures; (13) salacious titles and subtitles or advertising.[3] Industry trade papers saw NAMPI as an important step toward coordinating industry players.[4] Still, the organization was only an interim solution.

By December 1921 studio executives agreed that NAMPI's pointers were insufficient. Still hoping to stave off governmental involvement in the face of increasing state regulation and high-profile scandals, a new trade association was established: the Motion Picture Producers and Distributors of America (MPPDA). Enticed by a six-figure salary, Will Hays resigned from his cabinet post and in January 1922 signed on as the president of the MPPDA.[5]

Hays brought corporate organization to the motion picture industry. The freewheeling pioneering days became a distant era as Hays standardized and stabilized the relationship between producers, distributors, and exhibitors. By the end of his first quarter Hays had outlined a platform: "The industry must take its rightful place in the business world [and] in the educational world."[6]

Despite pressure on filmmakers to demonstrate restraint, it was controversial material that filled seats in theaters. Censors winced at *Fate* (1921), an autobiographical film starring Clara Hamon, who was acquitted of killing her millionaire husband despite her admission of shooting the railroad and oil magnate.[7] New York's censors refused to license *Voices of the City* (1921), a drama about police corruption starring Lon Chaney. There were some victories against the censors. Hal Roach raised the comedic ante in *Good Riddance* (1923). This picture featured a gag in which a stick of dynamite was tied to a donkey's tail. The donkey was then thrown out of an airplane. The censors claimed the *Jackass*-worthy stunt was "inhuman" and "would incite [viewers] to crime." In *Weathers v. Cobb* the court put the censors in their place, passing the film and insightfully commenting, "No doubt a good many of our restless and inciteable [*sic*] youth might imitate these things if they could get ahold of the airplane and the dynamite."[8]

Hays and the MPPDA tried to tone down controversial content to prevent the spread of state censorship. But the existing regulations remained firmly in place. Industry self-censorship had become an additional measure rather than a replacement for the patchwork of local ordinances. When the Hays office developed the "Formula" in 1924, yet another level of complexity was added.

The Hays Formula was a mechanism to vet source material prior to production. This proactive approach, moving regulation into the production phase rather than abridging inappropriate scenes after a film's completion, was intended to cut costs and save time. A producer would submit a synopsis of the film's content, and the commission would respond to the suitability of the material. The voluntary scheme was largely ineffective, prompting the Hays office to create a specialized subdivision: the Studio Relations Committee (SRC). The SRC was established in 1927 under the direction of Colonel Jason Joy. Joy's division called on production chiefs, including Irving Thalberg (MGM) and B. P. Schulberg (Paramount), to help refine the Formula into a set of rules that became known as the "Don'ts and Be Carefuls."[9] Internally referred to as the Magna Charta, these guidelines were adopted by the MPPDA on June 29, 1927.

The MPPDA's Magna Charta was similar to the Thirteen Points, only more detail oriented. The "Don'ts" included profanity, licentious or suggestive nudity, illegal traffic in drugs, sexual perversions, white slavery, miscegenation, sex hygiene and venereal diseases, scenes of actual childbirth, children's sex organs, ridicule of the clergy, or willful offense to any nation or race. The "Be Carefuls" revealed an even more granular listing. Special care was

cautioned for twenty-six subjects, including use of the flag, international relations (films were to avoid picturing another country's religion, history, insti-
tutions, prominent people, and citizenry in an unfavorable light), religion and
religious ceremonies, arson, theft, robbery, safecracking and the dynamiting
of trains and locales (bearing in mind the effect that a too-detailed description
of these may have upon the "moron"), brutality and possible gruesomeness,
technique of committing murder, methods of smuggling, actual hangings or
electrocutions, sympathy for criminals, branding of people or animals, the
sale of women or women selling their virtue, rape or attempted rape, first
night scenes, man and woman in bed together, deliberate seduction of girls,
surgical operations, use of drugs, and excessively lustful kissing, particularly
when one character is a "heavy."[10]

Unlike the vague and open-ended state censorship statutes, the MPPDA
offered specifically listed proscriptions. The SRC tinkered with the code, adding several new items, such as the use of liquor, dances that emphasize indecent movements, and the use of firearms. In a pamphlet entitled "A Code to
Maintain Social and Community Values in the Production of Silent, Synchronized, and Talking Motion Pictures," the MPPDA stated their guiding principles: "No picture shall be produced which will lower the moral standards
of those who see it. Hence the sympathy of the audience should never be
thrown to the side of crime, wrongdoing, evil or sin. Correct standards of life
shall be presented on the screen, subject only to necessary dramatic contrasts.
Law, natural or human, should not be ridiculed, nor shall sympathy be created for its violation."[11]

It did not take long for producers such as Cecil B. DeMille to game the
system, portraying sin, debauchery, and criminal behavior until the final reel,
when the criminal would be punished, the playboy married, the adulteress
abandoned, and the alcoholic reformed to become a teetotaler.

Still, the Hays Formula was better than NAMPI's Thirteen Points. The
SRC's "Don'ts and Be Carefuls" were more explicit than any previous method.
Despite the SRC's many prohibitions, the agency was lax in its enforcement.
State boards continued to censor films that slipped through the industry's self-
regulation process. It was not until 1933, when the Production Code Administration (PCA) was put under the direction of Joseph Breen, that industry
self-regulation became a systematic, compulsory process.

7

MIDNIGHT MOVIES AND
SANCTIONED CINEMA

—

Films of the 1910s can seem remote, with remnants of Victorian values, melodramatic plots, and exaggerated acting style. By contrast, cinema of the 1920s can be more accessible to modern audiences. Newly emancipated women appeared on the scene, storylines became darker, and acting became more naturalistic. Three genres that matured in the 1920s would have a lasting impact on American cinema: youth films, procedural crime dramas, and, outside the studio system, exploitation films.

The roots of the exploitation genre developed from pseudo-documentary pictures that chronicled sensational subject matter. *The Inside of the White Slave Traffic* (1913) and *Traffic in Souls* (1913) depicted the problems of prostitution. The horrific consequences of venereal disease emerged as a subgenre. *Damaged Goods* (1914) set the tone, portraying salacious content with an educational slant. *Damaged Goods* told the nightmarish story of a young man who contracted syphilis from a prostitute and passed it on to his family. Maryland's censor permitted the film but restricted admission to male audiences.[1] The lurid tale was a hit and influenced a wave of similarly provocative films, including classics of contagion such as *The Scarlet Trail* (1918), *Wild Oats* (1919), *Open Your Eyes* (1919), *The End of the Road* (1919), and *The Solitary Sin* (1919).[2]

Producer and presenter Samuel Cummins (1895–1967) emerged as a leader in the subgenre of VD films with *The Naked Truth* (1924). *Truth* built on the formula seen in *Damaged Goods*: reckless youth contracts VD, leading to madness and murder. A New York court summarized the film's plot in *Public Welfare Group Corp. v. Lord*: "The [*Naked Truth*] traces the lives of three young men from boyhood to manhood, and is intended to portray the dangers and results of association with lewd women. It shows a male and female in the nude, and, among other things, the progress of different venereal diseases and the effects thereof. Petitioner claims that it is educational. Defendant answers that it is obscene and indecent."[3] The court coyly underplayed some of the more colorful aspects of the plot. One syphilitic young man is forced to postpone his wedding to face medical treatment. Another hides his infection and gets married but without treatment loses his mind and kills his wife.

Cummins's *Naked Truth* provided an archetypal example of an exploitation film that combined moral and clinical education with a lurid story and shocking images. Supplementing the melodrama, *Truth* featured diagrams of the female reproductive system, animation of sperm fertilizing an egg, and graphic shots of diseased genitals showing the effects of syphilis and gonorrhea.[4]

Cummins's proto-exploitation film was released in New Jersey on a technicality. The Garden State censors ruled the film was not suitable for general exhibition, but it was granted a conditional pass for exhibition in noncommercial (i.e., educational) venues. Still not satisfied with the provisional pass, the producer appealed. In an instance of bureaucratic disorganization, the board failed to file a response. Public Welfare's petition was granted.[5] New Jersey censors would strive to avoid procedural mishaps in the future.

New York's handling of *The Naked Truth* was also noteworthy. Raising their noses at such lowbrow fare, New York judges refused to view the offending film. While this may seem to be a significant omission—neglecting to watch the film at issue—the court's refusal to screen the picture set a precedent.

Cummins claimed his film was educational; the censors called it indecent. Judge Edward C. Whitmyer deferred to the board: "It is not alleged, and does not appear, that the examining officials acted in bad faith, or capriciously, or arbitrarily, or without reasonable grounds for apprehending public morality, decency, or welfare. . . . Thus there is no question to review."[6] Cummins's complaint was dismissed.

Although *The Naked Truth* was banned in New York, Samuel Cummins continued to peddle provocative pictures for the next twenty-five years. He

Life in the fast lane: Helen Foster strips down in *The Road to Ruin* (1928).

imported titillating European titles, such as Kurt Gerron's *Girls for Sale* (1927) and Gustav Machatý's *Ecstasy* (1935), which introduced American audiences to the figure of Hedy Lamarr. Cummins also produced exciting lowbrow fare, such as *The Jungle Killer* (1932), and infotainment, such as *The Miracle of Birth* (1949). A late career magnum opus, Cummins's *10 Days in a Nudist Camp* (c. 1950) was an influential precursor to the "epidermis epidemic."

Emerging youth culture films became a target for the censors. In *The Road to Ruin* (1928), dircted by Mrs. Wallace Reid (Dorothy Davenport), a girl is introduced to life in the fast lane as she drinks, smokes, has sex, gets pregnant, has an illegal abortion, and then dies. A New Jersey court overturned the censors' ban as the *New York Times* lamented, "Film Censors Powerless."[7] While the picture played in the Northeast, *Road to Ruin* was banned in Birmingham. The distributor, True-Life Photoplays, attacked the Alabama ordinance as vague and ambiguous. This argument would prevail two decades later, but in *Brooks v. City of Birmingham* the court was not swayed: "It is difficult to imagine how a word description of a forbidden picture show could be more carefully drawn, in language more comprehensive and more definite in every particular, than that employed by the City Code."[8]

The Northern District Court of Alabama found the ban on *Road to Ruin* to be a valid exercise of police power. Applying the lowest level of judicial scrutiny, Judge Henry De Lamar Jr. opined, "The measures adopted have reasonable relation to that end and it is not open to the judiciary to interfere."[9] The days of such low-level "rational bias" scrutiny of laws that imposed restrictions on First Amendment rights would be numbered.

The Naked Truth was a precursor to the exploitation films that would flour-ish in the 1950s. But not all pictures cited by censors were at the bottom of the bill. Internationally acclaimed films such as Vsevolod Pudovkin's *The End of St. Petersburg* (1927) were banned in New York pending State Depart-ment approval.[10] New York's district attorney considered banning Dimitri Buchowetzki's German import *King of Kings* (1924) based on a provision of the state's penal code that made it a misdemeanor "to give a performance in which there is a living representation of the Deity."[11] Studio films were not exempt. First National's baseball picture *Babe Comes Home* (1927) was stopped in Chicago because of scenes in which the Bambino, Babe Ruth, was seen chewing tobacco.[12] Paramount's Academy Award–nominated *The Racket* (1928), a thinly veiled biopic of Al Capone, also had difficulty getting past Chicago censors. The film was ultimately permitted but only on an adults-only conditional pass.[13] United Artists' *Alibi* (1929) was recognized with three Academy Awards, including best picture and actor (Chester Morris), but criti-cal praise did not stop Chicago's ardent officials from condemning it.

Alibi was a police procedural that followed an urban crime unit as it hunted down a Prohibition-era gangster (Morris). The investigation is compromised when the gangster begins dating the detective's daughter (Mae Busch). The girl becomes a central figure in the criminal's alibi when a policeman is murdered.

The film was banned in Chicago. Like New York's *Naked Truth* court, the judge refused to view the film at issue. Instead, *United Artists Corp. v. Thomp-son* looked for guidance in familiar motion picture precedents: "The court, repeating the remarks made in the *Block* case concerning the necessity of protecting the more susceptible members of the audience, agreed that the film, which it did not view, could not fail to have a tendency to cheapen the value of human life in the minds of youthful spectators, and that its exhibi-tion would have a tendency toward immorality and to cause an increasing disrespect for the law and its officers."[14]

The case was not a total loss for filmmakers. The *Alibi* decision shined a light on the municipal ordinance. The court found the power of the city to permit films was a given; however, this power did not include punitive aspects. The court invalidated provisions of the ordinance that allowed con-fiscation without notice of unpermitted films in distribution.[15] The regula-tion stood, but a significant provision was expunged.

Exploitation filmmakers challenged the censors by producing and distrib-uting films on subject areas where most studio-made films feared to tread.

Samuel Cummins was early to adopt the strategy of marketing his pictures as "educational." This was a clever ruse designed to slip in otherwise objectionable footage. Reference to pubic regions was exciting, even if the context was venereal diseases or breeched babies—illicit images sold tickets. As crafty as Cummins's technique was, his arguments were defused when a court refused on principle to screen the challenged film. Filmmakers venturing outside accepted subject matter were in a difficult position. The *Mutual* precedent prevailed; censors had the upper hand, and courts deferred to the often arbitrary decisions of regional regulatory boards.

8

SOUND ENTERS THE DEBATE

—

As the motion picture industry developed, the legal system struggled to keep pace with new technology. Although films had been publicly exhibited for two decades before *Mutual*, the Supreme Court felt the need to legally define the medium: "The film consists of a series of instantaneous photographs or positive prints of action upon the stage or in the open. By being processed upon a screen with great rapidity there appears to the eye an illusion of motion. They depict dramatizations of standard novels, exhibiting many subjects of scientific interest, the properties of matter, the growth of the various forms of animal and plant life, and explorations and travels; also events of historical and current interest—the same events which are described in words and by photographs in newspapers, weekly periodicals, magazines, and other publications."[1]

That definition was sufficient for ten years. Prior to 1926 the censorship debate was a nagging inconvenience for developing studios, as jurisdictional boundaries could require different cuts made to a motion picture. With the coming of sound technology, these inconveniences became potentially lethal for a nationwide industry. Local censors, regional distributors, and individual exhibitors could easily alter a silent film. Sound technology drastically restricted film's malleability; with talkies, any subsequent editing destroyed synchronization. Thus the advent of sound films presented a make or break situation for filmmakers. Studios jumped at the chance to redefine their medium, with hopes they could circumvent censorship regulations.

On February 4, 1929, the Pennsylvania Supreme Court handed down two decisions on the issue of sound films that addressed the transformation of technology. These decisions were *In re Fox Film Corp.*, which addressed sound-on-film technology, and *In re Vitagraph, Inc.*, which addressed sound-on-disc technology.

Motion pictures had a storied history as an audio-visual medium. The first audio-visual experiment emanated from the Edison Laboratories in 1894. Using a Kinetophone, a hybrid device consisting of the Edison Kinetoscope and a wax cylinder phonograph, chief engineer W. K. L. Dickson produced and performed a squeaky violin solo for *The Dickson Experimental Sound Film* (c. 1894). Although the peephole-style viewing system lent itself to a solitary viewer wearing headphones, Edison did not pursue sound films. Sound amplification would have to wait.[2]

The wait was not long. In 1902 Gaumont debuted the Chronophone audio-visual system, and five years later, the improved Elgéphone system. Both were cylinder-based sound technologies (i.e., sound on disc). Pioneering female director Lois Weber directed and starred in several Gaumont sound films.[3] By 1907 Eugène Lauste had developed a rival technology: sound on film. Rather than using a secondary system such as a wax cylinder, Lauste's system transformed sound into light waves that were imprinted directly on the celluloid. Still, sound technology did not find widespread commercial use.

A decade later the experimentation with sound film continued. In 1919 the American inventor Lee de Forest patented a sound-on-film technology simultaneous with Germany's Tri-Ergon Company. Neither of these systems found commercial application. Nearly another decade would pass before the talkies would become an "overnight sensation."

Sound films burst out of Hollywood in the 1920s. The two competing technologies remained: sound on disc and sound on film. Western Electric, the manufacturing arm of AT&T Bell Laboratories, developed a sound-on-disc method for Warner Bros. The disc-based technology, dubbed Vitaphone, was unveiled in the non-sync-sound feature film *Don Juan* (1926), starring John Barrymore. Fox Film acquired rights to both De Forest's and Tri-Ergon's systems to market the Movietone sound-on-film technology. The first non-sync-sound Movietone feature was F. W. Murnau's Academy Award–winning *Sunrise* (1927). By 1929 Movietone and Vitaphone were competing for market share in the conversion to sound-film theaters.

Before sound technology, films could be censored in a piecemeal fashion by various state and municipal regulators. A silent film could survive for future exhibitions despite abridged, butchered, and condensed prints. The talkies presented a different scenario: neither sound on disc nor sound on film could survive a censor's cuts. Any alteration to the film's soundtrack would throw off synchronization, rendering the film unsuitable for exhibition. The network of nationwide censors now legitimately threatened filmmakers. The studios brought suit.

Fox was the first to challenge Pennsylvania's censorship statute (the film was unidentified in the court's opinion). The crux of Fox's argument rested on the common-law legal concept of *expressio unius est exclusio alterius*. That is, the expression of one thing excludes all others—when a series of items are listed, anything not explicitly stated is assumed to not be included. Relying on the Supreme Court's legal definition of motion pictures in *Mutual* and subsequent state statutes as a series of instantaneous photographs, the comprehensive description *excluded* any mention of audio-visual works. Therefore, Fox argued by parsing the legal language, the censorship statutes should not apply to sound films. "The basic and controlling question for determination is: Is the exercise of censorial powers of the board of censors over sound films— that is, spoken language films, to be displayed at public exhibitions—within the scope of the intent and purposes of the act of 1915?"[4] The court rejected Fox's interpretation; common sense would govern. A sound film could not be reasonably seen as "a thing so distinctly and intrinsically separate and apart from the object which the act of 1915 designates as a motion picture film, that it is fundamentally a new creation, and is not in fact a film. . . . [S]uch conclusion would lead into the realm of absurdity."[5]

Vitagraph attempted a similar legal sleight of hand: "Precisely the same basic question arises here that governed the *Fox Film* case: Has the board of censors, within the scope of the intent and purpose of the act of 1915, authority to require submission to it for approval or rejection of spoken language to be used as part of a motion picture intended for public exhibition?"[6] While Fox refused to submit their film on grounds that a talkie was fundamentally a different medium from a silent film, Vitagraph's technology permitted a different approach. Vitagraph submitted their *film* to the board of censors but not the accompanying disc that embodied the *soundtrack*. The censors received the image but not the companion audio. Vitagraph differentiated its claim from Fox in technological terms. While Fox's Movietone sound-on-film technology may fall within the statute's regulation of motion picture content,

Vitagraph argued, their own sound-on-disc was a wholly different technology and was outside the reach of censorship statutes. With little discussion the court disagreed: "The language was admittedly a part of the feature of the proposed exhibition, and as such came within the intent and purpose of the act of 1915."[7]

These filmmakers used ingenious methods and legal maneuverings to challenge the prevailing regulatory statutes. The courts, however, refused to allow studios to bootstrap their films with emerging technology as a means to escape the states' power to review motion pictures. Losing the legal battle, studios returned to strategic self-regulation with new determination as a last attempt to circumvent the censor's authority to alter their pictures.

9

TENSION INCREASES BETWEEN FREE SPEECH
AND STATE CENSORSHIP

—

As sound pictures entered the market in the late 1920s filmmakers were faced with increasing regulations on content. Conversely, print media was experiencing an era of greater freedom. The courts were beginning to review censorship of the press with greater scrutiny and liberate the written word from prior restraints.

Current notions of broad and unfettered free speech rights began evolving after World War I. Robert Goldstein's *The Spirit of '76* was not only censored as a film, but its producer was imprisoned for violating the Espionage Act of 1917. The state condemned both the speaker and his speech. Not long after the *Spirit of '76*/Goldstein debacle, the Supreme Court granted certiorari to *Schenck v. United States* (1919), which considered similar issues.

In 1917 the general secretary of the Socialist Party, Charles Schenck, printed fifteen thousand leaflets to oppose President Wilson's Conscription Act. Schenck intended to mail his broadsides to draftees. The circulars were undeniably political speech—close to the core guarantees of the First Amendment. Schenck's fliers may have been unpopular, but they did not advocate violent action; rather, his flamboyant rhetoric advised draftees to petition the repeal of the Conscription Act. Like Goldstein, Schenck was charged with conspiracy to violate the Espionage Act by attempting to cause insubordination in the military and to obstruct recruitment. The issue under consideration by the Supreme Court was simply whether Schenck's speech was protected under the First Amendment.

The answer was a swift and resounding "No." The unanimous 9–0 court spoke clearly: Schenck's speech fell outside of constitutional protections. Speaking for the Court, Justice Oliver Wendell Holmes opined that Schenck's speech created a "clear and present danger" such that Congress had a right to prevent.[1] The Court held that political pamphlets that might have been acceptable during peacetime could take on nefarious qualities during times of war. Holmes's influential "clear and present danger" test entered the lexicon to identify one type of unprotected speech.

Four years after *Schenck* the Court made another historic pronouncement in *Gitlow v. New York* (1925). Once again Socialists came under fire. Benjamin Gitlow published a periodical entitled the *Revolutionary Age*. Gitlow's arrest was incident to the distribution of the premier issue of the manifesto, which authorities claimed advocated the establishment of Socialism through labor strikes. Gitlow was convicted under New York's Criminal Anarchy Act of 1902. At trial Gitlow argued his speech should be protected under the First Amendment as the advocacy of a political position in the marketplace of ideas. The prosecution was unable to demonstrate any action resulting from the manifesto's publication. Gitlow's defense was that the *Revolutionary Age* manifesto did not present a clear and present danger.

The threshold issue was whether the First Amendment was a limitation solely on the federal government or whether it applied to states as well. A strict reading of the First Amendment sees an explicit directive to the federal government alone: "*Congress* shall make no law . . ." However, in *Gitlow* the Court took the opportunity to enunciate a broader interpretation of the First Amendment and adopted the doctrine of incorporation. The incorporation of the Bill of Rights is the process by which the courts have applied portions of the Bill of Rights to the states through the Fourteenth Amendment.

Under *Gitlow* a broad interpretation of the First Amendment would be construed: neither federal nor state government could abridge the freedom of speech. Even though the First Amendment would limit the government's ability to restrict speech, the rights of expression were not entirely unfettered. Writing for the unanimous Court, Justice Edward Terry Sanford opined, "It is a fundamental principle, long established, that the freedom of speech and of the press . . . does not confer an absolute right to speak or publish, without responsibility, whatever one may choose, or an unrestricted and unbridled license that gives immunity for every possible use of language and prevents the punishment of those who abuse this freedom." The Court balanced free speech with the state's powers to "punish those who abuse this freedom by utterances inimical to the public welfare, tending to corrupt public morals, incite to crime, or disturb the public peace."[2] *Gitlow* reiterated the rule seen in *Schenck*: the government had power to prohibit certain speech that embodied "dangerous tendencies."

After a series of cases that narrowed, circumscribed, and restricted the First Amendment, the tides began to turn with *Near v. Minnesota* (1931). *Near* clarified the Court's position on prior restraints of published material. "Prior restraint" refers to the state's authority to stop a communication before publication. This was always seen as strong medicine—silencing a speaker before he has spoken.

Jay Near published a tabloid newspaper in Minneapolis called the *Saturday Press*. His yellow journalism went mostly unnoticed until 1927, when the paper began attacking local officials. In banner headlines Near claimed the chief of police and other authorities were in the pocket of organized crime. A concurring opinion signed by three justices allowed Near's agitated copy to speak for itself: "There have been too many men in this city and especially those in official life who HAVE been taking orders and suggestions from JEW GANGSTERS, therefore we HAVE Jew Gangsters practically ruling Minneapolis. . . . Practically every vendor of vile hooch, every owner of a moonshine still, every snake-faced gangster and embryonic yegg in the Twin Cities is a JEW. . . . I simply state a fact when I say that ninety percent of the crimes committed against society in this city are committed by Jew gangsters."[3]

Under the theory that Near's paper presented a public nuisance, Minnesota officials obtained an injunction to stop the *Press*. The state called on a statute providing "that any person who shall be engaged in the business of regularly or customarily producing, publishing or circulating a newspaper, magazine or other periodical that is (a) obscene, lewd and lascivious or (b) malicious, scandalous and defamatory is guilty of a nuisance, and may be enjoined as provided in the Act."[4] The issue at bar was whether the Minnesota gag order violated the First Amendment by creating a prior restraint.

While not condoning Near's scandalous and possibly defamatory publication, the justices narrowly agreed in a 5–4 vote that the *Saturday Press* had the right to publish—even if the articles were untrue and motivated by malice. The Supreme Court held that Minnesota's statutory scheme was invalid under the First Amendment. The injunction against the newspaper was unconstitutional because prior restraint struck at the very heart of the First Amendment. With *Near v. Minnesota* the Court established that, with narrow exceptions, the state could not prohibit a publication even if the communication might be actionable after publication.

After *Near*, prior restraint of newspaper publication would be strictly scrutinized. Going forward, when regulating speech based on content the government would have the burden to demonstrate (1) a compelling interest that made it necessary to regulate, (2) narrowly tailored legislation to achieve that interest, and (3) the least restrictive means for achieving the state's interest. Never before had the press been guaranteed such expansive protection. As print media moved into a golden age of greater freedom, the circle of censorship tightened around the medium of motion pictures.

When Will Hays assumed leadership of the Motion Picture Producers and Distributors of America (MPPDA), the film industry was under fire from a series of scandals. Hays had three primary directives. First, he was charged with cleaning up Hollywood, controlling damage to the industry's moral standing that stemmed from high-profile divorces, rapes, murders, drug overdoses, and other forms of moral turpitude. Second, industry leaders relied on Hays to promote self-regulation as a means to stop the spread of regional censorship boards. As the studios coalesced into vertically integrated production-distribution-exhibition industrial units, regional censors would impede the celluloid assembly line. Third, as the studios evolved past the pioneering stage, they relied more on investment bankers and Wall Street financing. Hays served as a trustworthy, conservative voice, a functional guarantor and intermediary between filmmakers and investors.

While Hays was a politically savvy representative, his West Coast division—the Studio Relations Committee (SRC) run by Col. Jason Joy—created a code far too vague and voluntary to be effective. From the religious right, voices advocating censorship and self-regulation brought ideas of their own. Two key advocates were Martin Quigley and Father Daniel A. Lord.

Martin Quigley founded the *Exhibitors Herald* in 1915 and merged it with *Motography* in 1917. A decade later he acquired the *Moving Picture World*. Within four years he bought *Motion Picture News* and in 1931 merged all three trade papers into a single powerful voice: the *Motion Picture Herald*.[5] Quigley infused industry news with his conservative views. He was an advocate of self-regulation but found the early attempts, including the Don'ts and Be Carefuls, weak and insufficient.

Quigley found an ideological ally in Father Daniel A. Lord. A Jesuit professor of English at St. Louis University, Father Lord was summoned to Hollywood in 1927 to serve as an advisor on Cecil B. DeMille's *The King of Kings* (1927). Wandering among the plaster-of-paris pillars of Solomon's Temple and along the plywood Via Dolorosa, the cleric realized a cinematic pulpit could reach a far greater ministry. When Lord received a call from Quigley to help devise a new motion picture code, he must have seen providence. By 1930 Quigley and Lord hammered out a new production code geared to the moral uplift of motion pictures.[6]

While Quigley and Lord were collaborating on celluloid commandments, the MPPDA desperately needed an infusion of new energy. Col. Joy resigned from his post in 1932.[7] In his place New York censor James Wingate (1872–1961) was appointed. But Wingate never committed to a West Coast office, preferring his East Coast headquarters. It was during this period of disorganization that some of the most loved and notorious "pre-Code" films slipped past censors. Bela Lugosi's *Dracula* (1931) was red-banded as "adult entertainment which children will neither appreciate nor enjoy . . . not recommend[ed] for children under 15" but released unscathed by the SRC.[8] *Little Caesar* (1931) and *The Public Enemy* (1931) encouraged audiences to sympathize with gangster protagonists. Divorce, adultery, promiscuity, and prostitution looked glamorous when Marlene Dietrich went through the paces in *Blonde Venus* (1932) and *Shanghai Express* (1932). Tod Browning's *Freaks* (1932) brought disturbing images to the screen seen neither before nor since. *Tarzan and His Mate* (1932) depicted Maureen O'Sullivan's near-nudity in a jungle loincloth. Jean Harlow, Barbara Stanwyck, and Mae West relished their ability to use sex to control men in *Red-Headed Woman* (1932), *Baby Face* (1933), and *I'm No Angel* (1933). The censors tagged the ultra-violence of Howard Hawks's *Scarface: The Shame of a Nation* (completed 1931, released 1932),[9] but many images of sex, violence, and human abnormalities slipped past.

Disorganization and regime change in the SRC's West Coast office loosened the MPPDA's grip on studio pictures. Father Lord cited various morality violations: "26 of the pictures had plots built on illicit love, 13 were based on plots or main episodes in which seduction is accomplished, 18 characters lived in open adultery, 31 murders were committed."[10] All that was about to change. By the time Wingate vacated his post, his West Coast deputy had already usurped power. This administrator had informally led the commission since Joy's departure, but on July 6, 1934, Joseph I. Breen (1888–1965) was officially appointed head of the SRC.[11]

Three years earlier, Hays had poached Breen from Quigley's organization. At the MPPDA, Breen was the right man for the job: his outspoken conservative views gave him credibility with the proregulation crowd; his background in journalism fit perfectly with his position as Hays's public relations spokesperson. Breen's enthusiasm was apparent from the start. Two weeks after his appointment the *New York Times* reported that studios "scurried about trying to salvage some films [and] revise others. . . . Several million dollars is tied up in celluloid that has already been unofficially rejected by Joseph I. Breen, recently appointed morals director of the Hays office. His actions thus far threaten a shortage in pictures at the theaters unless studios can sufficiently whitewash the product already made."[12] Within three months Catholic leaders were publically praising the MPPDA's work—and endorsing 90 percent of the pictures passed.[13]

After a decade of ineffectual and sluggish administration, the SRC had lost its standing with moral reformers. Breen represented a much-needed infusion of integrity. He transitioned the SRC into a new entity: the Production Code Administration (PCA). The studios took Breen's comments seriously. Producers who contested Breen's decisions or proceeded with unapproved films found their actions reverberating in the investment community. Without PCA approval film financing was at risk. The Hays office under Breen operated under the guiding principle that content regulation was good business. Safe films equaled solid financing, and box office receipts justified Breen's rulings.[14]

As he took the reins at the PCA Breen was confronted by a new and powerful regulatory competitor: the National Recovery Administration (NRA). Under the NRA's oversight of trades and services, a subsection was created to oversee the motion picture industry.[15] Sol A. Rosenblatt became divisional administrator in 1933, and the grip of federal regulation was felt in the studios' front offices. Rosenblatt demanded strict oversight of the industry: "There are teeth in this reorganization . . . jail sentences and fines, and most important of all there is public opinion."[16] On January 27, 1934, Rosenblatt requested a meeting with the MPPDA and studio representatives at his Beverly Hills apartment.[17] After a tense discussion Breen emerged victorious. Breen's charisma, commitment to on-screen morality, and experience with the politics of film production won him Rosenblatt's confidence. While the threat of federal involvement remained a sword of Damocles hovering over the industry, the storm had passed. Joseph Breen, Hollywood's harshest critic, had saved the film industry from New Deal regulations.

There was little relief for filmmakers as Breen tightened the screws. With Breen in command, the studios diligently obeyed the regulator's directives— often allowing him to rewrite portions of their scripts. Harry Warner wired orders from New York: "If Joe Breen tells you to change a picture, you do what he tells you. . . . [I]f any one fails to do this—and this goes for my brother [Jack Warner]—he's fired."[18] Artistic freedom may have been restricted to gain the PCA's seal of approval, but the trade-off had benefits.

Quigley and Lord drafted the motion picture code; Breen was the muscle that implemented and energized their vision. Operating under the authority of the Hays office, these power brokers influenced a generation of Hollywood filmmaking. Filmmakers learned to "speak in code" to insinuate randy, bawdy, and banned behavior. While the code was restrictive, some of the most creative moments in Hollywood history resulted from working around the regulations. The code caused Betty Boop to cover up, killing her career, but other filmmakers mastered the art of omission. Paul Henreid pleasured Bette Davis with his seductive double-cigarette-lighting trick in *Now, Voyager* (1942). Innuendo sparked in *Double Indemnity* (1944), *The Postman Always Rings Twice* (1946), and *The Big Sleep* (1946). Alfred Hitchcock worked around the code's three-second kissing rule by having Cary Grant and Ingrid Bergman unlock their lips intermittently during a two-and-a-half-minute sequence in *Notorious* (1946).

Hays and Breen stood proud as the moral voices of Hollywood; however, as World War II ended, the balance of power in Hollywood shifted. After almost twenty-five years as president of the MPPDA, Will Hays retired in 1945. Breen left the PCA in 1941 for a stint at RKO Pictures but was back at the PCA office by the end of the year. He remained in command of the West Coast office until retiring in 1954. Father Lord died in 1954. Quigley continued publishing until 1965, long after his moral code had become an anachronism. Still, through his trade papers, Quigley had been an influential voice in the film industry for fifty years.

While Hollywood pictures were scrutinized by the PCA, movies made outside the studio system avoided Breen's comments. In the 1930s a wave of European films delivered a new level of sophistication to the American cinema and in the process riled state regulators. New York's board of censors in particular made a continuing effort to stamp out a string of Continental pictures with rousing titles such as *Ecstasy*, *Whirlpool*, and *Amok*.

10

THREATS FROM ABROAD AND
DOMESTIC DISTURBANCES

—

By 1934 Breen's office had tightened the screws on studio films but couldn't eliminate the threat of immoral, improper, sacrilegious, and un-permitted pictures. Several challenges came from socially progressive European film-makers. Artistic traditions on the Continent had long been comfortable addressing issues of infidelity, female sexuality, and male inadequacy—themes that alarmed prudish U.S. reformers. But the menace to morality was not only foreign: independent American moviemakers also avoided the oversight of the Production Code Administration (PCA). Bryan Foy and Al Christie were brought up in the Hollywood system before going rogue and operating independently. Skirting the code, they could produce fast, cheap exploitation films that defied regulations and were nimble enough in distribution and exhibition to mostly avoid getting caught. The regulations of the 1930s cleaned up studio films but also encouraged a counter industry that thrived on the forbidden.

As the PCA allocated its resources to scrutinize movies released by Hollywood's film factories, European pictures were reaching a heightened level of sophistication and social realism. Imported art films bypassed the PCA's mechanism for approval. One film in particular disturbed the status quo with adult themes, explicit nudity, a remarkable starlet, and an eye-catching title: *Ecstasy*.

Gustav Machatý, a native of Prague, began his career far from Hollywood in the Austrian-Hungarian Empire. He obtained an apprenticeship with fellow countryman Erich von Stroheim and assisted the notoriously temperamental director on *Foolish Wives* (1922). *Foolish Wives* incorporated elements of both Hollywood and European filmmaking. Dipping into Universal's deep pockets, von Stroheim commissioned extravagant sets, indulgent costumes, and meticulous scenic design. While these production values represented Hollywood at its very best, von Stroheim's complex screenplay drew from his European-influenced penchant for mature themes; the promiscuous social climbing of an aristocrat-poseur was not a typically American plot. After working with von Stroheim, Machatý returned to Bohemia to begin his own film career.

On his own, Machatý focused his camera on aristocratic debutants, promiscuous protagonists, and explicit nudity. *Kreutzerova sonáta* (1927) and *Seduction (Eroticon*, 1929) were successful films in Czechoslovakia. For his next project he discovered a nineteen-year-old named Hedwig Kiesler and built a scenario around her captivating beauty. *Extase (Ecstasy*, 1933) was the story of a young bride. She weds an older man who is unable to perform his wedding night responsibility. Before long she packs her bags and returns to her father's farm. "What happened?" asks her father. "Nothing," she responds sadly. Back on the family farm, passion and vitality return to the girl. One morning she skinny-dips in a secluded pond. Sensing a nearby filly, her horse runs off, and the girl gives naked pursuit—until she runs into a handsome young engineer employed by her father. That night she finds herself at the strapping young engineer's cabin. The two are drawn together as they lie back on a couch intertwined. Machatý's camera focuses on the girl's face as she achieves the eponymous ecstasy.

Promoted as "The Most Whispered About Picture In the World," *Ecstasy* became an international hit. At the Venice International Film Festival the picture was a runner-up for the Mussolini Cup, despite pans from the *Osservatore Romano*.[1] The Vatican reviewer denounced *Ecstasy* as "appealing to the lowest passion in human souls."[2] *Ecstasy* did not escape notice in America. Louis B. Mayer flew to Europe to meet the director and his raven-haired beauty. Signing them both to MGM, Mayer transformed Hedwig Kiesler into Hedy Lamarr. While Mayer claimed the starlet, Samuel Cummins, the impresario who had produced *The Naked Truth*, settled for *Ecstasy* itself. Cummins acquired the film's domestic distribution rights—a much more troublesome prize.

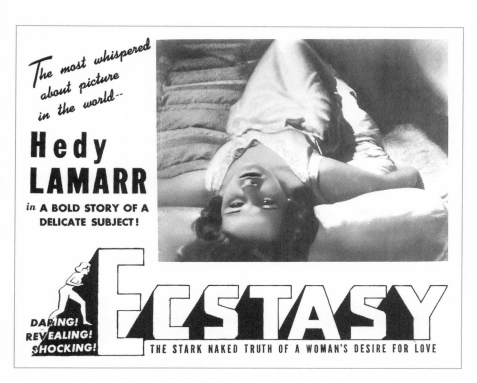

Gustav Machatý's controversial *Ecstasy* (1933).

Hedwig Kiesler a.k.a. Hedy Lamarr
(1914–2000), in *Ecstasy* (1933).

Ecstasy immediately ran into trouble when the picture was impounded at U.S. Customs. Under the Smoot–Hawley Tariff Act of 1930, officials were empowered to seize imported material and hold it pending an adjudication of possible obscenity: "All persons are prohibited from importing . . . any obscene book, pamphlet, paper, writing, advertisement, circular, print, picture, drawing, or other representation. No such articles . . . shall be admitted to entry . . . [and] shall be seized and held by the collector to await the judgment of the district court."[3] The film was shown to Judge John C. Knox and a panel of jurors. Verdict: the film was objectionable.[4] On appeal, the circuit court dismissed the action in *United States v. Two Tin Boxes* (1935).[5]

One year later the film's U.S. distributor was back in court in *Eureka Productions v. Lehman.* The distributor asserted that the state's regulations unduly burdened international commerce and discriminated against imported works. The commissioner of education countered that a permit was denied because the film was "indecent and immoral and would tend to corrupt morals."[6] Eureka's claim failed. The court opined, "All films, domestic and foreign, offered for exhibition in the state of New York, are subject to uniform regulations by the provisions of the statute. The statute did not deal differently with foreign films. All are required to meet the same standard of decency and morality."[7] The ban on *Ecstasy* remained intact on appeal, with the court concurring that the film "unduly emphasized the carnal side of the sex relationship."[8] As late as 1939 *Ecstasy* was still refused a permit.[9] In addition to New York, the film also ran into difficulties in Massachusetts and Maryland and remained banned in Pennsylvania until 1948.[10]

Ecstasy was imported just as the Breen regime began flexing its full muscle. By the 1930s a series of regulatory mechanisms monitored the film industry, from federal laws, such as the Tariff Act of 1930 and the lingering Espionage Act of 1917, to state and municipal censorship ordinances, together with the self-imposed code of the MPPDA and the vocal opinions of religious groups. This intense regulatory atmosphere did not discourage European filmmakers from confronting adultery, nudity, and impotence on-screen. A new wave of European-made films was about to test the U.S. censors.

Shortly after *Ecstasy*, another European art film, again focusing on the forbidden themes of impotence and adultery but also adding the taboo of suicide, caught the eye of New York's board of censors. *Remous* (*Whirlpool*, 1935) was directed by Edmond T. Gréville. Gréville launched his career as an assistant director for several masters of Continental cinema, including French visionary Abel Gance and German expressionist E. A. Dupont. In 1935 Gréville directed two films. The first was a Josephine Baker vehicle, *Princess Tam-Tam*

(1935), a musical comedy built around the performer's bubbly star persona; the second was a darker drama, *Remous*. In *Mayer v. Byrne* the New York Court dismissively summarized *Remous*: "The plot is practically the same as that of the picture *Ecstasy*."[11] This description was not entirely accurate, although the theme of an ineffective male and a lusty female ran through both films. *Remous* chronicles the life of a young married couple whose happiness is torn apart when the husband (Jean Galland) is crippled in an automobile accident. Unable to be satisfied by her impotent husband, the nubile newlywed (Jeanne Boitel) is drawn to an athletic lover. When the husband learns of her infidelity, he commits suicide—out of his love for her—in order to free her from the matrimonial bond. Not explicitly revealing any nudity or consummation, *Remous* was a bodice ripper.

Despite centuries of literary bodice ripping dating from *Moll Flanders*, such saucy content would not be tolerated on-screen. The court was offended by the film's frank portrayal of male incapacity and threatened by the portrayal of a voracious female libido. The "impotency of the husband and its effect upon the sex life of the wife resulting in her adultery and the husband's suicide is not regarded as a decent theme for screen portrayal. In this picture the wife apparently accepted the young athlete for no other reason than to satisfy her sex urge. . . . Such is not the subject matter for screen display. . . . The finding that *Remous* is immoral and would tend to corrupt morals is not arbitrary and the determination should be confirmed."[12]

A concurring opinion filed by Judge John Warren Hill focused on the presumption given to the administrative agency in the absence of an arbitrary or capricious ruling. Hill clarified that "the Moving Picture Division of the Department of Education may ban as immoral a film dealing with social sex problems, human biology or the procreative function even when not obscene or indecent."[13] The ban prevailed; independent distributors Arthur Mayer and Joseph Burstyn conceded defeat and cut down the film to produce an abridged version of it.[14]

Mayer and Burstyn had an eye for interesting films that offered audiences an alternative to glossy Hollywood fare. After *Remous*, they acquired U.S. exhibition rights for Jean Renoir's *Les bas-fonds* (*The Lower Depths*, 1936), Roberto Rossellini's *Roma, città aperta* (*Rome, Open City*, 1945) and Vittorio De Sica's *Ladri di biciclette* (*The Bicycle Thief*, 1948). Burstyn's true importance to the story of film and the First Amendment would be seen when the distributor brought his fight over a short film by Rossellini to the Supreme Court. Less than fifteen years after losing his battle over *Remous*, Burstyn would emerge as a major figure in the narrative of film and First Amendment rights.

The same year *Ecstasy* was winning praise at film festivals in Europe and condemnation at administrative agencies in New York, a picture entitled *Amok* (1934) was released. *Amok* was an international collaboration: a French film directed by a Russian émigré who had learned his craft in Weimar Germany and the Soviet film factories. Fyodor Otsep (also known as Fedor Ozep) started as a screenwriter for Russian filmmaker Yakov Protazanov on *Pikovaya dama* (*The Queen of Spades*, 1916) and the surreal *Aelita: Queen of Mars* (1924). Emigrating to Germany, Ozep immersed himself in expressionist techniques, directing Fritz Kortner in *The Brothers Karamazov* (1931) and *The Murder of Dimitri Karamazov* (1931).

Otsep's *Amok* was an exotic, psychological passion play set in the tropics that confronted issues of adultery, abortion, and suicide. In addition to these weighty subjects, the picture was augmented with nearly naked native girls. Otsep could not have consciously made a picture more likely to infuriate U.S. censors. In *Distinguished Films v. Stoddard*, the court characterized the film as

> designed to emphasize the oppressiveness of the jungle and to introduce [the protagonist] Dr. Holk as a man who, for obscure personal reasons, has banished himself to the jungle to work among the natives, the film portrays a tribal dance at which a native suddenly runs amuck [*sic*]. Just as the excitement is subsiding the leading lady, Mme. Helene Havilland [*sic*], apparently a lady of wealth and social position, comes into the doctor's residence. She explains that she has come to him for reasons of secrecy and offers him a large fee if he will grant her a personal favor. . . . [She] clearly indicates that the favor would be an illegal abortion and that the truth concerning the abortion must be kept from her husband at whatever cost. With a great show of indignation, the doctor at first refuses her request, but later indicates that he might be persuaded to illegally abort her for considerations other than pecuniary. . . . [T]he price for the abortion would be an adulterous relationship between them. . . . Further developments occur between the doctor and Mme. Havilland; he shows his infatuation for her and begs to perform the operation but she spurns his offer and instead goes to a native crone, an "herb doctor," of evil reputation. . . . Dr. Holk is called to the native woman's hut, but finds Mme. Havilland dying, evidently because of an illegal abortion; she extracts from him a promise to keep the cause of her death a secret from her husband.[15]

Dr. Holk (Jean Yonnel) confronts Mme. Haviland
(Marcelle Chantal) in *Amok* (1934).

The husband, once again played by Jean Galland—the same actor who had
played the crippled, cuckolded, martyred husband in *Remous*—returns to find
a dire situation: "On the husband's arrival the doctor informs him that the
cause of death was a heart attack; the husband refuses to believe this and
announces that he will take her body to Europe for post-mortem. As the casket is being lifted to the deck of the ship Dr. Holk clandestinely cuts the rope
and plunges into the sea with the casket."[16]

The film made a mark at the Venice International Film Festival and was
praised at its Paris premiere.[17] Despite its initial release in 1933, contemporaneous with *Ecstasy* and *Remous*, *Amok* was not brought to the United States
until 1946. When *Amok* did arrive it was immediately slapped with a ban,
deemed indecent, immoral, tending to corrupt morals and incite to crime.
In *Distinguished Films*, the court once again deferred to the censor's ruling:
"It is understandable . . . that some reviewing bodies would think this film
offended, thus there is doubtless some evidence to sustain the finding."[18]
Amok was too risqué, too dangerous, and ultimately too foreign for regulators to permit on domestic screens.

International films were not the only pictures to run afoul of the motion
picture regulators in the 1930s. Two U.S. producers who had been key players in the development of the American industry found their own pictures
rejected by the censorship boards. These unsung pioneers of Hollywood
were Bryan Foy and Al Christie.

Bryan Foy's early life unfolded not unlike the opening flashback sequence of *Singing in the Rain*. With his siblings, the Seven Little Foys, Bryan Foy (1896–1977) began his career on the vaudeville stage in 1912. By 1918 he left the family act for a job as a gagman for the stage and screen.[19] As a seasoned vaudevillian in New York in the 1920s, Foy was the right man in the right place at the right time. Sound pictures were emerging and Warner Bros. turned to Foy for his Rolodex of talent. Foy began directing Vitaphone shorts in 1927 and took the reins for Warner's first feature-length, all-talking motion picture, *The Lights of New York* (1928). Remaining in New York during the early experimental days of talkies, Foy became Warner's lead East Coast producer. While Jack Warner took credit as the more prestigious president of production on the Burbank lot, Foy was known in the industry as the "keeper of the B's," for the low budget films that he mass-produced.[20]

By the mid-1930s Foy resigned from Warner Bros. to produce B pictures independently. Leaving highfalutin production values to the well-funded film factories, Foy's expertise became grind-house films tailored to teen audiences. He produced the teasingly titled *What Price Innocence?* (1933) and *High School Girl* (1935), two films about teenage pregnancy. Importantly, neither of these films actually used the term "pregnancy," and they slipped past the censor's radar. That would not be the case for *Tomorrow's Children*.

Tomorrow's Children (1934) addressed the theme of eugenics. Sterilization was a hot topic; in 1932 the Human Betterment Foundation of Pasadena recommended the sterilization of eighteen million Americans deemed unfit to have children because of physical or mental disabilities or criminal propensities. Twenty-seven states enacted laws permitting sterilization.[21] Even the great justice Oliver Wendell Holmes came out in favor of eugenics in *Buck v. Bell*. The *Buck* decision denied the pleas of a woman unwilling to have the state hysterectomize her. Holmes penned the decision upholding the sterilization of the mentally challenged girl, opining that "three generations of imbeciles are enough."[22]

From the High Court's support of eugenics to the lowbrow sensationalistic treatment of *Tomorrow's Children*, Foy's film reveled in the tabloid-friendly topic. The court's plot summary in *Foy Productions v. Graves* reads as melodrama gone horribly awry. After a group of welfare workers are instructed in the benefits of sterilization, the scene switches to "a drunkard and his poverty stricken feeble-minded family, with its sick, crippled, and criminal members, and a normal attractive foster daughter. The welfare workers . . . [convince] the father and mother to submit themselves and their children to

Warner Bros.' "Keeper of the B's," Bryan Foy (1896–1977).
From the collections of the Margaret Herrick Library, Academy
of Motion Picture Arts and Sciences.

sterilization. . . . [T]he foster daughter . . . refuses to submit, escapes, is pursued, imprisoned, and is brought before the court, sentenced to submit to the operation, is seen on the operating table, prepared for the surgeon's knife, and finally released on the sudden discovery that she is not the natural child of the family, and therefore, there is no law permitting the mutilation of her body against her will."[23]

Unsurprisingly, the New York State board of censors denied a permit to *Tomorrow's Children*. The grounds of rejection: the picture was immoral, tended to corrupt morals, and incited to crime.[24]

On appeal, the New York court reliably deferred to the administrative authority. Speaking for the majority, Judge Daniel V. McNamee wrote, "Reproductive organs are the theme and their perversion is the topic of the picture, and without reference thereto the picture would have neither plot nor substance." Although the court's statement is true enough, it should be noted that reproductive organs were never explicitly seen in the picture. The court's main concern in *Foy Productions* was whether the censor's decision was arbitrary or capricious. If the Department of Education had acted reasonably, the court would not overturn their finding, citing the state's power to protect citizens from "evil influences": "Certainly there are some things which are happening in actual life today which should not have pictorial representation in such places of amusement as are regulated by this legislature, places where the audiences are not confined to men alone or women alone and where children are particularly attracted."[25]

Tomorrow's Children was banned. The Department of Education and the New York court deemed the topics of sterilization and eugenics—while newsworthy—unfit and improper for commercial entertainment.

In his dissenting opinion to *Foy Productions*, Judge James P. Hill discerned traces of valuable political speech in the low-budget exploitation film:

> The picture is a forceful and dramatic argument against the enactment of statutes which, under certain circumstances, permit enforced operations to prevent procreation. . . . The commissioner has found that the film was not obscene, indecent, inhuman, or sacrilegious . . . the film contains nothing lewd or lustful. No part of the human body is exposed to view, with the possible exception of a few square inches of the abdomen visible in the preparation for an operation. It would require a prurient imagination to find anything unchaste or indecent. . . . There were no facts before the commissioner upon which he could base a finding of immorality or that the film tended to corrupt morals.

In his well-reasoned conclusion Hill saw that "the theme of the film no more suggests sterilization as a means of birth control than a film showing the amputation of a leg would suggest that as a means to prevent persons from walking into danger."[26] To Hill, the censor's decision was overzealous; nevertheless, Foy's film was banned.

Bryan Foy ushered film into the sound era, but he was a relative newcomer compared to producer-director Al Christie. Christie (1881–1951) had been in Hollywood since inception. In 1910 Christie entered the business, working at David Horsley's Centaur Films in New Jersey. Horsley was an early independent manufacturer-exhibitor who had joined the nickelodeon craze in 1909 along with Carl Laemmle and William Fox. When he hired Christie, the Edison Trust was at the height of its power, using all the tools at its command, from legal action to intimidation and strong-arm thugs to crack down on

Al Christie (1881–1951) opened the first film studio in Hollywood. From the collections of the Margaret Herrick Library, Academy of Motion Picture Arts and Sciences.

independent filmmakers. Horsley decided to put distance between Centaur and the MPPC goons. The choice came down to moving operations to either Florida or the West Coast. One story—likely apocryphal—based the decisive factor on a coin flip. According to that legend, in 1911 Christie tossed the coin and headed to California, far from the Edison Trust's sphere of enforcement. Arriving in Los Angeles, Christie rented a cavernous space in a former tavern on the dusty corner of Sunset and Gower. Christening the West Coast branch of the company Nestor Productions, Christie opened the first film studio in Hollywood.[27]

Shortly after Nestor set up shop in Hollywood, Carl Laemmle acquired Horsley's interest in the studio and folded it, along with IMP, into Universal Pictures. In 1915 Laemmle purchased a large tract of land over the Cahuenga Pass, where he planned to consolidate his production units. Christie gave notice. The following year the Al Christie Film Company announced its slate of one- and two-reel productions in the *Moving Picture World*: "Long Time Comedy Producer Will Release One Single a Week and Two Doubles a Month."[28] Christie continued making movies for the next thirty years.

Christie commanded an assembly line, releasing no less than fifteen and up to forty films a year between 1935 and 1938. In 1937 the American Committee on Maternal Welfare commissioned him to produce an educational documentary to be called *The Birth of a Baby* (1938). In the picture, a girl believes she may be pregnant. She visits a doctor, who instructs her in the development of the fetus with the aid of diagrams. Nine months later she delivers as the film clinically records the entire event. Although *Birth* was intended for doctors as a teaching aid, the Committee was so impressed with Christie's work they decided to distribute the picture commercially. Still photos from the film were featured in *Life* magazine on April 11, 1938. By all accounts the film was a beautiful and sensitive document.

Not everyone agreed; censors in various states were not as pleased with the cinematic miracle of life. *Birth* was banned in Bakersfield, Cincinnati, Lynchburg, Moberly (Missouri), Omaha, and Springfield (Massachusetts).[29] In New York *Birth* was branded "indecent, immoral and would tend [to] corrupt morals within the meaning of section 1082 of the Education Law."[30]

Unlike the ban on the overtly sexual themes of European imports, censors conceded the worthwhile subject matter in *The Birth of a Baby*: "Undoubtedly, this picture may have scientific value. It is not inherently indecent in the ordinary accepted sense of the word, but it becomes indecent when presented in places of amusement. . . . [A] picture depicting the actual birth of a child becomes indecent when presented to patrons of places of public entertainment."[31] Like *Tomorrow's Children*, *Birth*'s subject matter—while topical, relevant, and educational—was unfit for commercial exhibition.

The New York court clarified its reasoning in *American Committee on Maternal Welfare v. Mangan*: "The 'show' business is clearly different from the newspaper business, and those who would engage in show business are none too likely to confine their productions to things which are just, pure, and of good report; but, in order to continue to attract patrons, many would cast discretion and self-control into the winds, without restraint, social or moral."[32] The issue turned on venue. A subject that may be deemed acceptable for the scientific community may not be appropriate for general audiences. "Even though the picture inculcates a lesson, it does not necessarily follow that the exhibition may not offend against public decency. However desirable it may be to disseminate such knowledge, it may well be doubted that it should be done by means of a picture show in a public playhouse."[33] Regulators feared that certain educational or scientific subjects could, in the hands of exploitation-minded filmmakers, be manipulated to appeal to an audience's prurient

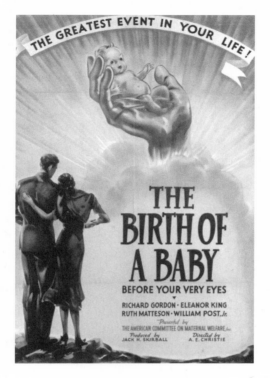

The Birth of a Baby (1938).

interests. Without viewing the film, the court deferred to the board of censors. Once again the mantra was repeated: in the absence of arbitrary or capricious behavior, the court would not disturb the censor's finding.

Two judges signed a dissenting opinion; this time Judge Hill was joined by Judge Christopher J. Heffernan, signifying slight momentum toward applying free speech concepts to motion pictures. The dissenting opinion stated, "The film *The Birth of a Baby* will give vital and needed information to pregnant women, many of [whom] fail to seek early and necessary advice. The authors treated the theme in a clean, dignified, and reverent manner. To limit the exhibition to educational and clinical groups will defeat the worthy purpose of the sponsors of the film."[34]

Ohio and Virginia fell in line with New York's majority opinion and denied the film commercial exhibition in *American Committee on Maternal Welfare v. City of Cincinnati* (1938) and *City of Lynchburg v. Dominion Theatres, Inc.* (1940).[35] On the other hand, Arizona, Indiana, Iowa, Oregon, Pennsylvania,

South Carolina, South Dakota, and Washington approved the film for public showings.[36] *The Birth of a Baby* would be permitted for exhibition in New York for clinical purposes.[37]

Al Christie and Bryan Foy were consummate old-school showmen from a pioneering era of motion picture history. They became involved in moviemaking when the medium was in its infancy. These two filmmakers were present at ground zero when Hollywood was founded and when talkies first spoke. Both men shared an entrepreneurial spirit, and when the industry coalesced into a studio system, they each left to strike out on their own with smaller independent films that appealed to young audiences. After run-ins with censorship boards, both Christie and Foy migrated back to the mainstream. Christie's later career saw a longstanding relationship with Hal Roach's Educational Pictures. His final films included *The Birth of a Star* (1944), with Danny Kaye and Imogene Coca, and *It Pays To Be Funny* (1947), with Bob Hope, Milton Berle, and Bert Lahr. Foy's late films included the hugely successful 3-D *House of Wax* (1953) and its less memorable follow-up, *The Mad Magician* (1954), both starring Vincent Price. Although their names may not be familiar to audiences today, Christie and Foy occupied a central role in the development of the American film industry. Both men challenged existing laws and made significant contributions to the story of film and the First Amendment. Together, Christie and Foy helped move the medium of motion pictures closer to constitutional protections.

Moving from Hollywood has-beens to the never-weres, Dwain Esper (1892–1982) and Willis Kent (1878–1966) dominated the exploitation circuit. Film censors could only ban films that were submitted for approval or films that were high profile enough to get noticed by municipal administrators. But regional regulators could not ban what they could not catch.

Esper and Kent were able to produce films quickly and cheaply—in a matter of days and for a matter of dollars. While the major studios dominated conventional cinemas with block booking and a systematic process of promotion and release, Esper and Kent mirrored the system on a microscopic scale. They raised capital and produced, distributed, and exhibited their own motion pictures, either skirting the censorship boards entirely or swooping into town for a limited engagement and exiting quickly before authorities could crack down on their sensationalistic code-breaking pictures.

This method of self-distributing dates back to George C. Hale's touring travelogues in 1905 and D. W. Griffith's *The Birth of a Nation* a decade later. But Dwain Esper took road showing and four walling (renting out a theater for short-term film exhibition) to a new level and helped to pioneer and popularize the genre of the exploitation film. Esper's films reveled in sex, drugs, adultery, abortion, and general debauchery not seen before on such a gratuitous scale. With earnings made during a successful career in construction, Esper bankrolled a production and distribution company, aptly incorporated as Roadshow Attractions. His first film, *The Seventh Commandment* (*The Sins of Love*, 1932), was tagged by censors in New York, Maryland, Massachusetts, Utah, and Virginia but escaped notice elsewhere.[38] Reviews were generally favorable, and one advertised, "See the strip poker parties and see what this gin mad generation is coming to."[39] From the establishment came a different reaction. Breen's office assessed the film as part of "an annual crop of smut which certainly violate[s] both the production and advertizing [*sic*] codes . . . these god-awful sex thrillers which attempt to preach a sermon while giving the morbidly curious public a close-up of an operation and a lot of vicarious thrills."[40]

Roadshow Attractions' output of exploitation films were generally constructed as cautionary tales that didn't skimp on titillating details. Esper released such titles as *Narcotic* (1933), *Maniac* (*Sex Maniac*, 1934), *Marihuana* (*The Weed with Roots in Hell*, 1936), *How to Undress in Front of Your Husband* (1937), *Slaves in Bondage* (1937), and *Sex Madness* (*Human Wreckage*, 1938). These showings mirrored mainstream film exhibition in an alternate reality: instead of beginning with a newsreel, standard in mainstream theaters, Esper offered audiences a series of shorts entitled *The March of Crime* (1936). Each fifteen-minute installment focused on a true-crime bio: Pretty Boy Floyd, Bonnie and Clyde, and John Dillinger. With a *Dragnet*-style voiceover, the featurettes showed grisly crime scene footage and deadpan reenactments.

Another producer, Willis Kent, had been churning out Poverty Row Westerns since 1930, when he stumbled on the low-cost, high-profit genre of exploitation B movies. Kent produced lowbrow films featuring drugs, prostitution, abortion, and white slavery to rival Esper's: *Cocaine Fiends* (*The Pace that Kills*, 1932), *Smashing the Vice Trust* (1937), *Wages of Sin* (1938), *Mad Youth* (1940), and *Confessions of a Vice Baron* (1943). New York's regents repeatedly denied *The Pace that Kills*, citing the film as indecent and immoral.[41] These films, however, are most notable, aside from their overblown content, for the surprising lack of censorial involvement.

One of the more shocking exploitation films of the era was Harry Revier's *Child Bride* (1938). *Child Bride* follows a schoolteacher (Diana Durrell) as she crusades against underage sex and marriage among the country folk of

Dwain Esper produced a series
of sensational titles including
Narcotic (1933),
The Seventh Commandment (1932),
and *Marihuana* (1936).

the Ozarks. One leering, lecherous hillbilly (Warner Richmond) is hot and bothered over a pubescent girl-child named Jennie. Jennie was played by Shirley Mills, a twelve-year-old actress who would appear as Ruth Joad in John Ford's *Grapes of Wrath* (1938) later that year. *Child Bride* went further than most pulps in its portrayal of female nudity when Mills appeared in an explicit skinny-dipping scene. *Child Bride* had the ingredients of a barely legal cult classic and emerged as one of the most successful road-show films. Kroger Babb, a producer, promoter, and presenter who would claim the title of top exploitation film maven in the following decade, began his career by reissuing *Child Bride* in 1945.

Esper, Kent, and Revier were not the only producers working on the periphery of the movie industry in the lucrative world of exploitation films. Their pictures fed the midnight market, often packaging sensational content as cautionary tales or infotainments. Michael Mindlin promoted *This Nude World* (1933) as "Guaranteed the Most Educational Film Ever Produced."[42] Like the nickelodeon boom of the 1910s, the demand for new product far exceeded supply. Films were made quickly and cheaply and tailored to satisfy the hunger of undiscerning audiences.

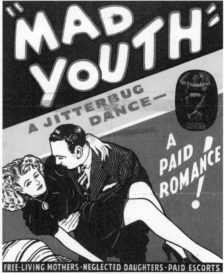

Willis Kent produced scandalous midnight movies: cocaine binges in
The Pace that Kills (1935) and prostitution rings in *Mad Youth* (1940).

Nudism on display in *This Nude World* or
This Naked Age (1933).

The Breen regime guided studio productions toward safe, sanitized, wholesome pictures. By contrast, the world of exploitation films thrived on salacious material. The PCA's strict rules, regulations, and production codes of "best practices" encouraged a new kind of moviemaker to produce cheap, fun, forbidden fare. These grind-house films may have lacked taste, quality, and artistic value, but they delivered entertainment that thrill-seeking audiences appreciated. As long as these pictures could barnstorm a theater, turn a profit on midnight shows, and disappear before they were caught or raided, the underground film trade could thrive. Exploitation filmmakers created a mirror industry that delivered guilty pleasures to eager audiences, filling the niche that the PCA's "better film" initiative had barred.

The PCA monitored mainstream material, but underground and international filmmakers dared to flout code, conventions, and, in at least one case, child protection laws. Throughout the 1930s the courts generally deferred to regulators, granting them the authority—in fact the duty—to protect the values, morals, and principles of their communities from the cinema's "capacity for evil." Independent producers and foreign filmmakers were the outliers who dared to challenge the system.

PART II

Freedom of the Screen

11

OUTLAWS AND MIRACLES

—

Once the Breen office began strict enforcement of Production Code Administration (PCA) regulations in June 1934, the effects rippled through the film industry. Hollywood was cleansed of the suggestive lewdness and overt violence that had previously slipped through the MPPDA. For the next six years the production code went unchallenged by the studio moguls. As long as sanitized cinema sold tickets, the PCA scheme worked. But by the early 1940s Joseph Breen's bureau faced its greatest challenge when Howard Hughes put muscle and money behind his fetishistic Western *The Outlaw*.

The clash between Breen and Hughes was foreseeable. Each man was unwavering and passionate about his cause. For Breen, it was film regulation and decency; for Hughes, it was the curvaceous female form. After a talent search that focused on anatomy as much as ability, Hughes began production on *The Outlaw* in 1940 without submitting a script to the PCA. When he turned in a cut for approval, the chief censor was gobsmacked. In a memorandum dated March 1941 Breen wrote, "In my more than ten years of critical examination of motion pictures, I have never seen anything quite so unacceptable as the shots of the breasts of the character of Rio. . . . Throughout almost half the picture, the girl's breasts, which are quite large and prominent, are shockingly emphasized, and in almost every instance are very substantially uncovered."[1] Baltimore judge E. Paul Mason expressed his disapproval that "Jane Russell's breasts hung over the picture like a summer thunderstorm spread out over a landscape."[2]

In many ways *The Outlaw* was a standard-issue Western. But other aspects of the film are a separate reality from serial sagebrush soaps or John Ford's desolate landscapes. In *The Outlaw*, Doc Holliday (Walter Huston) finds his friendship with lawman Pat Garrett (Thomas Mitchell) strained when Billy the Kid (Jack Buetel) enters the scene. After Billy is injured, Doc orders his courtesan Rio (Russell) to care for the young bandit. As Rio nurses Billy back to health, her cleavage is central to her caregiving. She is positioned horizontally throughout the picture and seems to thrive on Billy's manhandling. A psychosexual current runs through the film: characters are driven from homosexual yearnings to sadomasochistic cravings. Garrett feels slighted when Doc develops feelings for the young hustler. Rio is inflamed by Billy's mistreatment. Rather than a straightforward oater, *The Outlaw* is a series of interlocking love triangles.

Trouble was predictable when production began without an approved screenplay. After Hughes received Breen's notes, he complied with some requested changes and ignored others. It should not have come as much of a surprise to him when the Legion of Decency condemned the film, the PCA rejected the film, and several states, including Maryland, New York, Washington, and Wisconsin banned the film.[3] Facing failure due to the multiple mechanisms of censorship, Hughes fought back. He bankrolled a series of lawsuits aimed at either clearing his film for exhibition or stalling for time by papering the newly renamed Motion Picture Association of America (MPAA) with nuisance pleadings as the film played out in un-permitted exhibitions. In his complaint Hughes made two allegations. First, the MPAA conspired to dominate the market with monopolistic anticompetitive regulations. Second, the MPAA's ban on the film had a chilling effect on his freedom of speech. Hughes had the power, the money, and the single-minded resolve to pursue a test case that challenged the MPAA and pushed the agency to its limits.

In *Hughes Tool Co. v. Motion Picture Association of America* (1946) the mogul went on the offensive to protect his pet project. According to the facts stated in the opinion, Hughes submitted *The Outlaw* to the PCA, and after certain cuts were made, a seal was issued in 1941. In 1945 Hughes licensed distribution rights to United Artists. Promotional materials were submitted to the Advertising Code Administration (ACA), a sister organization to the PCA that oversaw marketing materials. After reviewing the promotions, the ACA rejected Hughes's campaign:[4]

Eight of the advertisements were pen and ink drawings, in which the breasts of the star were emphasized and exposed. The Administrator of the ACA suggested that these drawings could be rendered unobjectionable by a slight retouching, that is, by the raising of the blouse a fraction of an inch, which [Hughes] refused to do. Others were rejected because they showed a man and woman together in hay in a compromising horizontal position. Another was rejected because it exposed too much bosom and carried the line: "What are the two great reasons for Jane Russell's rise to stardom?" Eleven others were rejected because they contained what the Administrator terms was a false and misleading statement—"Exactly as filmed—not a scene cut." Four others were rejected because they contained the word "censored" displayed across the figure of the star with her anatomy exposed. There was also rejected the use of a type line, "How would you like to tussle with Russell?"[5]

Hughes's allegations against the PCA and ACA set the stage for a battle royal. The first of the mogul's claims was that his film exposed the MPAA's conspiracy to control motion picture distribution by engaging in monopolistic behavior in violation of the Sherman Antitrust Act. This was a heavy-handed accusation when it pertained to the obstruction of a single film. According to Hughes's complaint, the MPAA

> entered into an agreement and conspiracy to hinder and suppress competition in the interstate sale, distribution and showing of motion picture films, and to create a monopoly in the production and distribution of motion pictures of members and cooperating affiliated non-members; and by reason of the economic control centered in the seal, they have coerced and compelled a virtual totality of motion picture producers to submit all stories, scripts, and completed motion picture films and their titles, to its PCA for seal of approval, without which motion picture films cannot be shown in more than 90% of the motion picture theatres; by means of which producers are compelled to avoid controversial film treatment of social, political, economic, educational and public matters of importance, in contravention of the guarantee of free speech contained in the First Amendment.[6]

Despite Hughes's extravagant assertion, the court summarily rejected this argument: "These broad allegations have not been sustained by proof of facts."[7] Interestingly, the "proof of facts" would surface a mere two years later, in time for the government to prove its case in *United States v. Paramount Pictures, Inc.*[8]

Hughes's second allegation was a more practical attack on the regulatory agencies, claiming *The Outlaw* had been damaged by the PCA's and ACA's arbitrary and unfair decisions. New York's district court considered the narrow issue surrounding the rejection of advertising materials for *The Outlaw* but quickly snapped into its default position, deferring to the administrative agency. In the absence of arbitrary or capricious decision-making, the court's presumption would be difficult for Hughes to overcome. Writing for the majority, Judge John Bright reasoned, "The seal of approval was granted liberally . . . [and] governmental authorities in several communities subsequently required further deletions."[9] Furthermore, there was no evidence of discrimination against *The Outlaw*. Finally, the court stated that Hughes made his allegations with unclean hands. "It is further shown, without dispute, that plaintiff is now using not only rejected advertising material, but also material which has never been submitted to the defendant, both in newspapers and on sign displays. . . . Late in April 1946, it is alleged, and not denied, a sky-writing airplane wrote the words *The Outlaw* in the sky over Pasadena, and then made two enormous circles with a dot in the middle of each."[10]

Four years prior to *Hughes Tool Co.*, the Supreme Court had considered the limits on commercial speech. *Valentine v. Chrestensen* (1942) dealt with the distribution of handbills advertising the exhibition of a World War I submarine. *Chrestensen* demonstrated that all speech—even protected speech—was not equal under the First Amendment. Commercial speech, such as promotional pamphlets, did not receive the same heightened constitutional protections as politically motivated or creative speech. With the High Court's ruling on commercial speech, Hughes's claim crumbled. The court seized on a tagline used in many of *The Outlaw*'s promotional materials, "Exactly as it was filmed—not a scene cut," as false advertising.

In a final blow, the court revealed its understanding of Hughes's ultimate motive—to stall until the picture's box office vitality was played out: "Plaintiff obviously wants to prolong the present status until its picture has run its life, it will have received the profit from its exhibitions, and will no longer require the seal."[11] While Hughes's campaign ended in failure, he had succeeded in wearing down the MPAA's resources and energy.

Hughes followed this suit with another challenge to the New York State regents in *Hughes Tool Co. v. Fielding* (1947).[12] Judge Bernard Lloyd Shientag

Howard Hughes's pet project, *The Outlaw*,
tested the censors (1943).

sided with the censors, and once again Hughes was denied. But Hughes's legal battle was a war of attrition on censorship agencies. No mainstream producer had released a picture without the PCA's seal of approval since 1934, but as *The Outlaw* litigation played out, David O. Selznick released his own un-permitted fetishistic western. *Duel in the Sun* (1946) lingered over Selznick's paramour, Jennifer Jones, with obsessive detail in a manner similar to Hughes's fixation on Russell.[13]

Even with condemnation from regulatory agencies and seemingly endless litigation bills, *The Outlaw* was profitable. The film managed to recoup twice its prodigal production cost of $1.25 million: "Box Office Digest showed Hughes film at the top of all Hollywood pictures in box office returns and exhibitors demands."[14] *Variety* reported the film played successfully in foreign territories, adding up to cumulative box office receipts of over $5 million. By June 1968 the *Hollywood Reporter* estimated that *The Outlaw* had made over $20 million.[15]

State regulators held a dominant position in the 1930s, but that power began to shift in the 1940s, seen in a series of non-film-related decisions. In *Thomas v. Collins* (1945), a Texas judge ruled against a labor organizer for speaking at a union rally without a permit. The Supreme Court found the law unconstitutional.[16] The following year in *Hannegan v. Esquire* (1946), the Supreme Court cut into the Comstock Law, restricting the postmaster's authority to refuse mailings based on a personal finding of offensive materials.[17] Four months later the High Court ruled on another free speech case. In *Pennekamp v. Florida* (1946), First Amendment protections were extended to newspaper editorials. In line with *Near v. Minnesota*, which was directed to the prior restraints of newspaper publication, the *Pennekamp* Court reasoned, "the specific freedom of public comment should weigh heavily. . . . Freedom of discussion should be given the widest range compatible with the essential requirement of the fair and orderly administration of justice."[18]

The times were changing. By 1948 the Paramount Consent Decree formally dissolved the vertically integrated motion picture studios and prohibited anticompetitive practices such as block booking and blind buying. As hurtful as this decision may have been to the major Hollywood players at the time, the decision contained the seeds of a new era in filmmaking. In dictum, Justice William O. Douglas commented, "We have no doubt that moving pictures, like newspapers and radio, are included in the press whose freedom is guaranteed by the First Amendment."[19] Although not essential to the holding, this simple admission by the Court was an important step.

Coinciding with the groundswell of free speech rights was a wave of socially conscious films emerging in Hollywood. These pictures portrayed a grittier worldview with greater psychological depth. Social issues had been raised during the 1930s under Breen's watch, but serious concerns were generally not central to the types of films that Hollywood released during that era. *I Am a Fugitive from a Chain Gang* (1932) and Fritz Lang's *Fury* (1936) were notable exceptions.

The end of World War II brought darker films that addressed more realistic situations. Lang's *Scarlet Street* (1945) was a noir melodrama in which a henpecked man rescues a girl, only to find himself ensnared in her brutish boyfriend's criminal scheme. Although *Scarlet Street* was approved by the PCA, the Catholic Legion of Decency, censors in Maryland, New York, Ohio, Pennsylvania, the cities of Atlanta and Milwaukee, and New York's regents banned the film—a rare event for a studio picture. Within a week Universal complied with suggested cuts, and the film was permitted in the Empire State.[20] Other equally hard-hitting films met with less resistance. Billy Wilder's *The Lost Weekend* (1945) chronicled the torment of an alcoholic writer and won four Academy Awards. William Wyler's *The Best Years of Our Lives* (1946) dealt with the difficulties faced by war veterans and claimed seven competitive Academy Awards along with an honorary statuette for real-life paraplegic war vet actor Harold Russell.

Crossfire (1947) dealt with anti-Semitism within an army unit and was recognized with five Academy Award nominations. The RKO-produced film lost its Oscar expectations to 20th Century Fox's own anti-Semitic-themed entry, *Gentleman's Agreement* (1947), which boasted higher-wattage star power and won three Academy Awards along with five other nominations. In *Gentleman's Agreement*, Gregory Peck posed as a Jew to research a newspaper article. Once immersed in his alter ego, Peck experiences a hidden world of bigotry.

Following *Crossfire* and *Gentleman's Agreement* came a series of four films that confronted racial prejudice in America. Hitting a raw nerve, these films did not meet with the same accolades as the anti-Semitism-themed pictures.

The first film in this cycle was Stanley Kramer's *Home of the Brave* (1949). *Home* focused on an injured African American GI (James Edwards) and his friendship with a white soldier (Lloyd Bridges). In the film, a VA doctor uses the unorthodox technique of shouting racial slurs at the black vet to help him overcome his debilitating paralysis. Viewed from a contemporary perspective as insensitive and crass, at the time this scene was understood as a poignant symbol of liberation. Kramer negotiated with Breen's office to make an allowance for the use of the word "nigger." The epithet had been off-limits since the implementation of the code in 1934, but based on the context and the intended message of self-confidence, Breen uncharacteristically compromised.

Intruder in the Dust (1949) was based on William Faulkner's novel in which a white Mississippi boy (Claude Jarman Jr.) stood up for justice, protecting an innocent but curmudgeonly black man (Juano Hernandez).

The final two entries in this series of racially conscious films were the most controversial. In a quirk of casting, the leads in both films—which portrayed black people passing for white—were played by white actors of mixed-Irish descent passing for black. Cuban-Irish actor Mel Ferrer made his debut in *Lost Boundaries* (1949). Based on a true story, *Lost Boundaries* followed a fair-skinned African American doctor. Rejected by a Southern black medical clinic, he is forced to disguise his race and blend in at a Northern hospital. Unsurprisingly, this story met with fierce resistance in the South.

Lost Boundaries was produced and distributed by RD-DR Productions and Louis de Rochemont Associates. RD-DR and De Rochemont filed suit after Atlanta banned the picture. City censor Christine Smith commented that "because the film involved such a controversial subject . . . it is contrary to the public good"[21] and "detrimental to good order, good health or good morals."[22] Similarly, Lloyd T. Binford, chairman of the Memphis board of censors, refused to permit *Lost Boundaries*, dismissing the film with a homespun statement: "We don't take that kind of picture here."[23] The respective state courts upheld both municipal censors' decisions.

Georgia's district court echoed the *Mutual* precedent in *RD-DR Corp. v. Smith*: "Motion pictures are not to be regarded as a part of the press of the country or organs of public opinion and as such entitled to the protection afforded the press."[24] On appeal to the Fifth Circuit, Chief Justice Joseph Chappell Hutcheson Jr. not only affirmed the decision but in dictum dealt another blow to the medium:

We particularly disagree with, and dissent from, the view . . . [that the producers] advance: that moving pictures have now emerged from the business of amusement into instruments for the propagation of ideas and, therefore, like newspapers, freedom of assembly, freedom of speech, must be regarded as within the protection of the Fourteenth Amendment; that censorship of moving pictures by states or local communities is contrary to the new enlightenment and the trend of the new national opinion; and that the *Mutual Film* decision, standing in the way is now antiquated and tottering to its fall, and should be decently and finally interred.[25]

The Supreme Court declined to review the case,[26] and *Lost Boundaries* was a dead letter in Southern markets.

African American actresses Lena Horne and Dorothy Dandridge were considered for the leading role in *Pinky* (1949). Instead, Darryl F. Zanuck chose white actress Jeanne Crain to play the film's protagonist. The character of Pinky bridged two worlds divided by race. In one world she identifies as black, raised by her grandmother, a poor Southern black laundress (Ethel Waters). In the other world she passes as a white girl after studying to be a

Banned in the South: the true story of a black doctor passing as white in *Lost Boundaries* (1949).

nurse in the North. These worlds collide when Pinky returns home to care for her grandmother and a bigoted neighbor (Ethel Barrymore). The film premiered in Atlanta to great fanfare. This time Christine Smith, the censor who banned *Lost Boundaries*, found *Pinky* to be a strong and needed message to Southerners. She passed *Pinky*, stating, "I know this picture is going to be painful to a great many Southerners. It will make them squirm, but at the same time it will make them realize how unlovely their attitudes are."[27] At the Atlanta premiere the Roxy Theatre opened its balcony to African Americans, showing signs of social progress. The film surpassed box office expectations; scheduled for a standard one-week run, it was held over an additional two weeks.[28] Critical reception was equally positive; Academy Award nominations recognized Jeanne Crain in the leading actress category and both Ethel Waters and Ethel Barrymore in the supporting actress category. The picture was one of Fox's best performers of 1949.[29]

Such praise, however, did not dissuade Texas censors from banning the picture.[30] The Texas courts then upheld the ban. Fox helped finance an appeal whose verdict was handed down on January 30, 1952, in *Gelling v. Texas*. Despite the studio's efforts, the Texas censors prevailed, but the case was granted certiorari and would be reviewed by the Supreme Court. The final verdict arrived on June 2, 1952—just one week after the decisive *Miracle* decision. If not for that one-week lag, *Pinky* could have set the historic precedent. Perhaps it was more dramatic for the freedom of the screen to commence with a miracle rather than a pinky.

While *Home of the Brave, Intruder in the Dust, Lost Boundaries*, and *Pinky* each confronted the issue of race in America head-on, a comedy called *Curley* might have seemed less threatening. Instead, Hal Roach's kiddie picture became an important case, standing as the final instance of deferential treatment given to the state censors before the *Miracle* decision changed the legal landscape.

In 1947 United Artists submitted three films to the Memphis motion picture regulators for approval: a Hopalong Cassidy Western and two comedies produced by Hal Roach. Roach (1892–1992) had been making films since the 1910s, famous for producing the pictures of Harold Lloyd, Charley Chase, and Laurel and Hardy. But Roach's formulaic approach to kids' comedy was his greatest strength. Beginning in the mid-1920s Roach's studio, Educational Pictures, rounded up a group of charismatic children to create the *Our Gang* series, popularly known as *The Little Rascals* (officially, *Our Gang Comedies: Hal Roach presents His Rascals in . . .*). The silent-screen children were a modest

Cleared in Atlanta: Jeanne Crain starred in the story of a black nurse passing as white in *Pinky* (1949).

success, with character actors such as nice guy Mickey Daniels, chubby-cheeked Joe Cobb, and wild-haired Jackie Condon, along with racially diverse friends Sunshine Sammy and Farina. As the little rascals aged—or demanded higher wages—Roach simply substituted new gang members. Transitioning to sound pictures with *Small Talk* (1929), the series presented a new crop of child actors, including Jackie Cooper, "Chubby" Chaney, and bowler-wearing "Stymie" Beard. The best-known incarnation of the series featured "Spanky" McFarlane, "Alfalfa" Switzer, "Buckwheat" Thomas, and Pete the Pup. While the *Little Rascals* cast continually changed, one element remained consistent: longtime writer, director, and Roach right-hand man Robert F. McGowan. Most filmmakers shrink away from working with children and animals, but these were the elements that defined McGowan's career—it was reportedly not the kids or pets but the stage mothers who drove him from the field.[31] Without McGowan, Roach considered discontinuing the series but instead sold the property to MGM (where under Louis B. Mayer *Bored of Education* claimed an Academy Award for best short subject in 1936).

A decade after assigning the *Our Gang* rights to MGM, Roach and McGowan rebooted the concept of an ensemble cast of children with *Curley* (1947). Unlike the black-and-white *Little Rascals* short subjects, Curley and his gang premiered in a near-feature-length color film. Other than technical upgrades, the properties were very similar; in fact, the plot of *Curley* aped that of *Teacher's Pet* (1930), an *Our Gang* short that starred Jackie Cooper, "Wheezer" Hutchins, Stymie, and Farina. In both films the children's beloved blonde teacher gets engaged and plans to leave the school. This leads the gang to scheme up ways of getting rid of the substitute. Lo and behold, the new teacher is as young and pretty as the original. Order is restored. There was one major issue in *Curley*: the racial makeup of the classroom.

In the *Our Gang* shorts the children were racially integrated but generally seen after school or during weekend playtime. *Curley's* integrated ensemble was set in a classroom. The point was not lost on Memphis administrators. In *United Artists Corp. v. Censors of Memphis* the court explained, "The Board of Censors, following a private exhibition of the picture, wrote the following letter to United Artists. . . . The Memphis Board of Censors passes *The Marauders* and the Beebe [*sic*] Daniels Picture [*The Fabulous Joe*], but I am sorry to have to inform you that it is unable to approve your *Curley* picture with the little negroes as the South does not permit negroes in white school[s] nor recognize social equality between the races even in children. Yours truly, Lloyd T. Binford, Chairman."[32]

Memphis censor Lloyd T. Binford (1869–1956). *Memphis Press-Scimitar* photo, courtesy
Preservation and Special Collections, University Libraries, University of Memphis.

Like his kindred spirit, Maj. Funkhouser of Chicago, Binford was a zealous motion picture regulator. Appointed to the Memphis board of censors
in 1927, Binford quickly demonstrated his fervent censorial style. In 1928 he
disapproved of Cecil B. DeMille's portrayal of the Jews and the presentation
of the Passion in *The King of Kings*. Binford banned *Brewster's Millions* (1945)
because "it presents too much familiarity between the races." Even the greatest auteurs were not safe: Jean Renoir's *The Southerner* (1945) was sanctioned
for depicting rural whites in a negative light and Chaplin's *Monsieur Verdoux*
(1947) "for making murder a joke." But it was race relations that really riled
Binford. Celebrities such as Lena Horne, Duke Ellington, and Cab Calloway
disappeared from Tennessee screens. *Lost Boundaries* was barred, along with
Duel in the Sun and *Imitation of Life* (1934). "We don't have to give our reasons," Binford said.[33]

The mixed-race classroom in *Curley* set Binford off. United Artists challenged his ban. Declining to view the film, the court stood behind the *Mutual*
precedent: "The right to show a motion picture is merely a privilege. . . . [N]o

right of free speech has been denied petitioners."[34] The Memphis court also upheld the precedent set in *Mutual Film Corp. v. Hodges*. In *United Artists Corp. v. Censors of Memphis* the court asserted that United Artists was an interested party but the wrong plaintiff: the exhibitor alone had standing to bring a claim. Chief Judge Albert B. Neil commented, "We think the constitutionality of these statutes and ordinances cannot be questioned . . . except by someone who has the right to speak and is denied the privilege of speaking. . . . In the instant case no exhibitors of moving pictures in Memphis, to whom these ordinances and statutes apply, are claiming that they are denied freedom of speech or the right to contract with petitioners."[35]

United Artists petitioned the Supreme Court in May 1950 for a writ of certiorari to consider the *Curley* case. Five months later RD-DR Productions petitioned on behalf of *Lost Boundaries*. The High Court rejected both, a signal of their unwillingness to revisit the issue of motion picture censorship. That position would change in the coming year. The broadening of First Amendment protections, the growing popularity of socially realistic films, and the increasingly arbitrary and capricious decisions made by powerful censors such as Lloyd Binford and Christine Smith would prompt the Court to revisit the issue.

The first case to be granted certiorari was *Pinky*. While the picture was celebrated in Atlanta—even praised by the city's censor—it was banned in Marshall, Texas. In *Gelling v. State*, the exhibitor argued there had been a cultural evolution in First Amendment rights since *Mutual* was set thirty-seven years earlier, but the argument failed to persuade the Texas court: "Neither do we find in the reported cases that there is an indication in recent Supreme Court decisions that there has been a shift of emphasis in the court's attitudes."[36] While Texas judge Tom L. Beauchamp was convinced the *Mutual* precedent was applicable to *Gelling*, the Supreme Court was apparently less sure. Perhaps times had changed; the High Court granted certiorari to consider *Pinky*.

While *Pinky*, produced and distributed by Fox, was poised to challenge the long-standing legal precedent, a smaller independent picture was also navigating its way to the Supreme Court. That Italian production, a short film only forty minutes in length, would have a titanic impact on the American industry.

In the mid-1940s Hollywood was at the peak of its Golden Era. Studio-produced films boasted iconic stars, exquisite cinematography, luminescent lighting, and music by Europe's top conservatory-educated composers. While the apex of the art form was crafted on hermetic soundstages in

Hollywood, a group of Italian filmmakers took to the war-torn streets with untrained actors. One of the great innovators in this "neorealistic" technique was Roberto Rossellini (1906–1977). In his trilogy of *Roma, città aperta* (*Rome, Open City*, 1945), *Paisà* (1946), and *Germania anno zero* (*Germany Year Zero*, 1948), Rossellini captured postwar life with gritty realism.

Independent American film distributor Joseph Burstyn (1900–1953) was an early advocate of Italian neorealistic film, importing the stark pictures to American art houses. Burstyn was no newcomer to the film industry. Like the early film moguls, Burstyn's rise reflected the American dream—an immigrant's entrepreneurial success. Arriving in America from Poland, Burstyn migrated to midtown Manhattan and found work as a diamond polisher. By 1921 he moved on to publicity work for a Yiddish theater. Ten years later Burstyn got a break when a theater owner rented him an auditorium for $500. He sold $2,500 in tickets, which served as seed money to open a film import and distribution business.[37] With his partner, Arthur Mayer, Burstyn proved to be a great supporter of European cinema. In the 1930s the two men challenged New York's ban of *Remous* and distributed *Club de femmes* (1936) unlicensed and un-permitted.[38] A decade later Burstyn challenged Chicago's censors when they banned *The Bicycle Thief*.[39] The regulators prevailed, but Burstyn's spirit was not broken.

In the late 1940s Burstyn packaged three short films by preeminent European directors to create an omnibus feature. The vignettes were connected by a common theme reflected in the title: *L'amore* (*Ways of Love*, 1948). Opening with Jean Renoir's *A Day in the Country*, the first episode pictured a family's pastoral outing, "all clumsy enthusiasm, giggles, petticoats and parasols. At a provincial inn they encounter two arrantly flirtatious gents who . . . [seduce] the virginal daughter. . . . And under the spell of the country, the placid river and the summer clouds (all beautifully symphonized by Renoir), the innocent girl succumbs." Marcel Pagnol's *Jofroi* followed, depicting the "tale of a feud between two farmers over an orchard [and] reflective of love as a fundamental attachment to the soil." Rossellini directed the third film, *The Miracle*, which illustrated love sacred and profane.[40]

L'amore's production bypassed Breen's office since it was made outside of the MPAA's jurisdiction. The picture had not raised red flags when it premiered at the Venice Film Festival. The Italian censor stamped its approval. The Catholic Cinematographic Centre approved. *Il Popolo d'Italia*'s film critic praised the picture as a "beautiful thing, humanly felt, alive, true and without religious profanation as someone has said, because, in our opinion, the meaning of the characters is clear, and there is no possibility of misunder-standing."[41] When Burstyn applied for a permit, the picture was granted a license by the New York State Education Department on November 30, 1950. On December 12, 1950, *L'amore* premiered at the Paris Theater in midtown Manhattan.

The film received an excellent notice from the *New York Times*: "Judged by the highest standards, on either its parts or the whole, [the film] emerges as fully the most rewarding foreign-language entertainment of the year."[42] The New York Film Critics Circle awarded it best foreign-language film of the year.[43] But *L'amore* was polarizing. At the opposite extreme, Cardinal Francis Spellman condemned the film, urging the 1.25 million Catholics in his archdiocese to boycott. The next week over one thousand parishioners picketed the picture. Under pressure, the city's commissioner of licenses revoked its permit and demanded that Burstyn eliminate *The Miracle* from future screenings.[44]

Apart from the picture, Rossellini's personal life had become a magnet for moral criticism. After *The Miracle* he directed Ingrid Bergman in *Stromboli* (1950). Director and star were married—to different partners—when shooting began, but on set they began an adulterous affair. By the time the film was released, both were divorced, and in February 1950—the month *Stromboli* was released—their child was born. Three months later they married.

The scandal nearly eclipsed the film. Bergman had played a chaste nun on-screen in *The Bells of St. Mary's* (1945) and the saintly warrior in *Joan of Arc* (1948)—both roles recognized with Academy Award nominations. But in the court of public opinion she had fallen from virgin to whore. It is hard to imagine, in our scandal-saturated society, Congress taking note of a movie star's behavior, but Senator Edwin C. Johnson (D-CO) did just that. Denouncing Bergman, Johnson called for a morals probe to investigate "Hollywood's exploitation of immorality."[45] Tennessee's Lloyd Binford was not about to overlook an opportunity for moral outrage. He banned *Stromboli* "because of the moral character of the star."[46]

The Miracle unspooled as the swirl of controversy surrounding Rossellini and Bergman's behavior on *Stromboli* was reaching a fevered pitch.

While *Stromboli* continued Rossellini's neorealistic style, *The Miracle* was more picturesque. Leaving behind urban ruins and grimy street scenes, *The Miracle* opened with images of a majestic mountain range dropping steeply into the sparkling Adriatic Sea. Almost a part of the landscape, a peasant (Anna

Nannina (Anna Magnani) confides in a mysterious stranger (Federico Fellini) in the *Miracle* segment of *L'amore* (*Ways of Love*, 1948).

Magnani) minds her goat as a stranger passes. The stranger (Federico Fellini) is a welcome *paisano*. She confides in him her belief the world is plagued by demons and that he must have been sent by God to protect her. The stranger does not correct her; instead, with a sinister smile, he produces a bottle of wine. Saying nothing he pours her drinks until she slips into unconsciousness.

Justice Felix Frankfurter, a fan and supporter of the film, offered an in-depth plot summary in his concurring opinion in *Joseph Burstyn, Inc. v. Wilson*:

> A poor, simple-minded girl is tending a herd of goats on a mountainside one day when a bearded stranger passes. Suddenly it strikes her fancy that he is St. Joseph, her favorite saint, and that he has come to take her to heaven, where she will be happy and free. While she pleads with him to transport her, the stranger gently plies the girl with wine, and when she is in a state of tumult, he apparently ravishes her. (This incident in the story is only briefly and discreetly implied.) The girl awakens later, finds the stranger gone, and climbs down from the mountain not knowing

whether he was real or a dream. . . . Then, one day, while tending the village youngsters as their mothers work at the vines, the girl faints and the women discover that she is going to have a child. . . . In a scene of brutal torment, they first flatter and laughingly mock her, then they cruelly shove and hit her and clamp a basin as a halo on her head. Even abused by the beggars, the poor girl gathers together her pitiful rags and sadly departs from the village to live alone in a cave. . . . A goat is her sole companion. She drinks water dripping from a rock. And when she comes to the church and finds the door locked, the goat attracts her to a small side door. Inside the church, the poor girl braces herself for her labor pains. There is a dissolve, and when we next see her sad face, in close-up, it is full of a tender light. There is the cry of an unseen baby. The girl reaches towards it and murmurs, my son, my love, my flesh![47]

Bowing to public pressure, New York's licensing commission notified Burstyn of a new hearing. *The Miracle* set the stage for a showdown. Cardinal Spellman continued his crusade, calling the film "a vile and harmful picture, a despicable affront to every Christian."[48] On the other side, *New York Times* film critic Bosley Crowther used his pulpit to oppose the ban. The New York Civil Liberties Union and the Authors League of America supported the cause. The ACLU had been searching for a champion since *Lost Boundaries* and *Curley* had been denied certiorari by the Supreme Court. A test case against the New York board of censorship, while risky, presented the best reward because this regulatory agency was influential throughout the country. Precedent favored the commission. Only a few years earlier, when well-funded Howard Hughes had challenged the ban on *The Outlaw*, the court had upheld the agency's authority to impose moral judgments.

In this politically charged atmosphere, Joseph Burstyn retained Ephraim London (1912–1990). The *Miracle* case was London's first major First Amendment battle and would mark the beginning of the attorney's career as one of America's great free speech advocates. London would argue nine cases before the Supreme Court—winning them all. During the next decade London became instrumental in chiseling away governmental restrictions that burdened motion pictures as he argued on behalf of *Lady Chatterley's Lover*, *Mom and Dad*, *The Connection*, *The Lovers*, and *Language of Love*. London would become a key player in the story of film and the First Amendment; however, when Burstyn first hired the lawyer in 1951 there was only uncertainty, and the law did not favor the First Amendment cause.[49]

The Miracle came before the New York court in *Joseph Burstyn, Inc. v. Wilson* (1951). London based his defense strategy on two points. First, he challenged the statute as vague and overly broad. Second, he addressed the broader issue of whether film censorship under the *Mutual* precedent was out of date and no longer valid.

Looking first at the letter of the law, the censors were authorized to deny permits based on obscenity, indecency, immorality, inhumanity, sacrilege, or two vague catchalls: corruption of morals or incitement to crime. For its rejection of *The Miracle*, the board chose sacrilege as the prohibitive offense.[50] London seized on this ambiguous criterion, but the court just as quickly defused the allegation: "Accordingly, the claim that the word 'sacrilegious' does not provide a sufficiently definite standard may be passed without further consideration, since it is without substance."[51] Glossing over the issue, the court took judicial notice that the dictionary definition of sacrilege furnished a meaning clear enough to render the statute enforceable.

With his attack on the statutory construction defused, London turned to the constitutional argument. Once again, the court was not swayed: "Essentially, what petitioner would have us do is to predict that the Supreme Court will overrule the *Mutual Film* cases and so disregard them here, as well as our own holding in the *Pathé Exchange* case. But such was the position squarely taken in the *RD-DR Corp. [Lost Boundaries]* case, where the same arguments were presented as are here urged, and they were unequivocally rejected."[52] Writing for the majority, Judge Charles William Froessel acknowledged the Supreme Court's recent allusion to a possible extension of constitutional rights for film, but he just as quickly dispensed with this notion: "Some comfort is found by petitioner in a statement in *United States v. Paramount Pictures, Inc.* to the effect that moving pictures, like newspapers and radio, are included in the press. That was an antitrust case, freedom of the press was not involved, and the statement was pure dictum. . . . Were we to rely upon dictum, the concurring remarks of Mr. Justice Frankfurter in a subsequently decided free speech case . . . would be appropriate: Movies have created problems not presented by the circulation of books, pamphlets, or newspapers, and so the movies have been constitutionally regulated. However, dictum is a fragile bark in which to sail the constitutional seas."[53]

Judge Charles C. Desmond concurred in a separate opinion. He found the meaning of the term "sacrilegious" sufficiently definite but saw greater merit to the constitutional argument than the majority:

Motion pictures are, it would seem, not excluded from First Amendment coverage . . . but, since there was a reasonable ground for holding this film sacrilegious (in the meaning which the Legislature must have intended for that term), the film was constitutionally subject to control. . . . It fell within the well-defined and narrowly limited classes of speech, the prevention and punishment of which have never been thought to raise any Constitutional problem. . . . If not, then any prior censorship at all of any motion picture is unconstitutional, and the floodgates are open.[54]

Ephraim London argued that the *Mutual* precedent was out of date because both the medium of motion pictures and the First Amendment had undergone great refinement since 1915. His reasoning found traction with Judge Stanley Howells Fuld (1903–2003). In a lengthy dissenting opinion Fuld, joined by Judge Marvin Dye, displayed a progressive attitude that would influence the Supreme Court's decision.

Fuld's dissent focused on two issues. First, the judge parsed the statute to discern legislative intent:

The controlling statute, the Education Law, is significant both for what it says and for what it leaves unsaid. . . . For example, the statute expressly authorizes the regents to . . . revoke a motion picture license if it was obtained on a false application or if the licensee tampered with the film or if there is a conviction for a crime committed by the [film's] exhibition or unlawful possession. . . . But nowhere in the statute is there to be found any general grant of power to the regents to *revoke* a previously issued license. This omission is also to be contrasted with the further and explicit grant of such a power of revocation by the same Education Law as regards many other types of licenses issued by the Education Department. . . . Clearly, the legislature knew how to bestow the power of revocation when that was its purpose. . . . So, here, the regents' contention that they *must* have power to review and revoke in order to guard against error by the motion picture division in granting licenses, is not persuasive.[55]

Fuld cited the fact that in the commission's twenty-five-year history it had never before attempted to revoke a license or had even suggested the existence of such power. Having determined the board of education lacked authority to revoke the license, Fuld turned to the constitutional issue.

Judge Fuld contended that any state-authorized restriction on speech should be tailored to address a specific purpose. The confines of an indoor movie theater were relevant: "There is no captive audience; only those see the picture who wish to do so, and, then, only if they are willing to pay the price of admission to the theatre." Next, Fuld was wary of granting too much discretionary power to administrative officials. He belived state actors should not be allowed to censor speech based on mere personal disapproval:

> Invasion of the right of free expression must, in short, find justification in some overriding public interest, and the restricting statute must be narrowly drawn to meet an evil which the state has a substantial interest in correcting. . . . The statute before us is not one narrowly drawn to meet such a need as that of preserving the public peace or regulating public places. On the contrary, it imposes a general and pervasive restraint on freedom of discussion of religious themes in moving pictures, which cannot be justified on the basis of any substantial interest of the state. . . . [I]t is beyond the competency of government to prescribe norms of religious conduct and belief.[56]

Applying this reasoning to *The Miracle*, Fuld did not see any overriding public interest that warranted censorship: "The drastic nature of such a ban is highlighted by the fact that the film in question makes no direct attack on, or criticism of, any religious dogma or principle, and it is not claimed to be obscene, scurrilous, intemperate or abusive. Nor is there any evidence of any malicious purpose or intention on the part of the producers of the film to revile or even attack Catholic doctrine or dogma, and no suggestion of any reasonable likelihood of a breach of the peace resulting from the film's exhibition."[57]

After reviewing the statutory language and addressing the underlying constitutional issue, Fuld looked beyond the present issue to discuss the guiding principle of the *Mutual* precedent. For three and a half decades no court had addressed the elephant in the room: *Mutual* had denied First Amendment protections to motion pictures because the medium was "a business, pure and simple." This was an obvious ruse, since even in 1915 when *Mutual* was handed down it would have been inaccurate to say newspapers lacked a commercial purpose. "One reason for denying free expression to motion pictures, we are told, is that the movies are commercial," Fuld wrote, but newspapers, magazines and books are likewise commercially moti-vated, and that has never been an obstacle to their full protection under the First Amendment. . . . [T]he fact that the moving picture conveys its thought or message in dramatic episodes or by means of a story or in a form that is entertaining, makes the difference. . . . In an age when "com-merce" in the Constitution has been construed to include airplanes and electromagnetic waves, "freedom of speech" in the First Amendment and "liberty" in the Fourteenth should be similarly applied to new media for the communication of ideas and facts. Freedom of speech should not be limited to the air-borne voice, the pen, and the printing press, any more than interstate commerce is limited to stagecoaches and sailing vessels.[58]

For Fuld, *Mutual* not only was based on faulty reasoning but also was out of step with legal developments: "The consistent course of decision by the Supreme Court of the United States in recent years persuades me that the early decision of *Mutual Film Corp. v. Industrial Comm. of Ohio*—urged as estab-lishing that motion pictures are beyond the First Amendment's coverage—no longer has the force or authority claimed for it."[59] Then, in a bold and auda-cious move, the New York State judge disparaged Supreme Court precedent when he wrote,

The *Mutual Film* case should be relegated to its place upon the history shelf. Rendered in a day before the guarantees of the Bill of Rights were held to apply to the states, and when moving pictures were in their infancy, the decision was obviously a product of the view that motion pictures did not express or convey opinions or ideas. Today, so far have times and the films changed, some would deny protection for the opposite reason, that films are too effective in their presentation of ideas and points of view. The lat-ter notion is as unsupportable as the other and antiquated view; that the moving picture is a most effective mass medium for spreading ideas is, of course, no reason for refusing it protection. If only ineffectual expression is shielded by the Constitution, free speech becomes a fanciful myth.[60]

This was London's goal: not only a judicial declaration that protected his client's right to distribute the film, but also a legal triumph for Free Speech advocates and the medium of motion pictures. Unfortunately, this realiza-tion occurred in a dissenting opinion. Still, Fuld's commentary would prove influential.

Pinky was released over a year before the U.S. premiere of *The Miracle*. *Pinky* was banned, tried, appealed, and granted certiorari to the Supreme Court before the Italian film. And yet it was Rossellini's passion play that the High Court chose to review first. The Court delivered a resounding reversal.

Writing for the unanimous majority Justice Tom C. Clark acknowledged that cinema was no longer a nickelodeon attraction: "It cannot be doubted that motion pictures are a significant medium for the communication of ideas. They may affect public attitudes and behavior in a variety of ways, ranging from direct espousal of a political or social doctrine to the subtle shaping of thought which characterizes all artistic expression."[61]

Breaking the decades-long pattern of censorship decisions that doggedly deferred to municipal review boards, the High Court directly addressed the constitutional issue. Without dancing around the matter, Clark opened his opinion by stating, "The issue here is the constitutionality, under the First and Fourteenth Amendments, of a New York statute which permits the banning of motion pictures on the grounds that they are sacrilegious."[62]

Sacrilege was key. *The Miracle* was not banned for obscenity, fighting words, or incitement to crime, but rather for a vague and undefined violation of irreverence. The charge of sacrilege cut both ways, both strengthening the argument of free speech advocates as well as limiting the outcome of the decision. On the one hand the Court disapproved of the criterion of sacrilege in a regulatory ordinance: "In seeking to apply the broad and all-inclusive definition of 'sacrilegious' given by the New York courts, the censor is set adrift upon a boundless sea amid a myriad of conflicting currents of religious views, with no charts but those provided by the most vocal and powerful orthodoxies. New York cannot vest such unlimited restraining control over motion pictures in a censor."[63] On the other hand the Court limited the ruling to a narrow scope: "Since the term 'sacrilegious' is the sole standard under attack here, it is not necessary for us to decide, for example, whether a state may censor motion pictures under [a] clearly drawn statute designed and applied to prevent the showing of obscene films. That is a very different question from the one before us now. We hold only that under the First and Fourteenth Amendments a state may not ban a film on the basis of a censor's conclusion that it is sacrilegious."[64] The Court found that censoring a motion picture for sacrilege was invalid, but not censoring per se.

The *Miracle* decision was not a bombshell that eviscerated censorship. Rather, the decision's great value was that it brought the medium of motion pictures under the protection of the First Amendment. Thirty-seven years after *Mutual* the Supreme Court now understood "that expression by means of motion pictures is included within the free speech and free press guaranty of the First and Fourteenth Amendments." Furthermore, the Court wrote, "To the extent that language in the opinion in *Mutual Film Corp. v. Industrial Comm. [of Ohio]* is out of harmony with the views here set forth, we no longer adhere to it."[65]

Mutual had set a strong precedent with its unanimous decision; however, the *Miracle* Court spoke with equal force. Justice Frankfurter filed a long concurrence, which supplied doting details on the film. In a separate concurring opinion Justice Reed limited his comments to a concise statement: "This film does not seem to me to be of a character that the First Amendment permits a state to exclude from public view."[66]

One week later the Supreme Court handed down its decision on *Pinky*. Here, the Court issued an unsigned per curiam opinion, merely stating, "The judgment is reversed." The usually loquacious Justice Frankfurter authored a one-paragraph concurrence. His reasoning: "See my concurring opinion in *Burstyn v. Wilson*."[67]

The *Miracle* decision changed the legal landscape. But Rossellini's short film was not free and clear of its legal history just yet. Two years after the High Court's ruling Chicago's censors banned the film.

While the Supreme Court invalidated the "sacrilege" component of New York's censorship statute, the decision made it clear that motion pictures could be censored for appropriate reasons. The municipal code of the city of Chicago allowed the film commissioner to refuse a permit if he determined a motion picture was "immoral or obscene, or portrays depravity, criminality, or lack of virtue of a class of citizens of any race, color, creed, or religion and exposes them to contempt, derision, or obloquy."[68] Avoiding any reference to sacrilege, the commission banned *The Miracle* based on the similarly vague offense of immorality and the less elusive offense of obscenity. The American Civil Liberties Union stepped forward to address Chicago's sanction.

ACLU v. City of Chicago first affirmed the commission's power to require film submission and its authority to ban films deemed contrary to the ordinance. Then the court validated that the municipal ordinance was constitutional: a picture may be properly banned on grounds of obscenity. The next question was whether *The Miracle* was immoral or obscene. Here the appellate court punted, sending the film back to the lower court; this was a decision of fact not a matter of law: "The issue as to whether or not *The Miracle* is obscene must be submitted to a jury."[69]

First Amendment attorney Ephraim London (1934–1990) at his office at
1 East Forty-Fourth Street, New York, 1962. Courtesy of the *New York Daily News*.

The action was remanded and assigned to Judge John M. Tuohy. The film
was deemed to be obscene and banned.[70] The case was appealed again; this
time the court reversed the opinion, finding that the film was not obscene.
Back at the appellate level Judge Hugo M. Friend wrote, "It is not at all probable, it seems to us, that *The Miracle* would arouse sexual desires in the average,
normal individual. . . . [I]t appears unlikely that even the salaciously inclined
individual would be so affected by a film whose central character is clothed
only in rags and whose personality is devoid of any charm; there is no gloss
of glamour anywhere in the film."[71] Friend's panel then turned to the constitutional issue.

The Supreme Court had not been ready to preclude all censorship in the
Burstyn decision. The Illinois appellate court left that window open as well.
The court opined that regulators must censor with caution, narrowly tailor-
ing their objections and specifically focusing their cuts. Friend continued,

Under this rule the censoring authority, in refusing to issue a permit for showing the film, should be obliged to specify reasons for so doing; and upon trial of the issue whether the ban is justified, the trial court should require the censor to assume the burden of establishing the validity of his refusal. . . . To permit the banning of a motion picture film without requiring the censoring authority to substantiate his action runs directly counter to the spirit and the letter of the law relating to censorship. Freedom of expression is the rule, limitations upon it the exception.[72]

By 1957, nine years after its Venice Film Festival bow, seven years after its New York premiere, and five years after the Supreme Court's ruling, *The Miracle* was granted a permit to be screened in Chicago. That a forty-minute-long Italian art film was a catalyst for change in the development of First Amendment rights was a miracle in itself.

Censorship statutes still stood, but regulators no longer wielded near-unfettered power. The next phase in the story of film and the First Amendment would see the censor's authority grow more restricted still.

12

STATE CENSORSHIP STATUTES
ON THE DEFENSE

———

Post–World War II Hollywood faced new challenges and developments. The Paramount Consent Decree of 1948 put studios on notice that the era of vertical integration was over. While the industry's foundations were shaken, the theater screen was stretched—literally—with innovative formats such as CinemaScope, Cinerama, and stereoscopic 3-D. The star system was entrenched, but during the 1950s bankable screen icons were able to negotiate with greater clout, shifting the balance of power. The American cinema was revitalized with renewed energy, seen in *Singing in the Rain* (1952), fortified with smoldering intensity, seen in *On the Waterfront* (1954), and refined to technical perfection, seen in *Ben-Hur* (1959). But Hollywood also had increasing competition. Young audiences flocked to low-budget, lowbrow exploitation flicks, and worldly viewers gained access to international cinema.

The *Miracle* decision earned a place for film within the First Amendment. The films that followed pushed the boundaries of free speech even further.

Joseph Burstyn, Inc. v. Wilson was the first major blow to state censorship laws, but it did not signal the end of content-based regulations. The scope of the *Miracle* decision was narrow. The Court held that censorship based on sacrilege was insufficient to overcome First Amendment protections. Obscenity, immorality, indecency, nudity, and incitement to crime were still valid reasons to ban a film. The *Miracle* decision was still fresh when new challenges percolated up through New York and Ohio. The New York board of censors denied a permit to *La ronde* (1950), and Ohio banned a remake of *M* (1951). These two cases would be consolidated by the Supreme Court for the next major film censorship decision in *Superior Films, Inc. v. Department of Education* (1954).

Max Ophüls (1902–1957) directed *La ronde* (1950), a sophisticated comedy of manners. The New York court summarized the film in *In re Commercial Pictures v. Board of Regents*:

> The film from beginning to end deals with promiscuity, adultery, fornication and seduction. It portrays ten episodes, with a narrator. Except for the husband and wife episode, each deals with an illicit amorous adventure between two persons, one of the two partners becoming the principal in the next. The first episode begins with a prostitute and a soldier. Since the former's room is ten minutes walk from their meeting place on the street, and the soldier must hurry back to his barracks, they take advantage of the local environment. She informs him that "civilians" pay, but for "boys like you it's nothing." The cycle continues with the soldier and a parlormaid; the parlormaid and her employer's son; the latter and a young married woman; the married woman and her husband; the husband and a young girl; the girl and a poet; the poet and an actress; the actress and a count; and finally the count and the prostitute.[1]

The film featured French beauties Simone Signoret as the prostitute, Simone Simon as the maid, and Danielle Darrieux as the married woman. That *La ronde* was of the highest quality was evidenced by Academy Award nominations for writing and black-and-white art direction/set decoration. That the film did not offend standards of decency was attested to by the plaintiffs' testimony: "The film ran nearly two years in Paris, over a year in London which has quite rigid [censorship] standards in this respect. . . . It was exhibited for relatively long periods in Los Angeles, San Francisco, Washington, St. Louis and Detroit."[2]

Still, New York's appellate court upheld the censor's ban of *La ronde*, based on a finding that the motion picture "would tend to corrupt morals."[3] Despite the work of pioneering female jurist Florence Perlow Shientag, the state's regents won the day. In a throwback to the pre-*Miracle* cases the court deferred to the censoring authority, finding that "a ground sufficient to warrant interference with the Regents' judgment that *La Ronde* is immoral has not been shown."[4]

As Shientag was representing Commercial Pictures for *La ronde*, a similar action was developing in Ohio. The state's censors banned Joseph Losey's *M* (1951), a low-budget remake of Fritz Lang's classic film. Losey's B-movie version transplanted the story of a child murderer to Los Angeles and added noir ambience. Ohio objected, "This motion picture is filled with brutal crime. Two cold-blooded murders are presented, another implied and a third attempted. A schizophrenic killer is treated with sympathy and an under-world boss is depicted as vastly more efficient than the police. Twice, the methods for abducting children on the streets are elaborated."[5]

The Ohio court differentiated this case from the recent *Miracle* ruling. Sacrilege was not at issue—in the instant case the court considered whether *M* presented a clear and present danger to society: "As we view it, the United States Supreme Court has not *ipso facto* taken away all community control of moving pictures by censorship, and this court will not do so under the claim of complete unconstitutionality of censorship laws. The motion picture, *M*, as shown by the certificate was rejected for the following reasons, among others: 1. There is a conviction that the effect of this picture on unstable persons

Max Ophüls's merry-go-round of sex in *La ronde* (1950).

Joseph Losey turned in a low-budget, noir-infused remake of *M* (1951).

of any age level could lead to a serious increase in immorality and crime. 2. Presentation of actions and emotions of child killer emphasizing complete perversion without serving any valid educational purpose."[6] *M* was censured for presenting "dangerous criminal aspects" on-screen.

As the ban on *M* was sustained in Ohio, *La ronde* proceeded on appeal in New York. No friend to filmmakers, Judge Charles W. Froessel wrote the opinion as if *La ronde*'s story of interlinking assignations was a threat to the fabric of society:

> The Legislature may act to guard against such evil, though in so doing it overrides to a degree the right to free expression. . . . That a motion picture which panders to base human emotions is a breeding ground for sensuality, depravity, licentiousness and sexual immorality can hardly be doubted. That these vices represent a "clear and present danger" to the body social seems manifestly clear. The danger to youth is self-evident. And so adults, who may react with limited concern to a portrayal of larceny, will tend to react quite differently to a presentation wholly devoted to promiscuity, seductively portrayed in such manner as to invite concupiscence and condone its promiscuous satisfaction, with its evil social consequences.[7]

Sexual impropriety and films that could corrupt morals were seen as valid and important categories to regulate.

The dissenting voices in both New York's *La ronde* opinion and Ohio's *M* decision took broader views of the *Miracle* ruling, suggesting the statutes were invalid. In *Superior Films v. Department of Education* (the *M* case), Judge Kingsley Taft wrote, "The pronouncements of the law by that court in *Joseph Burstyn, Inc. v. Wilson* . . . and the later decision of that court in *Gelling v. Texas* . . . clearly require the conclusion that the Ohio moving picture censorship statutes are void because of the provisions of the Constitution of the United States."[8] Similarly, Judge Stanley H. Fuld eloquently wrote in *Commercial Pictures v. Board of Regents* (the *La ronde* case), "That the freedom of expression assured by the First Amendment is not limited to the air-borne voice, the pen, and the printing press . . . but extends as well to motion pictures, is now beyond dispute. . . . Here again, as in *Burstyn*, the censorship statute must fall because of the lack of a sufficiently definite standard or guide for administrative action."[9]

The Supreme Court consolidated *Superior Films* and *Commercial Pictures* to hear their third film censorship case in as many years. The screening habits of the justices served as a testament to the growing power and influence of motion pictures. Before *The Miracle*, the High Court had never screened a film; Rossellini's featurette was the first to be projected in the hall of justice. In 1953 a double feature not only unspooled but also preempted the president. According to the *New York Times*, "The nine black robed old men of the Supreme Court were too engrossed with a movie to bother with President Eisenhower's state of the union message. . . . The Justices could have knocked off to hear Ike if they wanted to but they elected to keep looking at the film. . . . Who wouldn't?"[10]

The screening took more time out of the Court's schedule than writing the opinion. The decision merely read, "The judgments are reversed. *Joseph Burstyn, Inc. v. Wilson*."[11] Justices Douglas and Black's concurring opinion was slightly more loquacious, when they noted, "The First Amendment draws no distinction between the various methods of communicating ideas. . . . In this Nation every writer, actor, or producer, no matter what medium of expression he may use, should be freed from the censor."[12] The burden for sustaining censorship of a motion picture shifted from filmmakers to the boards of review. While the *Miracle* decision struck sacrilege from the roster of permissible censorship acts, *Superior Films* and *Commercial Pictures* removed immoral and harmful imagery as standards for suppression.

Censorship laws were put on the defensive, and regulators in Ohio, Massachusetts, and Kansas found themselves in the crosshairs. The next challenge came from Howard Hughes. A decade earlier Hughes had lavished sums producing his fetish-Western, and even more in litigation. Now the mogul set in motion events that would take down Ohio's censorship law with two titillating titles: *The French Line* (1953) and *Son of Sinbad* (1955).

Hughes's infatuation with Jane Russell hadn't dimmed over the decade; *The French Line* starred the bodacious actress in scenes engineered to rile the regulators. The film cast Russell as an oil heiress, but the paper-thin plot was insignificant next to the widescreen 3-D Technicolor display of her ample assets. Ohio regulators particularly objected to the "obscene movements of body of the dancer, her bathycolpian posing in brief revealing costume, [and] accompanying lust provoking words of her song. . . . The words of the song and the method of presentation are so vulgar and obscene as to be unfit for publication in a court opinion."[13]

Russell was provocative in bubble-bath scenes in *The French Line*, but *Son of Sinbad* starred the burlesque actress who actually popularized the bubble-bath-onstage gimmick as the centerpiece of her act. Statuesque blonde Lili St. Cyr, called the "Anatomic Bomb," built her celebrity on a routine in which she disrobed onstage and stepped into a bubble bath. Ohio's regulators tried to throw ice water on St. Cyr's siren charms: "Portions of a picture entitled *Son of Sinbad* were excluded because certain dance scenes have no conceivable purpose except to be sexually stimulating and lust provoking."[14]

Hughes set his sights on the Ohio statute. Enacted in 1922, the statute provided for "the approval of films which in the judgment and discretion of the department of education are of a moral, educational, or amusing and harmless character or the rejection of those, or parts thereof, which, measured by the same judgment and discretion, do not fall into the class which the law authorized approved."[15] In *RKO v. Department of Education* Ohio's court struck down the thirty-two-year-old statute. A decade after *The Outlaw*, Hughes triumphed. Censorship was suspended in the state that had originated the *Mutual* decision.

Howard Hughes crossed the line in *The French Line* (1954).

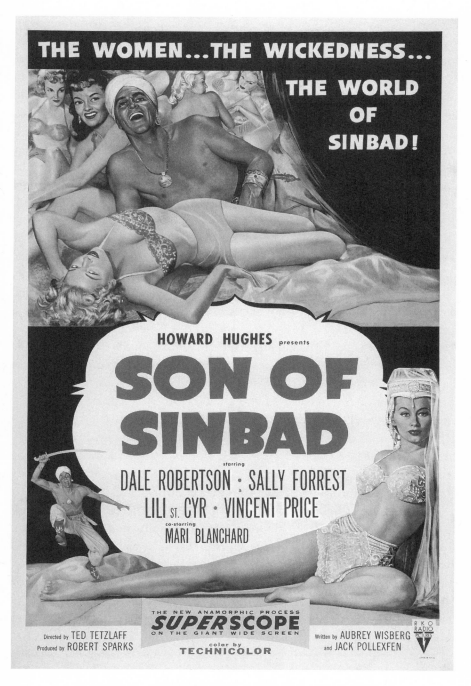

Vincent Price as Omar Khayyam opposite the "Anatomic Bomb,"
stripper Lili St. Cyr, in *Son of Sinbad* (1955).

Further challenges lay ahead. Film censorship ordinances were coming under attack with increasing regularity. Back in 1922 Massachusetts had passed "An Act Relative to the Examination and Licensing of Motion Picture Films to Be Publicly Exhibited and Displayed in This Commonwealth."[16] In addition to the regulation on content, Massachusetts also enforced exhibition through blue laws that shuttered theaters on Sunday.

Massachusetts invoked its blue laws to challenge Alf Sjöberg's Swedish production of *Miss Julie* (1951). Based on August Strindberg's play, *Miss Julie* dealt with social class, sex, and power, depicting an aristocratic girl's relationship with her servant. The film starred Anita Björk and was awarded the Grand Prix at Cannes in 1951. A success on the sun-soaked French Riviera, the film found less of a welcome in Middlesex County. Municipal regulators prohibited screenings of the film on Sunday. One exhibitor, fearing the loss of revenue as much as the specter of film censorship, challenged the regulation.

The owners of the Brattle Theatre argued that the film had played with a legal permit and without incident throughout the week. The court conceded that the modernist play "is not of such a character as to disturb the peace and quiet of the Lord's Day or to interfere with its due observance."[17] Brattle won the day, overriding and invalidating the blue laws. In *Brattle Films, Inc. v. Commissioner of Public Safety*, Chief Justice of the Massachusetts Supreme Court Raymond Wilkins opined, "We think [the regulation] is void on its face as a prior restraint on the freedom of speech and of the press guaranteed by the First and Fourteenth Amendments. . . . That the present controversy concerns exhibitions on only one day a week, and that day Sunday, does not seem to us to alter the governing rules of law. It is unthinkable that there is a power, absent as to secular days, to require the submission to advance scrutiny by governmental authority."[18] By July 1955 another censorship law had fallen.

The next major figure to push the envelope was Otto Preminger (1905–1986), a filmmaker who consistently made movies aimed at defying the censors. The famously temperamental director first came to popular and critical attention with his stylish film noir *Laura* (1944). Preminger didn't shy away from controversial themes; rather, he sought out hot-button topics. He took on adultery in *Daisy Kenyon* (1947), promiscuity in *The Moon Is Blue* (1953), heroin addiction in *The Man With the Golden Arm* (1955), and the details of rape in *Anatomy of a Murder* (1959). The state of Kansas brought the first challenge to a Preminger film, focusing on *The Moon Is Blue* in *Holmby Productions, Inc. v. Vaughn* (1955).

From a contemporary perspective it is difficult to identify why *The Moon Is Blue*, a bubbly screwball comedy, would have been so objectionable. A man-about-town (William Holden) pursues and picks up an outgoing girl (Maggie McNamara) on the way to the observation deck of the Empire State Building. He brings her home, not for sex—she states how proud she is of her virginity—but to make her dinner. Once in his bachelor pad she meets the neighbor, a competing lothario (David Niven). The film is a comedy of manners with saucy, suggestive dialogue. Sex is never seen, and nudity is never revealed, despite the insinuations of the two older men (for example, when Niven's ketchup squirts onto McNamara's blouse, he moves to wipe it off—then stops short).

Kansas censors rejected the film for precisely the reason the scenario was so entertaining: "On June 17, 1953, the board disapproved the film for the reasons [of] sex theme throughout, too frank bedroom dialogue [and] many sexy words; both dialogue and action have sex as their theme."[19] Preminger refused to make any compromises, saying, "I don't want to sound pretentious. I know that any comedy can survive a few cuts, but in this case I want to test a principle. I will make no cuts and I will make no deals. If anyone has the power to stop the picture from being played, then it won't be played."[20] Kansas regulators felt they had that power. The state's statute authorized censors to ban films deemed cruel, obscene, indecent, or immoral, or such as tend to debase or corrupt morals. *The Moon Is Blue* ran afoul of each of these charges except cruelty and was rejected.

Unlike the series of progressive decisions coming down from the Eastern courts, *Holmby Productions* deferred to the censors' administrative authority. The pre-*Miracle* mantra was repeated: "The board's action must be upheld unless it was fraudulent or so arbitrary and capricious as to be, in effect, fraudulent. . . . A court cannot substitute its opinion in place of the board's opinion as to the fitness of a film because our courts do not have such power conferred upon them by the legislature. . . . To have it any other way would be to destroy the vital marrow of our great concept of government."[21] Writing for the court, Judge Clair E. Robb next moved to address the constitutional issue: "The only question before us, then, is whether the statutes under consideration are unconstitutional because . . . they are couched in language so vague and indefinite as to offend due process."[22] The court wouldn't substitute its judgment for that of the board, but the authority of the regulators had come under review.

As opposed to sacrilege (*The Miracle*), immorality (*La ronde*), or incitement to crime (*M*), *Holmby Productions* focused on obscenity. The resulting judgment followed a familiar pattern. The ban was upheld. The producer appealed. The judgment was reversed: the U.S. Supreme Court invalidated the state's statute on grounds that it was unconstitutionally vague and overly broad.[23] The Kansas censorship ordinance was the third to fall in 1955.

Even before the Supreme Court tossed out the Kansas statute, United Artists took an unprecedented step for a major studio. Although *The Moon* was banned in Kansas—and earned a "C" condemned rating from the Legion of Decency—United Artists released the picture without an MPAA seal of approval. Despite cancellations in Connecticut, confiscations in New Jersey, and continuing Catholic outrage,[24] the un-permitted exhibition had little effect on box office. *The Moon* enjoyed a solid return. *Life* magazine called it a "Whopping Box Office Success," the *New York Times*, "a real smasheroo," and *Variety* saw "unusually strong domestic distribution," ranking the picture fifteenth for the year in terms of domestic box office.[25] *The Moon*'s success demonstrated that exhibitors would book a film even without the official seal. These elements exposed the weakening influence of the PCA, the municipal censors, and the Legion of Decency. Empowered by his victory, Preminger prepared another film, knowing that it would further stir the pot.

Preminger's next production to cross the censors was *The Man with the Golden Arm* (1955). *Golden Arm* followed the story of ex-heroin addict Frankie Machine (Frank Sinatra) as he struggled to stay clean. The picture was lauded for its serious, realistic approach to narcotics, a far cry from the crazed dope-fiend exploitation flicks of earlier eras. Because of the taboo subject, *Golden Arm* was denied a seal. Like *The Moon Is Blue*, *The Man with the Golden Arm* found its audience.

Maryland's board of censors was less understanding. The state's regulators had diligently followed the High Court's rulings on film and the First Amendment, striking the word sacrilegious and allowing for timely newsreels. The revised ordinance of 1955 provided, "The Board [of Censors] shall examine or supervise the examination of all films or views to be exhibited or used in the State of Maryland and shall approve and license such films or views which are moral and proper, and shall disapprove such as are obscene, or such as tend, in the judgment of the Board, to debase or corrupt morals. . . . All films exclusively portraying current events or pictorial news of the day, commonly called news reels, may be exhibited without examination."[26] The code further authorized censure of a motion picture if "its exhibition would tend to incite to crime[,] if the theme or the manner of its presentation presents the commission of criminal acts or . . . if it advocates or teaches the use of, or the methods of use of, narcotics or habit-forming drugs." United Artists submitted *The Man with the Golden Arm*, and Maryland's board pointed to a single scene that violated the statute: "This scene, which runs less than two minutes, shows Frankie Machine . . . taking a narcotic after six months in the United States Public Health Service Hospital for Drug Addicts at Lexington, Kentucky. Ostensibly he was cured, but all the pressures were there waiting for him. The scene shows him rolling up his sleeve, and tying a necktie around the upper arm, while a dope pusher prepares the drug for injection."[27] The board demanded that this scene be removed. United Artists refused. Preminger further baited the authorities stating, "I think that the film has a better moral point of view than some pictures which have been passed."[28]

The Baltimore court defended the ordinance and agreed with the censors. The scene was a violation of the code because it taught use of narcotics.[29] The Maryland court of appeals reversed the decision. Judge Edward S. Delaplaine had "no difficulty in finding from the record that the censored part of the film does not advocate or teach the use of, or the methods of use of, narcotics. On the contrary, the evidence is strong and convincing that the picture is likely to have a beneficial effect as a deterrent from the use of narcotics."[30] Preminger's provocative film received its license, and the ban was rescinded in Maryland, but the censorship law remained valid and on the books.

The following year the Baltimore board of censors banned a documentary that contained images of unclothed indigenous tribespeople in *Naked Amazon* (1954). The case went to trial, generating a discussion on the issue of nudity in film—nonsexual, nonpandering, nonprurient anthropological displays of the naked human figure. While Preminger's films challenged the censors on social issues, the on-screen display of nudity confronted regulators on a more primal level.

The legal discussion of nudity in mass media only began in the 1950s when a series of films and books exploited the growing popularity of nudism. The topic became so prevalent that *Variety* coined the phrase "epidermis epidemic."[31] A key ruling came down in *Parmelee v. United States* (1940) when the District of Columbia considered a ban on the import of a British book series entitled "Nudism in Modern Life." Looking to the history of the nude in art, medical treatises, and textbooks, the court arrived at the commonsense conclusion that "it cannot be assumed that nudity is obscene per se and under all circumstances."[32]

New York and New Jersey previously considered the issue of nudity in film in *Latuko* (1951). This British documentary focused on a tribe in Anglo-Egyptian Sudan. The film was banned in New York, and the *Times* reported, "The board did not elaborate on the reasons for its ruling but it was understood that the objections were to the nudity of the African natives depicted in the film."[33] New Jersey ultimately passed the film, with Judge Louis R. Freund holding that "only a narrow and unhealthy mind could find any depravity in the film. . . . [A] showing of the film revealed nothing suggestive, obscene, indecent or immoral in the lives of this tribe in its normal living state."[34] Garden State authorities continued to fight the permit, while in New York the documentary remained banned, shown only privately at the Museum of Natural History, the organization that had sponsored the picture.[35]

Maryland's censors considered a native-themed picture with far less of a prestigious pedigree than *Latuko* had. Baltimore's ban of *Naked Amazon* was based on the film's depictions of a Neolithic tribe living nearly unchanged since pre-Columbian times. In *Board of Censors v. Times Film Corp.* the court provided color:

> Zygmunt Sulistrowski, who is described as an explorer and photographer, and a man of adventure, headed an expedition to the Matto Grosso region of the Brazilian jungles. . . . When the group makes contact with the Camayura Indians, the scenes are entirely genuine and documentary. The Indians are aborigines who are said to bring to mind pictures of prehistoric man. . . . The natives are quite unaware that they are without clothing and the narration accompanying the scenes in no manner suggests that they are sexually excited, or exciting, rather, the photography and narration dwell on their unusual customs and rituals, which seemingly give the appearance of rather childlike games.[36]

While the court positioned the film as a documentary, *Naked Amazon* related less to the tradition of reality-based filmmaking than to "mondo" films, of which it was one of the first examples.

The genre of mondo film takes its name from *Mondo cane* (1962). *Mondo cane* used documentary techniques and found footage as a ruse to present titillating sex and graphically violent scenes. Despite the court's discussion of *Naked Amazon* as a (pseudo) documentary, the filmmakers were using these techniques to trade on exotic, erotic images.

Maryland's censors asserted that in *Naked Amazon*, "The showing of nudity . . . is calculated to arouse sexual desires of substantial numbers of people."[37] The film's producers responded by challenging the statute. Judge Hall Hammond opined,

> The parties meet head-on in their views as to constitutionality of the statute and as to whether it was rightfully applied by the Board. The Board says that prior restraint of motion pictures is constitutional; the producers that it is not. The Board says that the Maryland statute is tightly drawn and not subject to the infirmities of vagueness and lack of proper standards and, so, is valid; the producers [say] that it is vague and without tests that can constitutionally serve as measurements. The Board urges that it rightly interpreted the statute and properly applied its standards; the producers say that the Board misinterpreted and misapplied the statute and that, in any event, there was no basis in fact for the finding it made.[38]

Hammond's five-judge panel did not find the film obscene or pornographic; they ruled that the censorship board had misinterpreted and misapplied the statute: "There is no reasonable or substantial basis even on [the board of censor's] theory of the law, and certainly not under the statute as we read it, for a finding that the calculated purpose and dominant effect of the *Naked Amazon* was substantially to arouse sexual desires, based as it was only on the showing of primitive unprepossessing aborigines going about their daily lives in their native surroundings, unclothed, as is their custom, with no intimation of sexual activity or awareness."[39] The court did not address the constitutional issue, so the Maryland censorship statute remained on the books. The academic *Latuko* remained banned or controversial, while *Naked Amazon* quietly played uncut in the censor-friendly Old Line State.

The epidermis epidemic continued. New York tussled over another nudism film: *Garden of Eden* (1954), which was the subject of *Excelsior Pictures Corp. v. Regents*. With a plot that inadvertently suggested elements of *The Rocky Horror Picture Show*, *Garden of Eden* told the story of a woman and her daughter on the road. When their car breaks down they are forced to seek shelter—in a nudist camp. Shy and self-conscious at first, the women learn to love the freedom of "the lifestyle." *Garden of Eden* was directed by Max Nosseck, best remembered for his hardboiled classic, *Dillinger* (1945), a film which introduced tough guy Lawrence Tierney to film audiences. More objectionable than the sensational violence of *Dillinger*, *Eden*'s bucolic nudism set off the censors' alarms.

Rather than displaying nudists in their full-frontal natural beauty, *Garden of Eden* filtered private parts with diegetic—or naturally occurring—props. Breasts and buttocks were exposed, but naughty bits were always hidden behind a beach ball or well-placed flower pot or tucked just barely out of frame. The nudity in *Garden of Eden* was never dirty; the picture was tempting and titillating but frustratingly coy and prudish. This did not pass unnoticed at trial: "The specific and limited portions of the film to which the licensing authorities object are exposed portions of human bodies in scenes depicting a nudist colony. There is, however, no full exposure of any adult nude body."[40] The court rejected the censor's ban of the film but stopped short of addressing the constitutional issue, writing, "A majority of the court are of opinion that a decision striking down the entire statute as unconstitutional ought not be entered by an intermediate appellate court."[41]

Nudist holiday in *Garden of Eden* (1954).

Garden of Eden proved controversial in other jurisdictions. In Massachusetts the film was banned as indecent and impure, and exhibition was thought not in keeping with the character of the Lord's day.[42] Although the state's blue law had been overturned two years earlier in *Brattle Films*, the regulators relied on the same grounds in *Commonwealth v. Moniz*. The court disagreed, finding, "Apart from the showing of nudity, the picture is substantially free of erotic appeal."[43] The film was permitted to play. Kansas arrived at a different result. An exhibitor sought to enjoin regulators from interfering with the showing of *Garden of Eden* in *Dickinson Operating Co. v. City of Kansas City* (1958). While the lower court granted an injunction, this was overturned on appeal. The film was banned.[44] These varying results demonstrate the uncertain regulatory environment.

While the debate over nudity in *Garden of Eden* raged on, another controversial film with an equally innocent title was moving through the system: *Mom and Dad* (1945). *Mom and Dad* was a throwback to sex hygiene films such as *Damaged Goods* (1914). Exploitation and titillation masqueraded as education. Judge Philip J. Finnegan of the Seventh Circuit relished the details of the sensationalistic story:

At a high school dance, one evening the young lady encounters a slightly more sophisticated male applicant for the freshman class at a nearby college. A pastoral scene complete with falling leaves and orchestral crescendo symbolizes the transfer of this young uninformed girl from agonizing doubt into exaggerated certainty. . . . [P]art two, introduced as a film within a film, is a straightforward instruction on sex. Diagrams are used for explanations of post-insemination stages from embryo to fetus. Following these diagrams there are two separate inserts, one showing a normal delivery, and the other a Caesarian section. Both sequences focusing on surgical techniques, were apparently photographed at a hospital, and while each shows the birth of a human baby neither departs from its sterile medical environment. . . . Venereal disease is the subject of part three and consists primarily of photographs of the human ear, eye, nose and throat, showing the ravages of syphilis. Thousands of young men who served in our armed forces have, without a doubt, viewed much stronger versions of this same theme shown in required training films at basic training centers.[45]

Kroger Babb's sex-education/unwanted-pregnancy masterpiece of exploitation-infotainment, *Mom and Dad* (1945).

Master of the exploitation flick Kroger Babb (1906–1908). From the collections of the Margaret Herrick Library, Academy of Motion Picture Arts and Sciences.

Mom and Dad was the first film produced by Kroger Babb. Babb (1906–1980) was a colorful showman who would soon be recognized as a leading exploitation-cinema maven. He began his career by reissuing *Child Bride* in 1945 and followed up with *She Shoulda Said 'No'!* (1949). These pictures catered to young audiences with a hankering for scenes of sex, drugs, and the bizarre. For *Mom and Dad*, Babb ordered separate showings for men and women and interrupted each screening with a lecture presented by Dr. Elliot Forbes, a fake professor of sex hygiene. Accompanied by two nurses in white uniforms, the sexologist hawked his book, *The Secrets of Sensible Sex*.[46] One newspaper exposed Forbes as "a copyrighted stage name under which all lecturers with *Mom and Dad* shows work. . . . J. T. Woodruff, the Elliot Forbes of Unit No. 2 is considered by the company's local office personnel to be the best of all their lecturers."[47]

As lowbrow as Babb's production values were, the film's director, William Beaudine, boasted an impressive pedigree. After assisting D. W. Griffith on *The Birth of a Nation* and *Intolerance*, Beaudine launched his own career at Kalem in 1915. He built his reputation as a journeyman-director able to churn out a feature-length film under budget in a matter of days, unhampered by a personal style or artistic pretensions. By the 1920s Beaudine became a hired hand at the emerging studios, directing pictures for First National, Fox, Goldwyn, Metro, Paramount, and Warner Bros., as well as the Poverty Row factories Monogram and PRC.[48]

Mom and Dad was produced quickly and cheaply. Budgeted under $65,000, within four years the picture's box office brought in at least $8 million, and it continued its theatrical run into the 1960s.[49] *Mom and Dad* generated a solid return for Babb's Capitol Enterprises shingle. The film also left an impressive run of court decisions in its wake.

Mom and Dad first ran up against the regents in New York in 1956. The regulators objected to a scene that depicted a human birth. Citing section 122 of the education law's prohibition on indecent imagery, the board banned the film. Upon review the court denied the board, positioning "[t]he sequence [as] a biological demonstration, scientific in level and tone."[50] Furthermore, the court saw that the purported objectionable and indecent sequence constituted only a small portion of the narrative. This line of reasoning employed a judicial balancing act that looked forward to the *Roth* standard—handed down by the Supreme Court the following year—which weighed obscenity by looking at the work as a whole rather than isolated sections. Avoiding the constitutional issue, New York's five-judge panel found the film not indecent.

After the 1956 decisions for *Garden of Eden* and *Mom and Dad*, the legal landscape surrounding the issue and measure of obscenity drastically changed. This transformation stemmed from the Supreme Court's ruling in *Roth v. United States*. Prior to *Roth* obscenity had been judged by a formula that originated under English common law in *Regina v. Hicklin* (1868). The *Hicklin* test asked "whether the tendency of the matter charged as obscenity is to deprave and corrupt those whose minds are open to such immoral influences."[51] The focus of the test was on shielding young or salaciously inclined individuals from prurient influences. This benchmark for obscenity changed in 1957 when *Roth* replaced *Hicklin* in the United States. Under *Roth* material was deemed obscene if an average person applying contemporary community standards would view the dominant theme of the material taken as a whole as appealing to prurient—morbidly lewd and lascivious—interest. Furthermore, the work as a whole must be deemed to lack social importance. Rather than judging obscenity from a work's *possible* effect on the most susceptible person, *Roth* instructed the trier of fact to identify a work's effect on an average person. Secondly, *Roth* looked at the work as a *whole* rather than isolate any single objectionable aspect. Finally, the judge was instructed to apply contemporary community standards, which were intended to counterbalance pockets of regional bias.[52] As influential as *Roth* was, the obscenity standard would not be applied directly to motion pictures until 1964, seven years later. Despite that lag between the decision and its application to film, *Roth* remained an influential standard.

A year prior to *Roth*, both *Mom and Dad* and *Garden of Eden* were reluctantly permitted by New York's regents. An uneasy status quo was maintained. The films were approved, but the state's censorship statute also remained in place.

The next battleground returned to the city of Chicago and the Seventh Circuit. At issue was Claude Autant-Lara's *Le blé en herbe* (*The Game of Love*, 1957). French director Autant-Lara (1901–2000) began his career under French masters Jean Renoir and Marcel L'Herbier during the silent era. Autant-Lara transitioned to the talkies as a director but became best known for his outrageous comments and provocative political viewpoints. He was fond of claiming that "the [film] director must consider himself surrounded by enemies" and "if a film does not have venom, it is worthless."[53] Autant-Lara's art as a provocateur only increased as he aged, and his outspoken comments swung from strident Socialist propaganda to far-right, anti-Semitic diatribes.[54]

Autant-Lara's *Game of Love* was refused a license for exhibition in Chicago based on obscenity. In *Times Film Corp. v. City of Chicago*, Judge Elmer J. Schnackenberg wrote,

> The film, as an exhibit in this case, was projected before and viewed by us. We found that, from beginning to end, the thread of the story is supercharged with a current of lewdness generated by a series of illicit sexual intimacies and acts. In the introductory scenes a flying start is made when a 16-year old boy is shown completely nude on a bathing beach in the presence of a group of younger girls. On that plane the narrative proceeds to reveal the seduction of this boy by a physically attractive woman old enough to be his mother. Under the influence of this experience and an arrangement to repeat it, the boy thereupon engages in sexual relations with a girl of his own age. The erotic thread of the story is carried, without deviation toward any wholesome idea, through scene after scene. The narrative is graphically pictured with nothing omitted except those sexual consummations which are plainly suggested but meaningfully omitted and thus, by the very fact of omission, emphasized.[55]

Claude Autant-Lara's *Le blé en herbe* (*The Game of Love*, 1954).

The board of censors banned the film as obscene and immoral. The district court agreed. On appeal, the opinion was upheld; furthermore, the Seventh Circuit took the additional step of commenting on the validity of the censorship statute: "We hold that the public exhibition of obscene moving pictures may be barred. . . . The first and fourteenth amendments of the federal Constitution do not, and were never intended to, shield public peddlers of obscenity and immorality. The ordinance now under attack is not unconstitutional on the grounds asserted."[56]

The following year when Kroger Babb's *Mom and Dad* came under consideration in *Capitol Enterprises, Inc. v. City of Chicago*, the Seventh Circuit applied a test similar to the *Roth* standard: "A motion picture is obscene within the meaning of the ordinance if, when considered as a whole, its calculated purpose or dominant effect is substantially to arouse sexual desires, and if the probabilities of this effect [are] so great as to outweigh whatever artistic or other merits the film may possess. In making this determination the film must be tested with reference to its effect upon the *normal, average person*."[57] Chicago's censors deemed *Mom and Dad* to be obscene, and the district court agreed. These rulings were overturned by the Seventh Circuit. The court made a rare admission that censors and censorship laws must change with the times to remain relevant. Judge Philip J. Finnegan realized, "Early censorship cases serve very little in this modern setting. . . . Judges, no less than legislators should observe, without prejudice, what is going on in our changing society, averting through such alertness treating law as a petrified body of shibboleths."[58]

In *Capitol Enterprises*, the Seventh Circuit overturned the ban on *Mom and Dad* but left the statute intact:

> We have resolved plaintiff's appeal without passing upon the constitutional validity of the Ordinance because it is unnecessary to reach that problem. . . . Our decision rests on narrow but firm grounds for we are satisfied there was absent any sound basis for outlawing the film and the absence of any reasons by the censors for their classification is a foreboding guise for arbitrary censorship running afoul of the First and Fourteenth Amendments. Nothing has been put forward by the City indicating just what in this film are its inherent evils. . . . Consequently this censorship results in a curb on free expression and it is our view that the trial judge erred.[59]

Chicago's code would begin to unravel four months later when an Illinois district court considered *Desire Under the Elms* (1958) in *Paramount Film Distributing Corp. v. City of Chicago.*

Based on Eugene O'Neill's stage play, the film adaptation featured Burl Ives as Ephraim Cabot, the ruthless patriarch of a New England farm. His young bride (Sophia Loren) is pitted against a resentful son (Anthony Perkins) as they vie for the old man's inheritance. Even though the film adaptation strayed from the psychodrama of its source material, O'Neill's modernist writing demanded a mature audience. Perhaps the distributor should not have been surprised when the Chicago censors granted a permit limiting admission to persons over the age of twenty-one. It is doubtful that Paramount would have lost much of their audience due to the restrictive license; still, the studio sued for an injunction.

The district court handed down an unanticipated ruling. Taking a hard look at the ordinance, the court did not like what it saw. First, Judge Philip L. Sullivan considered the age classification and determined it was "an insufficient guide to either the censors or those who produce motion pictures." Sullivan continued, "A censorship statute is necessarily an invasion of the First Amendment right to freedom of expression. Although the City may under its police power limit that right to prevent an evil, any restrictive action must be reasonable, not capricious."[60] The court invalidated the contested provision of the city's censorship statute.

Meanwhile, Kroger Babb was continuing his streak after clearing *Mom and Dad* in New York and Chicago. He took on Pennsylvania's film regulators with his next picture. If *Mom and Dad* represented a throwback to social hygiene films, *She Shoulda Said 'No'!* (1949) was a return to the tried and trusted exploitation formula of crime, drugs, and reckless youth that saw a surge of popularity in the 1930s. *She Shoulda Said 'No'!* profited from a ripped-from-the-headlines casting coup. The film featured Lila Leeds, a former hatcheck girl at Ciro's Sunset Strip nightclub who achieved notoriety after getting busted with Robert Mitchum for marijuana possession. The quickie-cheapie film was released to theaters six months after the bust—quite a feat, as Leeds also served sixty days for the infraction during that time. Fast turnaround was a specialty of the film's director, Sam Newfield.

Newfield was a prolific B-movie maker who was never burdened by aspirations of quality. He made many films for his brother, Sigmund Newfield, President of PRC, one of the least prestigious low-budget film factories on Poverty Row. Sam Newfield's dubious film achievements included the all-dwarf Western *The Terror of Tiny Town* (1936), the ultra-low-budget actioner *The Invisible Killer* (1939), and the man-in-an-ape-suit jungle adventurer flicks *Nabonga* (1944) and *White Pongo* (1945).

She Shoulda Said 'No'! condemned—or glorified—the fast living of "today's teenagers," showing how "the use of the weed lead[s] to use of heroin, cocaine, opium, excites curiosity toward escape from reality . . . and actually leads to lives of sin, corruption, horror and murder."[61] The Pennsylvania censors demanded cuts to the film, including "the scene of two teenage couples, an open roadster on a hill overlooking Hollywood and being under the influence of the drug; each boy having a girl in his arms and smoking a marijuana cigarette . . . [t]he scene showing the party in Ann's home with Rita and the two men as they smoke marijuana cigarettes and under its influence deport themselves in an obscene manner . . . [and the] scene showing Rita dancing in an indecent fashion under the influence of the drug after smoking a marijuana cigarette."[62] Originally titled *Wild Weed*, the picture was rejected as immoral, indecent, improper, and tending to corrupt and debase morals. Babb made several cuts and changed the title to *Devil's Weed*. Rejected again, he merely "gave to the film the suggestive and odious title [*She Shoulda Said 'No'!*] and presented it once more to the Board of Censors which detected no change in the odor of the film because of the alteration of name and accordingly refused . . . to give it a license for distribution."[63] The producer argued the film was intended to depict the evils of narcotic use. The board didn't buy it, and the case went to trial as *Hallmark Productions, Inc. v. Carroll.*

From dope bust to starlet, Lila Leeds's short film career
peaked in *She Shoulda Said 'No'!* (1949).

The Supreme Court of Pennsylvania reviewed Babb's marijuana movie with a specific goal in mind: to determine whether the Motion Picture Censorship Act of May 15, 1915, was unconstitutional. The *Hallmark Productions* decision ultimately permitted the distribution of *She Shoulda Said 'No'!*, but Chief Justice Horace Stern signed off with the equivocal comment, "It is not necessary for us to consider . . . [the] constitutionality of our censorship statute" —precisely what the panel had been convened to decide.[64]

She Shoulda Said 'No'! received its license to play in Pennsylvania. The importance of this case is the introduction of a significant character to the story of film and the First Amendment: Judge Michael Angelo Musmanno (1897–1968), a zealous supporter of film censorship. Musmanno's dissenting opinions were fierce and fiery indictments against uncensored cinema. In his *Hallmark Productions* dissent, Musmanno wrote,

> If a picture is clearly indecent, offensive and injurious to the morals and welfare of the public, there can be no doubt that the proper authorities could seek an injunction in a court of equity against the nuisance, thus preventing harm from being done rather than waiting merely to punish after damage has already been accomplished. . . . It is no answer to a demand for motion picture censorship to say that if the people do not like a film they can stay away. How are people to know if a certain production is immoral and indecent? And why should anyone be required to be offended in a theatre with scenes that sting decent eyes and with language that shocks respectable ears? If one is to learn of impurities in water only after he has drunk it, the municipal authorities have done very little to protect the citizens who make up and maintain the municipality. . . . A worthy member of society, who is just as much concerned about mental purity as he is over bodily cleanliness, is grateful that the government which protects him from contact with physical contagion will also save him from association with moral trash and garbage.[65]

Interestingly, for a judge so adamant in his opposition to unregulated motion pictures, Musmanno was also the only judge thus far with a Hollywood credit. Musmanno wrote the story "Black Fury," a tale about a coal miner beaten to death by company goons, which was adapted for Paul Muni's 1935 picture of the same name. Musmanno's credit notwithstanding, the judge was the film industry's greatest threat in Pennsylvania during the late 1950s.

The next motion picture to provoke Musmanno's wrath was *Undercover Girls* (1950). *Undercover Girls* unspooled at Martin Blumenstein's Ideal Drive-In Theatre in Lackawanna County.[66] Musmanno summarized the film with characteristically colorful language: "The pictures depicted a series of dancing acts, which were definitely cheap, lewd, obscene and indecent. By their very nature they would corrupt the morals of the immature and the weak, appealing only to those of depraved taste and the lowest of human instincts. To seek and entice dollars through the promotion of lust and immorality manifests the worst kind of greed of money."[67] Situated in a rural township, the Ideal did not cater to a mainstream movie audience but to the trenchcoat brigade. The theater had previously been cited for showing titles such as *Blondes for Sale* (n.d.), *Bare Facts* (1954), *Naughty Paris Nights* (1951), *The Rage of Burlesque* (1951), *Love Life of a Gorilla: An Expose of Strange Jungle Life* (1937), and *Children of the Sun: The Sensational Story Filmed in a French Nudist Camp* (1933).[68]

Judge Michael Musmanno (1897–1968) speaking at a rally, August 3, 1954. Courtesy of the Special Collections Research Center, Temple University Libraries, Philadelphia, Pennsylvania.

Despite Musmanno's descriptive opinions, the ban was overruled on appeal in *Commonwealth v. Blumenstein*. Citing the *Hallmark Productions* case of the previous year, the *Blumenstein* decision took the next step, invalidating the state's motion picture censorship act. Once again, Musmanno penned an ardent dissent: "In . . . *Hallmark Productions, Inc. v. Carroll* . . . this Court dismantled the siege guns of the Motion Picture Censorship Act of 1915 which for 41 years had stopped those invading forces at Pennsylvania's borders. Now, there is nothing left with which to save clean-minded, clean-thinking men, women and children of this State from the vulgarities, obscenities and indecencies which some moving picture producers are determined to inflict on the public for the sake of a greed-soaked dollar."[69]

July 2, 1959, the same day that judgment on *Blumenstein* came down, Musmanno continued in a similar vein in his dissent in *Kingsley International Pictures Corp. v. Blanc*. The majority had granted a permit for the French film *. . . And God Created Woman*. Perhaps inspired by the upcoming patriotic holiday, Musmanno's dissent would represent the apotheosis of his procensorship polemic.

Et Dieu . . . créa la femme (*. . . And God Created Woman*, 1956) was the directorial debut of writer-director Roger Vadim (1928–2000). Of Russian-French extraction and born into an exiled aristocratic family, Vadim saw his family's fortunes dwindle during World War II. After the war Vadim found work in the French film industry as an assistant to director Marc Allégret. Nine years later Vadim made his directorial debut with *. . . And God Created Woman*. The film made its star, and Vadim's first wife, Brigitte Bardot, an international sex symbol.

Set in Saint-Tropez, Vadim's *. . . And God Created Woman* chronicled the sexual awakening of an eighteen-year-old beauty. While Musmanno refused to watch the film, he was sure the content could not be clean, and this he asserted with style: "I make no comment on the merits or demerits of the film since I have not seen it nor have I read any judicial description of it. I would say, however, that the fact it has met with financial success is no proof to me that it is lily white pure. There can be little doubt that there were many people in the days of the Augean Stables who would gladly have paid an admission price to see them because, although difficult to explain, there do exist people who enjoy that type of scenery and effluvium."[70]

In *Kingsley International Pictures*, the distributor prayed for an injunction to prevent the state from interfering with the exhibition of the picture. The lower court denied Kingsley's petition. That decision was reversed on appeal.

Brigitte Bardot, irresistible in *Et Dieu . . . créa la femme*
(*. . . And God Created Woman*, 1956).

An injunction is considered strong legal medicine; necessary to the equitable relief is a demonstration that the applicant would suffer irreparable harm if not for the remedy. Kingsley Pictures argued that interference with exhibition would have a devastating financial impact with regard to distribution of the film. Musmanno disagreed: "If the verdicts established the film not to be obscene the most the plaintiff would have suffered would have been the loss of several weeks' receipts which unquestionably it would immediately have recouped. If, on the other hand the film would have been proved obscene, then Kingsley would have had no property rights to be protected because, obviously, as I must repeat, no one can have property rights in an illegal thing."[71] The statement that "several weeks' receipts" would have been immediately recouped demonstrates an opinion both naive to the business of filmmaking as well as legally unsound (that a property owner should face a penalty prior to final legal judgment because it may be "easily recovered").

Brigitte Bardot's beachfront bikini frolic struck a raw nerve with the Pennsylvania judge. Musmanno further expressed concern for constituents of the commonwealth with a colorful comparison that equated cinema with venomous vipers: "The Majority completely ignores the rights of the public in this matter. The public has the right to be protected from lewd, lascivious and immoral exhibitions. . . . Suppose Kingsley had owned a couple of poisonous snakes which it wished to exhibit on an admission fee basis. And suppose the municipal authorities concluded that the mere presence of the snakes in public constituted a mortal danger to spectators and bystanders. Would this Court, in such a situation, be concerned only with protecting the property rights of Kingsley and ignore the public peril presented by the snakes?"[72] Snakes represent a demonstrable threat, an *actual* hazard to *all* people. Even the most objectionable movies—far seedier than an art film set on the sun-kissed French Riviera—only present a *possible* hazard to *some* people. Musmanno's hyperbolic argument denied a realistic consideration of the public interest.

Having exhausted an arsenal of legal ammunition and creative solutions, Musamanno resigned himself to defeat on the subject of motion picture censorship in *Kingsley International Pictures*. The film . . . *And God Created Woman* would be permitted for exhibition in Pennsylvania. The judge signed off with a sigh of dismay and a dramatic flourish:

It is with a great deal of melancholy that I survey . . . the efforts . . . to keep immoral and obscene motion pictures out of [Pennsylvania]. . . . Unless the General Assembly comes to the aid of the people with renewed legislation and William Penn comes down from his pedestal atop City Hall to protect the State he founded against the forces of immorality at our borders, far more damaging to the welfare of the people than the Indians he encountered, the fair Commonwealth which he dedicated to religious freedom, civic liberties and moral purity, may well be on the way to a cinematic Gomorrah.[73]

Musmanno's crusade against the degenerate morality of motion pictures had reached its conclusion. Kingsley Pictures, however, soldiered on, engaging First Amendment legal warrior Ephraim London to lead the charge in the company's next challenge.

The subject of the next debate was Marc Allégret's adaptation of *Lady Chatterley's Lover* (1955). Written by D. H. Lawrence and first published in 1928, the novel chronicled the sexual frustration of an upper-class woman and her adulterous relationship with a working-class man. Lawrence's vulgar descriptions had moved U.S. censors to ban the book and postmasters to criminalize shipments of the manuscript. Allégret's motion picture adaptation

Immoral influence? Danielle Darrieux relaxes in the arms of
Erno Crisa in *Lady Chatterley's Lover* (1955).

featured Danielle Darrieux, who had appeared in *La ronde* several years earlier. The New York court of appeals provided a detailed summary of the picture in *In re Kingsley International Pictures Corp. v. Regents* (1958):

> This film deals with the relationships of Lady Chatterley with her hus-
> band, Sir Clifford Chatterley, and her lover, Mellors. Sir Clifford returned
> to his wife from the wars as a cripple doomed to a life in a wheelchair.
> His war injury rendered him impotent to father offspring. . . . This led
> him to propose to his wife . . . that she have sexual relations with another
> man of her own choosing so that she might bear an heir for Sir Clifford.
> . . . It was not long before Lady Chatterley and Mellors indulged in adul-
> tery. Scenes of their passion were portrayed. Their *affaire*, climaxed by
> the pregnancy of Lady Chatterley, unfolded through a series of clandes-
> tine bedroom scenes during which the two were shown lying in bed in a
> state of apparent undress before, and again after, acts of adultery; during
> which Mellors assisted Lady Chatterley in her preparations for the sexual
> act by unbuttoning her blouse and unzipping her dress; during which
> Mellors expressed his passion by caressing her buttocks.[74]

While the film neither depicted nudity nor scenes of sexual intercourse, the New York regents found the picture immoral because it presented adultery as desirable and acceptable. The film was censored based on its theme of immorality. This ban could not abide. The "presentation of adultery or similar immoral acts . . . is not a permissible standard under the United States Constitution for prior restraint."[75] Relying on a case litigated by the same court eight months earlier, *Kingsley International Pictures v. Regents* held, "The opinions in the *Excelsior Pictures* [*Garden of Eden*] case so thoroughly and completely analyze all of the authorities which are pertinent here it seems unnecessary to discuss them further. We have viewed the picture under consideration here and do not think it can be considered obscene as that term is now judicially defined. Hence, the license denial was unconstitutional."[76]

The decision was reversed on appeal. Citing the same *Excelsior Pictures* precedent, New York's court of appeals noted that censorship based on sexual immorality *could* be a valid exercise of the regents' authority. The opinion concluded with a statement similar in tone to Musmanno's dramatic writings: "If our people must be exposed to mass sexual immorality, if the very fabric of our society is to be laid bare to such corrosive influences, it must be at the command of our people themselves. Their command, however, has been to the contrary by virtue of this enactment."[77] Judges Marvin Dye and Stanley Howells Fuld dissented, voicing their disagreement with censorship based solely upon the criterion of immorality.

The battle over *Lady Chatterley's Lover* would be appealed to the Supreme Court in 1959, but the film distributor and its tireless free speech advocate, Ephraim London, had one more stop on the way to Washington: Rhode Island.

The Rhode Island censors used a system similar to Massachusetts's blue laws: "There are two types of licenses which are issued by the Providence Bureau of Licenses for the showing of motion pictures. One is for Sunday exhibitions as provided under . . . the Rhode Island General Laws 1956, and the other is for weekday exhibitions."[78] Under the blue law ordinance, Rhode Island banned *Lady Chatterley's Lover* and . . . *And God Created Woman*. Kingsley Pictures, the domestic distributor of both films, sent London to challenge the licensing bureau. After a procedural win in which London prevailed over the bureau's motion to dismiss, the Rhode Island action was preempted as the Supreme Court granted certiorari. All eyes turned to Washington.

Seven years earlier, in 1952, the Supreme Court handed down *Joseph Burstyn, Inc. v. Wilson* to establish the *Miracle* precedent. The landmark decision was narrowly tailored: content-based film censorship may be permitted, but bans based solely on sacrilege would not be allowed. Now the Court again overturned a New York ruling, this time in *Kingsley International Pictures, Inc. v. Regents*. This decision closed the decade, definitively asserting that censorship based on immorality, like that based on sacrilege, would not be accepted.

The High Court's ruling was another victory for free speech advocates; *Kingsley* was the broadest application yet of film and First Amendment rights. Justice Potter Stewart spoke for the Court when he stated, "What New York has done . . . is to prevent the exhibition of a motion picture because that picture advocates an idea—that adultery under certain circumstances may be proper behavior. Yet the First Amendment's basic guarantee is of freedom to advocate ideas. The State, quite simply, has thus struck at the very heart of constitutionally protected liberty."[79]

While *Kingsley* was unanimous, it was not monolithic, logging four concurring opinions. Justices William O. Douglas and Hugo Black boldly asserted their stance that all censorship violated constitutional protections. Douglas wrote, "I can find in the First Amendment no room for any censor whether he is scanning an editorial, reading a news broadcast, editing a novel or a play, or previewing a movie."[80] Black skipped the screening. The details were inconsequential; as a matter of law, censorship was wrong: "I have not seen the picture. My view is that stated by Mr. Justice Douglas, that prior censorship of moving pictures like prior censorship of newspapers and books violates the First and Fourteenth Amendments."[81]

Less radical than Douglas's and Black's views, Justices John Marshall Harlan II, Felix Frankfurter, and Charles Evans Whittaker struggled to maintain the legitimacy of the state's statute. Their feeling was that censorship could be defended but in this instance was improper. In Harlan's words, "Although I disagree with the Court that the parts of . . . the New York Education Law . . . are unconstitutional on their face, I believe that in their application to this film constitutional bounds were exceeded."[82] Frankfurter believed the statute was valid but had been incorrectly applied to this specific film. He penned a folksy concurrence that professed amazement that such a mild film would rattle the regents: "As one whose taste in art and literature hardly qualifies him for the *avant-garde*, I am more than surprised, after viewing the picture, that the New York authorities should have banned *Lady Chatterley's Lover*. To assume that this motion picture would have offended Victorian moral sensibilities is to rely only on the stuffiest of Victorian conventions."[83] *Kingsley* was the Court's strongest statement on film and the First Amendment, but issues still remained. The plurality was troubling; division among the justices over whether the Court should articulate a bright-line rule or continue to consider censorship on a case-by-case basis would unfold in future actions.

Mere months after *Kingsley*, the thirty-year-old novel was back in the news. Despite its initial publication in 1928, *Lady Chatterley's Lover* had never received broad distribution in the United States because it was held

> to be obscene and non-mailable pursuant to 18 U.S. Code § 1461. The Postmaster General wrote . . . [that the] contemporary community standards are not such that this book should be allowed to be transmitted in the mails. The book is replete with descriptions in minute detail of sexual acts engaged in or discussed by the book's principal characters. These descriptions utilize filthy, offensive and degrading words and terms. Any literary merit the book may have is far outweighed by the pornographic and smutty passages and words, so that the book, taken as a whole, is an obscene and filthy work.[84]

In the early 1950s publisher Barney Rosset (1922–2012) used his Grove Press to introduce avant-garde authors to U.S. audiences and push the limits of censorship. By mid-decade he was championing *Lady Chatterley's Lover*.

Grove Press v. Christenberry challenged New York to determine whether the novel was obscene within the meaning of the law. Overruling the postmaster's ban, the district court's decision was affirmed on appeal. The Second Circuit held that "modern intellectual standards and morals neither require nor permit such a restriction."[85] The classic novel prevailed over the censors. By the end of the decade, as regulators saw their control over content diminish, *Lady Chatterley's Lover* was available as a book and a film.

The issue with the film adaptation of *Lady Chatterley's Lover* was the *idea* of immorality. Lady Chatterley's adulterous affair was not explicitly shown on-screen, but the topic of adultery alone had set off the censors. In the next challenge, the fleshy display of naked bodies would be considered. *Garden of Eden* came before the Chicago regulators, who promptly slapped a ban on the nudist classic.

New York permitted *Garden of Eden* in *Excelsior Pictures* (1956) before *Roth* standardized the measure of obscenity. By 1960 *Roth* was the rule. For the Illinois court, the exercise became whether *Garden of Eden* taken as a whole appealed to the prurient interest of the average person applying contemporary community standards. The verdict was that it did not: "Nudity in itself and without lewdness or dirtiness is not obscenity in law."[86] The film was not obscene under *Roth*. If the film was not obscene, then it fell within the purview of First Amendment. If the film fell within the purview of the First Amendment, then it was protected free speech and was shielded from the content-based regulations of municipal censors. The court concluded that since *Garden of Eden* was neither obscene nor immoral within the meaning of the Chicago ordinance, the denial of a license by city authorities was an infringement of Excelsior's freedom of speech.[87]

The ghost of Maj. Funkhouser would have railed against this decision. Forty years after Funkhouser's retirement, nudist bodies—albeit partially obscured by beach balls, inflatable rafts, and flowerpots—were seen on-screen, licensed, and permitted in neighborhood theaters. As Funkhouser might have feared, once depictions of nudity were freed from the shadow of legal obscenity, the floodgates opened. Now vetted in two important jurisdictions—New York and Chicago—a pent-up wave of nudist camp films burst forth after the *Garden of Eden* decision. Led by Samuel Cummins's *10 Days in a Nudist Camp* (1952) and low-budget auteur Edgar G. Ulmer's *The Naked Venus* (1959), a fleshy parade followed. Doris Wishman directed *Hideout in the Sun* (1960), *Diary of a Nudist* (1961), *Nude on the Moon* (1961), and *Gentlemen Prefer Nature Girls* (1963). Herschell Gordon Lewis and David Friedman produced a series that included *Living Venus* (1961), *Daughters of the Sun* (1962), *Nature's Playmates* (1962), and *Goldilocks and the Three Bares* (1963).

These nudist films—or rather, informational pictures promoting the naturalist lifestyle—could be made on shoestring budgets; production costs amounted to the price of film stock, since sets, lighting, and of course costumes were virtually eliminated. Featuring varying levels of filmmaking skill, other notable titles of the "nudie cutie" genre were *Nudist Paradise* (1959), *Not Tonite, Henry!* (1960), *Nudist Life* (1961), *Nudes of the World* (1962), and *My Bare Lady* (1963). Twenty-three-year-old Francis Ford Coppola turned in *The Bellboy and the Playgirls* (1962) and *Tonight for Sure* (1962). Ulmer, Wishman, and Lewis operated under the radar, churning out dirty little films to a hungry audience; their existence rested on the work of Ephraim London, Kroger Babb, and the exploitation and mainstream filmmakers who had stood up to the censors.[88]

The producers of *Garden of Eden* had overcome censorship laws in New York, Massachusetts, and Illinois. While ordinances remained on the books, *Garden of Eden* was instrumental in liberating nudity from the taint of obscenity and bringing the unclothed body under the protection of the First Amendment.

The "epidermis epidemic" took off with Doris Wishman's *Hideout in the Sun* (1960)
and *Nude on the Moon* (1961), Herschell Gordon Lewis's *Living Venus* (1961),
and Rat Packer Hank Henry in *Not Tonite, Henry!* (1961).

The majordomo of the nudie cuties was Russ Meyer (1922–2004). Meyer served as a combat cameraman during World War II in the 166th Signal Photographic Company and was deployed at the Battle of the Bulge.[89] In civilian life he transitioned to glamour photographer, shooting cheesecake pinups and several early centerfolds for *Playboy*.[90] Meyer moved into motion pictures with a low-budget independent feature that he wrote, directed, shot, and edited entitled *The Immoral Mr. Teas* (1959).

Shot in four days, *Mr. Teas* told the tale of an average American man (played by Bill Teas, who had served with Meyer in the war). Coming down from an anesthetic taken for dental surgery, Mr. Teas discovers that he has developed X-ray vision. His newfound ability allows him to see through women's clothing. *The Immoral Mr. Teas* was one of the first "aboveground" movies in decades to show nudity without the pretext of an anthropologic documentary or informational tract on naturism. The nudity in Meyer's film fit within the parameters of *Roth*, narrowly skirting the prurient interest of an average person or offending community standards.[91] *Mr. Teas* was so silly and nonthreatening that it escaped municipal bans, which turned a blind eye on Meyer's comically obsessive attention to large breasts.

Meyer's films were wildly successful. In 1971 an Ohio court wrote, "*The Immoral Mr. Teas* has now grossed $1,200,000 on a $26,500 investment. That's a 40–1 return . . . second in film history only to *Gone With the Wind*. Meyer's subsequent films have done nearly as well. Both *Lorna* (1963) and *Eve and the Handyman* (1961) have grossed nearly a million, and not one of his 20 films have failed to return four times its original cost."[92] These films, along with *Mudhoney* (1965) and Russ Meyer's masterwork, *Faster, Pussycat! Kill! Kill!* (1965), were more outrageous than Hollywood fare but didn't descend into pornography. Meyer's movies remained within the ambit of First Amendment constitutional protections.

New genres emerged in 1950s as the legal restraints that fettered movies with self-imposed production codes and state-enforced censorship began to crumble. There was a changing of the guard; after years of authority, chief enforcers such as Joseph Breen and Lloyd T. Binford were retiring (in 1954 and 1955, respectively). Breen's successor, Geoffrey Shurlock, was far more liberal. By 1956 Shurlock revised the production code to allow "some treatment (if tasteful) of previously banned topics like drug trafficking, prostitution, abortion, kidnapping, childbirth, and miscegenation. Words like *hell* and *damn* were also permitted if not used excessively."[93]

As the code became more flexible, a new crop of filmmakers became more daring. Working inside Hollywood, Otto Preminger took on sophisticated themes and dared to distribute pictures without the seal of approval. Outside the mainstream, Kroger Babb and Russ Meyer made exploitation flicks that spoke to teen audiences.

Teens and taboos began to dominate American cinema. No longer relegated to supporting roles and sidekick parts, young adults took center stage in *Rebel Without a Cause* (1955), *The Blackboard Jungle* (1955), *King Creole* (1957), and *High School Confidential* (1958). Sexuality came into focus, whether coy, such as Carroll Baker sucking her thumb and wearing a slinky teddy in *Baby Doll* (1956), or bold—Mamie Van Doren shaking her hips and skinny dipping in *Untamed Youth* (1957). Even quintessential everyman James Stewart began uttering previously verboten language, such as "bitch," "panties," "rape," and "slut" in *Anatomy of a Murder* (1959). Mainstream comedies became exuberantly risqué and horror more intense. Considered cinema classics today, both Billy Wilder's *Some Like It Hot* (1959) and Alfred Hitchcock's *Psycho* (1960) were released without PCA approval.

B films had existed at the bottom half of the marquee for decades, but the 1950s saw an explosion of grindhouse pictures. No one embodied the values of independent moviemakers better than Samuel Z. Arkoff, his American International Pictures (AIP), and its top director, Roger Corman. Corman's movies thrived on flaming passion, weird adventure, and cartoony violence, as in *Swamp Women* (1955), *Attack of the Crab Monsters* (1957), and *A Bucket of Blood* (1959). AIP crafted its own code, the ARKOFF formula: Action, Revolution, Killing, Oratory, Fantasy, and Fornication.[94] Arkoff's code provided a contrast to the Don'ts and Be Carefuls of the PCA and reveled in the prohibitions of the prior era.

The 1950s were a dramatic chapter in the story of cinema and censorship. As the decade began, the *Miracle* decision put regulators on the defense. Within ten years filmmakers enjoyed far greater rights. But the bare bodies frolicking in *Garden of Eden* were an innocent prelude to what would soon be seen on-screen.

13

DEVIL IN THE DETAILS

Film and the Fourth and Fifth Amendments

—

Between 1951 and 1961 a shift changed the landscape of film and the First Amendment. Prior to *Joseph Burstyn, Inc. v. Wilson* motion pictures fell outside the First Amendment. The *Miracle* decision broke the censor's stronghold. *Kingsley* (*Lady Chatterley's Lover*) widened that crack and *Excelsior* (*Garden of Eden*) differentiated nudity from the obscene. The scope of state regulatory power narrowed.

The next battleground would be waged on two fronts: obscene content and proper procedure. The Supreme Court broke away from common law customs to create a test to define obscenity in *Roth v. United States*. The second issue dealt with censorship statutes on procedural grounds. Filmmakers claimed that bans by municipal boards without a fair hearing were a violation of due process under the Fifth Amendment; furthermore, confiscation of motion picture prints without a fair hearing was an illegal seizure under the Fourth Amendment.

The courts recognize that "the essence of justice is largely procedural."[1] The Fifth Amendment provides, "No person shall . . . be deprived of life, liberty, or property, without due process of law." This language is mirrored in the Fourteenth Amendment, ensuring that due process applies to the states—which included municipal administrative organizations such as the board of regents or departments of education or censorship.

Procedural due process mandates that when an individual is faced with deprivation of life, liberty, or property by a state entity, that individual shall be entitled to adequate notice, a hearing, and a neutral magistrate having jurisdiction over the matter. When a state actor encroaches on a fundamental individual liberty, such as freedom of expression, the courts will apply the highest level of review. Applying strict scrutiny to the law in question, the courts are charged with determining whether the law is narrowly tailored, using the least restrictive means to further a compelling state interest.

As a threshold matter, due process only applies to state actors. A film studio, the MPAA, the PCA, or the National Board of Review can freely censor. But state regents, municipal regulatory boards, and administrative agencies empowered to restrict motion pictures based on content are state actors, and the due process provisions of the Fifth Amendment are triggered to control any abuse of authority.

Times Film Corporation disputed Chicago's censorship ordinance in 1957 and brought the first significant post-*Miracle* legal challenge based on procedural grounds. Times applied for a permit to exhibit a motion picture entitled *Don Juan* (1955). They tendered the fee but refused to submit the film for examination. The regents rejected the application for a permit.

Don Juan was based on Mozart's opera *Don Giovanni*. The picture was the third in a series based on the works of classical composers and written and directed by Austrian filmmaker Walter Kolm-Veltée (1910–1999). Prior to *Don Juan*, Kolm-Veltée had produced the biopics *Eroica* (1949), based on the life of Beethoven, and *Franz Schubert* (1953). *Don Juan* was the conclusion to this "great composers" trilogy. While the content of *Don Juan* was not controversial in the least, the film claims the dubious honor of being the first to prompt the Supreme Court to favor the censors since *Mutual* over fifty-five years earlier.

Times brought suit in the Seventh Circuit to challenge section 155-41 of the municipal code of Chicago, which required submission of all motion pictures for examination prior to their public exhibition. At trial, content was not at issue; the focus was entirely on procedure. In *Times Film Corp. v. City of Chicago* (1960), the Supreme Court wrote,

There is not a word in the record as to the nature and content of *Don Juan*. We are left entirely in the dark in this regard, as were the city officials and the other reviewing courts. Petitioner claims that the nature of the film is irrelevant, and that even if this film contains the basest type of pornography, or incitement to riot, or forceful overthrow of orderly government, it may nonetheless be shown without prior submission for examination. The challenge here is to the censor's basic authority; it does not go to any statutory standards employed by the censor or procedural requirements as to the submission of the film."[2]

The sole grounds for Don Juan's denial was the distributor's refusal to submit the film for examination.

Times Film Corporation banked on a theory of absolute freedom of speech—a proposal that the Court had rejected on many occasions: "Petitioner would have us hold that the public exhibition of motion pictures must be allowed under any circumstances. The State's sole remedy, it says, is the invocation of criminal process under the Illinois pornography statute . . . and then only after a transgression. But this position, as we have seen, is founded upon the claim of absolute privilege against prior restraint under the First Amendment—a claim without sanction in our cases."[3] The Supreme Court concluded that the submission requirement prior to public exhibition was not an infringement on speech.

By a 5–4 vote the High Court found the city's ordinance remained within constitutional limits. While this was a loss for free speech advocates, the decision fired up passionate dissenting opinions. Chief Justice Earl Warren, joined by Justices Hugo Black, William Douglas, and William Brennan, saw the holding as an administrative backdoor to greater censorship. Warren wrote, "To me, this case clearly presents the question of our approval of unlimited censorship of motion pictures before exhibition through a system of administrative licensing. Moreover, the decision presents a real danger of eventual censorship for every form of communication, be it newspapers, journals, books, magazines, television, radio or public speeches. The Court purports to leave these questions for another day, but I am aware of no constitutional principle which permits us to hold that the communication of ideas through one medium may be censored while other media are immune."[4] Warren's dissent framed the issue differently than the majority. The majority contemplated whether motion pictures were entitled to absolute freedom. By contrast, Warren saw a narrow question: whether a state actor may require submission of a film for a licensing scheme and censorship prior to public exhibition.

Chief Justice Warren's dissenting opinion launched into an in-depth chronicle of film censorship in America. This judicial history lesson pointed out the arbitrary and capricious decisions that local authorities had imposed on motion pictures over the years. His point was that many locally enforced, content-based restrictions clearly violated the spirit of the First Amendment, the letter of the law, and the intentions of the Founding Fathers:

> Chicago licensors have banned newsreel films of Chicago policemen shooting at labor pickets and have ordered the deletion of a scene depicting the birth of a buffalo in Walt Disney's *Vanishing Prairie* . . . . Before World War II, the Chicago censor denied licenses to a number of films portraying and criticizing life in Nazi Germany including the *March of Time's Inside Nazi Germany* . . . . Recently Chicago refused to issue a permit for the exhibition of the motion picture *Anatomy of a Murder* based upon the best-selling novel of the same name, because it found the use of the words "rape" and "contraceptive" to be objectionable. . . . *It Happened in Europe* was severely cut by the Ohio censors who deleted scenes of war orphans resorting to violence. . . . The Memphis censors banned *The Southerner*, which dealt with poverty among tenant farmers because "it reflects on the South." *Brewster's Millions*, an innocuous comedy of fifty years ago, was recently forbidden in Memphis because the radio and film character Rochester, a Negro, was deemed "too familiar." . . . *No Way Out*, the story of a Negro doctor's struggle against race prejudice, was banned by the Chicago censor on the ground that "there's a possibility it could cause trouble." The principal objection to the film was that it showed no reconciliation between blacks and whites. . . . Memphis banned *Curley* because it contained scenes of white and Negro children in school together. . . . Atlanta barred *Lost Boundaries*, the story of a Negro physician and his family who "passed" for white, on the ground that the exhibition of said motion picture "will adversely affect the peace, morals and good order" in the city. . . . *Scarface*, thought by some to be the best of the gangster films, was held up for months; then so badly mutilated that retakes costing a hundred thousand dollars were required to preserve continuity. The New York censor banned *Damaged Lives*, a film dealing with venereal disease, although it treated the difficult theme with dignity and had the sponsorship of the American Social Hygiene Society. The picture of Lenin's tomb bearing the inscription "Religion is the opiate of the people" was excised from *Potempkin*. From *Joan of Arc* the Maryland Board eliminated Joan's exclamation as she stood at the stake: "Oh God, why hast though forsaken me?" and from *Idiot's Delight*, the sentence: "We the workers of the world, will take care of that." *Professor Mamlock* was

produced in Russia and portrayed the persecution of the Jews by Nazis. The Ohio censors condemned it as "harmful" and calculated to "stir up hatred and ill will and gain nothing." . . . *Spanish Earth*, a pro-Loyalist documentary picture, was banned by the board in Pennsylvania. . . . Charlie Chaplin's satire on Hitler, *The Great Dictator*, was banned in Chicago, apparently out of deference to its large German population. . . . Ohio and Kansas banned newsreels considered to be pro labor. . . . The Pennsylvania censor disapproved the duration of a kiss. The New York censors forbade the discussion in films of pregnancy, venereal disease, eugenics, birth control, abortion, illegitimacy, prostitution, miscegenation and divorce. . . . A member of the Chicago censor board explained that she rejected a film because "it was immoral, corrupt, indecent, against my . . . religious principles." . . . A police sergeant attached to the censor board explained, "Coarse language or anything that would be derogatory to the government—propaganda" is ruled out of foreign films.[5]

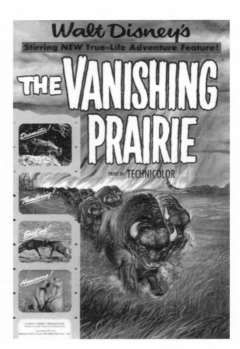

Chief Justice Earl Warren's lesson on film censorship in America included *The Spanish Earth* (1937) and *The Vanishing Prairie* (1954).

Warren's film history of censorship was damning evidence of local authorities' capricious rulings. He called for greater protection against these abuses.

Justice Douglas wrote his own dissenting opinion, more philosophical in nature. His dissent served as a springboard to discuss the history of censorship from Socrates and Hobbes to the contemporaneous Communist regimes and French colonial powers in North Africa. The evil of censorship, according to Douglas, was the ease with which it could erode fundamental liberties: "Yet as long as the First Amendment survives, the censor, no matter how respectable his cause, cannot have the support of government. . . . It is not permissible, as I read the Constitution, for the government to release one movie and refuse to release another because of an official's concept of the prevailing need or the public good."[6]

While Chicago's ordinance survived Times Film Corporation's attack, the Court stipulated that "many complex issues still remain unsettled." Within six months the Seventh Circuit heard a new challenge to the code in *Zenith International Film Corp. v. City of Chicago* (1961). *Zenith International Film* expanded on the issue of procedural due process.

Zenith International held domestic distribution rights for a French film entitled *The Lovers* (1958). This picture would prove to be a gadfly to various censorship boards. After Chicago banned *The Lovers*, Zenith first appealed to Mayor Richard Daley. Unsurprisingly, Daley upheld his censors' ruling. Trying another tactic, Zenith next contested the procedural aspect of the ban. Zenith claimed they had been denied their right under the Fifth Amendment to a fair administrative hearing prior to the state's denial of a license.

At trial, unsavory details of the licensing and permitting process in Chicago came to light. The court noted that neither Mayor Daley nor the police commissioner nor the censoring committee had viewed the film in its entirety.[7] The only group to screen the film was the film review board. Hence, the only group that could legitimately apply the proper criterion under *Roth*—looking at the work as a whole—was the review board, but the ban came from the police commissioner, who merely concluded the film was immoral and obscene. Furthermore, Zenith was not served with a particularized statement of why a permit was denied. The court stated, "The record before us is completely devoid of any rationalization by the City why it should in this particular case interfere with the free expression of ideas."[8] The film was simply rejected out of hand.

The chief judge of the Seventh Circuit, John Simpson Hastings, found this practice unacceptable—the very antithesis of a fair determination under the law. When a license is declined, the censoring authority is obligated to specify reasons. When expression is censored by a municipal agency, the state actor must bear the burden of demonstrating the reasons for the ban. "To summarize," the court held,

> Zenith has been deprived of its right to a full and fair hearing in the comprehensive Chicago licensing procedure. There was no opportunity for any sort of fair hearing before municipal authorities at any level of the proceedings; Zenith had no opportunity to present evidence of contemporary community standards; the responsible city officials failed to view the film as a whole and thus could under no circumstances apply the proper standard of obscenity; there was no de novo hearing before the Mayor; the sole group that saw the film was a Film Review Board whose procedure does not allow for a hearing; there are no standards for selection of such Board and no safeguards to preclude an entirely arbitrary judgment on its part; and finally, there was no indication given to Zenith why the city found the film to be obscene and immoral.[9]

But the court still did not strike the statute down. Instead, it cautioned the city to follow proper procedure and articulate clear reasons when imposing restraints on distribution of a film.

Leaving the Midwest, the next focus in the ongoing censorship battle shifted back to Maryland. In 1957 the court overruled the board of censors on *Naked Amazon* but left the law intact. Maryland's motion pictures regulatory commission soon faced new challenges. In 1965 Russ Meyer's film *Lorna* (1964) was banned; once again the court of appeals overruled the administrative authority in *Dunn v. Board of Censors* (1965). Next, the French motion picture *La jeune folle* shed light on the procedural predicament that ultimately brought down the Maryland statute and influenced procedural aspects of censorship across the nation.

Few siblings have shaken up the American film industry as the frères Allégret. Yves Allégret (1907–1987) directed *La jeune folle*. Within two years of the film's release, Yves's older brother Marc (1900–1973) brought his adaptation of *Lady Chatterley's Lover* to U.S. theaters. While Marc's fame as a filmmaker became more widely known, the movies of both brothers raised significant issues regarding free speech in America that ultimately reached the highest court.

La jeune folle (*Revenge at Daybreak*, 1952) was set in civil-war torn Ireland and centered on a conflicted nun. As the plot unfolds she makes the gut-wrenching discovery that her brother was killed as an informer by the IRA

PART II: FREEDOM OF THE SCREEN

leader she has come to love.[10] Neither immorality nor obscenity was evident—Maryland's censors conceded the picture did not violate statutory standards; rather, the case turned on a purely procedural issue.

Four years earlier, Times Film Corporation had challenged the submission requirement for *Don Juan* in the Seventh Circuit and lost. Times, now the distributor of *Revenge at Daybreak*, took a more focused approach in *Freedman v. Maryland*:

> Unlike the petitioner in *Times Film*, appellant does not argue that [section 2 of the state censorship statute] is unconstitutional simply because it may prevent even the first showing of a film whose exhibition may legitimately be the subject of an obscenity prosecution. He presents a question quite distinct from that passed on in *Times Film*; accepting the rule in *Times Film*, he . . . focuses particularly on the procedure for an initial decision by the censorship board, which, without any judicial participation, effectively bars exhibition of any disapproved film, unless and until the exhibitor undertakes a time-consuming appeal to the Maryland courts and succeeds in having the Board's decision reversed.[11]

In plain English: the *Don Juan* case failed because its attack was too broad, challenging the statute for the mere requirement of submitting a film. *Freedman* raised the issue of timing; the Maryland statute rose to the level of a prior restraint on free speech due to the burden of an ill-defined process of review: "Risk of delay is built into the Maryland procedure, as is borne out by experience; in the only reported case indicating the length of time required to complete an appeal, the initial judicial determination has taken four months and final vindication of the film on appellate review, six months."[12] Several years earlier Judge Musmanno had expressly rejected this very argument in *Kingsley International Pictures* (. . . *And God Created Woman*). Now the Supreme Court opined on the matter and repudiated the Pennsylvania jurist's stance.

The *Freedman* ruling centered on the procedural logistics of due process and film censorship. Under *Freedman*, ordinances that regulated motion picture content were required to meet a three-pronged test. "A system of movie censorship must contain at least three procedural safeguards if it is not to run afoul of the First Amendment: (1) the censor must have the burden of instituting judicial proceedings; (2) any restraint prior to judicial review can be imposed only briefly in order to preserve the status quo; and (3) a prompt judicial determination of obscenity must be assured."[13] Within a few years courts weighed the third prong heavily, scrutinizing state ordinances for a proper timeline. In one such case, the court wrote, "In order for censorship to be valid, the exhibitor must be assured . . . by statute or authoritative judicial construction, that the censor will, *within a specified brief period*, either issue a license or go to court to restrain showing the film."[14]

The *Freedman* ruling struck down a central provision of Maryland's censorship statute. Recognizing the statute's scheme did not satisfy timely due process, the Court held that a regulatory board possessed the power to *approve* a film, but the administrative agency lacked authority to unilaterally impose a ban without a fair hearing.

Adding to the court's unanimous ruling, Justice Douglas penned a concurring opinion. His unwavering viewpoint on free speech clearly addressed the issue of procedural delay: "I do not believe any form of censorship—no matter how speedy or prolonged it may be—is permissible. . . . I would put an end to all forms and types of censorship and give full literal meaning to the command of the First Amendment."[15]

Less than six months after *Freedman v. Maryland*, the Old Line State was considering a new challenge in *Trans-Lux Distributing Co. v. Board of Censors*. Here the court explained, "After the Supreme Court . . . invalidated Maryland's statute requiring licensing by the Maryland State Board of Censors of motion pictures prior to their exhibition, by its decision in *Freedman v. Maryland* . . . the General Assembly of Maryland enacted Chapter 598 of the Acts of 1965 as an emergency measure which became effective upon its signature by Governor [J. Millard] Tawes on April 8, 1965."[16] Despite the High Court's annulment of the state's censorship statute, Maryland went only a month before a replacement passed through the legislature. The fix was simple and practical: "The new Section 19 provides that any film duly submitted to the Board for examination and licensing shall be reviewed and approved within five (5) days."[17] This provision was intended to address timely due process.

The first film to face this revised ordinance was an intense Danish production directed by Johan Jacobsen entitled *En fremmed banker på* (*A Stranger Knocks*, 1959). The picture opened with a biblical quote about the mark of Cain, foreshadowing the story's climatic moment. Along a bleak seacoast a lone figure seeks shelter at an isolated cottage. The cottage's inhabitant, a young woman, invites the stranger in. A voiceover explains that the woman has lived alone in the cottage since the end of the war. She retreated to a solitary existence after her husband was tortured to death by Nazis. After the stranger arrives, a relationship develops between the two loners. Their bond is then consummated:

The man is lying on the sand and the woman walks over to him and lies down beside him. They kiss and he fondles her. The scene clearly implies that they are having sexual intercourse, but there is no showing of nude figures. . . . As she reaches a climax the bite-shaped scar on the man's arm is revealed. She realizes that he is her husband's murderer. . . . She is horrified as he admits that he was a collaborator with the Nazi SS during the war and that they tortured and killed her husband. "We shot him in the neck." . . . As he is about to run out the door, she shoots him in the back. As he dies he says, "One animal kills another."[18]

Critics found the sexual relationship important to the film's revelation. One wrote, "There's nothing lewd about this stark two-character drama of love, hatred and revenge in postwar Denmark."[19]

The picture was banned in Maryland but overturned upon review. The court found the film to be a serious work of art with social importance that did not appeal to the prurient interest: "The film deals with sex . . . [but] does not go beyond the customary limits of candor."[20] The court was silent on issues of procedural process, indicating the revised statute satisfied constitutional requirements.

Whereas Maryland permitted *A Stranger Knocks*, and the picture played without incident in Washington and San Francisco,[21] New York reached a different conclusion on the same film in *In re Trans-Lux Distributing Corp. v. Board of Regents*. Writing for the majority, Judge Adrian P. Burke opined, "It is my view that a filmed presentation of sexual intercourse, whether real or simulated, is just as subject to State prohibition as similar conduct if engaged in on the street. . . . I take it to be conceded that New York may constitutionally prohibit sexual intercourse in public."[22] While *A Stranger Knocks* unspooled in Maryland, distribution was restricted in New York.

Other legislatures had been watching the proceedings with interest and revised their respective codes to comply with the new standard. In New York a new rule was adopted on March 26, 1965, providing for review within five days of a film's submission.[23]

Chicago similarly added time-sensitive procedural safeguards. The new provisions were tested when Chicago moved to ban two exploitation films, *Rent-A-Girl* (1965) and *Body of a Female* (1964).[24] The revised ordinance directed its municipal regulators to inspect a film and either grant or deny an exhibition permit within three days. Any challenge had to be addressed within fifteen days, and another hearing had to be scheduled. After that the board

Vibeke (Birgitte Federspiel) and Han (Preben Lerdorff Rye) in
En fremmed banker på (*A Stranger Knocks*, 1959).

was given five days to consider its findings.[25] Despite the elaborate scheme, the Supreme Court found Chicago's ordinance still flawed in *Teitel Film Corp. v. Cusack* (1968): "The Chicago censorship procedures violate [the *Freedman* rule's] standards in two respects. (1) . . . [T]he procedure must assure that the censor will, within a specified brief period, either issue a license or go to court to restrain showing the film. (2) The absence of any provision . . . [to] assure a prompt final judicial decision."[26]

The Kansas censorship ordinance came under attack on procedural grounds in *Londerholm v. Columbia Pictures Corp.* The state law had been revised after Preminger's 1955 challenge. In 1965 Columbia Pictures informed the Kansas Board of Review that it would no longer submit films for approval. The studio assumed that the *Freedman* decision rendered the Kansas Motion Picture Censorship Act unconstitutional. Columbia distributed *Bunny Lake Is Missing* and *Bedford Incident* to several Kansas theaters without certificates of approval.[27]

Neither of these films contained indecent or controversial content. Directed by the censor-baiting Otto Preminger, *Bunny Lake Is Missing* (1965) told the story of a woman who reported her daughter missing. As the mystery unfolds, no evidence the young girl ever existed comes to light. *The Bedford Incident* (1965) was a Cold War naval thriller featuring Richard Widmark and Sidney Poitier. The Kansas court promptly dismissed any issue regarding either film's content. "The facts are not in dispute, and neither film is challenged as being obscene. The sole question presented is one of law: Is the Kansas Motion Picture Censorship Act constitutional?"[28]

Relying on the Supreme Court's precedent in *Freedman*, Kansas stressed their presumption against any restraint on freedom of expression. Judge Harold R. Fatzer made short work of the state's argument: "It is readily apparent the Kansas procedural scheme does not satisfy the criteria of *Freedman*. First, once the Board disapproves a film, the exhibitor is required to assume the burden of instituting judicial proceedings. . . . Second, once the Board has acted against a film, exhibition is prohibited pending judicial review, however protracted. . . . Third, no assurance is provided for a prompt judicial determination. . . . These are the same procedural defects *Freedman* declared existed in the Maryland statute."[29] The Kansas censorship law, which had been one of the strongest arbiters of movie censorship in the Midwest for nearly five decades, fell in 1966.

Proper procedure had become an Achilles heel for many of the municipal censorship boards. Maryland's ordinance fell in 1965 with *Freedman*. Within months Virginia's law was invalidated in *Victoria Films v. Motion Picture Department of Censorship* when the censors attempted to ban a nudist film entitled *Traveling Light* (1961).[30] The Kansas ordinance was invalidated the following year in *Londerholm v. Columbia Pictures*, and Chicago followed in 1968 with *Teitel Film v. Cusack*.

Complementing the Fifth Amendment's guarantee of due process is the Fourth Amendment's protection against illegal seizures. The Fourth Amendment provides for "the right of the people to be secure in their persons, houses, papers, and effects, against unreasonable searches and seizures." The Constitution mandates that the state obtain a valid warrant based on probable cause that describes the objective of the search and seizure.

Even with the *Freedman* decision instructing courts to keep a watchful eye on proper procedure, issues still arose. As statutes fell based on defective due process issues Damon Huskey (1924–2004), the high sheriff of Rutherford County, North Carolina, took a unilateral approach, boldly ignoring any process at all. On June 19, 1969, Sheriff Huskey raided the Midway Drive-In Theatre and confiscated the exploitation flicks *A Piece of Her Action* (1968) and *The Ramrodder* (1969). Two months later deputies returned to seize the

Richard Burton/Clint Eastwood war thriller *Where Eagles Dare* (1968). Next, Huskey's henchmen impounded an updated version of Voltaire's *Candide* entitled *Candy* (1968), a film memorable only as an all-star fiasco with Marlon Brando, Richard Burton, John Huston, Walter Matthau, and Ringo Starr. The lawman crusaded to clean up theaters in his county, boldly announcing that "he intended to enforce the North Carolina statutes against obscenity; that he considered as obscene and unlawful any motion picture which depicted any nude woman or any act of sexual intercourse; that he considered all adult films to be obscene; that he considered all X and all R films to be obscene; that anyone showing films in those categories would be prosecuted and the film would be confiscated."[31] The sheriff believed Hollywood's decadence was undermining the morals of Rutherford County. Unfortunately, audiences were not interested in the cleaned-up screens: "The district judge found from the evidence that the public, faced with a steady diet of G movies, stayed away in droves, and that the effect of the ban would have been to put the plaintiff out of business."[32]

In *Drive In Theatres, Inc. v. Huskey* (1970), the issue of obscenity was never raised; the Fourth Circuit cited *Freedman v. Maryland* and *Teitel Film v. Cusack* to condemn the sheriff's actions on a procedural level. While *Freedman* was intended to protect exhibitors from arbitrary and capricious state seizures prior to or without an adversarial hearing, in practice that rule quickly eroded.

Huskey's actions were extreme, but such seizures were not isolated instances. In St. Louis plainclothes policemen visited a theater showing Russ Meyer's *Vixen!* (1968). They seized four reels of the film print without warrants. Meyer's company "asserted that they [were] being harassed by a bad faith prosecution . . . and that the seizure of the films and other materials was unlawful for lack of prior notice and of an adversary hearing on the issue of obscenity."[33] In *Eve Productions, Inc. v. Shannon* (1971) the Eighth Circuit disagreed, refusing to see any evidence of bad faith enforcement or harassment.

The Beverly Hills police attempted a less hostile and more effective method. In 1970 the Monica Theater in West Hollywood prepared to run *Motel Confidential* (1969), a film directed by Stephen C. Apostolof (1928–2005). Apostolof was a Bulgarian-born filmmaker whose *Journey to Freedom* (1957) was drawn from his own experiences fleeing Eastern Europe. Once in Hollywood Apostolof met Ed Wood Jr. shortly after the cult filmmaker's *Plan 9 from Outer Space* (1959). Teaming up, Apostolof and Wood made a series of Z-grade grindhouse erotica, including *Orgy of the Dead* (1965), *Drop Out Wife* (1972), and *Fugitive Girls* (1974). *Motel Confidential* was the final installment

The sex Western *The Ramrodder* (1969) included two future
Manson-family members in its cast.

of Apostolof's "Confidential" trilogy that also included *Suburban Confidential* (1966) and *College Girl Confidential* (1968). These exploitation films purported to be exposés on the sex habits of certain demographics—businessmen, housewives, and coeds.

After receiving a complaint about *Motel Confidential*, a police officer visited the theater and watched the film. Once the credits rolled, he returned to his desk and dutifully applied for a warrant, which the magistrate issued—no questions asked and without seeing the picture. The officer returned to seize posters and film print and to arrest the theater's owner.[34] The theater owner argued the warrant was invalid: the magistrate issued the warrant without viewing the film, and no adversarial proceeding was held to consider the picture's alleged obscenity. The court denied the theater's claim, finding the officer's detailed summary of the film sufficient for the magistrate's reliance. Based on the description, "the film and photographs were probably obscene," wrote the court, which found "that the issuance of the warrant . . . did not constitute either a prior restraint on communications, a denial of due process, or a violation of constitutional seizure provisions."[35]

Law enforcement techniques varied. Authorities in North Carolina and St. Louis could not be bothered by procedural formalities before seizing motion pictures. Other authorities at least went through the motions, even if validity of the warrant was dubious.

In *State v. Eros Cinema, Inc.* (1972), Louisiana authorities superficially complied with the procedural formalities. *Eros Cinema* centered on the seizure of several films, including *Four Women in Trouble*, *Studs Galore*, and *Zodiaction*. *Four Women in Trouble* (1970) featured legendary performer John Holmes playing an abortion doctor in one of his first credited performances; no information is available regarding the other films. Rather than discussing any issues of content relating to possible obscenity in the program, the focus of *Eros Cinema* was the validity of the warrant.

Looking to the Supreme Court for guidance, Louisiana cited *Quantity of Books v. Kansas* (1964), in which the High Court held that the seizure of materials prior to an adversarial determination of obscenity was unconstitutional. Without reaching the question of whether the novels at issue were legally obscene, the Court found that the issuance of a warrant prior to an obscenity hearing was unconstitutional.[36]

Differentiating *Eros Cinema* from *Quantity of Books*, the Louisiana court attempted to circumvent procedure by citing legal needs: "We hold that the seizure of a single copy of an allegedly obscene motion picture . . . may be had without a prior adversary hearing. . . . If a person is in fact exhibiting an obscene film, notice to the exhibitor that he is required to appear in court for a hearing to determine whether the film might be seized as evidence affords him an opportunity to destroy the evidence of his crime."[37] Despite *Freedman*, which placed the burden on regulators to mandate prompt judicial determination prior to any declaration of a film's obscenity, Louisiana rationalized the warrantless seizure of offending motion pictures under the pretext of preserving evidence.

In Virginia a similar episode occurred. The Lee Art Theatre was showing *A Smell of Honey, a Swallow of Brine* (1966). This film centered on a sadistic female who seduced men and then accused them of rape, leaving a trail of ex-boyfriends financially ruined, emotionally destroyed, or locked in prison. The siren meets her match when she turns on a misogynistic thug who reacts to her teases with tough love. *A Smell of Honey* was the second of seven films made during the collaboration of producer David F. Friedman and director Byron Mabe. Friedman had started his film career during the sun-kissed nudie cutie craze of the 1950s. Mabe (1932–2001) brought a darker edge to the partnership. He carved out a corner of the sexploitation market with his rough S&M-themed films, including *She Freak* (1967), *The Acid Eaters* (1968), and *The Big Snatch* (1971). In *Lee Art Theatre, Inc. v. Virginia* (1968), the state attempted to enter *Smell of Honey* into evidence, but the exhibitor argued the seizure was improper: "The seizure was under the authority of a warrant issued by a justice of the peace on the basis of an affidavit of a police officer which stated only the titles of the motion pictures and that the officer had determined from personal observation of them and of the billboard in front of the theatre that the films were obscene."[38] The Virginia court of appeals admitted the film into evidence but was overturned by the Supreme Court. Evidence based on a faulty warrant could not be properly admitted.

By 1972 the Supreme Court was closely scrutinizing the procedural deficiencies and aggressive seizures that had arisen since *Freedman*. Two key cases centered on allegedly obscene films on drive-in theater screens: *Rabe v. Washington* (1972) and *Roaden v. Kentucky* (1973). Both were resolved with unanimous decisions favoring the exhibitor.

In *Rabe v. Washington* the manager of the Park Y Drive-In Theatre in Richland, Washington, had exhibited *Carmen, Baby* (1967). The picture was a funky, modernized adaptation of Bizet's opera *Carmen*. While noting several sexually charged scenes, the Court saw that "no instances of sexual consummation [were] explicitly portrayed."[39] *Carmen, Baby* was one of the

Tough love in Byron Mabe's *A Smell of Honey,
a Swallow of Brine* (1966).

---

first pictures written and directed by Radley Metzger (b. 1929) after nearly a decade of importing titillating titles from Europe. Metzger would become one of the pioneering directors of "prestige" adult films. This was clear in his production of *Carmen*. *Carmen* was not a low-budget, sleazy stag film: it was a widescreen, stylishly psychedelic motion picture that appealed to mainstream art house theaters. On two successive evenings a local policeman viewed the film from outside the theater fence. The officer obtained a valid warrant and arrested the theater owner for violating the state's obscenity statute. The

Washington Supreme Court did not evaluate the motion picture's content; rather, it held that the film was obscene in the *context of its exhibition* at a drive-in.[40] The fact that the material was exhibited on an outdoor screen was sufficient to justify a seizure in the opinion of the state. The obscenity statute was interpreted such that an exhibitor could show the film to consenting adults in an indoor theater, but exhibition on an outdoor screen—even with no children present—was prohibited. The U.S. Supreme Court effortlessly overturned this decision: "The statute, so construed, is impermissibly vague as applied to petitioner because of its failure to give [petitioner] fair notice that criminal liability is dependent upon the place where the film is shown."[41]

In its following session the Supreme Court considered the seizure of another film without a valid warrant in *Roaden v. Kentucky*. The sheriff of Pulaski County, Kentucky, had purchased tickets to a local drive-in, where he watched a film entitled *Cindy and Donna* (1970). Once the credits rolled, the lawman concluded the film was obscene and that its exhibition violated the state statute. A substantial part of the film was also observed by a deputy from a vantage point on the road outside the theater.[42] Like the film at issue in *Rabe v. Washington*, *Cindy and Donna* was also a Radley Metzger production. *Cindy and Donna* depicted a grindhouse version of the tried and true saga of a young girl's sexual awakening. Fifteen-year-old Cindy (Debbie Osbourne) is innocent, while her seventeen-year-old half sister Donna (Nancy Ison) is more experienced in the ways of men. Overcoming her inhibitions, Cindy smokes marijuana and engages in a lesbian scene. Finding her newly awakened appetite insatiable, she seduces her sister's boyfriend. Donna discovers the lovers in flagrante delicto and runs hysterically into the street, where she is killed by a passing car. The film ends with Cindy's realization that unrestrained carnal desires result in death and punishment.

After watching *Cindy and Donna*, the sheriff stormed the theater's projection booth to confiscate the picture and arrest the projectionist and theater manager. The question in the case was whether the seizure of allegedly obscene material contemporaneous with an arrest for the public exhibition of such material could be accomplished without a warrant. The Louisiana court had answered this question in the affirmative in *State v. Eros Cinema, Inc.*: the film could be seized based on the need to preserve evidence.

The Supreme Court differed. *Cindy and Donna* was seized "solely on a police officer's conclusions that the film was obscene. . . . Nothing prior to seizure afforded a magistrate an opportunity to focus searchingly on the question of obscenity."[43] The statute fell short of procedural requirements and violated the illegal seizure provisions of the Fourth Amendment. The decision was reversed.

Having brought motion pictures under the guarantees of First Amendment protections, the Supreme Court had turned to illegal seizures and due process under the Fourth and Fifth Amendments. The three-pronged *Freedman* rule focused on proper procedure, tasking the state to provide a prompt hearing and determination prior to seizing a film. While *Freedman* remained the governing authority, several states found ways to undermine and avoid the rule. In North Carolina Sheriff Huskey simply confiscated all but G-rated movies. Kentucky's courts permitted impossibly vague interpretations of obscenity statutes to shutter undesirable films. California, Louisiana, Virginia, and Washington permitted evidence obtained pursuant to varying degrees of defective warrants. Each of these instances violated constitutional protections, skirting procedural issues with creative litigating until the Supreme Court closed the loopholes in *Lee Art Theatre*, *Rabe*, and *Roaden*. Having scrutinized the codes and corrected state courts for procedural shortfalls, the next stage would refocus on substantive issues.

PART III

Dirty Words, Filthy Pictures, and Where to Find Them

14

DIRTY WORDS

Profanity and the Patently Offensive

Chicago passed a municipal film ordinance in 1907; New York followed (1908) and then Portland (1915), Atlanta (1920), and Memphis (1921). Pennsylvania began regulating on the state level in 1911. Censorship boards sprang up in Ohio (1913), Kansas (1913), Maryland (1916), Missouri (1919), New York (1921), Virginia (1922), Florida (1922), and Massachusetts (1922). Three decades later, as these regulations were tested in court, the laws began to fail. Even statutory prohibitions that were not directly challenged became suspect. The Maryland court of appeals remarked that the state code's "definition of 'incite to crime' is highly suspect, if not entirely invalid."[1]

All eyes turned to the next subject of debate: obscenity. But what was obscenity? Justice Potter Stewart memorably commented "I know it when I see it" in his concurring opinion to *Jacobellis v. Ohio*.[2]

On film, obscenity could take two forms: dirty words and filthy pictures.

Dirty words were not new to the cinema. Victor McLaglen had raised the eyebrows of lip-readers with his salty talk in the silent film *What Price Glory?* (1926). It wasn't difficult to see "goddamnits" on the lips of dogfighting pilots during aerial combat scenes in the Academy Award–winning *Wings* (1927). The Hays Commission responded by cracking down on profanity with the production code of 1930, which prohibited "obscenity in a word, gesture, reference, song, joke or by suggestion . . . even when likely to be understood only by part of the audience . . . [and] profanity (this includes the words God, Lord, Jesus Christ—unless used reverently—Hell, S.O.B., damn, Gawd), or every other profane or vulgar expression however used."[3] Even with these mechanisms in place, a swear word could be negotiated, as Clark Gable's famous line in *Gone with the Wind* (1939), "Frankly, my dear, I don't give a damn," could attest. The MPPDA's policy was to maintain plausible deniability, refusing to comment on the record and writing confidentially, "It is important that all Board members avoid any statements seeming to indicate that the Code has been amended for a particular purpose or in connection with any particular picture."[4]

Two decades after *Gone With the Wind*'s noteworthy "damn," Lenny Bruce became the prime mover in obscenity law. After a 1961 show at the Jazz Workshop in San Francisco, Bruce was charged with violating California's obscenity law. The comedian was acquitted. The following year California brought suit after a show at the Troubadour in West Hollywood. In December 1962 Bruce was arrested again after a gig in Chicago. Charged with violating the Illinois obscenity statute, Bruce was convicted in absentia.[5]

As Bruce's legal troubles accumulated, New York's courts began contemplating dirty words in motion pictures. Shirley Clarke's *The Connection* was the test case. Clarke (1919–1997) had begun her career as a dancer but met with greater success as a director of avant-garde short films. In the Greenwich Village scene of the late 1950s she mingled with trendsetters of the independent film movement, including Maya Deren and Jonas Mekas. In the shadow of *Ben-Hur*, Clarke's documentary *Skyscraper* (1959) received an Academy Award nomination. Her next film, which was released in 1962, was *The Connection*, a gritty jazz-inflected docudrama.

The Connection (1961) was set in a dilapidated loft where junkies, musicians, and assorted hipsters anxiously awaited the arrival of their drug dealer—their connection. Clarke's black-and-white DIY style drew from cinema verité and French New Wave techniques. Adding to the realism was the characters' street slang. The jonesing characters "need some shit." In the context of the film "shit" referred to heroin. Lacking requisite hipness, the New York board of regents balked at the excremental explicative. Clarke called on Ephraim London. London argued that the word was not used in an obscene manner but rather as argot intended to enhance verisimilitude. The defense prevailed, and the attorney added another win to his record. Judge Francis Bergan opined, "The sole ground for refusing a license to show the motion picture is premised on obscenity in the use of the word 'shit.' In most instances the word is not used in its usual connotation but as a definitive expression of the language of the narcotic. At most, the use of the word may be classified as vulgar but it is not obscene . . . and the determination of the Board of Regents is annulled."[6]

In addition to defending the right to use indecent language in the film, London took aim at the statute, claiming that New York's censorship law violated the First Amendment. The court dismissed this theory with a single sentence: "The presumption that the section is constitutional prevails."[7]

London continued to protect and expand First Amendment rights. Lenny Bruce engaged London after another arrest following a performance at New York's Café Au Go Go. But as the trial became protracted Bruce's personal issues interfered. He dismissed London to represent himself pro se. The strategy did not work. Bruce was convicted. Appling *Roth*, the court found Bruce's performances "were obscene, indecent, immoral, and impure. The monologues contained little or no literary or artistic merit. They were merely a device to enable Bruce to exploit the use of obscene language."[8]

Despite Bruce's conviction, dirty words were becoming a louder and more frequent occurrence in American culture. Elizabeth Taylor, the icon of Hollywood refinement, spewed coarse language on-screen in *Who's Afraid of Virginia Woolf?* (1966). According to *Life* magazine, *Virginia Woolf* contained "eleven 'goddamns,' seven 'bastards,' five 'sons of bitches,'" and "assorted graphic phrases such as 'screw you,' 'up yours,' and 'hump the hostess.'"[9] The film arrived at an auspicious time for First Amendment advocates; the MPAA was in flux.

After Will Hays retired in 1945, Eric Johnson (1896–1963) filled his post at the newly renamed Motion Picture Association of America. Johnson's administration saw a loosening of the production code. When Johnson died in 1963, the MPAA's top post remained vacant for three years. In 1966 Jack Valenti (1921–2007) was selected to head the organization. Under Valenti the Hays Code was finally put to rest, but the new rating calibration would not be finalized until 1968. It was during this interim that *Virginia Woolf* slipped through the system with a mere "Suggested for Mature Audiences" proviso. *Virginia Woolf* was released at an opportune moment.

Whereas Lenny Bruce's vulgar vocabulary was punished, *Virginia Woolf* opened the door for certain words and phrases that had been previously considered indecent. The next challenge would become a cultural touchstone. *FCC v. Pacifica Foundation* centered on a broadcast of comedian George Carlin's satiric twelve-minute monologue entitled "Filthy Words." This case would define indecency and determine when and where regulation of content would be permitted.

Carlin's monologue was broadcast on a Pacifica-owned radio station in New York around 2:00 p.m. on October 30, 1973. Prior to the broadcast the station warned listeners that the monologue included "sensitive language which might be regarded as offensive to some." The warning was accurate, if understated: Carlin riffed on and exuberantly repeated the words shit, piss, fuck, cunt, cocksucker, motherfucker, and tits. A few weeks later the Federal Communications Commission (FCC) received a complaint. Although the commission had been authorized to regulate the airwaves since 1948, as had its predecessor, the Federal Radio Commission, since 1927, the agencies had not exercised their influence.[10] Carlin's "Filthy Words" woke the sleeping giant.

New York's court upheld the FCC's authority to regulate radio transmissions. The case was appealed and granted certiorari by the Supreme Court to determine whether the FCC's regulation amounted to state-sponsored, content-based censorship that contravened the First Amendment. The Court was faced with defining indecency vis-à-vis obscenity. *FCC v. Pacifica Foundation* construed indecency as a mechanism to protect young audiences. Justice Stevens wrote, "The concept of indecent is intimately connected with the exposure of children to language that describes, in terms patently offensive as measured by contemporary community standards for the broadcast medium, sexual or excretory activities and organs, at times of the day when there is a reasonable risk that children may be in the audience."[11] Indecent language was not obscene but may be subject to certain regulations.

The Supreme Court construed the issue narrowly, determining only whether the First Amendment prevented a state actor (the FCC) from restricting the public broadcast of indecent language. The *Pacifica* decision catalogued several types of speech that fell outside constitutional protections, such as communications calculated to provoke a fight, see *Chaplinsky v. New Hampshire* (1942), or incitement to imminent lawless action, see *Brandenburg v. Ohio* (1969). These could readily be regulated by state actors. The Court recognized limitations on commercial speech as well as defamation, libel, and blackmail. Obscenity was also in the unprotected category. But Carlin's cursing fell into none of these classes.

At first the *Pacifica* decision seemed to favor Carlin's freedom to spew indecent speech. The Court recognized that "the fact that society may find speech offensive is not a sufficient reason for suppressing it. Indeed, if it is the speaker's opinion that gives offense, that consequence is a reason for according it constitutional protection. For it is a central tenet of the First Amendment that the government must remain neutral in the marketplace of ideas."[12] Then the prevailing winds changed direction: "In this case it is undisputed that the content of Pacifica's broadcast was vulgar, offensive, and shocking. . . . [W]e must consider its context in order to determine whether the Commission's action was constitutionally permissible."[13] From here it was downhill for Carlin. Due to the pervasiveness of broadcast media, its accessibility to children, and the logistical impossibility of completely shielding listeners with prior warnings, the FCC's regulations—construed as time, place, and manner restrictions, not as government censorship of content— were permissible. Although Carlin's monologue was protected speech—both parties agreed that it was not obscene—it was nevertheless subject to certain regulation.

Regulations on the time, place, and manner of speech receive intermediate scrutiny. Intermediate scrutiny is a lesser level of review than that imposed upon regulations geared to the *content* of speech. Under intermediate scrutiny the state may impose reasonable restrictions on otherwise protected speech, provided that the restrictions (a) are content neutral, (b) are narrowly tailored to serve a significant government interest, and (c) leave open alternative channels for communication.[14] *Pacifica* came down to 5–4 vote. The narrow holding considered relevant factors such as the audience, medium, time of day, and method of transmission as well as the availability of limited sanctions that could be constitutionally invoked against a broadcast of offensive words.

Nearly simultaneous with *Pacifica*, the MPAA was revamping its rating structure. By 1972 the MPAA abandoned the production code in favor of a tiered rating system that categorized motion pictures based on age-appropriate content.[15] This was not a new idea. In the early 1960s New York assemblyman Luigi Marano (R-Brooklyn) introduced a bill to recalibrate the rating system.[16] Marano was not alone. In 1963 the city's chief censor, Dr. Hugh Flick, also proposed reclassifying movies based on age.[17] Both plans were tabled a full decade before the MPAA ultimately adopted similar measures.

Age-based ratings replaced the outdated production code in 1972, but the new system proved to be a slippery endeavor. Within six years the system was overhauled. Six years after that, in 1984, the system was again fine-tuned and a new rating introduced, PG-13, for increased levels of violence and coarser language that did not reach the R-rating threshold. By 1990 NC-17 was introduced and the single "X" was phased out.

The rating system slid toward more permissive regulations. Just three years after PG-13 was established, harder profanity was permitted; *Adventures in Babysitting* (1987) dropped the F-bomb two times. By 1988 sporadic F-words slipped into several PG-rated films, such as *Big* (1988) and *Beetlejuice* (1988), despite the availability of the PG-13 rating. By 2002 PG-13 movies were permitted the use of one nonsexual "fuck." But even this rule was flexible. *The Hip Hop Project* (2006), a documentary on mentoring troubled teens, used the F-word seventeen times. *Gunner Palace* (2004), a documentary on soldiers in the Gulf War, dropped the F-bomb forty-two times. The MPAA assigned PG-13 ratings to both films but maintained that these were exceptions to the rule regarding profanity in PG-13 motion pictures: "The official edict from the MPAA's Classification and Ratings Administration's guidelines lays out that, [a] motion picture's single use of one of the harsher sexually-derived words, though only as an expletive, initially requires at least a PG-13 rating. More than one such expletive requires an R rating, as must even one of those words used in a sexual context." The agency went on to qualify this rule: "The guidelines also add that if two-thirds of the ratings board members hold the view that multiple F-words are being used in a legitimate context or manner or are inconspicuous, the film is still eligible for its PG-13 rating."[18]

As curse words were slipping into PG-rated films, cable channels gleefully released torrents of profanity on the small screen. While broadcast networks were subject to the FCC, cable TV was beyond the agency's reach. Trey Parker and Matt Stone taunted the commission in a *South Park* episode airing on Comedy Central. "It Hits the Fan," (2001) used the word "shit" and derivatives such as "shitty," uncensored, 162 times—or an average of once every eight seconds for the duration of the twenty-two-minute program. Additionally, the word was seen written another thirty-eight times, bringing the total to two hundred shits. On HBO an episode of *The Wire* entitled "Old Cases" (2002) used the word "fuck" thirty-eight times in a period of three minutes and forty-five seconds. As cable and satellite channels grew more popular, the FCC was powerless to enforce regulations against them.

The commission's oversight was restricted to broadcast television, where an equilibrium was maintained. From 1978–1987 no indecency actions were filed;[19] but moving into the new millennium, the FCC renewed its mission, targeting the broadcast of fleeting expletives. At the 2002 Billboard Music Awards, Cher commented in an acceptance speech, "I've also had my critics for the last forty years saying that I was on my way out every year. Right. So fuck 'em." The remark was broadcast on Fox unedited. At the 2003 Billboard

Music Awards Nicole Richie, promoting her reality show *The Simple Life*, joked, "Why do they even call it *The Simple Life*? Have you ever tried to get cow shit out of a Prada purse? It's not so fucking simple." Again the comment was broadcast on Fox before it could be bleeped. At the 2003 Golden Globe Awards, broadcast on ABC, U2 won best original song, and singer Bono accepted the award, saying, "This is really, really, fucking brilliant." [20]

The FCC initially denied complaints from the Parents Television Council (PTC) that the statements were indecent or obscene. The remarks were deemed not actionable because they "did not describe, in context, sexual or excretory organs or activities and . . . the utterance was fleeting and isolated." [21] Abiding by the *Connection* rule, the commission deemed the majority of the celebrity curses expressive, not descriptive. Furthermore, they were live, improvised, and not repeated. The PTC did not relent. Bowing under pressure, the commission revised its stance in March 2004: "Given the core meaning of the F-Word, any use of [the] word or a variation, in any context, inherently has a sexual connotation." [22] The FCC filed claims against the networks. [23]

Prior to the FCC's revised 2004 policy, fleeting, unrepeated profanities were overlooked. As early as 1978 the FCC held that the single use of an expletive in a program that aired at 5:30 p.m. would not trigger an action under the holding of *Pacifica*. [24] The commission reaffirmed the policy in 2001, holding that material was not indecent if an utterance is a mistake or isolated: when a newscaster mistakenly said, "Oops, fucked that one up," the FCC held that there was no indecency because of the accidental nature of the broadcast. [25] With the 2004 policy change, the commission would ban even a single, fleeting, accidental use of such a word.

Fox challenged the commission's revised policy but was rejected by the Supreme Court. In *FCC v. Fox Television Stations, Inc. ("Fox I")*, Justice Antonin Scalia spoke for the 5–4 majority: "The Commission's change in policy and its order finding the broadcasts actionably indecent were neither arbitrary nor capricious. . . . The agency's reasons for expanding the scope of its enforcement activity were entirely rational . . . the [F-]word's power to insult and offend derives from its sexual meaning. And the Commission's decision to look at the patent offensiveness of even isolated uses of sexual and excretory words fits the context-based approach we sanctioned in *Pacifica*. Even isolated utterances can be made in pandering, vulgar and shocking manners." [26] While Scalia's opinion was consistent with the time, place, and manner restrictions enunciated in *Pacifica*, *Fox I* overrode the guiding rationale that had been effective since the *Connection* case. Previously, when an indecent word or profanity was used in a nonliteral sense (e.g., "fucking brilliant," "I need some shit"), the fleeting, nonrepetitive utterance was not considered actionable indecency. Scalia changed this presumption. He wrote it was "certainly reasonable to determine that it made no sense to distinguish between literal and nonliteral uses of offensive words."[27] The case was remanded to consider constitutional issues surrounding the fleeting and nonrepetitive expletive rule.

The second round (*"Fox II"*) returned to the Supreme Court in 2012. This time the Court parsed the regulation with three issues in mind: first, whether it was sufficiently clear to put broadcasters on notice; second, whether the regulation complied with due process under the Fifth Amendment; third, whether the FCC's de facto censorship complied with the First Amendment. The majority found that Fox did not have sufficient notice of proscribed language despite the commission's contention that the network should have known Cher's and Nicole Richie's comments were actionably indecent even before the 2004 code revision. Without sufficient notice, the FCC's actions violated due process under the Fifth Amendment. On the issue of free speech, the Supreme Court punted: "Because the Court resolves these cases on fair notice grounds under the Due Process Clause, it need not address the First Amendment implications of the Commission's indecency policy."[28]

As dirty words were filtered out of broadcast media, motion pictures moved in the opposite direction. Trending over four decades, profanity intensified in the cinema. In Brian De Palma's *Scarface* (1983), the word "fuck" was uttered 207 times during the film's 170-minute duration, for an average of a curse every forty-nine seconds. *Scarface* was one of the final films to be marked with the prohibitive X rating,[29] but this was negotiated down to an R rating and thus began a slippery slope. Less than a decade later *Goodfellas* (1990), with a running time of 146 minutes, threw down three hundred "fucks"—averaging a curse every twenty-nine seconds. Scorsese bested himself with *The Wolf of Wall Street* (2013), which contained a record 506 "fucks" during its 180-minutes running time—or a fuck every twenty-one seconds.[30]

An interesting example of calibrating the intensity of various vulgar words was seen in *The King's Speech* (2010). The MPAA assigned an R rating to the film based on its frequent use of profanity. In the picture, an unconventional therapist (Geoffrey Rush) guides King George VI (Colin Firth) to overcome his stammer by repeating curse words. The streams of profanity are relevant, possibly fact-based, and arguably essential to the plot and character development. After winning four Academy Awards for the film, the

Weinstein Company prepared a PG-13 version to make the film accessible to a wider audience. Negotiating with the MPAA, changes were made to the pivotal scenes of profuse profanity. Weinstein replaced the rapid-fire F-bombs with forty-two "shits." Working out a metric to calibrate curse words, Weinstein was able to achieve the desired PG-13 rating based on shit's lesser vulgarity value. The question of whether this was a meaningful determination remains debatable.

According to Weinstein, the rationale for this alteration was to reach out to families and children. According to their press release, "The release of *The King's Speech* PG-13 offers families nationwide access to a positive story about stuttering and overcoming obstacles and social stigmas."[31] Six months later Weinstein was less willing to negotiate with the MPAA over excluding profanity in the documentary *Bully* (2011).

Bully focused on the lives and deaths of two children, ages eleven and seventeen years old. Both committed suicide as a result of bullying. Directed by Lee Hirsch, the film unflinchingly documented the vulnerable students and their families. *Bully* drew strong reaction for scenes that vividly captured verbal and physical abuse. The film's target audience was school-age children; however, due to the amount of profanity the MPAA assigned the picture an R rating. Standing their ground, filmmaker and distributor appealed the MPPA's decision, petitioning for a PG-13 rating. Weinstein prevailed, claiming the victory made the film easier for younger audiences to see.[32]

Curse words and profanity can be categorized as indecent expression, which was initially viewed as a subset of obscenity. While expletives were uttered in motion pictures even before the talkies, the issue came to the forefront in the 1960s. *The Connection* made nonliteral use of the expletive "shit" to describe drugs; such evocative use would be permitted. This was an arbitrary legal construction to be sure. Lenny Bruce began pushing the limits of free speech, but it was George Carlin's "Filthy Words" that generated the landmark *Pacifica* decision that outlined time, place, and manner restrictions on speech in broadcast media. Whereas indecent language in broadcast media was contained by the FCC, self-regulation was ineffective against the rising tide of curse words in film. As the debate over indecent language continued, obscenity developed its own methodology of calibration.

15

FILTHY PICTURES

Obscenity from Nudie Cuties to Fetish Films

———

By the late 1950s American audiences watched as a new type of cinema unspooled across theater screens. European imports such as *Lady Chatterley's Lover* and *. . . And God Created Woman* delivered mature subject matter. Exploitation filmmakers Russ Meyer and Kroger Babb churned out nudie cuties. Hollywood insiders such as Otto Preminger broke through cultural taboos with sophisticated dramas.

While Preminger tended to address socially relevant themes, director Billy Wilder incorporated code-breaking content into mainstream comedies. *Some Like It Hot* (1959) poked fun at cross-dressing and bisexuality. Despite its light-hearted treatment the Legion of Decency condemned the film.[1] Wilder's next release was the Academy Award–winning *The Apartment* (1960). This picture focused on the action at Jack Lemmon's flat, which he loaned out for what the film coyly called "assignations." Two years later Wilder revisited the taboo topic of sexual liaisons more directly. In *Irma la Douce* (1962) Shirley MacLaine played a kind-hearted Parisian prostitute. Finally, Wilder took the play on prostitution to its comic extreme in *Kiss Me, Stupid* (1964). Here, a struggling songwriter (Ray Walston) schemed to offer his wife to a popular singer (Dean Martin) in exchange for the singer performing his compositions. *Kiss Me, Stupid* aroused the Legion of Decency to issue another C rating.[2]

While Wilder merely hinted at naughty exploits, blonde bombshell Jayne Mansfield took titillation to the next level. Mansfield's career rested on her noteworthy bosom, on display in films such as *The Girl Can't Help It* (1956) and *Will Success Spoil Rock Hunter?* (1957). The platinum blonde voluptuary left little to the imagination in *Promises! Promises!* (1963), becoming the first mainstream Hollywood starlet to reveal her bare breasts and buttocks on screen since the silent era. The following year the MPAA gave its seal of approval to *The Pawnbroker* (1964), even though the picture included two nude scenes.[3] The administration permitted the exception, they explained, based on the film's socially relevant content. The MPAA, which was once so powerful, had lost its teeth. By the 1960s the MPAA's claim to be Hollywood's moral guardian survived in name only.

During the decades-long battle of attrition, First Amendment advocates wore away many state censorship statutes. Courts tossed out bans based on sacrilege and immorality. Offenses of indecency could be couched in the calculus of time, place, and manner restrictions shielding children from inappropriate content. Although enumerated in many statutes, the offense of inhumanity remained untested in court. The prohibition would unlikely have passed muster. The remaining threat to the moral fabric of filmgoing America was obscenity.

Until 1957 American courts relied on the common law definition of obscenity. But prohibitions on obscenity stretched back to the colonial days. Puritanical New Englanders passed the first antiobscenity ordinance in 1712 when Massachusetts made it illegal to publish "any filthy, obscene, or profane song, pamphlet, libel, or mock sermon in imitation of religious services."[4] Nearly a century later Pennsylvania recorded the first obscenity case in *Commonwealth v. Sharpless* (1815). In *Sharpless*, the defendant was charged with exhibiting a "certain lewd, wicked, scandalous, infamous, and obscene painting representing a man in an obscene, impudent, and indecent posture with a woman."[5] Antiobscenity statutes were enacted throughout the states in the 1840s. Meanwhile in England an influential ruling was passed down: *Regina v. Hicklin* (1868).

Hicklin would be the defining case on obscenity in the United Kingdom and the United States for nearly a century. The facts of the case surrounded a publication alleging depravity in church confessionals. Presiding over the matter was a colorful larger-than-life figure, Lord Chief Justice Sir Alexander Cockburn (1802–1880). Along with power and prestige in the royal courts,

Sir Cockburn was proud of his widely known reputation as a libertine. In his later years he boasted, "Whatever happens, I have had my whack."[6] Cockburn handed down the landmark decision that would become known as the *Hicklin* rule: "I think the test of obscenity is this, whether the tendency of the matter charged as obscenity is to deprave and corrupt those whose minds are open to such immoral influences, and into whose hands a publication of this sort may fall."[7] Two aspects of the *Hicklin* rule are significant. First, *Hicklin* defined obscenity by a publication's *possible* influence on the *most vulnerable* audiences as opposed to an average person or a community standard. Second, the rule applied to *any* portion of a given work, even taken out of context. If an isolated excerpt could influence the target audience, the entire work could be banned for obscenity.

In the United States *Hicklin* became a powerfully persuasive authority. Under this rule modernist literary milestones were turned away from American shores. Among the influential novels banned were D. H. Lawrence's *Lady Chatterley's Lover* (1928), James Joyce's *Ulysses* (1933), and Henry Miller's *Tropic of Cancer* (1934).[8] The *Hicklin* rule remained in place until the Supreme Court formulated its own obscenity standard in *Roth v. United States* (1957).

Samuel Roth (1893–1974) was a purveyor of adult books based in New York City. After sending a publication entitled "American Aphrodite" by mail, he was convicted of distributing obscene materials. The Supreme Court consolidated this case with *Alberts v. California*, in which the defendant violated a similar statute. Writing for the 6–3 majority, Justice William Brennan repudiated *Hicklin* in favor of what would be the new *Roth* standard: "The early leading standard of obscenity [*Regina v. Hicklin*] allowed material to be judged merely by the effect of an isolated excerpt upon particularly susceptible persons. . . . [We hereby adopt and endorse] this test: whether, to the average person, applying contemporary community standards, the dominant theme of the material, taken as a whole, appeals to prurient interest."[9]

While *Roth* became the authorized calibration for obscenity in 1957, it would be seven years before courts applied the test directly to motion pictures in *Jacobellis v. Ohio*. Film producers and distributors who challenged a ban based on obscenity between 1957 and 1964 found themselves in an area of ambiguity post-*Hicklin* and pre-*Jacobellis*.

Capitol Enterprises, Inc. v. City of Chicago was one of the first motion picture cases that cited the *Roth* standard. Here, the Seventh Circuit reviewed Kroger Babb's exploitation film *Mom and Dad* and declared, "*Roth* bristles with explanations and interpretations of [obscenity] and pruriency, but none of them encompasses the film involved here. . . . We think the censor's classification of *Mom and Dad* [as obscene] was unwarranted."[10] Shortly afterward, in *Excelsior Pictures Corp. v. City of Chicago (Garden of Eden)*, the court expanded the dialogue: "This Court further finds that nudity per se is not immoral or obscene within the meaning of the ordinance."[11] In *Excelsior Pictures* the court reasoned that, were this not the case, art museums and galleries would be in continual breach of the law due to graphic depictions of the nude body.

Even before the Supreme Court applied *Roth* to motion pictures, several of the hard-line pro-censorship states had begun to show greater flexibility. In Maryland another nudism-themed film was considered in *Fanfare Films, Inc. v. Motion Picture Censor Board*. Judge Hall Hammond explained,

> *Have Figure—Will Travel* [1963] is in form a travelogue portraying the story of three girls, two of whom are confirmed nudists, who take a vacation cruise through the inland waterways from upper New York to Florida on a cabin cruiser belonging to the father of one of the girls. Scenes are shown during stops at New York City and Charleston and at nudist camps in New Jersey and Florida. The third girl becomes a convert to nudism as the trip—and the film—progresses. The Board passed the scenes in the nudist camps, in which there were both unclothed men and women, but it disapproved the scenes of the girls on the boat.[12]

The chairman of the board of censors appears to have enjoyed the film, going on record to state that the photography was good, the dialogue was unobjectionable, and the picture had artistic value. What he objected to were scenes of nudism *outside* the confines of the camp. Nudity *in* the camp was not obscene, but nudity on the boat was obscene "because in that locale it was not a normal way of life, normal people would not so comport themselves and there was no reason for its portrayal except to arouse sexual desires in the viewers."[13] Maryland's court of appeals rejected this argument and permitted scenes of nautical nudism.

While Maryland permitted nude scenes in *Have Figure* and allowed simulated sex in *A Stranger Knocks*, New York's courts struggled with similar issues. Dealing with themes of isolation, sexual power, and physical vulnerability, the Swedish revenge-drama *A Stranger Knocks* clearly aimed for an art cinema audience. Still, the New York authorities rejected the film. And yet, three months later a very different result was reached when the less high-brow and more salacious French film *Les collégiennes* (*Twilight Girls*, 1957) was challenged.

Contrasting with the artistic intentions of *A Stranger Knocks*, *Les collégiennes* aimed to titillate. In the film, a beautiful teenager (Marie-Hélène Amaud) is sent to boarding school. On her voyage of self-discovery, she indulges in various sexual encounters, including with an older businessman, a handsome young musician, and a female classmate. Radley Metzger's Audubon Films picked up *Les collégiennes* for American distribution. The New York censors objected to the nudity and lesbianism, contending the scenes were "deliberately inserted to appeal to the prurient interest." Audubon countered that the scenes were an "artistic presentment."[14] The appellate court surprisingly ruled in Audubon's favor, holding, "The parts of the motion picture directed by the Board of Regents to be eliminated as obscene, in our opinion do not constitute an appeal to prurient interest in violation of the statute."[15] The wartime psychodrama was banned in New York while the sexy schoolgirl confection played on.

Jacobellis v. Ohio would become the defining case on the issue of obscenity in film. This case centered on Nico Jacobellis (1923–2001), manager of several motion picture theaters in Cleveland Heights, Ohio. Jacobellis had been convicted on two counts of possessing and exhibiting an obscene film in violation of Ohio's code.[16] The film at issue was Louis Malle's *Les amants*.

Les amants (*The Lovers*, 1958) featured Jeanne Moreau in what had become a typical art house drama: a woman who rediscovers true love in an adulterous relationship. While the tale was controversial, it was not new—the screenplay was based on an eighteenth-century bodice ripper penned by Dominique Vivant. Malle's treatment was recognized with a special jury prize at the 1958 Venice Film Festival. The motion picture found a less celebrated reception in the United States. Censorship boards in Maryland, New York, and Virginia, as well as municipal regulators in Boston, Chicago, Memphis, Portland, and Providence, objected to the film's prolonged love scenes. Ohio's board of censors was particularly offended.

The Ohio court described the film in colorful language:

In the motion picture *Les Amants* (or *The Lovers*) the dominant theme of sex is brought into sharp focus early in the film. After the stage has been set and the characters have assumed their relationships to each other,

In Louis Malle's *Les amants* (1958) adultery triggers true love.

Jeanne (Jeanne Moreau) and her lover Raoul (José Luis de Vilallonga)
in *Les amants* (1958).

there is evident a calculated, concentrated, and determined effort to portray the sexual theme basely and wantonly. In a tantalizing and increasing
tempo, the sexual appetite is whetted and lascivious thoughts and lustful
desires are intensely stimulated. The apex is reached when the wife of the
publisher and the itinerant archeologist engage in protracted love play,
give full vent to their emotions and indulge themselves in sexual activity.
Very little, if anything, is left to the imagination. Lurid details are portrayed to the senses of sight and hearing. After the narrative has reached
this carefully built up and long-anticipated climax, it scurries to a hasty
conclusion.[17]

After screening the film, the court applied the test set forth in *Roth*: whether
to the average person applying contemporary community standards, the
dominant theme of the material, taken as a whole, appealed to prurient interest. The Ohio court answered yes.

Their holding was affirmed on appeal. The state's high court had a low
opinion of Malle's film. Judge Gerald E. Radcliffe spoke for the panel:

This court viewed *Les Amants* (*The Lovers*). The film ran for 90 minutes.
To me, it was 87 minutes of boredom induced by the vapid drivel appearing on the screen and three minutes of complete revulsion during the
showing of an act of perverted obscenity. *Les Amants* (*The Lovers*) was not
hard-core pornography, i.e., filth for filth's sake. It was worse. It was filth
for money's sake. The producers, distributors and exhibitors evidenced
so little responsibility in connection therewith that they have no right to
assert constitutional guaranties which require a high degree of responsibility from those who seek their protection.[18]

The court stated a "degree of responsibility" was necessary for those seeking constitutional guarantees of free expression. This was an unprecedented
interpretation of the First Amendment and perhaps the trigger that moved
the Supreme Court to hear the appeal.

Jacobellis v. Ohio was the seventh case in twelve years to come before the
Supreme Court that pitted motion picture producers, distributors, and exhibitors against state and municipal censors. Attorney Ephraim London had
proven his value twice over before the High Court with *Burstyn* and *Kingsley*,
as well as numerous times in various state courts. Once again he was called
on to represent filmmakers in a fight for First Amendment freedoms.

Justice Brennan, who wrote the majority opinion for *Roth*, also spoke for the Court in *Jacobellis*. He began by referencing *Burstyn* and the proposition that motion pictures now fell within the guarantees of free speech. Brennan clarified that under *Roth*, obscenity fell outside constitutional protections. If *The Lovers* was obscene, it could be censored. If the film was not legally obscene, then it was subject to constitutional protections, and content-based regulations would be strictly scrutinized. In its reasoning the Court conceded that the "application of an obscenity law to suppress a motion picture . . . required ascertainment of the 'dim and uncertain line' that often separates obscenity from constitutionally protected expression."[19] After watching the film, the Court found the line less dim and uncertain: the Court held that *Les amants* was not obscene under the *Roth* standards.

The holding for *Jacobellis*, that the film fell within constitutional protections and could not be arbitrarily banned by a state regulator, was less significant than several pronouncements included in the opinion. First, the majority reaffirmed *Roth* as the proper test for obscenity in motion pictures. Second, Brennan reinforced the importance of the adjective "utterly." Courts were instructed that a work must be utterly, completely, entirely without social importance to be banned. Third, *Jacobellis* clarified the expectations of contemporary community standards. Brennan explained that the calibration referred "not to state and local communities, but rather to 'the community' in the sense of society at large . . . the public, or people in general. . . . [T]he concept of obscenity would have a varying meaning from time to time—not from county to county, or town to town."[20]

Justice Potter Stewart's concurring opinion contained one of the most pithy and memorable one-liners in all jurisprudence. Regarding pornography, he wrote, "I know it when I see it."[21] Stewart's one-paragraph statement also contained another prescient comment: "I have reached the conclusion . . . that under the First and Fourteenth Amendments criminal laws in this area are constitutionally limited to hard-core pornography."[22]

Justice Arthur Goldberg also submitted a brief concurring opinion. In his estimation, the board of censors had merely exaggerated the offensive elements in *The Lovers*: "I have viewed the film and I wish merely to add to my Brother Brennan's description that the love scene deemed objectionable is so fragmentary and fleeting that only a censor's alert would make an audience conscious that something questionable is being portrayed."[23]

In his dissent, Justice John Marshall Harlan II asserted that the individual states should be given latitude to calibrate and proscribe obscenity: "The more I see of these obscenity cases the more convinced I become that in permitting the States wide, but not federally unrestricted, scope in this field, while holding the Federal Government with a tight rein, lies the best promise for achieving a sensible accommodation between the public interest sought to be served by obscenity laws and protection of genuine rights of free expression."[24] Harlan's dissent articulated conservative values by championing the state's authority within its sovereign borders, but it also directly contradicted Brennan's conception of national community standards representing society at large.

Following *Jacobellis* in 1964, the Supreme Court cited procedural deficiencies to strike down Maryland's censorship statute in *Freedman*. Maryland fixed the deficiencies and ratified a new motion picture censorship law.[25] Six months later the state censors were back in action, refusing to license Russ Meyer's *Lorna* (1964).

Meyer was already notorious for his nudie cutie films featuring buxom women. *Lorna* starred the curvaceous Lorna Maitland, a former Las Vegas showgirl who would go on to headline two more Meyer films: *Mudhoney* (1965) and a pseudo-documentary on San Francisco strippers entitled *Mondo Topless* (1966). The title character in *Lorna* is sexually unsatisfied by her husband. After skinny-dipping in a river, she is raped by an escaped convict, but the assault serves only to awaken her long-frustrated desires. She continues the aggressive and adulterous relationship with the convict until her husband discovers the lovers and a tragic ending ensues. Meyer's film was a softcore sexploitation version of the popular theme of a woman's sexual awakening already seen in *Lady Chatterley's Lover*, . . . *And God Created Woman*, *Les amants*, and *Les Collégiennes*.

A Stranger Knocks made it through the Maryland censors on the technicality of a procedural defect in the statute. Under the new—and constitutionally valid—law *Lorna* was banned. The board made the same finding, word for word, for *Lorna* as it had for *A Stranger Knocks*. In *Dunn v. Board of Censors* Judge Hall Hammond, who had written the opinions for *Naked Amazon* and *Have Figure—Will Travel*, turned his attention to *Lorna*. Overruling the state's censors, Hall wrote, "We found the picture *Lorna*, despite its implied showings of sexual intercourse . . . and of female nudity to be tiresome, boring, cheap, often vulgar and sometimes revolting, but we do not feel qualified to say . . . that to the average person applying either local or national contemporary community standards the dominant theme of *Lorna* was an appeal to prurient interest, or that the picture exceeded customary limits of candor in its representations of sex or the sexual mores of the community pictured or that it was utterly without redeeming social importance or literary or artistic value."[26] Citing *Roth* and *Jacobellis*, the Maryland court found that despite poor taste, *Lorna* did not rise to the level of legal obscenity.

Under *Roth*, obscenity was legally defined by whether an average person applying contemporary community standards would view the dominant theme of the material taken as a whole as appealing to the prurient interest. A significant element in *Jacobellis* was Brennan's comment that the work must be *utterly* without social importance, which ratcheted up his previous comment in *Roth* that the work must lack social value. This element would be taken up in the Court's next major pronouncement on obscenity, *A Book Named "John Cleland's Memoirs of a Woman of Pleasure" v. Attorney General of Massachusetts* (1966). While *Roth* was more permissive than *Hicklin*, *Memoirs* permitted courts to increase the censor's power for the remainder of the decade.

First published in 1748, *Memoirs of a Woman of Pleasure* has been considered the first prose example of pornography in the English language. The novel followed an orphan girl named Fanny Hill whose great expectations come to an end as she finds work as a prostitute in London. Fanny's progress includes an exceptional variety of fetishes:

> [The] book detail[s] her initiation into various sexual experiences, from a lesbian encounter with a sister prostitute to all sorts and types of sexual debauchery in bawdy houses and as the mistress of a variety of men. . . . These scenes run the gamut of possible sexual experience such as lesbianism, female masturbation, homosexuality between young boys, the destruction of a maidenhead with consequent gory descriptions, the seduction of a young virgin boy, the flagellation of male by female, and vice versa, followed by fervid sexual engagement, and other abhorrent acts, including over two dozen separate bizarre descriptions of different sexual intercourses between male and female characters.[27]

This road of excess ultimately leads Fanny to her true love and a respectable marriage, from where she recounts her sordid past. *Memoirs of a Woman of Pleasure* was written with graphic descriptions rendered in explicit detail despite the antiquated English: "My thighs, now obedient to the intimations of love and nature, gladly disclose, and with a ready submission, resign up the soft gateway to the entrance of pleasure . . . oh! [M]y pen drops from me here in the ecstasy now present to my faithful memory!"[28] The perversity of the prose is epic and audacious, especially considering that Fanny Hill's story came out four decades before the Marquis de Sade picked up his plumed pen. The author, John Cleland, serving time in debtor's prison when the book was published, renounced the erotic novel when charged by the royal censors. The forbidden book went underground. Despite its obscene and illegal content, *Memoirs* was quietly traded in men's clubs and women's parlors in the United States by the early nineteeth century. In 1963 G. P. Putnam's Sons published an unabridged edition that was promptly banned in Massachusetts. Within three years, *Memoirs v. Massachusetts* rose to the Supreme Court. The case was brought in rem, meaning that the proceeding placed the book itself on trial but not its publisher or distributor.[29] The next landmark decision on the issue of obscenity would pit eighteenth-century erotica against William Cowin, the assistant attorney general of the state of Massachusetts.

Justice Brennan stood as the Supreme Court's leading voice on obscenity issues. In his first year on the bench he had penned the majority opinion for *Roth*. Seven years later he wrote *Jacobellis*. In 1966 he spoke for the majority once again in *Memoirs*. *Memoirs* expanded on the point addressed in *Jacobellis* that a work could not be banned unless it was found to be *utterly* without redeeming social value.[30] Under *Memoirs*, even if a work included obscene elements, to be banned by a state actor it must also utterly lack all social, literary, or historical value. As long as a work had significance aside from a prurient purpose, it would not be deemed legally obscene. The Massachusetts court credited a modicum of literary and historical value to the book. This slim assessment was enough: *Memoirs of a Woman of Pleasure* was rescued from the dustbin of obscene publications, and the new standard for legal obscenity was clarified.

While Justice Brennan's hand in the leading obscenity decisions provided continuity, there were shifts on the Court. Justices William Douglas and Hugo Black both dissented in *Roth* but concurred with the majority in *Memoirs*. Douglas favored a strict interpretation of the First Amendment: "Whatever may be the reach of the power to regulate conduct, I stand by my view in *Roth v. United States* . . . that the First Amendment leaves no power in government over expression of ideas."[31]

Justice Tom C. Clark penned the *Miracle* decision and voted with the majority in *Roth* but seems to have been offended by the nature of the material in *Memoirs*. In his dissenting opinion, he stated, "My study of *Memoirs* leads me to think that it has no conceivable social importance. The author's obsession with sex, his minute descriptions of phalli, and his repetitious accounts of bawdy sexual experiences and deviant sexual behavior indicate the book was designed solely to appeal to prurient interests."[32] The examination of obscenity can too easily cross the line from legal analysis to personal reaction. With the continuous and increasing flow of pornographic issues, Clark hit a wall: "I have stomached past [obscenity] cases for almost 10 years without much outcry. Though I am not known to be a purist—or a shrinking violet—this book is too much even for me."[33]

Representing the states-rights perspective, Justice Harlan scored a trifecta, dissenting in *Roth*, *Jacobellis*, and *Memoirs*. In *Memoirs* he elaborated on comments made in *Jacobellis*, identifying the two standards in his analysis of pornography. Federal suppression, he opined, should be limited only to hardcore pornography. States, however, should be allowed a different threshold: "State obscenity laws present problems of quite a different order. The varying conditions across the country, the range of views on the need and reasons for curbing obscenity, and the traditions of local self-government in matters of public welfare all favor a far more flexible attitude in defining the bounds for the States."[34] Harlan disagreed with the broad community standard of *Jacobellis* in favor of empowering local populations to create their own standard. His opinion would find greater weight in future rulings on obscenity.

In the aftermath of *Memoirs* one thing was clear: there was very little agreement among the plurality of opinions. If the Highest Court couldn't reach a clear consensus, how could they provide guidance? Harlan recognized this, opening his dissent with the comment, "The central development that emerges from the aftermath of *Roth v. United States* is that no stable approach to the obscenity problem has yet been devised by this Court."[35] There was little consistency between the states; even within a state there were differing standards for obscenity. This lack of uniformity would be the rule for the remainder of the 1960s as motion pictures became more sexually explicit and dared regulators with ever more provocative content.

American moviegoers discovered a new wave of European films. Lighting up marquees were celebrated names of La Nouvelle Vague, including directors Truffaut, Godard, Chabrol, Rivette, and Rohmer. A growing number of independently produced European pictures represented a wide range of aesthetics from refined to risqué—seen in the films of Malle and Vadim. There was also shoddy and shocking fare by Italian filmmakers such as Paolo Cavara and Gualtiero Jacopetti (including *Mondo cane*, 1962). Exciting new voices emerged from elsewhere in Europe, including Great Britain: Tony Richardson (*The Loneliness of the Long Distance Runner*, 1962) and Lindsay Anderson (*If. . . .*, 1968); Poland: Roman Polanski (*Knife in the Water*, 1962); the USSR: Andrei Tarkovsky (*Andrei Rublev*, 1966) and Sergei Parajanov (*Shadows of Forgotten Ancestors*, 1964); and West Germany: Volker Schlöndorff (*Young Torless*, 1966), Werner Herzog (*Signs of Life*, 1968), and Rainer Werner Fassbinder (*Love Is Colder Than Death*, 1968). But the enfant terrible of the continental cinema of the 1960s was Swedish director Vilgot Sjöman (1924–2006).

Sjöman began his film career apprenticing with Sweden's greatest filmmaker, Ingmar Bergman. He assisted the master on *Winter Light* (1963) and shot a documentary behind the scenes: *Ingmar Bergman Makes a Movie* (1963).[36] Moving out of Bergman's shadow, Sjöman found that his next film had no trouble drawing notice on its own.

Sjöman's *491* (1964) focused on several alienated youths as they descended into depravity. The title derives from Matthew 18:21–22, where Peter asks Jesus how many times a sinner may be forgiven. Peter offers a limit on redemption—perhaps after seven sins? To which Jesus replies, "I say not . . . seven times: but, until seventy times seven." From this numerical dogma derives the equation $7 \times 70 = 490$. The suggestion is that while 490 sins could be forgiven, the 491st would constitute an unforgivable sin.

491 (1964) searches for the unforgivable sin.

The film is presented as a sociological experiment. Six young delinquents are placed in a private home instead of being institutionalized. The purpose is to determine whether the youths may be reformed by living in an atmosphere of kindness and forgiveness.[37] The housemaster, Krister, while kind and supportive, is also conflicted. Each character in *491* is faced with inner challenges while Sjöman poses the question of whether the youths are beyond redemption.

Initially the hoodlums commit acts of masochism: "One boy cuts a piece out of his hand. Another boy holds his hand over the fire in a fireplace until it is charred." Soon their ire is turned on Krister. They steal and pawn his belongings to purchase alcohol and a prostitute. Full of drink and terror the boys engage in an orgy that culminates in acts of sodomy and bestiality upon the prostitute. "The movie stops just short of showing the culmination of sexual relations, but all of the witnesses who testified as to that happening testified that the culmination of the sexual relations was not left as a matter of mere speculation." Meanwhile, another hoodlum finds himself alone with Krister and seduces the preceptor into "homosexual love-making. . . . [Krister] is shown with his head between the thighs of the boy. The movie stops just short of showing the culmination of the homosexual act."[38]

As cartons containing motion picture prints of *491* were passing through customs, officials halted the import. The picture's American distributor, Janus Films, responded to claims by editing out a scene depicting the prostitute fornicating with a dog. Janus then sought a declaratory judgment that *491* was not legally obscene. The abridgement of the canine copulating sequence did not satisfy the district court. Judge Henry Graven was unimpressed, writing, "The film was exhibited to me. It is a thoroughly nasty work. Sordid and brutal from beginning to end, it is highlighted by scenes of homosexuality, rape, prostitution and sodomy. If it has any social significance, as claimant says it has, that significance can only be the author's thesis that human beings are vile. I incline to the view that even this dreary message is merely a sham, and that it is the pornography upon which the maker and the importer rely to sell the picture."[39] Despite Graven's antipathy toward the film, he did not rule on legal obscenity: "Whether or not the film is obscene is a question of fact. Claimant asks me to hold as a matter of law that no reasonable trier of the fact could find this film to be obscene. This contention seems to me to be without merit. I believe that a reasonable trier of the fact could find this film to be obscene. Whether it is so found or not must await decision at the trial."[40] That trial was only three months away.

Janus retained Ephraim London. The timing of the *491* case and its subsequent appeal is critical to the analysis. When Graven's district court ruled on obscenity, the Supreme Court had not yet heard *Memoirs v. Massachusetts*. The appeal to the Second Circuit, on the other hand, occurred subsequent to *Memoirs*.

The Second Circuit presided over by Chief Judge J. Edward Lumbard perceived some value in *491*.

> If *491* is viewed solely as an exhibition on the screen of a series of sexual acts (1) sodomy (buggery); (2) intercourse with a prostitute; (3) a homosexual act; (4) intercourse between the prostitute and a dog; and (5) of self-mutilation then the picture might well be characterized as utterly without redeeming social significance or utterly devoid of social value. But to attribute to this two-hour picture, attempting to deal with social problems which in 1966 are not only on our own doorstep but very much over the threshold, such a purpose is completely to misunderstand and misview the picture and its message.[41]

London couldn't convince the court to appreciate or enjoy the film, but he did persuade the panel to see the picture in a larger tradition of seamy but accomplished artworks. Lumbard continued, "Repulsive, revolting, disgusting—all words used by witnesses in describing *491*—feelings assuredly shared by this court and the district court after having seen the film. . . . [But] Oedipus, Richard III, Macbeth and Hamlet are not exactly pleasant. . . . [T]he drama of life is not always to be paraded on a stage in light musical comedy or in operettas with happy endings."[42] Placing Sjöman's *491* with such company might seem disproportionate, but London had demonstrated the film had value, or, rather more likely, that the film did not *utterly* lack social value or worth. Judge Sterry Robinson Waterman reluctantly admitted to this in his concurring opinion: "I contribute this bit with real regret, the film cannot truthfully be said to be utterly without redeeming social importance. It attacks broadside the Christian ethos, [and] it exemplifies the worthlessness of humans devoid of innate spiritual resources."[43] Under the guidance of Ephraim London, *491* escaped the taint of obscenity.

In his next film Sjöman again pushed the boundaries of acceptability. *Syskonbädd 1782* (*My Sister My Love*, 1966) drew on unlikely source material for a New Wave film: a seventeenth-century play entitled *'Tis Pity She's a Whore*. The drama undoubtedly ruffled the already ruffled collars of its first audiences. *'Tis Pity* is the tragic tale of incestuous siblings whose forbidden passion ends in murder and suicide. Sjöman's adaptation starred Bibi Andersson and Per Oscarsson. *Syskonbädd* appears to have been imported and exhibited without the Sturm und Drang that accompanied *491*. The film even received positive reviews. Judith Crist, writing for *New York* magazine reported, "*My Sister My Love* had no court-inspired publicity but it had beautiful Bibi Andersson, breasts-buttocks-and-bellies."[44] It was Sjöman's next film that placed the Swedish director in history books for better or worse.

Jag är nyfi ken—en film i gult (*I Am Curious [Yellow]*, 1967) was Sjöman's radical avant-garde pseudo-documentary mash-up of sex and politics. The verité-style film centers on a Swedish girl named Lena who navigates through topical issues and questions whether social activism is a passion or a passing fashion. In a series of vignettes, the picture touches on Marxism, feminism, civil protest, sexuality, nuclear paranoia, monogamy, voyeurism, teen angst, eating disorders, sexually transmitted diseases, Eastern religion, and Franco's dictatorship in Spain. Indeed, wrote one court, "It would perhaps not be demonstrably wrong to say that [the film] is concerned with that subject which has become such a commonplace in contemporary fiction and drama, the search for identity."[45] Within this flurry of activism and activity Sjöman captured Lena and her lover Borje in frank and unglamorous full-frontal nudity as well as in simulated (admittedly acrobatic) scenes of sexual intercourse. Writing for *Life* magazine, film critic Richard Schickel observed, "This movie does in fact go further than any previously theatrical film in showing male and female genitals nude and functionally employed (there is also a little—very little—oral sex). Ten—even five—years ago they would have been shocking esthetically and culturally, not to mention morally. But we have, in every area of thought and art, been brought so teasingly close to this level of explicitness that it is a relief to arrive there and finally be done with it."[46] While *I Am Curious (Yellow)* was shocking and scandalous in its day, it now seems a tame, even quaint compendium of 1960s youth trends. There is nudity—approximately "10 minutes out of 120," according to Chief Judge Lumbard[47]—but Lena is hardly presented as a sexual object of desire.

Barney Rosset, editor-in-chief and publisher at Grove Press imported *I Am Curious* to the United States. Rosset built his career by championing avant-garde authors—even going to court to fight for the right to publish certain books. Rosset introduced American readers to notable talents. When no other American publisher would touch them, Rosset printed the work of Samuel Beckett, William S. Burroughs, Jean Genet, Henry Miller, and Pablo

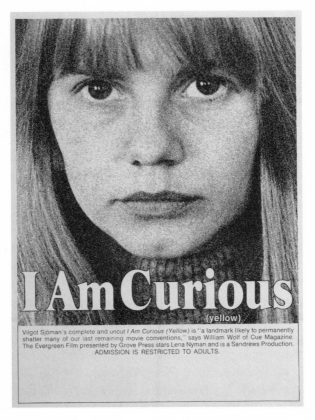

Jag är nyfi ken—en film i gult (*I Am Curious [Yellow]*, 1967).

Lena (Lena Nyman) and her lover Borje (Borje Ahlsted) broke down barriers in *I Am Curious (Yellow)* (1967).

Neruda. Rosset's Grove Press defended several significant twentieth-century novels against charges of obscenity in landmark legal actions, including D. H. Lawrence's *Lady Chatterley's Lover* in *Grove Press, Inc. v. Christenberry* (1960); Henry Miller's *Tropic of Cancer* in *Grove Press, Inc. v. Gerstein* (1964); and William S. Burroughs's *Naked Lunch* in the last major literary censorship case in the United States, *Attorney General v. A Book Named "Naked Lunch"* (1966).[48] Empowered by the press's winning record in court, Grove began importing European art films. Consistent with Rosset's brand, many of these pictures were controversial, including Jean Genet's *Un chant d'amour* (1950), Gabriel Axel's *Det kære legetøj* (*Sex and the Law*, 1968) and Sjöman's *I Am Curious (Yellow)*. In later years Rosset reflected on his impulsive decision to purchase distribution rights to Sjöman's film: "During the Frankfurt book fair, I read an article in the Manchester Guardian about this Swedish film, *I Am Curious (Yellow)*. I thought, that's for us, how do we get it? So Christine, my wife, and I got on a plane from Frankfurt. I bought it right there on the spot for a hundred thousand dollars. That was a lot in those days."[49] Rosset was enthusiastic about the film. Censors were less so.

Contemporary critics were not particularly kind to Sjöman's cocky and self-consciously "revolutionary" motion picture. Judith Crist found it was "a pretentious film that exploits sexual intercourse in all its varieties," and yet she admitted "it has some lovely moments."[50] Vincent Canby commented in the *New York Times*, "[It] is a good, serious movie about a society in transition."[51] To Andrew Sarris, on the other hand, "*I Am Curious (Yellow)* . . . struck me as all wind-up and no delivery."[52] Roger Ebert gave the film a thumbs down: "If your bag is shelling out several bucks to witness phallus (flaccid), then *I Am Curious (Yellow)* is the flick for you. But if you hope for anything else (that the movie might be erotic, for example, or even funny), forget it. It's a dog. A real dog."[53] Richard Schickel voiced the most unkind cut: "To tell you the truth, I don't think that I would be taking up your time—and mine—with a review of *I Am Curious (Yellow)* if the censors had not made such a thing out of it. . . . I should say that the sight of Lena Nyman, [the] leading lady, naked is one of the best earnests [*sic*] of Sjöman's seriousness. A panderer would have picked a prettier creature."[54] One Midwestern reviewer described the leading lady's "ponderous breasts and massive bottom [as] on rather extensive display."[55]

Critics hurled snarky comments, but municipal regulators responded with self-righteous outrage. Like *491*, *I Am Curious* was seized at customs in New York. The film was confiscated under the Tariff Act of 1930 as "immoral articles." Rosset appealed to the Second Circuit, and the film was permitted entry. But similar cases sprang up around the country in Alabama, Arizona, Georgia, Maryland, Massachusetts, New Jersey, and Ohio.[56] The film was seized from five Los Angeles theaters.[57] The Legion of Decency condemned the picture.[58] These objections fixated on Lena's nonchalant nudity and her simulated sex scenes.

Lena's naked body is untoned, unmanicured, and decidedly unglamorous. It can hardly be intended as arousing when she strips down to be scrubbed for scabies treatment. Still, the courts treated her onscreen nudity with talismanic importance. One court observed, "Several scenes depict sexual intercourse under varying circumstances, some of them quite unusual. There are scenes of oral-genital activity."[59] Another boldly provided greater detail: "The sex scenes leave very little to the imagination. One unusual scene is an episode of copulation in the crook of a very large old tree. . . . There is also a scene of intercourse on the balustrade of the Royal Palace in Stockholm, in rhythm to the Swedish National Anthem while a palace guard endeavors to stand at attention watching the antics of the lovers."[60] It was evident to all and conceded by Grove that the picture contained nudity and sexual content. The question was whether the film exceeded the limits established by the courts. Was the film legally obscene?

In 1968 the gauge for calibrating obscenity in the United States was *Memoirs*. *Memoirs* incorporated *Roth*: whether an average person applying contemporary community standards would find that the dominant theme of the material taken as a whole appeals to the prurient interest. To this *Memoirs* added three additional considerations: (a) whether the material was patently offensive; (b) whether the material constituted hardcore pornography; or (c) whether the material was *utterly* without redeeming social value. This often-subjective calculus led to *utter* inconsistency within the courts as to what was or was not legally obscene.

The first decision on *I Am Curious (Yellow)* came down from the Second Circuit. The three-judge panel, including Chief Justice Lumbard, listened to a parade of professional witnesses that included film critics, English professors, a minister, sociology professors, psychiatrists, and a novelist—each testifying as to the social value of the film.[61] The court applied *Roth-Memoirs*. First, the *Roth* elements were considered: "Although sexual conduct is undeniably an important aspect of the picture and may be thought of as constituting one of its principal themes, it cannot be said that the dominant theme of the material taken as a whole appeals to a prurient interest in sex. Whatever the dominant theme may be said to be . . . it is certainly not sex. Moreover, not only is the sexual theme subordinate, but it is handled in such a way as to make it at least extremely doubtful that interest in it should be characterized as prurient."[62] Next, the *Memoirs* elements were incorporated to determine whether the picture was utterly without redeeming social value: "It is . . . clear that *I Am Curious* is not utterly without redeeming social value. Whatever weight we may attach to the opinions of the experts who testified to the picture's social importance, and whether or not we ourselves consider the ideas of the picture particularly interesting or the production artistically successful, it is quite certain that *I Am Curious* does present ideas and does strive to present these ideas artistically. It falls within the ambit of intellectual effort that the first amendment was designed to protect."[63] *I Am Curious (Yellow)* was adjudicated by the Second Circuit as not obscene and therefore within the constitutional guarantees of free expression. But this win was not unanimous. Lumbard dissented: "While the sex is heterosexual . . . these acts bear no conceivable relevance to any social value, except that of box-office appeal. . . . Obviously the only interest aroused for the average person is a prurient interest."[64]

Eleven months after *I Am Curious (Yellow)* was cleared for exhibition in New York, a roller-coaster ride of legal clearance began. The film became engaged in a series of lawsuits. These cases demonstrate the uncertainty that surrounded what constituted obscenity and the inconsistency between various jurisdictions.

Despite the influential Second Circuit's ruling, several states arrived at a contrary conclusion. In Maryland, a state notorious among film distributors for its rigorously enforced regulations, *Wagonheim v. Board of Censors* came down in October 1969: "It is our judgment that [*I Am Curious (Yellow)*] is utterly without redeeming social value. . . . Finding nothing in this film that merits the protection of the First Amendment of the United States Constitution, we are of the opinion that it should be disapproved for licensing."[65] The guiding rationale behind Maryland's decision was the understanding of "contemporary community standards" as a local measure, not a national average. With an epic intonation, Judge Thomas B. Finan declared that "when a State seeks to clean the Augean stables of obscenity or . . . prevent the offending material from accumulating, it should be able to consider and apply the community standard of its own community, and not be required to attempt to evaluate the standards of other communities not under its jurisdiction."[66] Applying a similar reasoning, the Supreme Court of Georgia also found *I Am Curious (Yellow)* to be obscene in *Evans Theater Corp. v. Stanton*. "After viewing the film ourselves, we state without hesitation that the trial judge did not err in finding it obscene, whether viewed by the standards of our local community or national standards."[67] The reasoning of both Maryland and Georgia, which based their ruling at least in part on localized community standards, ran contrary to Justice Brennan's direction to consider community standards on a national level as expounded in *Roth* and *Jacobellis*.

Rather than relying on community standards, Arizona found that *I Am Curious (Yellow)* qualified as hardcore pornography. As defined by the statute, hardcore porn was sexually morbid, grossly perverse, and bizarre, without any artistic or scientific purpose or justification. By deeming a film to be hardcore porn, the court avoided the need to analyze any social value. In *NGC Theatre Corp. v. Mummert*, the Supreme Court of Arizona held, "There is . . . a class that social values cannot redeem. This is the fourth category; this is the so-called 'hard core pornography' which is obscene on its face and is not protected by the First Amendment. . . . We have no difficulty in placing the film *I Am Curious (Yellow)* in the fourth category and holding that the trial court did not commit error in failing to consider the social value doctrine as a separate independent test in determining that the film was not protected by the First Amendment."[68]

Protecting his investment in *I Am Curious*, Rosset took preemptive action in several jurisdictions, but with little success. In Ohio Grove sought a declaratory judgment based on the Second Circuit's finding that the film was not obscene as a matter of law. In *Grove Press, Inc. v. Corrigan* Ohio's court recognized the authority of the Second Circuit but gave greater deference to Lumbard's dissent. The declaratory judgment was declined.[69] In Alabama Grove sought an injunction to prevent a county sheriff from seizing the film or interfering with the exhibition of the picture prior to an adversary hearing on the question of obscenity. This was a reasonable request in light of the *Freedman* and *Trans-Lux* rulings. Alabama declined to enjoin the Department of Law Enforcement, holding in *Grove Press, Inc. v. Bailey*, "We are of the opinion that no special circumstances have been shown in this case which would justify the granting of equitable relief by way of injunction. . . . We find no basis for the charge that the defendants have acted out of a desire to injure the business and reputation of the plaintiff. . . . The court is convinced from the evidence that the alleged threats of arrest and seizure were not made in bad faith and for the purpose of depriving the plaintiff of its First Amendment freedoms."[70]

Southern and rural jurisdictions tended to find *I Am Curious (Yellow)* obscene by their community standards. The film was distributed with less resistance in Northern markets. In New Jersey Judge Nelson Mintz was skeptical of the film's value but was ultimately—and reluctantly—fair. "While I do not unqualifiedly accept everything the experts for the defense had to say on whether or not the film is utterly without redeeming social value, I believe that their collective testimony was clearly more persuasive than that of plaintiffs and amply reflects the required modicum of social value."[71] Despite his pro-speech holding in *Lordi v. UA New Jersey Theatres, Inc.*, Mintz felt obliged to record his personal opinion of the picture for posterity: "To this captive onlooker [the film] was a continuous and unrelieved boredom [and] except for the sexual scenes, it is almost impossible to remember anything about it. . . . [I]ts only interest to the viewer arises from the uncertainty of the method of mutual sexual gratification in which hero and heroine will next indulge."[72] Notwithstanding his personal opinion of the film, this judge recognized that subjective distaste was not a proper basis for a finding of obscenity.

In Massachusetts authorities threatened to seize the motion picture print from a theater. Serafim Karalexis (b. 1944), the manager of Cinema 1 & 2, and its owners, Film Distributors Incorporated, brought suit, praying for an injunction.[73] In *Byrne v. Karalexis* the district court held that Karalexis had a probability of success in having the statute declared unconstitutional and granted a temporary restraining order.[74] The state appealed. In an anticlimactic conclusion the Supreme Court vacated and remanded for reconsideration in light of two recent judgments handed down that same session, *Younger v. Harris* and *Samuels v. Mackell*,[75] which considered the issue of federal abstention from actions pending in state court. Karalexis proceeded with his planned exhibition of *I Am Curious (Yellow)* as the judicial process played out. By the time the state was prepared to review the case on remand, the issue was moot; the film had long since closed.

Perhaps even more anticlimactic was Maryland's appeal, which came down in the same Supreme Court session, only two weeks after *Karalexis*. *I Am Curious (Yellow)* had been deemed obscene by the appeals court in *Wagonheim v. Board of Censors*. Grove Press encouraged an appeal. Unfortunately for Grove, its subsidiary imprint, Evergreen Press, had published Justice Douglas's *Points of Rebellion*.[76] Due to his relationship with the publisher, Douglas recused himself. The result was an equally divided court, which affirmed the lower court's holding by default.[77]

Despite these hurdles, Grove reaped financial success from *I Am Curious (Yellow)* in the short term. The distributor was flush with cash. It purchased a building in Greenwich Village and picked up U.S. distribution rights for more controversial European pictures. As Rosset recalled, *"I Am Curious (Yellow)* was a big success. But it was a disaster for us in many ways. Because we made a lot of money, I went and bought a lot of foreign films—which were no longer commercially viable because all the art theaters had closed down, overnight, in 1970. They had started showing X-rated porno films. There had been a big market for foreign films in this country, and suddenly it was gone. After *I Am Curious (Yellow)* played, that was the end. We killed our own market."[78]

Grove's success with *I Am Curious* stood on the cusp of a precipice. An emerging era of hardcore pornography and explicit fetish films was around the corner.

Simultaneous with the distribution of *I Am Curious (Yellow)*, Grove picked up another European avant-garde film. This title met with very different results. Produced in France over fifteen years before its U.S. release, *Un chant d'amour* (1950) was an experimental film by Jean Genet (1910–1986). Genet was an influential and controversial French intellectual, playwright, author, and activist whose work challenged mainstream values by celebrating criminals and gay culture. Underlying much of Genet's work is the struggle between outcasts and their oppressors. Each of these elements—gay, criminal, the struggle against an oppressor—was incorporated into his poetic film. In *Landau v. Fording*, the California court summarized the film:

> *Un chant d'amour* is an 8mm silent film of about 30 minutes duration. . . . The setting is an unnamed prison cell block in an unnamed place. The principal characters are a guard and four prisoners. At the outset, the guard is walking outside the prison walls. Each prisoner is alone in his cell engaging in various acts of self-love and masturbation. The prisoners are also shown communicating with each other by knocking on the walls and by the passage of a straw through a hole in the thick wall between and the blowing of smoke through a straw. Two of the prisoners are clearly involved in a homosexual relationship. The guard in the course of his duties looks into each of the individual cells through peepholes and observes the prisoners. Their acts of sexual perversion and particularly the conduct of one hairy-chested prisoner arouse the guard's voyeuristic and latent homosexual tendencies. The film reaches a climactic ending in a sadistic beating of the hairy-chested prisoner by the algolagnic guard.[79]

Jean Genet's paean to homoerotic prison love
in *Un chant d'amour* (1950).

———

Saul Landau (1930–2013) sublicensed *Un chant d'amour* from Grove and road showed the picture through Santa Barbara, San Francisco, and Berkeley. As he prepared for a return engagement in Berkeley, Landau was arrested and the film confiscated. In the resulting case, the issue at bar was whether *Un chant d'amour* was obscene within the meaning of the California penal code. *Roth-Memoirs* was applied. The court found

> that to the average person applying contemporary community stan-
> dards, the predominant appeal of the film as a whole was to prurient
> interests, i.e., a shameful and morbid interest in nudity and sex, substan-
> tially beyond customary limits of candor in the description or represen-
> tation of such matters. The court further found that the film explicitly
> and vividly revealed acts of masturbation, oral copulation, the infamous
> crime against nature (sodomy), voyeurism, nudity, sadism, masochism,
> and sex and that it was nothing more than cheap pornography calculated
> to promote homosexuality, perversion, and morbid sex practices, that it
> fell far short of dealing with homosexuality, perversion, masturbation, or
> sex from the scientific, historical or critical point of view, was completely
> lacking in the exposition of any ideas of social importance, and had no
> value as art or otherwise to give it redeeming social importance.[80]

On appeal Judge Wakefield Taylor stated that the problem with *Un chant d'amour* was one of form and not content—an effective and dramatic film about homosexuality and sadism in prisons could be made that avoided obscene matters, but *this* film amounted to "nothing more than hardcore pornography."[81]

After stepping through *Roth-Memoirs* and determining that the picture was utterly without redeeming social importance, the court took a step further. California resurrected the antiquated argument that motion pictures required special care and additional attention due to the medium's capacity for evil. The capacity for evil argument initially appeared as the rationale for regulating motion pictures in *Mutual Film Corp. v. Industrial Commission of Ohio*. Now fifty-one years later the justification was relevant once again. Differentiating censorship of print from film, Judge Taylor commented, "Because of the nature of the medium, we think a motion picture of sexual scenes may transcend the bounds of the constitutional guarantee long before a frank description of the same scenes in the written word."[82]

After California deemed Genet's film legally obscene, the case was appealed to the Supreme Court. In a 5–4 decision and no recorded reasoning whatsoever, the High Court affirmed California's ruling. The complete text of the opinion read, "The petition for a writ of certiorari is granted and the judgment of the Court of Appeal of California, First Appellate District, is affirmed."[83] Dissenting were the Court's reliable proponents of broad First Amendment rights, Justices Black and Douglas, joined by Stewart and Fortas. With little written record, the pendulum had swung back toward stricter enforcement of censorship.

Grove Press brought an artistic and cultured sensibility to U.S. theaters by acting as a counterpoint to mainstream programming. But *Un chant d'amour* was too outré. It was too avant-garde. Its unabashed homoerotic imagery was too challenging outside of art house or college campus audiences. *I Am Curious (Yellow)*, on the other hand, could reach a broader audience with its blend of high and low culture. *I Am Curious* incorporated many elements standard in art films: nonlinear editing, self-reflexive style (i.e., making a film about making a film), casual easiness with nudity both male and female. For B-movie credibility, *I Am Curious* offered teen angst and rebellion. The nonchalance regarding sexual issues seen in the film proved to be a short-lived phenomenon.

I Am Curious (Yellow) did not achieve widespread acceptance in the United States; rather, it was found to be obscene and in contravention of community standards in half the jurisdictions where it played. Still, the film had made inroads where it was cleared of obscenity charges. This demonstrated to film-makers and exhibitors not only that sex sells, but more importantly from a commercial standpoint, that sex sells to a mainstream audience. In 1967 Sjö-man's daring film ushered in a new era of sensual sophistication and sexual explicitness. By 1968 that era had turned sour with violent and misogynist depictions of fetishism and sexual deviance.

Odd Tastes (1968) masked degrading content in the trappings of a New Wave film. The film was directed by Donald A. Davis (1932–1982), who had begun his career in Ed Wood's troupe as a production assistant and had per-formed a cameo in *Plan 9 from Outer Space*.[84] *Odd Tastes* purported to be the "sexual biography" of Charles Odham; however, the filmmaker's main inter-est was sexual degeneracy on-screen. The film opens with fantasies of incest, "with Ruthie opening her breasts to the infant Charles, and then, if imagina-tion hasn't caught on already, going through a routine with her mouth and lips that is highly suggestive of fellatio to the infant."[85] The scenes become increasingly exotic and bizarre: Charles's "love affair in Malaya is succeeded by a homosexual affair in a Swiss school, culminating in the accidental death of his masochistic French teacher. Later, discovering his childhood sweet-heart in a Hong Kong brothel, Odman [sic] is driven by guilt into an opium and sex orgy with the madam. His lust for bizarre pleasures takes him to Africa's jungles and Timbuktu's slave markets. Becoming increasingly per-verted, he ultimately falls victim to his own devices: he is destroyed in a sadis-tic experiment with a . . . vibrator."[86] Running through the *Roth-Memoirs* test, Maryland found the film to be obscene "hard core pornography and as such, could be proscribed by the Maryland statute."[87] *Odd Tastes* was deemed legally obscene, despite the fact there were no explicit sex scenes, no images of pen-etration, and none of the trappings that define hardcore today. Expert testi-mony that the film's perverted themes did not address "the normal sex drive of heterosexual relations" was sufficient to categorize the film as hardcore.[88]

Maryland also banned *Love Camp 7* (1969). *Love Camp 7* was the first film in the esoteric subgenre of "Nazi sleaze sexploitation."[89] The man behind *Love Camp 7*, Lee Frost (1935–2007), was no stranger to the bizarre and titilating, having previously directed *Mondo Bizarro* (1966). Frost's partner, Bob Cresse (1936–1998), wrote and produced *Love Camp 7* as well as played the central role of the sadistic Nazi commandant. The love camp was a stalag where European beauties were enslaved, stripped and whipped, and degraded and raped "for the pleasure of the 3rd Reich," according to the film's promotional materials. Presiding over the Maryland court of appeals, Judge Marvin H. Smith observed, "There was a depiction of violence through the cruelty of the officers and the guards and a violence which was directed to sexual matters. That is to say, the humiliation so frequently was a humiliation of a woman's body. Now I don't mean in terms of sexual intercourse necessarily. . . . It seemed to me a combination here of the violence and of the sexual. It was the violence which offended me more than the seeing on the screen of the nude bodies or even of, let's say, the final rather orgiastic party of the officer."[90] Applying *Roth-Memoirs* in *Hewitt v. Board of Censors*, the court found *Love Camp 7* obscene. Judge Smith's opinion quoted an expert's testimony: "I had the feeling that I was attending a sideshow where the barker was saying, in effect, 'I have here some terrible things to show you; they are horrible, beyond comprehension; they will revolt you; they are terribly upsetting, but I want you to see them' . . . recognizing that by his speech he was not turning the people away but inducing them to come in and share in prurient satisfaction."[91]

While Maryland historically favored film regulators, the Second Circuit could be more permissive. The court found *I Am Curious (Yellow)* not obscene in 1968. The following year, however, the court became less lenient as sex and violence drastically increased. An example is seen in *United States v. A Motion Picture Film—Pattern of Evil* (1969). "Claimant has argued that because the sexual activity portrayed in *Pattern of Evil* is (in claimant's view) portrayed less explicitly than similar activity in *I Am Curious*, the film cannot lawfully be found to go beyond customary limits of candor. Claimant's argument is unpersuasive for two reasons. The Court in *I Am Curious* ruled that the film possessed a modicum of social value and for that reason could not be declared obscene; this ruling made it unnecessary to reach the question of whether it was patently offensive."[92] *Pattern of Evil* (*Fornicon*, 1971) was an S&M-themed fantasy from the mind of children's book author Tomi Ungerer (b. 1931). In his book *Fornicon* Ungerer designed fanciful sex devices rendered in erotic line drawings. In the hands of director G. Harrison Marks (1926–1997) these drawings became full-fledged fetish gear. Marks began directing "beaver films" such as *As Nature Intended* (1961) during the naturalist craze of the early 1960s. After a flirtation with nudie cutie comedies such as *The Nine Ages of Nakedness* (1969), the director was drawn to darker proclivities in *Stinging Tails* (1992), *Whip Tricks* (1993), *The Spanking Game* (1993), and *Flogging the French Maid* (1994).

The Nazi-fetish sexploitation film *Love Camp 7* (1969) was cowritten by Bob Cresse, who also played the camp commandant, seen here hog-tying a victim. Maria Lease (the bound woman) and Kathy Williams (held at gunpoint) played U.S. WACs who volunteer for an undercover mission in the German joy divisions.

BY 1970
ANYTHING
GOES... —N.Y. POST

1968 From Sweden: "I am Curious Yellow"
1969 From Denmark: "Without a Stitch"
1970 From England where the new
Permissiveness started...

REPRINTED FROM THE
"HOLLYWOOD REPORTER"
February 9, 1970

'FORNICON'
Pattern of Evil
Ruled Not Obscene
In N.Y. Trial

New York. — The importer of the British-made "Pattern of Evil" was victorious in Federal Court Friday, when a jury held that the film was not obscene and could not be confiscated by Customs. The film, described as a spoof on sex exploitation pictures, was imported by Chelsea Productions and was seized by Customs last year for obscenity.

A jury of seven women and five men deliberated four and one-half hours before returning the verdict. Federal Judge John M. Cannella, who presided at the trial of Chelsea's suit contesting the forfeiture, charged the jury that, if the picture unanimously passed one of three tests, as outlined by the U.S. Supreme Court, it should be cleared.

Herald Price Fahringer, constitutional lawyer from Buffalo, successfully argued the case for Chelsea in a trial that lasted five days. Judge Cannella granted Fahringer's request to have the jury also see two Scandinavian sex pictures, "Without A Stitch" and "I Am Curious (Yellow)," to demonstrate what contemporary community standards might be.

JERALD INTRATOR presents a Film by GEORGE HARRISON MARKS

FORNICON

PATTERN OF EVIL

IVONE PAUL · CINDY NEAL · RENA BRONSON · PAUL HOLCOMBE · IN **COLOR** · A MARVIN FILMS RELEASE

Tomi Ungerer's erotic line drawings became operational sex
machines in *Fornicon* (*Pattern of Evil*, 1971).

Not finding the requisite modicum of social value in *Fornicon*, the New York court deemed the picture to be obscene. Judge Milton Pollack wrote, "After viewing the film, the Court finds that it is highly doubtful that a genuine plot or theme exists and it is fairly arguable that, devoid of plot, the purpose, intent, and effect of the film are obscenity for the sake of lewdness and lasciviousness."[93]

Contrasting with the sexual biography of *Odd Tastes* was the story of an insatiable girl in *Nympho: A Woman's Urge* (1965). Although the film was released only four years prior to *Odd Tastes*, *Love Camp 7*, and *Pattern of Evil*, *Nympho* seems dated, a relic of a different and far more innocent era. *Nympho* was shot in black and white and cut to a jazzy score, teeming with suggestive images of licking lips, fondling, groping, and heavy petting. While *Odd Tastes* served up shameless sexual debauchery, *Nympho* coyly posed a question to eager audiences: "How many nights of love does it take to satisfy [a girl's] tortured cravings?"

Set as a case study told to a psychologist, *Nympho* explored the sexual biography of Laura (Maude Ferguson), who grew up on a farm where she was frequently disciplined by her father with sexualized spankings. Moving to New York, Laura dives wholeheartedly into a hedonistic scene. She experiences an array of sexual situations, including a lesbian relationship, orgies, and relations with throngs of young men. *Nympho* was banned in Michigan, where in *People v. Bloss* the court of appeals found that "the film deals with the problems of a seemingly over-sexed young woman. Although it has a pseudo-psychoanalytical approach, its primary appeal is to a prurient interest in sex. This prurient appeal is the dominant theme of the movie as a whole. The film is utterly without redeeming social value. Further, we find that it goes beyond the contemporary national community standards in its descriptions and representations of sexual matters."[94] While both *Odd Tastes* and *Nympho* purported to be sexual biographies, they are stylistically very different; the comparison of these two films demonstrates how screen morals devolved over a four-year span. One thing the perverted male of *Odd Tastes* and the voracious girl of *Nympho* shared was that both were found obscene and banned in 1969–1970.

While hardcore pornography was banned under *Roth-Memoirs*, a shadow genre of softcore arose that was able to skirt the edge of sexual explicitness without falling into proscribed conduct. The master of this softcore style of sensual film was Radley Metzger.

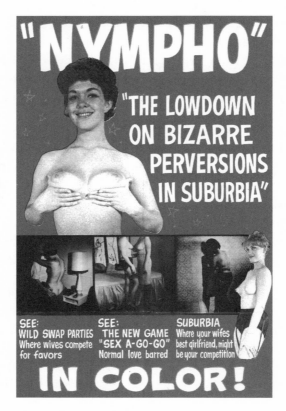

A jazzy nudie pictured in *Nympho: A Woman's Urge* (1965),
directed by Amin Q. Chaudgri.

Metzger emerged in the late 1950s, importing European titles for the
U.S. market through Audubon Films. In 1957 he presented *Les collégiennes*,
a French film set in an all-girls dormitory that offered lesbian scenes to art
house audiences. Amazingly, Metzger was able to prevail against New York's
censors. Encouraged by this win, Metzger searched the globe for erotic, exotic
cinema that tested legal boundaries but stayed on the right side of censorship guidelines. He imported the sensual Spanish-language *Soft Skin on Black
Silk* (1959) and the Japanese *The Warped Ones* (1960). Riding on the wave of
interest in Scandinavian sex films that followed *I Am Curious (Yellow)*, Metzger
found Mac Ahlberg's *I, a Woman* (1966) to be a solid investment. *I, a Woman*
featured svelte Swedish ingénue Essy Persson in the now-typical story of a
young girl's sexual awakening. The film was directed with Nouvelle Vague

panache, including quick nonlinear cuts and scenes photographed through beveled glass to present teasing images of the young girl's body. Along with artistic cinematography, the picture contained requisite sexual deviance. In addition to a spanking scene, incest is alluded to in a sequence where the girl appears to be pleasuring herself while listening to her father play his virtuoso violin. While handled with sophistication and appreciated in New York, Chicago's censors cried foul.[95] The film was seized without a warrant or adjudication on the subject of obscenity, as mandated in *Freedman*. Although the Seventh Circuit made no ruling on the substantive issue of obscenity, the court ordered the film returned, and it played without further incident.[96]

As Metzger moved from distribution to production, he looked to Persson as his star. His picture *Therese and Isabelle* (1968) was another rendition of the time-tested tale of sexual awakening, this time at a Swiss all-girls' boarding school. Theresa (Persson) is abandoned by her parents and sent to a dormitory, where she finds herself captivated by the older, more worldly Isabelle (Anna Gael). Their friendship culminates in Sapphic caresses shot in a slow and sensual style. Pennsylvania regents objected, but in *Duggan v. Guild Theatre, Inc.*, the court found that *Therese and Isabelle* passed crucial elements of the *Roth-Memoirs* test. "The dominant theme of the work is that of loneliness, the loneliness of a young girl, not wanted by her mother, who turns to another young girl for affection. As a result of this lack of maternal affection, the movie tells us, the girl becomes entwined in a homosexual relationship. Does this then make the dominant theme of the work as a whole a sexual one? Taking the evidence in a light favorable to the movie's dissemination, as we must, we cannot say that it does."[97] The exhibitor called a former New York State film censor as an expert witness. He "testified that the movie points up the destructive effect that the lack of parental love has on a young person. It shows how young people caught in this kind of situation can very easily, in their search for affection or love, become involved in this kind of exploratory or transitory homosexual relationship."[98] The court found *Therese and Isabelle* not obscene. Metzger was empowered by his legal victories. His films became harder and more sexually explicit, finally going the full distance in *Camille 2000* (1969) and *The Lickerish Quartet* (1970). These titles catered to an art house audience that desired a more risqué edge.

Upon its release in 1958 Louis Malle's *Les amants* was seen as scandalous and obscene. Once *The Lovers* was cleared of obscenity in *Jacobellis*, even mainstream Hollywood began to embrace the new morality. That Hollywood had entered a new era was evident when Liz Taylor squeezed into a white teddy

PART III: DIRTY WORDS, FILTHY PICTURES

to play a promiscuous "party girl" in *Butterfield 8* (1960). The decade ended with Natalie Wood and Dyan Cannon contemplating a swinging four-way sex swap in *Bob & Carol & Ted & Alice* (1969). *Newsweek* ran a cover story in November 1967 featuring Jane Fonda's nude torso (pictured from behind), promoting an article entitled "Anything Goes: The Permissive Society."[99]

The 1960s saw the final nail in the coffin of the production code. By the end of the decade the *New York Times* reported that of 360 films distributed in the United States in 1968, only 160 were submitted for code approval.[100] In a notable act of defiance, the Academy celebrated the X-rated *Midnight Cowboy* (1969) as best picture.

As immense as the cultural shift was from 1960 to 1969, another epochal change would occur during the brief period from 1970 to 1973. An influx of European hardcore along with the unexpected success of a low-budget American pornographic feature film and yet another revised test for obscenity would redefine the limits of censorship and acceptability for motion pictures in the United States.

16

THE PORNO CHIC

From Danish Loops to Deep Throat

—

Alberto Ferro (b. 1936) was the scion of an aristocratic Italian family, the multilingual son of a dignitary and diplomat. After graduating from a Swiss college, Ferro studied law at the University of Milan. By 1960 he opened a legal practice; his specialty was representing clients charged with distribution or possession of obscene materials. One client introduced Ferro to his source of illicit books and photographs, a tobacco shop in Belgium. The following year Ferro began importing materials to Italy using his family's diplomatic immunity to pass through customs. He found the pornography disappointing. The images were disgusting and degrading, and even worse they were poorly produced, shoddy, and blurry. The lawyer discovered a new calling.

Ferro established a base of operations in Denmark, where regulations on pornography were less strict. By the mid-1960s the Danish criminal code's sections on pornography were amended to permit the possession, distribution, and sale of obscene materials to adults over fifteen years old.[1] Assuming a Scandinavian identity, Ferro transformed himself into Lasse Braun and began producing sex loops on 16mm film. Braun shot a color adaptation of *Madama Butterfly* entitled *Golden Butterfly* (1966) in Monte Carlo, followed by *Chains of Eroticism* (1968) in Sweden and *Tropical Paradise* (1969) in Trinidad. Distancing his work from the sleazy sex loops of the clandestine stag film trade, Braun produced films that were professionally photographed in exotic locations and featured beautiful girls. Instantly successful, the filmmaker rein-vested his profits to produce elaborate costume dramas: *Orgie in Rome* (1970), *Delphia the Greek* (1970), and a Viking trilogy that consisted of *In the Name of Odin* (1971), *The Way to Valhalla* (1971), and *Victory for the Queen* (1971). Braun packaged his titles with glossy cover art, a far cry from the brown paper wrap-ping of earlier pornography. Expanding beyond the backrooms of tobacco shops, Braun established a mail order operation, AB Beta Film. His business boomed, servicing fifty thousand clients by 1969.[2] The commercial pornogra-phy industry was born.

Pornography began appearing in mind-boggling varieties, from highbrow and respectable to outrageously exploitative and debasing. At the lowest rung were the films of Danish performer Bodil Joensen. In 1968–1969 Joensen appeared in unnamed loops that featured explicit bestiality. The loops were presented in a pseudo-documentary directed by Shinkichi Tajiri entitled *Bodil Joensen—en sommerdag juli 1970 (A Summer Day July 1970*, 1970); the film played at an Amsterdam film festival. Joensen was the most depraved example of hardcore; one exhibition of portions of her film in San Francisco resulted in a conviction and jail sentence.[3] At the other end of the spectrum were clinical studies that aspired to document the liberation of formerly forbidden images. These films had scholarly titles, such as John Lamb's *Sexual Freedom in Denmark* (1970) and Alex de Rezny's *Censorship in Denmark: A New Approach* (1970), which was reviewed by Vincent Canby for the *New York Times*.[4] Some were banned, as was Jorgen Lyhne's *Pornography: Copenhagen 70* (1970), an exploitation documentary found obscene in Missouri and Illinois in *United States v. Strand Art Theatre Corp.* (1970) and *Movies, Inc. v. Conlisk* (1971), respec-tively.[5] Others, such as Torgny Wickman's *Ur kärlekens språk (Language of Love*, 1970) met greater success—perhaps for this film in particular because its dis-tributors engaged Ephraim London to defend it against charges of obscenity in *United States v. 35mm Color Motion Picture Film Entitled "Language of Love"* (1970).

Language of Love presented itself as infotainment, an educational "white-coater" presented by sexuality experts. The Second Circuit described the film as "a movie version of the marriage manual. . . . Assuming . . . that the path to marital euphoria and social utopia lies in the perfection and practice of clinically correct and complete sexual technology, this film offers to light that path in a way the masses can understand. It purports to be a veritable primer of marital relations, or perhaps the Kama Sutra of electronic media. . . . *Lan-guage of Love* stars four of what are apparently leading Scandinavian sexual

Swedish scientists studied modern sex in
Ur kärlekens språk (*Language of Love*, 1969).

technocrats, with brilliant cameo roles for the functioning flesh of various unnamed actors."[6] Censors decried the film as sexploitation masquerading as science. Ephraim London was able to convince the court that the film did not treat its subject matter in a debasing, shameful, or morbid manner but was instead intended as a celebration of human sexuality. The court accepted London's argument: "To conclude otherwise would be to suggest that the human body and its functions are in themselves somehow 'dirty' or unspeakably offensive. There is no logic in such a position, and we reject it. . . . The erotic instinct and the apparent desire for sex education are in the ascendancy in our society, and in the sensitive area of constitutional adjudication of individual rights we must be careful to distinguish between the arousal of sexual instincts and the perversion of those instincts to morbidity."[7] *Language of Love* opened the door for explicit representations of sexuality, but the images were still marked as a seedy and seamy business.

In the porno underground, one man distinguished himself above all others: Reuben Sturman. Viewing a bootlegged copy of Braun's *Delphia the Greek*, Sturman was inspired. Where some saw smut, Sturman saw opportunity.

Sturman (1924–1997) began his career distributing comic books. He expanded to racy short stories and soon published pulpy paperbacks through his Satan Press. By the early 1970s Sturman engineered a prototype for the modern peep show. In the backrooms of adult bookstores, Sturman installed single-person cabins that contained an 8mm projector, a small screen, and a lock for privacy. He charged twenty-five cents for two-minute views of an adult film. But he needed content. So in 1971 Sturman journeyed to Copenhagen to call on Braun. They established a partnership. The European pornographer found his American counterpart prepared to handle distribution and exhibition. Over the next decade Sturman's grosses from porn loops alone may have exceeded $2 billion.[8] An accurate accounting of Sturman's profits cannot be known because he seldom paid taxes on these illegal imports.[9]

Sturman was a singular figure in the shadow history of underground films. By the mid-1980s he was identified by the Justice Department as the number one distributor of hardcore pornography in the United States. The attorney general's Commission on Pornography (1986) identified Sturman as not only the most prolific producer and distributor but also the wealthiest pornographer. The FBI and IRS targeted the sleaze merchant.[10] He beat an obscenity charge in Florida in *United States v. Sturman* (1982)[11] but shortly after was indicted on sixteen counts of tax evasion. He was convicted in 1989 in one of the largest tax evasion cases in the history of the IRS.[12] The pornographer's luck had run out. In 1992 he was busted with a shipment of films featuring "humans eating excrement, women having sex with horses, pigs, chickens and other animals, and acts of sadomasochism."[13] Sturman was found guilty of transporting obscene materials across state lines and sent to prison. He escaped and was apprehended two months later. In a new proceeding Sturman was convicted on extortion charges and sentenced to an additional nineteen years in *United States v. Sturman* (1995).[14] Sturman died on October 29, 1997, two years into that sentence. In the pre-Internet days of pornography, Sturman was able to transform filthy pictures into lucre. He brought dirty movies out of the shadows and to a much wider audience. This pornographer's part in the story of film and the First Amendment may not have been an admirable role, but he prepared the way for a cultural shift that accepted—even eagerly awaited—access to sexually explicit materials.

Coinciding with an increase in the availability of pornographic books and movies was the trend of easing prosecution for possession of obscene materials. A trilogy of cases came down in consecutive Supreme Court sessions: *Redrup*, *I.M. Amusement* and *Stanley*.

In 1967 the Supreme Court consolidated three cases involving sale of illicit publications in *Redrup v. New York*. In the first action, Robert Redrup had been working at a New York newsstand when he sold two pulp paperback books, *Lust Pool* and *Shame Agent*, to a patrolman. Other separate actions consolidated in *Redrup* included a case against a defendant who sold two skin magazines, *High Heels* and *Spree*, to a woman in Paducah, Kentucky. A third came from Arkansas, where the state moved to have several magazines declared obscene, including *Gent*, *Swank*, *Bachelor*, and *Modern Man*. Because each of the publications was sold neither to minors nor to unwilling audiences in any of the actions, the Court held that "the distribution of the publications in each of these cases [was] protected by the First and Fourteenth Amendments from governmental suppression, whether criminal or civil, *in personam* or *in rem*."[15]

The following year the High Court extended protection from newsstands to cinemas in *I.M. Amusement Corp. v. Ohio*. Here the Court issued a succinct ruling: "The judgment of the Supreme Court of Ohio is reversed. *Redrup v. New York*."[16]

The third case was *Stanley v. Georgia*. *Stanley* was significant because the Court found *possession* of obscene materials could be protected. In a search of Robert Stanley's house pursuant to a valid warrant, federal agents found three reels of 8mm film. Using a nearby projector they viewed the loops and concluded they were obscene. Ruling in Stanley's favor, the Court held that while obscene materials were outside of constitutional protection, "the First and Fourteenth Amendments prohibit making mere private possession of obscene material a crime."[17] Under this trilogy of cases, obscene materials, whether print, graphic, or audiovisual, could be sold to consenting adults and possessed privately in one's home. But could they be *distributed* for exhibition at movie theaters?

Although the answer to that question was not immediately apparent, the thriving pornographic film industry was expanding to meet the needs of voracious audiences.

Cinema's descent into hardcore can be seen in the microcosm of Russ Meyer's career. Meyer was best known for nudie cuties in the late 1950s. In the 1960s Meyer moved into a phase of more serious filmmaking with *Lorna*.

Vixen! marked another turn in Meyer's oeuvre. Before *Vixen!* Meyer's buxom models retained a certain sweetness or innocence—his women were presented as iconic symbols of fleshy feminine beauty. With *Vixen!* Meyer captured the grunting, grinding, and writhing of the ultimate act, though not explicitly. Despite the nonexplicit sex, Meyer's seamy direction was enough to earn *Vixen!* the MPAA's first X rating.

In *Vixen!* (1968) a young woman (Erica Gavin) lives with her sexually inadequate husband in the wilds of British Columbia. Each male she meets, including a Canadian Mountie, a leather-clad motorcycle tough, and a man fleeing the draft, falls victim to her insatiable sexual appetite. The Supreme Court of Ohio summarized, "The movie is approximately 70 minutes long, out of which approximately one-half deals with incest, adultery, and lesbianism, which are graphically portrayed through facial and bodily expressions indicative of orgasmic reaction. The remaining one-half of the movie leads the viewer through such contemporary issues as racism, anti-militarism, communism and airplane hijacking. It should be noted that, although the players are frequently shown nude and at full length, at no place are their genital parts exposed to the leering lens of the camera."[18]

As one of the first X-rated films, *Vixen!* was a prime target for the remaining municipal censors. Local law enforcement officials in Florida, Ohio, Georgia, Illinois, Michigan, North Carolina, Oklahoma, Utah, and Wisconsin attempted to ban the picture.[19] Florida State Attorney T. Edward Austin brought suit but was defused when the district court declared Florida's obscenity ordinance unconstitutional.[20] Ohio mounted a stronger case under the guidance of Charles H. Keating.

Keating had been an antiporn crusader in Ohio since the 1950s. In 1958 he founded Citizens for Decent Literature, which grew into one of the largest antismut organizations in America. By 1970 he took his campaign to the national stage when President Nixon appointed him to serve on the Commission on Obscenity and Pornography. On his way to Washington Keating brought one last action in his home state. Establishing his standing to sue on behalf of the morality groups that he chaired, Keating tried to ban *Vixen!*.

Keating's *Vixen!* case is notable because it straddled the *Roth-Memoirs* standard for obscenity and the Supreme Court's revised test in *Miller v. California* (1973). *Vixen!* came before the Ohio court in 1971, where it was adjudicated under *Roth-Memoirs*. Relying on the then-authorized "utterly without redeeming social value" gauge, Ohio determined the film to be obscene. Judge Joseph James Patrick Corrigan unenthusiastically dissented: "Although

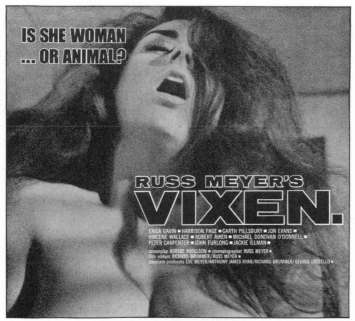

IS SHE WOMAN
... OR ANIMAL?

RUSS MEYER'S
VIXEN.

ERICA GAVIN ■ HARRISON PAGE ■ GARTH PILLSBURY ■ JON EVANS ■
VINCENE WALLACE ■ ROBERT AIKEN ■ MICHAEL DONOVAN O'DONNELL ■
PETER CARPENTER ■ JOHN FURLONG ■ JACKIE ILLMAN ■
screenplay ROBERT RUDELSON ■ cinematographer RUSS MEYER ■
film editors RICHARD BRUMMER/RUSS MEYER ■
associate producers EVE MEYER/ANTHONY JAMES RYAN/RICHARD BRUMMER/ GEORGE COSTELLO ■

IN EASTMANCOLOR ■ **RESTRICTED TO ADULT AUDIENCES** ■ AN EVE PRODUCTION

One of the first films to receive an X rating, Russ Meyer's
Vixen! featured Erica Gavin (1968).

I can agree . . . that the dominant theme of the film is sex, it does not follow
. . . that it is therefore obscene. In my opinion the film, taken as a whole, at
least contains sufficient commentary on matters of some social importance
to bring it within the ambit of the protection of the First and Fourteenth
Amendments."[21] The case was appealed to the Supreme Court and remanded
in light of the recent *Miller* decision that recalibrated the legal standard for
obscenity.

In the meantime Lasse Braun and Reuben Sturman's black-market trade in
hardcore pornography was having an effect on mass-market entertainment.
Nineteen seventy saw the wide release and distribution of the first mainstream porn film in the United States. The film, directed by Howard Ziehm
(b. 1940) and Michael Benveniste (1946–1982) and entitled *Mona: The Virgin
Nymph* (1970), was recognized by *Variety* as "the long-awaited link between
stag loops and conventional theatrical fare. . . . [*Mona*] was the first hard-core
film to be known by name and promoted nationwide."[22] The picture centered

on a young woman who was encouraged by her father to save her virginity for her wedding night. She understands Dad's advice as an open invitation for oral intimacies. The film grossed over $2 million.

Another cinematic landmark was achieved the following year with Wakefield Poole's *Boys in the Sand* (1971). Poole (b. 1936) had been a Broadway dancer and choreographer. While advancing his career on the legitimate stage he also became a pioneering film director of gay pornography. *Boys in the Sand* premiered at the 55th Street Playhouse in New York, bringing explicit homosexuality to an "aboveground" screen for the first time.[23]

Shot on Fire Island, *Boys* consisted of three vignettes. The *Village Voice* marveled at the picture's "Adonises rising, Venus-like, from the frothing Atlantic, set within a travelogue document of everyday life on the secluded gay paradise."[24] *Boys* was a critical and commercial success. On December 22, 1971, *Variety* ran its first-ever review of a gay pornographic film. The film was advertised in the *New York Times* beside notices for John Cassevetes's *Minnie and Moskowitz* (1971) and Elizabeth Taylor's *X, Y and Zee* (1972). Gay porn had not been so mainstream before or since. Riding high on this accomplishment, Poole released his next project, a film that proved to be the strangest genre-hybrid of the porno chic era, if not of all time: a heterosexual, sexually explicit biblical epic entitled *Wakefield Poole's Bible* (1973). In his *Bible*, Poole envisioned Adam and Eve, David and Bathsheba, and Samson and Delilah as X-rated fare.[25]

In addition to the taboo-busting imagery in *Mona* and *Boys*, sexual liberation was embraced on-screen by both mainstream Hollywood and independent filmmakers. Fox contracted Russ Meyer to produce a big-budget studio sex comedy, *Beyond the Valley of the Dolls* (1970, scripted by Roger Ebert). Columbia Pictures picked up *The Last Picture Show* (1971), which revealed starlet Cybill Shepherd without bikini bottoms at a swinging pool party. MGM distributed Michelangelo Antonioni's *Zabriskie Point* (1970), which featured a surreal scene of hundreds of naked bodies undulating on a desert landscape. United Artists made headlines with Bernardo Bertolucci's *Last Tango in Paris* (1972). Warner Bros. released Stanley Kubrick's X-rated masterwork *A Clockwork Orange* (1971), leaving the director's ultraviolent rape scene untouched in the final cut. While Paramount delivered a restrained version of Henry Miller's *Tropic of Cancer* (1970), the studio leased soundstages to producers of hard- and softcore movies.[26] In addition to the major studios, independent filmmakers also played up sex, violence, and general deviance in such films as *Carnal Knowledge* (1971), *Straw Dogs* (1971), *Pink Flamingos* (1972), and *Sweet*

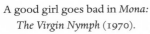

A good girl goes bad in *Mona:
The Virgin Nymph* (1970).

Gay porn had a moment of mainstream
recognition with Wakefield Poole's
Boys in the Sand (1971).

Sweetback's Baadasssss Song (1971), which director Melvin Van Peebles promoted as "rated X by an all white jury."[27]

The Supreme Court recognized the cultural shift and in 1973 redefined
its test for obscenity for the third time since *Roth*. In *Miller v. California* the
Court opined, "One can concede that the sexual revolution of recent years
may have had useful byproducts in striking layers of prudery from a subject
long irrationally kept from needed ventilation. But it does not follow that
no regulation of patently offensive hard core materials is needed or permissible; civilized people do not allow unregulated access to heroin because it is
a derivative of medicinal morphine."[28]

Marvin Miller ran a mail order business in California that distributed
adult books. He printed brochures advertising several titles, including *Sex
Orgies Illustrated* and *An Illustrated History of Pornography*, and sent out a mass
mailing. One of the unsolicited pamphlets went to a restaurant in Newport
Beach, California. The manager and his mother opened the catalog and called
the police.

Miller made two significant changes to the prior obscenity rulings. First, *Miller* struck the "utterly without redeeming social value" language of *Memoirs*. Second, *Miller* renounced the "national community standards" that Justice Brennan had expounded in *Jacobellis* in favor of focusing on local community standards as defined by applicable state law. Speaking for the Court, Chief Justice Warren Burger handed down a new rule: "The basic guidelines for the trier of fact must be: (a) whether the average person, applying contemporary community standards would find that the work, taken as a whole, appeals to the prurient interest . . . (b) whether the work depicts or describes, in a patently offensive way, sexual conduct specifically defined by the applicable state law; and (c) whether the work, taken as a whole, lacks serious literary, artistic, political, or scientific value."[29] All three conditions must be satisfied for material to be deemed obscene.

The federal determination of obscenity would now reference state law. The "utter lack of social value" prong was replaced by a determination that material at issue "lacked *serious* literary, artistic, political, or scientific value" as a matter of law (i.e., to be determined by the judge not a jury).

Miller was a 5–4 split, with the chief justice in the slim majority with Justices White, Blackmun, Powell, and Rehnquist. Justices Brennan, Stewart, and Douglas found themselves on the opposite side. These three dissenters in *Miller* had been among the strongest voices in the majority for *Memoirs*.

Justice Douglas remained steadfast, arguing in his dissenting opinion for the broadest interpretation of the First Amendment. In his view, protections on speech and expression were intended to invite dispute and spark debate, to "create dissatisfaction with conditions as they are, and even to stir people to anger." The framers of the Constitution did not carve out obscenity from the freedom of speech; hence, there are no constitutional guidelines for deciding what is and is not obscene. Douglas continued, "What shocks me may be sustenance for my neighbor. What causes one person to boil up in rage over one pamphlet or movie may reflect only his neurosis, not shared by others. We deal here with a regime of censorship which, if adopted, should be done by constitutional amendment after full debate by the people."[30]

The Supreme Court took up the *Miller* standard on June 21, 1973. That same day the Court also handed down three related decisions on obscenity: *Paris Adult Theatre I v. Slaton* (appealed from the Supreme Court of Georgia), *United States v. Orito* (appealed from the Eastern District of Wisconsin), and *United States v. 12 200-Ft. Reels of Film* (appealed from the Central District of California). Each of these rulings was equally as divisive as the *Miller* decision. Justices Douglas, Brennan, Stewart, and Marshall dissented in each case.

In *Paris Adult Theatre I*, the Supreme Court of Georgia enjoined a theater from showing two films. The theater had displayed conspicuous warnings, including a sign on the door that announced, "Adult Theatre—You must be 21 and able to prove it. If viewing the nude body offends you, Please Do Not Enter."[31] The films at issue were *It All Comes Out in the End* (1970) and *Magic Mirror* (1970). *Magic Mirror* featured Swedish siren and prolific sexploitation starlet Uschi Digard. Digard's curvaceous figure would be featured by Russ Meyer in *Supervixens* (1975) and *Beneath the Valley of the Ultra-Vixens* (1979). Each of these films—including *It All Comes Out in the End* and *Magic Mirror*—were softcore; there was no explicit depiction of sexual intercourse. Indeed, the trial court observed that "the sexual activity depicted in these films is merely simulated, and that, being such, it is not obscene."[32] Georgia's Supreme Court saw things differently: "Actors cavorting indiscriminately in the nude, in a manner designed to appeal to the prurient interests; they depicted simulated acts of intercourse and fellatio. . . . The films in this case leave little to the imagination. It is plain what they purport to depict, that is, conduct of the most salacious character."[33] An injunction was issued.

The Supreme Court affirmed, differentiating *Paris Adult Theatre I* from *Redrup*. *Redrup* permitted consenting adults to purchase obscene materials. In *Paris I* the Court found that "the States have a legitimate interest in regulating . . . exhibition of obscene material in places of public accommodation, including so-called adult theaters from which minors are excluded."[34] The majority opinion rested on the premise that the states' power to protect health, safety, welfare, and morals "to maintain a decent society" could reach the urban blight of adult theaters. In a jurisdiction where pulpy paperbacks might be permissible under *Redrup*, the "rising tide of commercialized obscenity" in motion pictures could be proscribed by states.

In *United States v. Orito*, George Joseph Orito was caught transporting eighty-three reels of filthy films from San Francisco to Milwaukee. Here, the Court differentiated the present case from *Stanley*, which protected possession of obscene materials in a specified zone of privacy. "The Constitution extends special safeguards to the privacy of the home . . . but viewing obscene films in a commercial theater open to the adult public . . . or transporting such films in common carriers in interstate commerce, has no claim to such special consideration."[35] Possession of obscene materials in one's home was protected, but interstate transport could be risky.

Finally, in *United States v. 12 200-Ft. Reels of Film*, a California resident, Mr. Paladini, was returning from a trip to Mexico when customs officials at LAX found films, slides, and photographs that were allegedly obscene. Whereas

Orito was moving materials interstate, Paladini was transporting materials internationally. Once again the *Stanley* holding was narrowed. "We have already indicated that the protected right to possess obscene material in the privacy of one's home does not give rise to a correlative right to have someone sell or give it to others. . . . Nor is there any correlative right to transport obscene material in interstate commerce . . . It follows that *Stanley* does not permit one to go abroad and bring such material into the country for private purposes."[36] In *12 200-Ft. Reels of Film* the Court held that Congress could prohibit importing obscene material, even if it was intended for private, personal use and possession.

June 21, 1973, was an important day in the story of film and the First Amendment. *Miller* shifted the power to determine whether materials were obscene back under state control, thereby complicating commercial distribution of media on a national platform. *Paris Adult Theatre I* gave power to the states to regulate theaters exhibiting obscene materials, even if consumers were restricted to consenting adults. *Orito* and *12 200-Ft. Reels of Film* demonstrated that even though materials may be protected in the privacy of one's home, they could not enter the stream of commerce or be transported without substantial risk. As motion picture content became more daring, states could respond with more stringent regulations.

Only three months after the *Miller* decision, *Vixen!* returned to court. Ohio's magistrates had considered the action in 1971 and applied *Roth-Memoirs* to find Meyer's film obscene. Remanded for reconsideration, the state now applied *Miller*. Under the new measure they reached the same result. "Doubt can no longer remain that the depiction of purported acts of sexual intercourse on the movie screen and the public exhibition thereof for commercial exploitation rather than for a genuine, scientific, educational, sociological, moral, or artistic purpose is forbidden by Ohio law. Here, there is no dispute as to the fact that *Vixen!* does depict numerous acts of purported sexual intercourse, and obviously it does so for a commercial purpose. . . . Therefore, where scenes in a motion picture film depict purported acts of sexual intercourse and are exhibited for commercial exploitation, those scenes are violative of [the Ohio obscenity statute] . . . constitute a nuisance . . . and their exhibition may be enjoined."[37]

Acting on behalf of the Ohio Anti-Obscenity League, Charles Keating had prevailed. Coinciding with the *Vixen!* decisions, Keating himself had ascended to the national stage. Appointed by President Nixon to the Commission on Obscenity and Pornography, he served as the voice for conservative values.

The commission had been organized under Lyndon Johnson in response to *Stanley* and the social problem of rampant pornography. One of the commission's directives was to determine whether exposure to pornography degraded morality. After intensive research and analysis, the eighteen-member panel concluded that there was no demonstrable correlation between pornography and sex crimes. Keating did not accept the result, and he was not alone: the Senate voted 60–5 (with 35 abstentions) to reject the commission's findings. Nixon was displeased as well, stating, "So long as I am in the White House there will be no relaxation of the national effort to control and eliminate smut from our national life."[38] Like the president, Keating would not to be swayed by the empirical findings of a systematic, scientific, and well-funded study. With the aid of Nixon speechwriter Pat Buchanan, Keating compiled a report that countered the commission's data with homespun and creative reasoning. "As Marcellus said in Hamlet, 'Something is rotten in the State of Denmark.' One can consult all the experts he chooses, can write reports, make studies, etc., but the fact that obscenity corrupts lies within the common sense, the reason, and the logic of every man."[39] Speaking for socially conservative antiobscenity moralists, Keating's response poo-pooed the commission's findings—he was unconvinced by data because common sense should dictate. This nonscientific opinion proved influential and was even referenced in the *Paris Adult Theatre I* decision: "Although there is no conclusive proof of a connection between antisocial behavior and obscene material, the legislature of Georgia could quite reasonably determine that such a connection does or might exist."[40]

The postscript for the two key players in the *Vixen!* action are significant. Russ Meyer's film was successful enough to bring Darryl Zanuck calling. Ailing and in need of a hit, 20th Century Fox greenlit *Beyond the Valley of the Dolls* (1970) with a $1 million budget, by far Meyer's biggest film. *Dolls* delivered $9 million.[41] Despite the changing times, Meyer continued his style of filmmaking on a smaller scale, independently producing *Supervixens* and *Beneath the Valley of the Ultra-Vixens*. Meyer spent the 1980s and 1990s securing his legacy as "King Leer" by releasing his films on video and penning an autobiography, *A Clean Breast*.

Subsequent to *Vixen!* and the pornography commission, Keating catapulted from civic duties to corporate governance. He too found financial success until coming under SEC investigation in 1976. A decade later, his gamble on high-risk investments resulted in a magnificent fall. By 1991 he was convicted of fraud, racketeering, and conspiracy. The man who fought for increased regulation on speech worked equally hard to ensure deregulation of financial markets.

Keating prevailed in his quest to ban *Vixen!* in Ohio. He also overcame his opponents on the federal level by suppressing the results of the Commission on Obscenity and Pornography in order to publish his own analysis. These short-term successes only prolonged the on-screen inevitable. Racy, indecent, sexually explicit materials increasingly infiltrated mainstream entertainment. As *Vixen!* was debated in the judicial halls of Ohio and the corrosive influence of obscenity was being mulled on Capitol Hill, a cheaply made and shoddily produced little film (at sixty-one minutes) was released in New York City on a sweltering summer day.

Variety compared *Deep Throat* (1972) to "the *Ben-Hur* of porno pix." The *New York Times* saw *Deep Throat* as "pornography's *Gone With the Wind*."[42] These were not the best comparisons. *Deep Throat* was the *Jazz Singer* of its era. There were talkies before *The Jazz Singer*, but the film was a revolutionary and game-changing success. Likewise, *Deep Throat*, with color, scripted dialogue, and a comedic plot, attained a staggering level of mainstream recognition. On June 12, 1972, *Deep Throat* opened at the World Theater, 153 West Forty-Ninth Street, in New York City. Less than a week later, on June 17, a security guard at the Watergate Hotel in Washington, D.C., inadvertently exposed a political scandal that reached the highest levels. Journalists Bob Woodward and Carl Bernstein adopted the name of the popular porno—and naughty play on words—for their deep-cover contact in the administration. The words "Deep Throat" became synonymous with scandal—from dirty movies, obscenity, and First Amendment issues to political intrigue.

With the imbroglios still simmering, an R-rated *Deep Throat II* (1974) was released. The second installment was followed by *Linda Lovelace for President* (1975), which conflated the two simultaneous but unconnected scandals. *Linda Lovelace for President* was released in three versions: X-rated film, R-rated cut, and a sanitized PG-rated picture. The latter edit raises the question: what is the point of a PG-rated stag film? The answer lies in Lovelace's uncanny acceptance by the mainstream market—everyone wanted to see the girl-next-door with sword-swallowing skills, even if X or R was too spicy.

The cultural significance of *Deep Throat* went beyond *The Jazz Singer* in terms of the legal history of the American cinema. *Deep Throat* introduced a new awareness of First Amendment rights to the general public. In 1951 films lay outside constitutional guarantees of free speech. By 1972 mainstream theatergoers had developed a level of sophistication to ask whether *anything* should be banned—should the government decide what I want to watch? It was an abbreviated evolution—in less than twenty years the medium of motion pictures was embraced with constitutional protections as an inalienable right.

Deep Throat became the cornerstone in the short-lived but highly publicized and culturally influential "porno chic" era. Ralph Blumenthal wrote an article for the *New York Times Magazine* entitled "Porno Chic: 'Hard-Core' Grows Fashionable—And Very Profitable." Published in January 1973, the column reported on the surprising box office from *Deep Throat, Behind the Green Door* (1972), and *The Devil in Miss Jones* (1973).[43] Sexually explicit films, once limited to all-male, sleazy, raincoated audiences, were now lauded by the likes of Norman Mailer, Truman Capote, and Gore Vidal and in periodicals such as the *New York Times* and the *New Yorker*. Anyone culturally astute, hip, and with it simply had to see *Deep Throat* and Linda Lovelace's much-hyped skill.

A forty-four-year-old former hairdresser from Queens named Gerard Damiano (1928–2008) directed *Deep Throat* under the pseudonym Jerry Gerard. In the late 1960s Damiano directed grindhouse flicks such as *We All Go Down* (1968) and *Teenie Tulip* (1970). His career changed when a colleague named Chuck Traynor demonstrated his wife's virtuosic talent. The woman was Linda Boreman (1949–2002). Under Traynor's guidance she took the name Linda Lovelace. Damiano claimed that he instantly knew he could make the girl and her singular sex act a star.

Damiano secured funding from Louis "Butchie" Peraino a.k.a. Lou Perry (1940–1999), the son of Anthony "Big Tony" Peraino (1915–1996). Big Tony was a member of the Columbo family whose biography was not unlike a character out of the Corleone saga. A first-generation Sicilian immigrant, Big Tony branched out from standard mafia-dominated areas of narcotics and labor racketeering to new business ventures that included dry cleaning and pizza parlors. In the 1960s Big Tony invested in peep show pornography. This side business proved extremely lucrative with the innovations of Reuben Sturman's private cabana-stalls. When Butchie petitioned for a loan to produce Damiano's film, Big Tony readily invested in the $25,000 production budget.[44]

With a shoestring budget and a starlet open to suggestion, Damiano drove to Miami for the shoot. He hired a minimal crew that included an assistant cameraman/production assistant/struggling actor named Herbert Streicher (1947–2013). Under the name Harry Reems, Streicher would personify the iconic 1970s mustachioed porn stud.

Judge Joel Tyler (1921–2012) called *Deep Throat* "a Sodom and Gomorrah gone wild before the fire." Courtesy of Allyn Baum / *New York Times* / Redux.

In the first recorded decision against *Deep Throat*, New York Judge Joel Tyler called the picture "a Sodom and Gomorrah gone wild before the fire," the "nadir of decadence," and "a feast of carrion and squalor."[45] Tyler described the motion picture more fully in his opinion: "Following the first innocuous scene ('heroine' driving a car), the film runs from one act of explicit sex into another, forthrightly demonstrating heterosexual intercourse and a variety of deviate sexual acts. . . . The camera angle, emphasis and close-up zooms were directed . . . toward a maximum exposure in detail of the genitalia during the gymnastics, gyrations, bobbing, trundling, surging, ebb and flowing, eddying, moaning, groaning and sighing, all with ebullience and gusto."[46] The film's plot focused on "a young woman whose clitoris is in her throat. . . . [She] consults a buffoon psychiatrist who diagnoses her amazing deformity and prescribes fellatio to achieve an orgasm. The balance of the film deals with the young woman serving as the doctor's assistant by engaging in sexual acts with him and his patients."[47] The slight scenario served to string together Lovelace's varied couplings; still, the comedic plot helped to elevate the picture above the stag loops that had preceded it.

First Amendment advocates argued for the film's social significance and plausible value. In Massachusetts experts from various fields praised the film's "tragicomic disparity between the female star's sexual yearning and attaining" and saw Linda Lovelace "as an allegorical figure . . . representing the plight of women unable to achieve sexual gratification, or as a step forward in the women's liberation movement."[48] In New Jersey "testimony was given that the film takes sexual variations and techniques out of the closet and allows the viewers to see men and women enjoying what is done by the majority of people in private. A psychiatrist testified that exhibition of the film would allow people to engage in enjoyable sexual acts without shame and guilt and presumably thereby improve mental health. It is argued that the motion picture establishes the right of a woman to enjoy sex in her own way."[49] None of these theories had any effect on the court. Instead, Judge Tyler's opinion looked to *New York* magazine's film critic for guidance.

> Judith Crist characterizes the production [as] "idiot moviemaking" and the actors "awful" (*New York Magazine*, Feb. 5, 1973, p. 64). I agree, except to add that a female who would readily and with apparent, anxious abandon, submit to the insertion of a glass dildoe [*sic*] container into her vagina, have liquid poured therein and then drink it by means of a tube, as was done here to and by the "superstar," is not a reflection merely upon her thespian ability, but a clinical example of extraordinary perversion, degeneracy and possible amentia. Whatever talent [the] superstar has seems confined to her magnificent appetite and sword-swallowing faculty for fellatio.[50]

Any argument for *Deep Throat*'s social value was undercut by the sheer amount of sexual content.

> In its explicitness *Deep Throat* goes beyond any film which has been examined by the courts, and probably beyond anything thus far exhibited in public theatres in this country. . . . The explicit sexual activity displayed is hardly comparable to other films considered by the federal courts and found to be non-obscene. Compare *Jacobellis v. Ohio* (one explicit love scene on last reel of film); *United States v. 35 MM. Motion Picture Film Entitled "Language of Love"* (explicit sexual scenes, a close-up of a gynecological examination done by bona-fide Swedish physicians, and an explicit sequence of female masturbation); *United States v. One Motion*

Picture Film Entitled "I Am Curious Yellow" (explicit sexual scene taking 10 minutes of a total of 120); *United States v. One Carton Positive Motion Picture Film Entitled "491"* (act of sodomy, homosexuality, self-mutilation, prostitution); *United States v. One Carton Positive Motion Picture Film Entitled "Technique of Physical Love"* (demonstration by models of various positions of sexual intercourse, no explicit sexual activity).[51]

Linda Lovelace's on-screen, explicit sexual stunts were seen as so shocking and outrageous that the discussion of social significance or educational value was overshadowed and eclipsed by the demonstration of her extraordinary ability.

It has been claimed that *Deep Throat* was a financial success, but how successful the picture was can never be known with any degree of accuracy. For a purported $25,000 production budget plus $15,000 for postproduction and music, the picture cost approximately $40,000 (excluding prints and advertisement). The cast and crew received a pittance. According to Damiano, Lovelace was paid $1,200 and Reems $250. Once *Deep Throat* began making money, the Perainos bought out Damiano's share with an offer he couldn't refuse. When a *New York Times* reporter commented to Damiano that he may have received unfavorable terms in the deal, the director replied, "I can't talk about it." When the journalist persisted, Damiano said, "You want me to get both my legs broken?"[52]

Peraino maximized profits by four walling exhibition of the film, that is, renting theaters and keeping the box office. In many engagements tickets were never issued—after a cash exchange the customer was simply admitted to the theater. Records were intentionally kept minimal. This strategy resulted in a conviction for tax evasion for one exhibitor in *United States v. Thetford* (1982).[53] But the dearth of data has not stopped speculation even from reputable industry and academic sources: "The opening-week run of *Deep Throat* at the New World Theater . . . pulled in $30,033, a record at the time for a porn title playing on a single screen. . . . End of the year figures for 1972 were astonishing: reported grosses for *Deep Throat* exceeded $3 million (after just six months in limited release)." "*Deep Throat* . . . grossed over $3.2-million in more than 70 theaters across the country, including some $700,000 in New York alone . . . making it the greatest porno ever." "*Deep Throat* grossed five million dollars within a year of its release." "[*Deep Throat* was the] eleventh highest grossing film of the year and earn[ed] $20 million in rentals." "*Deep Throat* has made to date roughly $25 million." "*Deep Throat* [spent] ninety-six weeks on *Variety*'s list of fifty top-grossing films and earn[ed] more than $100 million in theater and video revenues worldwide." According to starlet Linda Lovelace, "The box office receipts from one theater alone, the one in San Francisco, have come to more than $6.5 million. The total take? Experts have estimated the gross at more than $300 million." Finally, the documentary *Inside Deep Throat* (2005) provided the most optimistic estimate: "*Deep Throat* became a $600-million global phenomenon that's considered the most profitable film in history."[54] The only thing certain about *Deep Throat*'s profitability is that there is (purposefully) no certainty.

We can be sure that *Deep Throat*'s profitability was offset by the litigation that cascaded down on the picture wherever it opened. Between March 1, 1973, and October 30, 1973, the film was repeatedly challenged in court. The first decision came down in Judge Tyler's criminal court in New York, ruling the film obscene. Similar actions followed: *Deep Throat* was deemed obscene by the Fifth Circuit in *Eastin v. City of New Orleans* (March 8, 1973), the First Circuit in *United States v. One Reel of Film* (July 16, 1973), and the district court of Georgia in *Sanders v. McAuliffe* (October 3, 1973). New Jersey found the picture obscene in *Coleman v. Wilson* (March 21, 1973); however, four months later the state's obscenity statute was held to be unconstitutional in *Hamar Theatres, Inc. v. Cryan* (July 26, 1973). Two months after *Hamar Theatres*, *Throat* reopened at a theater near Princeton with no legal interference.[55] The Seventh Circuit found the film was obscene, but local authorities conducted an improper seizure that denied the exhibitor due process in *Ricciardi v. Thompson* (June 25, 1973).

The following year courts continued stamping out the film wherever it opened. State supreme courts in Georgia, Florida, and Arkansas approved bans on *Deep Throat*, deeming the film to be legally obscene under local ordinances, in *S.S.W. Corp. v. Slaton* (February 18, 1974), *State v. Aiuppa* (May 1, 1974), and *Herman v. State* (July 1, 1974), respectively. Several Texas courts banned the film, the first instance occurring in *Dexter v. Butler* (November 11, 1974). Maryland banned *Deep Throat* in *Mangum v. Board of Censors* (November 25, 1974). California enjoined the film but was reversed on appeal to the Supreme Court, where the state's obscenity statute was found unconstitutional in *Pussycat Theatre Hollywood v. Hicks* (June 4, 1974). The campaign against *Deep Throat* continued. The supreme courts of Nebraska, Michigan, Massachusetts, Kentucky, and North Dakota each deemed *Deep Throat* obscene, in *State v. American Theater Corp.* (June 5, 1975), *State ex rel. Wayne v. Diversified Theatrical* (April 1, 1976), *Commonwealth v. 707 Main Corp.*

(November 23, 1976), *Western Corp. v. Commonwealth* (November 18, 1977), and *State v. Spoke Committee University Center* (September 29, 1978), respectively. The Sixth Circuit upheld a ban in *United States v. Marks* (July 30, 1975).

The Supreme Court of South Dakota found *The Devil in Miss Jones* obscene under state law. At trial, defendant Mini-Kota Art Theatres offered evidence from a prior unrelated action. In Sioux Falls, *Deep Throat* had previously been found not obscene by a jury. The defendant in *City of Sioux Falls v. Mini-Kota Art Theatres, Inc.* argued this evidence had probative value to demonstrate that *The Devil in Miss Jones* was not obscene. The court differed, rejecting the evidence as irrelevant.[56] Hence, in the Mount Rushmore State, *Deep Throat* was permitted in at least one county while *The Devil in Miss Jones* was banned statewide.

Then in 1975 the tide began to turn. Three of the strongest film censorship jurisdictions invalidated their obscenity laws in cases concerning *Deep Throat*: the Supreme Court of Pennsylvania in *Commonwealth v. MacDonald* (October 30, 1975), the Seventh Circuit in *Grandco Corp. v. Rochford* (June 8, 1976), and the Maryland court of appeals in *Wheeler v. State* (December 12, 1977). The Supreme Court of Colorado, sitting en banc, also invalidated the state obscenity statute as fatally defective in *People v. Samuel Tabron* (January 5, 1976).

Justice Brennan had written in *Jacobellis*, amplifying his statements in *Roth* and *Memoirs*, that community standards should be construed as a broad term that encompassed dominant modes of thought and prevailing attitudes. *Miller* renounced this and defined community standards by a localized measure. The question arose, on what level are (local) community standards defined? State level? City level? Neighborhood level? One poetic justice—Owen McGivern—commented that *Behind the Green Door*'s display of "multiple and variegated ultimate acts of sexual perversion would have been regarded as obscene by the community standards of Sodom and Gomorrah."[57] McGivern's appellate court in New York managed to rein in the standard to a more reasonable radius: "the average person in New York State, City or County."[58] In *United States v. Marks*, the Sixth Circuit approved of a regional standard "when the District Judge instructed the jury that the contemporary community standards would be comprised of the Eastern District of Kentucky, as opposed to the national standard, or even the Cincinnati-Covington area."[59] In Florida's *State v. Aiuppa*, which deemed *Deep Throat* to be obscene, the dissenting opinion took note of inconsistencies stemming from varying community standards: "Juries in Jacksonville and Key West, Florida, have rendered verdicts that the movie *Deep Throat* does not offend local standards. Other trial courts have held provisions of the state obscenity acts void for vagueness and over-breadth or, as in this case, have refused to enforce such acts until an authoritative opinion on their constitutionality has been rendered by this Court."[60] *Variety* picked up on this phenomenon, noting that *Deep Throat* was banned in Manhattan by Tyler's court while a jury 185 miles north in Binghamton, New York, found the film not obscene.[61] Film exhibitors were put in the position of forum shopping for districts, areas, or regions that implemented more permissive community standards and avoiding less open-minded constituencies.

The inconsistencies of community standards remained an issue for a decade. A corner was turned in *United States v. Various Articles of Obscene Merchandise* (1982). *Various Articles* centered on a shipment of confiscated video-cassettes. A decade after Judge Tyler's decision, Judge Robert W. Sweet took judicial notice that since *Deep Throat* was widely available, it had been enveloped into the community standards.[62]

The Southern District of New York found the film not obscene. The state appealed. On May 18, 1983, the Second Circuit reaffirmed Sweet's ruling and provided thoughtful commentary on the notion of community standards.

It is true that the mere availability of similar materials in the Southern District of New York does not demonstrate that they are acceptable to the average member of the community. . . . [Previously,] we held that evidence of availability of similar materials is not by itself sufficiently probative of community standards to be admissible in the absence of proof that the material enjoys a reasonable degree of community acceptance [c.f. *City of Sioux Falls v. Mini-Kota Art Theatres, Inc.*]. However, where the availability and public viewing of the same or comparable materials in the New York area is widespread, as appears to be the case here (e.g., the motion picture *Deep Throat* was exhibited to paying patrons in numerous New York theatres), the trial judge was entitled to draw the inference therefrom that the challenged articles enjoy a reasonable degree of community acceptance. Thus, while the existence of enclaves of tolerated obscenity does not by itself create a community standard, judicial notice of widespread community availability and patronage of such works may be accepted as circumstantial evidence of contemporary community standards. At some point a work widely available must be considered inferentially acceptable.[63]

Community standards were an unpredictable liability in the cycle of *Deep Throat* cases until the tide of pornography reached a critical mass. Despite inconsistent regulations on dirty films, obscene audiovisual materials steadily crept into American culture. Once porn became widely available to main-stream viewers outside of isolated enclaves, then it achieved a level of accept-ability. Over time the bar was lowered, and interest and access to hardcore pornography gave way to a new community standard.

One technological development that enabled *Deep Throat* to gain trac-tion with consumer culture was the rise and increasing importance of the home video market. The rise of home media coincided precisely with porno chic and *Deep Throat*'s 1972 theatrical release. Sony introduced the U-Matic in 1971. The significance of this clunky machine was that magnetic videotape was contained in a cassette as opposed to the unwieldy reel-to-reel format in use for decades. The cassette casing made the media more manageable. As *Deep Throat* ignited film screens and censors, consumer-electronics manufac-turers engaged in their own struggle. Philips introduced the N1500 video-cassette recorder in 1972; Sanyo rolled out the V-Cord in 1974; Sony's Beta-max and Panasonic/Quasar's VX "Time Machine" debuted in 1975; finally, JVC, in a collaborative effort with Sony and Matsushita/Panasonic, unveiled VHS in 1977. VHS quickly dominated. This home video market immediately embraced pornographic films.

Home video and sexually explicit materials were seemingly made for each other. A symbiotic relationship developed for two reasons: first, the common-sense comfort of viewing these materials in one's home as opposed to a filthy theater; second, and more significant to a legal history, the safe harbor that had been carved out to favor home consumption of obscene materials. In *Redrup* the Supreme Court folded the sale and distribution of obscene publications into First Amendment protections. In *Stanley* the High Court decriminalized possession of obscene material in the privacy of one's home. Taken together, *Redrup* and *Stanley* encouraged the home video market at a time when nui-sance and zoning laws as well as crime and disease were marginalizing the theatrical market for sexually explicit and obscene materials. Lasse Braun's professionally designed, glossy cardboard packaging and extravagant produc-tions helped to raise the genre out of peep show perversions. Ensconced in the safety and safe harbor of the private zone of one's home, high-priced porn videocassettes sat atop VCRs across the nation. Pornography "con-stituted over half of all sales of pre-recorded tapes in the late 1970s."[64] The price of prerecorded videotapes was kept artificially elevated due to demand

and the gray-market status of the materials, but the list price—which could reach $80 to $120 for a single movie—did not dissuade consumers.[65] The market was insatiable; by 1978 industry estimates had pornographic videotapes accounting for up to 70 percent of rentals and sales.[66] It is perhaps this invisible majority of porn consumers that the Second Circuit was referring to in *United States v. Various Articles of Obscene Merchandise* when the court permitted evidence of obscene materials' penetration into mainstream culture to be considered as a gauge of acceptance into community standards. By 1985, within two years of the *Various Articles* decision, home video sales equaled that of domestic theatrical box office.[67] Litigation no doubt had a chilling effect on the theatrical market for pornographic films, but these materials seemed better suited to home media both on a human level as well as under the legal standards of *Redrup* and *Stanley*.

Deep Throat was such anathema that municipalities were determined to prevent the picture's exhibition using any legal theory at their disposal. Having exhausted obscenity statutes, several jurisdictions applied laws creatively. In 1975 Michigan filed an action against film exhibitors under the state's public nuisance act in *State ex rel. Wayne County Prosecutor v. Diversified Theatrical Corp.* The law proscribed places of lewdness or prostitution as public nuisances. Diversified Theatrical prayed for Michigan to reconsider whether the statute could be properly applied to motion picture theaters. The Michigan Supreme Court reversed, reasoning, "The statute was intended to apply to houses of prostitution and not motion picture theatres where sexual acts are not committed but are portrayed on the screen."[68]

In Texas a Houston district court consolidated over twenty cases. In addition to seizing physical prints of the film, magistrates had issued a warrant for projectors as "criminal instruments" under the Texas penal code. The court struck down this overreaching theory, holding, "[The] statute clearly indicate[s] that a criminal instrument is not equipment which is designed, made, or adapted for a lawful use, but which incidentally may be used for the commission of a crime. There are many, many common, ordinary, everyday objects which can be used to commit crimes, but these are not criminal instruments."[69] Federal prosecutor Larry Parrish crafted perhaps the most creative cause of action in the cycle of *Deep Throat* cases, which he argued before the Fifth Circuit.

Soon after graduating from the University of Tennessee, Parrish became an assistant district attorney and launched a crusade against pornography. Unlike Tennessee's curmudgeonly censor Lloyd T. Binford, who relied on homespun philosophy and old-school prejudice to guide his regulation of film, Parrish was a new breed of activist who employed aggressive enforcement and imaginative lawyering. The first film Parrish set his sights on was *School Girls* (1970). He coordinated with FBI agents to seize prints of the picture as soon as it entered Memphis.[70] The officer sent to confiscate *School Girls* first sat through several trailers at the theater. "He saw previews to a film nobody had ever heard of called *Deep Throat*, and when he came back he told us about it," Parrish recalled. "He didn't even know the name of it. But we knew it was a film that deserved to be prosecuted."[71] Parrish's next crusade had begun.

Deep Throat had few points of contact with Memphis, but with inspired legal thinking a conspiracy took shape. Parrish imagined a network of filth purveyors intent on perverting the status quo and the Christian values of the region. "The indictment, cleverly drafted by Parrish, charged 117 persons and corporations with a nationwide conspiracy to create an obscene film and distribute it throughout the United States. The crime had thus been committed in each and every district where the film *could have* been shown. Under the theory of this indictment, any local United States Attorney could decide the most appropriate district in which to prosecute. . . . Of the 117 individuals and corporations named in the indictment, only 18 were actually prosecuted."[72] One of those alleged coconspirators was Harry Reems. According to the indictment, the conspiracy began in February 1971, a year before Reems's involvement, and continued through June 1975, three years after Reems's performance in the film. Although Reems's role was limited, under the law, once a person joins a criminal conspiracy, he is liable for all acts in furtherance of that conspiracy. Parrish's theory was inspired, but the Tennessee prosecutor found himself facing an equally imaginative attorney. Reems engaged a young lawyer named Alan Dershowitz.

With a home-field advantage, Parrish won the first round. The Sixth Circuit held, "It was not necessary that the films be judicially determined to be obscene before any conspiracy to violate Section 1465 could exist. In our opinion there was substantial evidence to support the conviction of the appellants on the conspiracy count."[73] On April 30, 1976, a Memphis jury found Reems and sixteen other codefendents guilty of conspiracy to transport obscene materials across state lines for distribution.[74] This was the first time an actor had been convicted for appearing in an American film.

Dershowitz was prepared to appeal what he called "a very serious and important civil liberties case."[75] The lawyer discovered a flaw in Parrish's

Larry Parrish crafted a porno conspiracy to put Harry Reems behind bars in Tennessee. *Memphis Press-Scimitar* photo, courtesy Preservation and Special Collections, University Libraries, University of Memphis Libraries.

———

Mustachioed porn stud
Harry Reems (1947–2013).

———

allegations: what Reems had done was legal at the time he did it. On appeal, defense pointed out that at the time *Deep Throat* was produced, *Roth-Memoirs* governed the standard for obscenity. Under this test, courts were directed to look at a national community standard. Parrish's action hinged on defining obscenity on a local or regional standard, the law under *Miller*. Hence, "Harry Reems was not being tried under the law as it existed at the time he acted in *Deep Throat*, but rather under a new set of standards that had come into existence a year and a half after it had been completed. The general rule is that a defendant must be tried under the law that was applicable *at the time he committed his alleged criminal conduct.*"[76]

A bold effort, but once again Parrish prevailed. The case was granted certiorari. Finally the tables turned in Reems's favor. The Supreme Court reversed the prior rulings, reasoning that the filmmakers had no fair warning of the changing standards for obscenity. "We have taken special care to insist on fair warning when a statute regulates expression and implicates First Amendment values. . . . We therefore hold . . . that the Due Process Clause precludes the application to petitioners of the standards announced in *Miller v. California*, to the extent that those standards may impose criminal liability for conduct not punishable under *Memoirs*."[77] Harry Reems was freed.

Besides *Deep Throat*, two other pictures, *Behind the Green Door* and *The Devil in Miss Jones*, helped to establish porn in popular culture. While *Deep Throat* was a comedy with explicit sex, *Behind the Green Door* (1972) had aspirations as an art film. Directed by Jim (1943–2007) and Artie Mitchell (1945–1991), *Green Door* told the story of a girl-next-door who was kidnapped and taken to an underground sex club, where she performed various acts onstage before masked spectators. The Mitchells elevated their film with an inspired casting choice: an all-American, clean-cut, fresh-faced actress named Marilyn Briggs (1952–2009). Before 1972 Briggs's most notable accomplishment was as cover girl for Ivory Snow's box, innocently smiling and snuggling a chubby baby. Adopting the name Marilyn Chambers, the model shed her sweet image. Chambers did not have a signature erotic expertise like Linda Lovelace; instead, a notable pairing elevated Chambers into the pantheon of porn. Chambers engaged in an interracial sex scene, a taboo-busting sequence that shocked even the most hardened contemporary viewers. Ivory Snow quickly withdrew their detergent boxes.[78]

The Mitchells' filthy film received favorable reviews. It became the first American porno picture to compete for the Palme d'Or at Cannes.[79] The Mitchells, next film, *Resurrection of Eve* (1973), also starred Chambers. *Sodom*

The porno chic: *Deep Throat* (1972),
Deep Throat II (1974), and
Behind the Green Door (1972).

and Gomorrah: The Last Seven Days (1975) followed, but each subsequent film cost more and earned less. *Sodom* was produced on a $1 million budget and opened with Judge Tyler's quote from *People v. Mature Enterprises, Inc.* comparing porn to "a Sodom and Gomorrah gone wild before the fire." The film was a career-crushing bomb. It would be a decade before the Mitchells would direct another feature-length film.

Coming off his success with *Deep Throat*, Damiano released *The Devil in Miss Jones*, which completed the porno chic triumvirate. Shedding the low comedy of *Throat*, *Miss Jones* strived for highbrow cultural references. In the opening scene Miss Jones (Georgina Spelvin) commits suicide by cutting her wrists and lying in her bathtub for an extended nude and gory episode. She finds herself in purgatory. Unable to ascend to heaven she is fated for the inferno. Before her descent, an angelic bureaucrat permits her to return to Earth to engage in the lustful activities she avoided while alive. Before her reincarnation, she receives sexual education from Harry Reems. In the end Miss Jones finds herself trapped in a room with a man (Damiano) uninterested in sex, echoing Sartre's *No Exit*. *Miss Jones* is dark and somber, replacing the funky hipness of *Deep Throat*.

By the mid-1970s the porno chic had transformed into a home video revolution. After a brief period in the spotlight, the three primary starlets receded back to the margins of adult entertainment.

Georgina Spelvin, née Michelle Graham (b. 1936), was a thirty-six-year-old musical stage performer when she appeared in *Miss Jones*. Unsuccessful in her previous acting career, she was hailed by the *Village Voice* as "the new Greta Garbo of copulation."[80] Spelvin continued to appear in hardcore films through the 1980s, authoring a 2008 autobiography entitled *The Devil Made Me Do It*.

Linda Lovelace reached her maximum exposure in *Linda Lovelace for President*. After the picture bombed and mainstream interest in the porno chic dimmed, the sword-swallowing starlet worked to prolong her fifteen minutes of fame by penning two pro-porn biographies, *Inside Linda Lovelace* (1974) and *The Intimate Diary of Linda Lovelace* (1974), followed by two antiporn screeds, *Ordeal* (1980) and *Out of Bondage* (1988). By the late 1980s Lovelace reemerged as an outspoken opponent of pornography, exploitation, and violence against women. She had a complicated relationship with adult media: while maintaining her position as an antiporn crusader she also posed for magazines such as *Leg Show* as late as 2001.

Marilyn Chambers attempted a transition to mainstream cinema, appearing in David Cronenberg's *Rabid* (1977). But the crossover proved too ambitious for the time. Chambers returned to sex films with *Insatiable* (1980). She continued as an erotic performer for nearly two more decades.

Gerard Damiano's career also lasted long past its prime. The director of *Deep Throat* continued to churn out explicit videos, such as *Splendor in the Ass* (1989). Lou Peraino's distribution entity, Bryanston Pictures, presented several notable films after *Deep Throat*, including *Andy Warhol's Frankenstein* (1973) and *The Texas Chainsaw Massacre* (1974). The final chapter of the Mitchell brothers saga presented a far darker tale. The brothers produced several more films but concentrated more on live shows at their O'Farrell Theater in San Francisco. Artie battled substance abuse, which threatened the brothers' joint ventures. In February 1991 Jim shot Artie dead. Convicted of manslaughter, Jim served half of a six-year sentence.[81]

The Mitchells' *Behind the Green Door* was produced on a $60,000 budget. The film reported theatrical grosses over $25 million, doubling that for home video sales.[82] *The Devil in Miss Jones* was similarly successful. Roger Ebert's contemporary review called it "the best hard-core porno film that I've ever seen, and although I'm not a member of the raincoat brigade, I have seen the highly touted productions like *Deep Throat* and *It Happened in Hollywood*."[83] *Miss Jones* had a budget comparable to *Green Door* and went on to gross $15 million at the box office, placing tenth at the box office for 1973.[84] *Deep Throat* has been enshrined as the centerpiece of the porno chic because of the picture's speculative reputation as the most profitable film in history as well as its identification with Woodward and Bernstein's naughty code name.

As sexually explicit film rose to mainstream prominence, distribution and exhibition presented serious risks. After *Miller*, community standards were decentralized to a point that an exhibitor could hardly know if the film would be deemed obscene until after assuming the risk of renting and opening the picture.

The porno chic was a short-lived fad. Damiano foresaw the end in an interview with Roger Ebert in July 1974: "The only thing that's kept hard-core going this long is the FBI and the Nixon administration. . . . Without censorship to encourage people's curiosity the whole thing would have been over six months ago."[85] Unsimulated on-screen sex in mainstream movies gave up its dying gasp in 1975–1976. Directors Pier Paolo Pasolini (1922–1975) and Nagisa Oshima (1932–2013) attempted to elevate hardcore to legitimate cinematic art in *Salò, or the 120 Days of Sodom* (1975) and *In the Realm of the Senses* (1976), respectively. *Salò* focused on four fascists as they reveled in violence, sadism, and sexual torture. *Senses* told the story of a man and a geisha, leaving little to the imagination in their expressions of passion and depravity. Bob Guccione's *Caligula* (1979) bookended the era of tolerance for explicit sex in mainstream, theatrically released movies.[86]

Theatrical adult films enjoyed mainstream acceptance from 1972 to 1976. The emerging video market allowed consumers to enjoy explicit materials in the cleaner, safer comforts of home. And the consumer's appetite proved ravenous. Home media exploded with varieties of cinematic kink that developed into more deviant sexual acrobatics—while meanwhile providing a wildly profitable investment for video distributors. The porno chic was a short-lived fad but had a wide-ranging influence on film and video productions in terms of content, profit expectations, and the development of new technology.

17

JUST NOT HERE

Content Regulation through Zoning

—

In response to the porno chic, states intensified their efforts to regulate the rising tide of explicit media. Legislatures and local authorities fought the increasingly difficult battle to control motion pictures with a threefold strategy: (1) enforcing censorship laws; (2) challenging adult theaters under nuisance laws; and (3) employing zoning ordinances to regulate the time, place, and manner of exhibiting undesirable content.

New York State remained a powerful gatekeeper with the ability to prevent or delay import of foreign films containing controversial content. On June 6, 1972, customs officials seized an animated short produced in Great Britain entitled *Sinderella* (1972). This cartoon was directed by David Grant a.k.a. Terry Gould (1937–1991), the self-proclaimed British king of sexploitation who specialized in fractured fables such as *Snow White and the Seven Perverts* (1972). Judge Jacob Mishler summarized the animated film as follows:

> The general outline of the plot is the story of Cinderella interspersed with bits and parts of Little Red Riding Hood, Puss N' Boots and Goldilocks and The Three Bears. While the narrator recites the script with the tonal wonderment of a fairy tale free from vulgarity, the film depicts sexual organs and sexual acts. The first scene shows Sinderella in the woods; she finds something on the ground which upon her urging becomes an

erect phallus, she then inserts it between her legs in masturbation. Other scenes depict Sinderella performing sexual acts with the above-mentioned fairy-tale characters as well as with the prince in a bedroom of the palace and shadowy outlines indicating The Three Bears having sexual relations with Sinderella in rapid succession. There is hardly a frame of the film that does not show genital organs, the sexual act, or movement from which sexual activity is suggested.[1]

The district court sided with customs officials and condemned the cartoon under the Tariff Act.

On appeal to the Second Circuit, Judge Leonard Page Moore affirmed. In his decision Moore acknowledged a longstanding linage of illustrated obscenity:

> Fortunately, we do not have to decide upon the permitted range of pornography which judging by the frescoes of the early dynasties of Egypt, the relics of Pompeii, the temples of India and the ancient prints of Japan has not been altogether unknown throughout the ages. Our problem is only does this film come within the ban of [tariff law] and the *Miller* guidelines. [*Sinderella*] has no redeeming value whatsoever and should be banned. It may be true that in the field of pornography things have gone about as far as they can go but this does not justify adding another import to our fast accumulating collection.[2]

At the other end of the artistic spectrum from Grant's silly sketches were the bohemian art films of Andy Warhol (1928–1987). The pioneering pop artist moved from silk-screen paintings to motion pictures with his series of "static films" produced in the early 1960s: *Blow Job* (1963), which depicted a man's face as he purportedly received oral stimulation, and the self-explanatory *Sleep* (1963), *Eat* (1963), and *Kiss* (1963). Warhol moved into comparably epic filmmaking with *Empire* (1964), which was still a static shot, but this time an eight-hour-long recording of the Empire State Building. By the mid-1960s the artist transitioned to narrative filmmaking, transforming his factory workers into "Superstars." Candy Darling, Ultra Violet, Edie Sedgwick, Nico, and Viva basked in the glory of their fifteen minutes of fame. Warhol's active participation in filmmaking waned by the end of the decade. *Blue Movie* (1969) was the last film he personally directed.

Blue Movie imposed epic length (140 minutes) on a mundane premise. The film records a stream-of-consciousness dialogue between Viva and Louis Waldon as they discuss topics ranging from fashion to Vietnam and relationships to television. Their small talk switches to sex and performance anxiety.[3] While the film's sex scene was not explicit, Viva and Louis's coitus was unsimulated. Perhaps unknowingly, Warhol had created a motion picture ideally suited to test the third prong of *Memoirs* standard, which hinged on whether a work was utterly without social value.

Two weeks after the film opened on Bleecker Street, it was seized by Deputy Public Morals Inspector Charles Smyth and charged with obscenity.[4] When New York challenged *Blue Movie*, obscenity was calibrated under the *Memoirs* standard. The court had little problem with the first two prongs. Dominant theme taken as a whole appeals to a prurient interest in sex: check. Patently offensive material as judged by contemporary community standards: check. The third prong was the sticking point: was the material *utterly* without redeeming social value?

The majority of *Blue Movie*'s running time saw Warhol's performers discussing social issues. This dialogue brought a modicum of social value to Warhol's film. Theater manager Saul Heller told the *New York Times*, "I saw other pictures playing around town and this was a kiddie matinee compared to them."[5] In *People v. Heller* the court viewed things differently. Finding that the film held no social value, the court declared *Blue Movie* obscene. Judge Fuld, the reliable advocate of First Amendment protections, filed a dissenting opinion that maintained his position on broad free speech rights even if he personally disliked the content of the speech. Fuld wrote, "If I were to judge the film before us in terms of my personal views of its social value, of its moral and aesthetic worth, I would condemn it for its vulgarity no less than for its banality."[6] His point: speakers should have the right to be vulgar and banal. The case was appealed to the Supreme Court in *Heller v. New York* (1973) and remanded back to the appeals court.[7]

On remand, *Miller* had replaced *Memoirs*, but the result did not change. The court dismissed the picture's sheen of social value and again condemned *Blue Movie* as obscene.

The utterly lacking test was abandoned in *Miller* because of the difficulty in proving such an extreme. The clever pornographer need only infuse some social or political content into the work to escape successful prosecution. However, this court, as it must have when the *Heller* case was here before, has applied the utterly without test within the realm of reason. Thus, we found *Blue Movie* obscene even though the pornographic activities depicted were interspersed with some political and social dialogue. We cut through the form, as it were, to the substance and the substance of the film was and remains hard core pornography.[8]

Warhol's experimentation at the crossroads of art, cinema, and pornography had reached a conclusion. His flirtation with filmmaking was over. As the *Blue Movie* drama unfolded, six subway stops uptown, *Deep Throat* began its run.

Overt sexual themes were not only seen in the extremes of porn flicks and art films but also in mainstream Hollywood movies. After testing the MPAA with *Who's Afraid of Virginia Woolf?* Mike Nichols directed *Carnal Knowledge* (1971). Starring Jack Nicholson, Ann-Margret, Candice Bergen, and Art Garfunkel, *Carnal Knowledge* focused on changing sexual relationships. In *Jenkins v. Georgia* the Supreme Court provided a plot synopsis:

Two young college men, roommates and lifelong friends forever [are] preoccupied with their sex lives. Both are first met as virgins. Nicholson is the more knowledgeable and attractive of the two. . . . Art Garfunkel is his friend, the nice but troubled guy. . . . He falls in love with the lovely Susan (Candice Bergen) and unknowingly shares her with his college buddy. As the safer one of the two, he is selected by Susan for marriage. The time changes. Both men are in their thirties, pursuing successful careers in New York. Nicholson has been running through an average of a dozen women a year but has never managed to meet the right one . . . [until] he finds Ann-Margret, an aging bachelor girl with striking cleavage. . . . [As for] Garfunkel. . . . [t]he sparks have gone out of his marriage, [and] the sex has lost its savor.[9]

The film is obviously "about" sex. Despite the theme and occasional nudity, depictions of carnal knowledge were tastefully handled in typical Hollywood style with bodies tussling under thin sheets.

Southern regulators felt that the film's direct approach to young love and sexual experience fell outside of contemporary community standards. *Carnal Knowledge* was deemed obscene in Georgia under *Miller* and banned. Upon appeal to the Supreme Court, the justices viewed the film and disagreed.

Writing for a unanimous panel, Justice Rehnquist stated, "Our own viewing of the film satisfies us that *Carnal Knowledge* could not be found under the *Miller* standards to depict sexual conduct in a patently offensive way. . . . While the subject matter of the picture is, in a broader sense, sex, and there are scenes in which sexual conduct including 'ultimate sexual acts' is to be understood to be taking place, the camera does not focus on the bodies of the actors at such times. There is no exhibition whatever of the actors' genitals, lewd or otherwise, during these scenes." In an important statement Rehnquist went on to declare, "There are occasional scenes of nudity, but nudity alone is not enough to make material legally obscene under the *Miller* standards."[10]

Rehnquist's statement was the capstone to the decades of attrition against motion picture regulatory law. The *Miracle* decision stood for the proposition that states could not ban a motion picture based on sacrilege. *Kingsley* expanded film freedom to cover immoral ideas. *Superior Films* demonstrated that a movie could not be censored for tending to corrupt morals. *Excelsior* declared that nudity was not per se obscene, but *Jenkins* finally addressed the "elephant in the room." Under *Jenkins*, the Supreme Court ruled that nudity alone was not enough to transform an otherwise legitimate motion picture into censorable obscenity.

The following year the Supreme Court considered a case at the intersection of obscenity and nuisance law. This area would prove to be the next great hurdle in the legal history of motion pictures.

Richard Erznoznik was the manager of the University Drive-In Theatre in Jacksonville, Florida. In March 1972 his theater showed an R-rated film entitled *The Class of '74*. The coming-of-age comedy contained scenes of softcore nudity. Unfortunately for Mr. Erznoznik these scenes played on his outdoor screen. Parishioners at the nearby Resurrection Catholic Church were distracted and called in authorities.[11] Erznoznik was charged with violating the municipal code for exhibiting a motion picture in which "the human male or female bare buttocks, human female bare breasts, or human bare pubic areas are shown . . . visible from any public street or public place."[12] The film was identified as a public nuisance and banned.

Erznoznik argued the municipal ordinance constituted a prior restraint on First Amendment rights. Jacksonville countered that the intent of the city code was to protect citizens from unwilling exposure to offensive materials; however, as drafted the law singled out all films containing any nudity. Erznoznik claimed the ordinance was overbroad—it sweepingly forbade any film depicting uncovered buttocks or breasts in all contexts. The law would

Class of '74 (1972).

---

bar a film "containing a picture of a baby's buttocks, the nude body of a war victim, or scenes from a culture in which nudity is indigenous. The ordinance also might prohibit newsreel scenes of the opening of an art exhibit as well as shots of bathers on a beach. Clearly all nudity cannot be deemed obscene even as to minors."[13]

Nonetheless, the state upheld the statute as a reasonable exercise of police power. On appeal the Supreme Court differed. While clearly understanding the desire to shield minors, motorists, and churchgoers from such distractions, the Court insisted that when "First Amendment freedoms are at stake we have repeatedly emphasized that precision of drafting and clarity of purpose are essential. These prerequisites are absent here."[14] Florida's nuisance statute overreached legitimate state interest. Content-based restrictions on expression must be narrowly tailored to specifically address the issue.

A similar drama played out with nuisance statutes in Louisiana, seen in actions against two films, *The Stewardesses* and *Last Tango in Paris*. *The Stewardesses* (1969) was a softcore 3-D confection that surprised at the box office.

Produced for approximately $200,000, the picture earned nearly $7 million in 1969 and went on to claim $25 million worldwide.[15] That the film appealed to prurient interest was not contested. Louisiana's Supreme Court agreed: "At the outset we hold that we agree with the trial judge and decide that *The Stewardesses* is obscene."[16]

The Stewardesses was a happy amalgamation of Chris Condon's two interests: aviation and stereoscopic sexploitation. Condon (1923–2010), born Christo Dimitri Koudounis, served in the Air Force as a combat cinematographer and earned four Bronze Battle Stars. After the war he settled in North Hollywood and opened an optics company devoted to telephoto and specialty lenses. He developed a friendship with Andre De Toth and, at the one-eyed director's insistence, developed a high-quality 3-D lens for motion picture cameras. In 1953 Condon patented his system. Within a decade Condon's company, Magnivision 3-D, developed a single-camera system that streamlined unwieldy 3-D camera technology. Magnivision was influential in the second phase of 3-D films that took off with *The Stewardesses*. With windfall profits from the sexy film, Condon founded Trans Sierra Airlines. He split his time between flying and filming, supplying 3-D lenses to *Andy Warhol's Frankenstein* (1973), *Mr. Howard's Crazy Airline* (*International Stewardesses*, 1974), *The CIA Girls of Capitol Hill* (1977), and *The Volcano Creature and the Surfer Girls* (1978). When the third wave of 3-D hit, Condon's system had become an industry standard and was used in *Jaws 3-D* (1983), among other pictures.[17]

In the case of *The Stewardesses*, the issue was not whether the film was obscene—that was uncontested on appeal to the state's supreme court—the issue was whether Louisiana's nuisance law violated the First Amendment. The statute was enacted for red light abatement, deeming that any place where prostitution or obscenity occurred was a nuisance and could be shuttered for up to a year.[18] Antiprostitution vice legislation had become common by the turn of the twentieth century, but only in the 1970s were such laws finessed to address movie theaters that exhibited allegedly obscene materials. The Louisiana Supreme Court construed the vague language in the public nuisances statute broadly enough to reach theaters and squelch undesirable exhibitors. Judge Frank W. Summers, writing for the majority in *State v. Gulf States Theatres of Louisiana, Inc.*, stated, "Some prior restraint is necessary if the efforts of states to regulate obscenity are to be enforceable."[19]

Judge Mack Barham, a progressive voice in the conservative state on civil rights as well as First Amendment issues, filed a dissenting opinion. Barham saw the ordinance as defective. He then noted that the tribunal had

The friendly skies in *The Stewardesses* (1969).

not viewed *The Stewardesses* before deeming it obscene. Barham concluded, "While the exact legal guidelines for determining whether, when, and how obscene expressions are protected by the First Amendment are in a state of flux, it is certain that our statute does not meet the minimum standards now required by the United States Supreme Court."[20]

A year later Louisiana revisited the issue; however, this time the tables were turned. Barham now wrote for the majority while Summers dissented. In this case, Gulf Theatres exhibited *Last Tango in Paris* (1972). *Tango* raised eyebrows across the country with its adventurous sexual content. None of the amorous acts were explicitly depicted, but the suggestion alone earned the film an X rating.

Once again Louisiana's public nuisances statute was invoked, this time in *Gulf States Theatres of Louisiana, Inc. v. Richardson*. Barham looked at the legislative history of the statute: "A history of the development of the statutes casts light upon the consideration of the constitutional attacks. The statutes originated with Act 47 of 1918, which was an act to declare houses of prostitution and their contents nuisances and to provide means to enjoin and abate them. All seven provisions, R.S. 13:4711–4717, remained unchanged for over 40 years. In 1960 the Legislature attempted . . . to amend Section 4711 to include obscenity with prostitution in the definition of a nuisance."[21]

The state's rationale in citing the nuisance statute as opposed to an obscenity ordinance was strategic. The obscenity laws required an analysis of the film at issue, costly and time consuming for both the state and the exhibitors. Declaring a theater to be a public nuisance eradicated this problem at its roots: condemning the theater eliminated the need for a film-by-film analysis. Barham saw through this canny strategy, writing, "We are constrained to find that R.S. 13:4712 is unconstitutional on its face because it authorizes the total *ex parte* [i.e., without all parties present] suppression of alleged obscenity without any independent judicial determination on facts that the expression is probably obscene."[22] Judge Summers remained unconvinced, writing, "I adhere to the reasons assigned for our decision on this identical issue in *State of Louisiana v. Gulf States Theatres of Louisiana, Inc.*"[23] Over Summers's reservations, a year after *The Stewardesses* was banned, *Last Tango* was permitted in Louisiana. The state's nuisance statute imposed an impermissible prior restraint on First Amendment rights by sidestepping the procedural requirement of a full and fair hearing on the issue of obscenity.

While Louisiana's courts monitored the (mis)use of red light abatement statutes to regulate movie theaters, the practice continued for several more years in Alabama. Radley Metzger imported European erotica in the 1950s and produced artistic adult films in the 1960s. Influenced by the porno chic of the 1970s, he moved into hardcore filmmaking under the name Henry Paris. *The Opening of Misty Beethoven* (1975) has been considered Metzger/Paris's porn masterpiece. Produced on a lavish budget and shot in Paris, Rome, and New York, *Misty Beethoven* was a sexually explicit version of *My Fair Lady*. When the film opened in Huntsville it was quickly deemed obscene and shuttered. Rather than invoking an obscenity ordinance, Alabama authorities cited the state's red light abatement act to brand the theater a public nuisance. The case rose to the state supreme court as *Trans-Lux Corp. v. State ex rel. Sweeton*.

Alabama's code defined a nuisance as "any place in or upon which lewdness, assignation or prostitution is conducted, permitted, continued or exists and the personal property and contents used in conducting or maintaining any such place for any such purpose."[24] The court was unable to speak in a singular voice; instead, the holding was a plurality with eight separate concurrences and two dissents. Turning in a per curiam opinion, the Alabama Supreme Court "conclude[d] that 'lewdness' includes the exhibition of an obscene motion picture in a public place, such as an enclosed motion picture theater."[25] Six years after Louisiana overruled misuse of nuisance statutes, Alabama permitted use of its red light abatement act to enjoin the exhibition of obscene films.

Alabama was not the only state to strategically combat obscenity. In *State v. "Without a Stitch"* Ohio enjoined exhibition of a Danish film entitled *Uden en trævl* (1968). *Without a Stitch* told the story of a girl unable to achieve sexual climax. Her doctor suggests she keep a diary of her sexual encounters—a crafty dramatic device that justified a montage of explicit scenes running the gamut from German sadism to lesbian coupling. Unlike the Alabama statute, the Ohio red light abatement act specifically addressed motion pictures.[26] While Louisiana reigned in expansive use of nuisance laws, in Alabama and Ohio red light abatement statutes were either tailored to movie houses or broadly construed to reach bothersome theaters.

Despite Alabama's and Ohio's use of red light abatement laws to control exhibition of allegedly obscene films, this approach was a disfavored method of regulating speech. Instead, other states relied on zoning laws to regulate the time, place, and manner of undesirable speech. As opposed to nuisance and red light statutes that aimed to shutter theaters and silence improper films, zoning laws banished unwanted exhibitors to sectors of industrial use.

The issue of whether zoning ordinances and time, place, and manner restrictions on speech had a chilling effect on First Amendment rights was raised in *Young v. American Mini Theatres, Inc.* Detroit's city code defined an adult mini-theater as "an enclosed building with a capacity for less than 50 persons used for presenting material distinguished or characterized by an emphasis on matter depicting, describing or relating to Specified Sexual Activities or Specified Anatomical Areas . . . for observation by patrons."[27] Zoning laws threatened American Mini Theatre's Pussy Cat adult movie theater franchise: "Instead of concentrating adult theaters in limited zones, [Detroit's] ordinances require that such theaters be dispersed. Specifically, an adult theater may not be located within 1,000 feet of any two other regulated uses or

Scandinavian sex comedy *Uden en trævl*
(*Without a Stitch*, 1968).

within 500 feet of a residential area."[28] The district court of Michigan found
the zoning ordinance was a rational attempt to preserve the city's neighborhoods. On appeal, the Sixth Circuit reversed, finding the law an impermissible prior restraint.[29] The Supreme Court disagreed, siding with the lower
court and recognizing that the content of speech could be a valid classification for zoning purposes.[30] In *Young v. American Mini Theatres, Inc.* Justice Stevens spoke for the 5–4 majority, reasoning, "The 1,000-foot restriction does
not, in itself, create an impermissible restraint on protected communication.
The city's interest in planning and regulating the use of property for commercial purposes is clearly adequate to support that kind of restriction applicable
to all theaters within the city limits. In short, apart from the fact that the ordinances treat adult theaters differently from other theaters and the fact that
the classification is predicated on the content of material shown in the respective theaters, the regulation of the place where such films may be exhibited
does not offend the First Amendment."[31] The zoning scheme requiring dis-
persal of adult businesses in order to protect and maintain the quality of life
in a community qualified as a legitimate and compelling state interest, such
that speech could be regulated based on its adult content.

American Mini Theatres was reaffirmed a decade later in *City of Renton v. Playtime Theatres, Inc.* In *Playtime Theatres*, a Washington State town implemented a regulation prohibiting adult theaters within one thousand feet of residential zones, churches, and parks and increased the prohibited zone to one mile in the case of schools.[32] In 1982, a year after the zoning regulation was ratified, Playtime purchased two theaters with the intention of exhibiting adult films. These venues happened to be located within the proscribed zone. The theater owners challenged the regulation, filing suit to seek a declaratory judgment against the ordinance.

While *American Mini Theatres* upheld the state's regulation with a 5–4 plurality, *Playtime Theatres* was more decisive at 7–2. The majority in both cases was composed of Chief Justice Burger joined by Justices White, Powell, Rehnquist and Stevens (with Stevens penning *American Mini Theatres* and Rehnquist authoring *Playtime Theatres*). The core dissenters were Justices Brennan and Marshall.

In *Playtime Theatres*, the Court was able to speak in a stronger voice when it declared that the zoning regulation at issue did not have a chilling effect on First Amendment protections. Rehnquist reasoned that Renton's ordinance did not entirely ban adult theaters but merely zoned a distance between such businesses and residential areas. Therefore, the ordinance should be analyzed as a time, place, and manner regulation.[33] Triggering this lower level of scrutiny, the Court could more easily uphold the validity of the zoning law despite the potential to chill certain expression in certain locations. Presuming that the municipality's intentions were unrelated to the suppression of free speech, Rehnquist continued, "The ordinance by its terms is designed to prevent crime, protect the city's retail trade, maintain property values, and generally protec[t] and preserv[e] the quality of neighborhoods, commercial districts, and the quality of urban life, not to suppress the expression of unpopular views."[34] The Court positioned Renton's ordinance as intended to stopgap secondary effects of adult-oriented businesses, which might include depreciation of property values, crime, and transient persons.

Even with the Supreme Court's approval to zone undesirable theaters away from residential districts in *American Mini Theatres* and *Playtime Theatres*, the enforcement of content-based zoning restrictions was still carefully scrutinized. By the late 1970s New York's stylish porno chic had deteriorated into an urban blight. When the Bryant Theatre on Forty-Second Street between Broadway and Sixth Avenue announced it would exhibit adult pictures as a grind house operating from 8:00 a.m. to 2:00 a.m., the city commissioner moved to stop the show, invoking chapter 32 of the administrative code of the city of New York, section B32-26.0, paragraph 5(a)(2). The district court kept the city in check. In *Natco Theatres, Inc. v. Ratner,* Judge Gerald L. Goettel wrote, "The Court has not been unaware of the problems facing New York City in regards to adult movie theatres. The 42nd Street–Times Square Area has become an ugly wormhole in the Big Apple. The Court is cognizant of the blighting effect such establishments have upon neighborhoods, and would applaud innovative approaches developed by the city to deal with such problems. However, such approaches must be consistent with the dictates of the Constitution . . . [and] the Administrative Code of the City of New York [has] gone beyond permissible constitutional boundaries."[35] Despite the decline of the historic and once grand neighborhood, the court invalidated the regulation for its overreaching and chilling effect on constitutionally protected speech.

After watching Times Square transform into a hub for porno playhouses, other areas around the country attempted to control the spread of adult businesses. When a suburb of Chicago moved to ban Studio Eleven Cinema from showing Russ Meyer's *Beneath the Valley of the Ultra-Vixens,* the Seventh Circuit disapproved. In *Entertainment Concepts, Inc., III v. Maciejewski,* Judge William J. Bauer scolded, "The Village of Westmont does not even attempt to advance a legitimate governmental interest to support the zoning ordinance. The Village admits in its brief that it enacted the ordinance to regulate the showing of sexually explicit movies. Since its aim (and the ordinance's language) sweeps beyond unprotected obscenity, the Village's expressed aim is the suppression of speech."[36]

Minneapolis attempted to zone adult theaters into obscurity with a complex regulatory scheme that not only consolidated the regulated uses but also restricted the adult-oriented businesses from operating within five hundred feet of one another. Minneapolis Code of Ordinances section 540.410 was intended to drive adult operations out of business, and in *Alexander v. City of Minneapolis* the court ruled the regulations unconstitutional.[37]

Unlike these schemes, one Michigan town's zoning was able to pass muster. In 1973 the city of Warren enacted zoning ordinance section 14.02(C) for the purpose of minimizing urban blight and the adverse impact of adult-entertainment uses. The district court parsed the legislative act and approved provisions that affected zoning of adult cinemas. The ordinance was challenged in *15192 Thirteen Mile Road, Inc. v. City of Warren.* "While it would be unconstitutional for a municipality to zone adult uses into swamps, warehouses, or shipyards, where there are few access roads and where the locations are poorly lit and perhaps unsafe . . . the evidence in the case does not show a deliberate attempt to zone adult uses into a set of commercially impracticable sites. The fact that a plaintiff may not be able to afford renovation or construction costs does not persuade the Court that Ordinance 14.02(C) is invalid. For although Warren may not constitutionally act to ensure the commercial failure of adult uses, it is not required to ensure their success."[38] Distinguishing the ordinances of Westmont in *Maciejewski* from Warren in *15192 Thirteen Mile Road*, a rule emerged: blatant attempts to ban adult businesses through the ruse of a zoning scheme would be disallowed. However, the systematic regulation of these adult businesses was permitted, notwithstanding potential hardships that may emerge as byproducts of the regulations.

American Mini Theatres and *Playtime Theatres* demonstrated that content of speech could be a valid classification underlying zoning laws. In subsequent cases courts would balance a municipality's desire to maintain neighborhood standards with constitutional protections, slapping down egregiously overreaching ordinances. The integrity of a community's health, safety, and welfare and the control of urban blight and proximity to residential areas were valid concerns to support zoning, despite the chilling effect on free expression. But what if a theater exhibited an occasional adult film? What if a theater exhibited an X-rated film for a single showing?

An occasional X-rated film or an annual festival would not yield the secondary effects of adult-oriented businesses that zoning laws were intended to control. A single showing of *Last Tango in Paris* on a neighborhood screen would not cause a depreciation of property values. An annual festival that included a one-night engagement of *Midnight Cowboy* or *A Clockwork Orange* would be unlikely to affect safety in a local community. Could the rationale supporting zoning laws be focused on a single showing?

The city of Covina, California, attempted to make this argument. In 1977 a neighborhood art house announced a series of French pictures that had been marked with the MPAA's scarlet letter, X. The films at the center of this controversy starred Sylvia Kristel (1952–2012) as Emmanuelle. *Emmanuelle* had been a successful franchise of softcore erotica that featured more heavy breathing and long languorous shots of the ingénue's lithe figure in the nude than of explicit acts. The first installment, simply titled *Emmanuelle* (1974), was set in Bangkok. The beautiful young model is a student in the art of love, learning from her older husband as well as a revolving bedroom door of extramarital affairs. The sequel relocated Emmanuelle, her husband, and their activities—this time focusing on Sapphic studies—to Hong Kong in *Emmanuelle: L'antivierge* (*Emmanuelle II* or *The Joys of a Woman*, 1975).

The Covina cinema scheduled a limited showing of *Emmanuelle* and *Joys of a Woman*. The theater announced that aside from this programming, no more X-rated films would be shown at the venue.[39] The exhibitor was an upscale cinematheque catering to film buffs and movie lovers—not to the raincoaters that characterized urban blight. Nevertheless township authorities attempted to zone the theater out of its location.

The court recognized Covina's overreach. In *Pringle v. City of Covina* (1981), Judge Robert D. Potter opined that the regulation

> could not be justified by the city's interest in preserving the character of its neighborhoods. . . . While defendant certainly has an important and substantial interest in maintaining the stability of its neighborhoods, we cannot conclude that defendant could reasonably have determined that a single showing of a sexually explicit film produces adverse secondary effect[s] destructive of the general quality of life in the neighborhood. . . . Indeed, we would have to conclude that the ordinance was not rationally tailored to support its asserted purpose as a necessary zoning regulation to prevent neighborhood blight but was instead a misconceived attempt directly to regulate content of expression by using the power to zone as a pretext for suppressing expression.[40]

The court construed the statute to preserve its validity: it could be enforced against theaters that usually, habitually, and customarily exhibited such films. Hence, "the ordinance cannot be enforced against the Cinema unless, contrary to its representations and previous policy, the Cinema presents a preponderance of films in which the dominant theme is the depiction of the ordinance's enumerated sexual activities."[41] Zoning could not be used to banish theaters that exhibited the occasional adult film. Or could it?

The most recent statement came down from the Supreme Court of New Mexico in *City of Albuquerque v. Pangaea Cinema*. The Guild (Pangaea) Cinema is an independent theater located in Albuquerque's Nob Hill neighborhood near the University of New Mexico. In 2007 the Guild scheduled a weekend festival of erotic films called "Pornotopia." Attempting to block the event, the city called on zoning laws that prohibited public screenings of adult films outside specified areas.[42] The Guild conceded the scheduled films featured explicit sex but challenged the validity of the ordinance.

Event organizers claimed the programming was artistic and educational, despite titles such as *Couch Surfers: Trans Men in Action*. The city countered,

Sylvia Kristel distracts her husband, played by Umberto Orcini, in the second installment, originally titled *Emmanuelle: L'antivierge* (1975).

———

Emmanuelle proved she was open for suggestion in *Emmanuelle: The Joys of a Woman* (1975).

———

Dutch actress Sylvia Kristel became a softcore sex symbol with *Emmanuelle* (1974).

———

citing precedent that "zoning power over adult amusement establishments . . . are not regulating the content of the entertainment . . . but rather the negative secondary effects that such adult material produces in the surrounding community, such as crime and sex offenses."[43] The theater responded that secondary effects such as prostitution, crime, and depreciation of property values should not be an issue for a festival occurring once a year.[44]

Noting that the code did not ban adult establishments entirely, the court concluded the law was content neutral. Since content was not the subject of the regulation, the less demanding time-place-manner analysis was applied. Moving through its analysis the court found the zoning law a valid exercise of police power tailored to protect the significant interest of combating negative secondary effects of adult entertainment.[45]

Pangaea appealed and a final decision came down in 2013. New Mexico's Supreme Court recognized that cities were allowed to impose different zoning requirements on adult theaters than mainstream theaters, per *American Mini Theatres* and *Playtime Theatres*. However, the court was also persuaded by the Ninth Circuit and California's state court, which had found it unconstitutional to place zoning restrictions on businesses that occasionally feature adult entertainment.[46]

The prior decision was reversed, allowing Pornotopia to proceed. New Mexico's highest court reasoned, "If the City Council wishes to expand the ordinance so that rare, occasional, or incidental exhibitions of adult material will render a business an 'adult amusement establishment,' it must produce some evidence linking these occasional showings to negative secondary effects."[47] Within two months of the decision, on November 1, 2013, the Guild presented a five-film festival that included *Vulvalicious, Teach Me, Beat Me,* and *Rock Hard Gay Love.* Pornotopia has continued as a yearly event.

Municipalities struggled to regulate availability and control public exhibition of obscene materials. As First Amendment rights expanded, several techniques attempted to avoid the strict scrutiny of speech issues. By construing red light abatement statutes broadly enough to reach theaters, several states shuttered adult entertainment establishments. This technique was disfavored. Nuisance statutes could more easily reach unwanted theaters by focusing on negative secondary effects. But nuisance statutes were limited, as *Pangaea Cinema* demonstrated: an annual festival could not be reined in as a nuisance based on secondary effects alone. But could a monthly festival or a weekly program? These questions remain unanswered as the balance between speech and regulation continues on a region-by-region, case-by-case basis.

PART IV

Censorship Today

18

IS CENSORSHIP NECESSARY?

—

The story of film and the First Amendment charts a steady course toward creative freedom. Within one hundred years, motion pictures developed from an amusement into an art form and from a revolutionary technology into an industrially produced mass media. More accessible to large audiences and more powerful in delivering a message than any previous medium, the movies transcended their origins as entertainment to become a cultural experience.

During the first decade of the twentieth century a web of local and regional censors crisscrossed the country. These regulators intended to protect the morals of their communities, but the effect of their activism created a patchwork of inconsistent standards. Harry Aitken of the Mutual Film Corporation rose to challenge the state's authority to censor and delay his films. Aitken was less of a First Amendment warrior than a practical businessman. As he saw it, regional censorship held up his company's timely newsreels. By 1915 Aitken had an answer, but it wasn't the result he had hoped for. The Supreme Court unanimously held that motion pictures did not qualify for First Amendment protections. The Court's reasoning hinged on two points. First, "the exhibition of moving pictures is a business, pure and simple, originated and conducted for profit." States had long regulated and citizens had long accepted standards governing stage productions, parades, and circuses.

Second, the Court saw films as "vivid, useful and entertaining no doubt, but . . . capable of evil, having power for it, the greater because of their attractiveness and manner of exhibition."[1] Because the silver screen transfixed audiences with a hypnotic power unlike any other medium of expression, the Court found it well within the state's rights to regulate.

With a legal framework in place to support state censorship, the film industry rethought its approach. Motion picture producers and distributors turned to self-regulation in an effort to avert governmental interference. Studio executives appointed Will Hays to lead the effort. The initial solution proposed by the Hays office was a list of Don'ts and Be Carefuls for sensitive on-screen subjects. Soon a production code was hammered out; however, enforcement was lax until Joseph Breen took control of the PCA in June 1934. Under Breen, gangster dramas like *Scarface* were squelched and cunning sexual innuendoes from the likes of Mae West were silenced. Hollywood filmmakers were forced to convey naughty moments with elliptical references: a tight embrace, a fade to black, a train going through a tunnel.

On the one hand the production code limited the subject matter and maturity of the movies; on the other hand the code sought to forestall state censorship. By joining the MPAA, studios sacrificed autonomy hoping to avoid governmental regulators. In exchange the MPAA lobbied in Washington to maintain the film industry's independence. This symbiotic relationship helped studios position their films as safe investments for financiers. Challenges to the status quo would not come from within the studio system: it was up to independent and international filmmakers to fight the battle for film's First Amendment rights.

The showdown arrived in 1952. Roberto Rossellini's *The Miracle* played in Italy without incident, but once it arrived in the United States censors sharpened their scissors. New York's board of regents banned the picture, but domestic distributor Joseph Burstyn championed the short film up to the Supreme Court. In a verdict that was impossible to predict, the Court reversed its long-held position. Thirty-seven years after excluding film from the constitutional guarantees of free speech, the *Miracle* decision brought movies under the First Amendment. Wrote the Court, "It cannot be doubted that motion pictures are a significant medium for the communication of ideas. Their importance as an organ of public opinion is not lessened by the fact that they are designed to entertain as well as to inform. . . . That the production, distribution, and exhibition of motion pictures is a large-scale business conducted for private profit does not prevent motion pictures from being a form of expression whose liberty is safeguarded by the First Amendment."[2]

Burstyn scratched out a small safe harbor for film under the First Amendment. By the end of the decade motion pictures had been accepted as legitimate speech protected under the First Amendment. The censors had one remaining cause of action: obscenity.

But how would the courts measure obscenity? The question was answered in *Jacobellis*, which applied *Roth* to motion pictures. As the standard evolved from *Roth* to *Memoirs* to *Miller*, so would the analysis for film. Ultimately, "all ideas having even the slightest redeeming social importance—unorthodox ideas, controversial ideas, even ideas hateful to the prevailing climate of opinion—have the full protection of the [First Amendment] guarantees."[3]

But even *Miller* was not a stationary standard. The test was refined in subsequent decisions. In the following term, the Court clarified "community standards" in *Hamling v. United States* (1974). *Hamling* involved the mailing of a brochure deemed obscene; the case was heard by the Ninth Circuit and affirmed by the Supreme Court. Justice Rehnquist opined that standards should be determined by the community where the jury was selected.[4] This took the test one step further away from Brennan's direction to judge obscenity by a national standard.

Three years after *Hamling* the Court revisited *Miller* in *Ward v. Illinois* (1977). In this case, Wesley Ward was charged with distributing two allegedly obscene publications: *Bizarre World* and *Illustrated Case Histories, a Study of Sado-Masochism*. The publisher argued that since the S&M-themed content was not *specifically* prohibited by the obscenity ordinance, it should be permitted. Justice White speaking for a slim 5–4 majority held that an obscenity statute was not required to exhaustively enumerate the list of materials deemed offensive.[5] White continued to mull over the statutory construction of obscenity ordinances in *Brockett v. Spokane Arcades, Inc* (1985). Here, the "prurient interest" requirement became the focus. A Washington State statute declared that any place where lewd films were publicly exhibited as a regular course of business could be deemed a moral nuisance. The statute defined lewd and prurient matter as "that which incites lasciviousness or lust." Spokane Arcades sold and showed sexually explicit books and movies: inciting lasciviousness or lust was their core business. The smut purveyor challenged the statute on First Amendment grounds and claimed the ordinance was unconstitutionally overbroad. Spokane Arcades argued that by enumerating "lust" the law reached material that may arouse normal, healthy, natural sexual interests. The Court agreed, severing the overbroad provision "lust" and sending the case back to the state for reconsideration.[6]

After tweaking the first two prongs of *Miller*, the Court turned to the third factor. The question of whether a work was devoid of serious literary, artistic, political, or scientific value had always been a slippery criterion. *Pope v. Illinois* (1987) helped to clarify this step of the obscenity test. In this case, attendants at a Rockford, Illinois, adult bookstore sold allegedly obscene magazines to undercover law enforcement officers. Defendants claimed that *value* should be judged according to community standards—in which they might not be obscene. The Court disagreed—once again in a decision penned by Justice White—and clarified that value should be determined on an objective standard: "There is no suggestion in our cases that the question of the value of an allegedly obscene work is to be determined by reference to community standards. . . . The proper inquiry is not whether an ordinary member of any given community would find serious literary, artistic, political, or scientific value in allegedly obscene material, but whether a reasonable person would find such value in the material, taken as a whole."[7] By 1987 the Court completed its tour of the *Miller* standard, refining the cogs in the mechanism by which obscenity would be judged.

While the Court had recalibrated its test for obscenity, municipal regulators around the country were less open to change. The first wave of censors was composed of social activists rallying to rid their communities of filth. Anthony Comstock, founder of the New York Society for the Suppression of Vice and special agent for the Post Office Department, believed obscenity was the greatest threat to youth and society. He lobbied Congress to enact what would become known as the Comstock Law in 1873, which made it illegal to send any obscene, lewd, and lascivious materials, including contraceptive devices and information on abortion, through the Postal Service.[8] Mayor George McClellan Jr. attempted to shutter New York's nickelodeons in 1908 to protect the health, safety, welfare, and morals of his city. State censors saw themselves as crusaders for their cause. Maj. M. L. C. Funkhouser was the moral custodian for Chicago from 1907 to 1918. Dr. Ellis Oberholtzer was protector of Pennsylvania from 1915 to 1921. Susannah Warfield supervised Ohio's board of censors from 1922 to 1954. Lloyd T. Binford defended Tennessee's values from 1928 to 1955.

The second wave of censors may have been slightly more reasonable. Christine Smith's control of cinema in Atlanta could be unpredictably levelheaded during her two-decade term, 1945–1964.[9] Mrs. Russell Wagers, Lollie Whitehead, and Margaret K. Gregory began their tenures as Virginia's regents in 1949 and remained until the board was defunded in 1966.[10] Helen Tingley served as Maryland's movie czar from 1943–1948, her short term dominated by Howard Hughes's unyielding campaign to clear *The Outlaw*.[11] Damon Huskey, the high sheriff of Rutherford County, North Carolina, from 1958–1986, was the most militant of the second wave, banning all but G-rated films in his jurisdiction.[12]

Mary Avara joined the Maryland board in 1960 and remained active until her post was decommissioned in 1981. Even as the office closed, Avara insisted that censors played an important role in the cultural well-being of the community. Avara relished her reputation, appearing on Johnny Carson, Merv Griffin, and Dick Cavett, but the *Baltimore Sun* reported that her best performance was before the Maryland Senate. Defending her department's budget, "she would fling her arms toward the heavens, point her fingers at the lawmakers like some avenging angel, and then unleash a tirade against pornography. 'Do you like filth? . . . Do you like violence? Do you want your children to see this?'"[13] The final film to pass through Avara's office was *For Your Eyes Only* (1981); but by that time her board had long been a relic from an earlier era of film history.

Although Avara's position as state censor was discontinued, her motivating question remained relevant. Is censorship necessary?

In *Jacobellis*, Ohio's Supreme Court articulated why it felt censorship was important. "History is replete with examples of nations that lost positions of eminence in the world and whose citizens lost their freedom due to decay of their moral fiber resulting in degeneracy and depravity. Legislative bodies must continue to pass laws which attempt to protect the morality of the people from themselves and from their own weaknesses."[14] By contrast, New Jersey's court stated in *UA New Jersey Theatres* that "while the State has an interest in and may prevent the dissemination of material deemed harmful to children, that interest does not justify a total suppression of such material, for to do so would reduce the adult population to seeing and reading only what is fit for children."[15] Each position presents a valid argument.

Certain materials are more easily outlawed. Child pornography has an outlier status that is difficult if not impossible to dispute. In 1982 the Supreme Court unanimously ruled in *New York v. Ferber* that the First Amendment did not forbid states from banning the sale of materials depicting children engaged in sexual activity. The motivation was protection of children. But

Ferber left a loophole for would-be child pornographers: "If it were necessary for literary or artistic value, a person over the statutory age who perhaps
looked younger could be utilized."[16]

Congress intended to close this loophole with the Child Pornography Prevention Act of 1996 (CPPA). The act addressed content that simulated child
pornography either by using adults who look like minors or by rendering
with digital effects.[17] While *Ferber's* main focus was protecting children, the
CPPA addressed consumers of this prohibited material.

The Court shot the CPPA down in *Ashcroft v. Free Speech Coalition*. The act
was deemed overbroad since it restricted works of historic and artistic value.
Wrote Justice Kennedy, the themes of

> teenage sexual activity and the sexual abuse of children have inspired
> countless literary works. William Shakespeare created the most famous
> pair of teenage lovers, one of whom is just 13 years of age. . . . Contem-
> porary movies pursue similar themes. Last year's Academy Awards fea-
> tured the movie, *Traffic*, which . . . portrays a teenager, identified as a 16
> year-old, who becomes addicted to drugs. The viewer sees the degrada-
> tion of her addiction, which in the end leads her to a filthy room to trade
> sex for drugs. The year before, *American Beauty* won the Academy Award
> for Best Picture. . . . In the course of the movie, a teenage girl engages in
> sexual relations with her teenage boyfriend, and another yields herself to
> the gratification of a middle-aged man.[18]

The High Court was reluctant to regulate content that played to perversions
but avoided actual child endangerment.

Another area concerned with protecting innocent victims is animal cruelty. Should depictions of deliberate pain and inhumane treatment of animals
be protected as free expression, or is there a valid interest in excluding such
works from the First Amendment?

Hollywood has a long history of improper treatment of animals. Reports
that as many as one hundred horses had died during the production of *Ben-
Hur* (1925) were hushed by MGM.[19] Westerns, particularly low-budget,
quickly produced B-movie sagebrush soaps, made use of trip wires, pitfalls,
and chutes to make horses fall or coerced the animals into dangerous stunts.
In 1940 the American Humane Association (AHA) objected to these practices, but enforcement of ethical treatment of animals was haphazard until
the 1980s. The AHA's greater involvement was triggered in part by two inci-
dents: the on-camera slaying of a water buffalo in *Apocalypse Now* (1979) and

the accidental killing of a horse during a choreographed explosion in *Heaven's Gate* (1980). After these instances of intentional and negligent cruelty, the AHA developed guidelines and was permitted access to monitor treatment of animals on unionized productions.

These measures of self-enforcement only applied to unionized pictures. More recently, two independent productions prompted renewed inquiry into animal cruelty. One of these events was a viral video, the other an underground fetish film.

In March 2008 a seventeen-second video was posted to YouTube depicting a U.S. marine in combat gear in Iraq. He stands on a desert precipice holding a white and brown puppy by the scruff of its neck. He then hurls the pup off the cliff. The video lit up the web with comments of disbelief and disgust. Three months later reports surfaced that the soldiers involved had been disciplined and discharged.[20] The Internet can harbor sinister sexual predators, but the destruction of a puppy united a virtual lynch mob.

The Marine Corps handled the puppy incident internally, dispensing penalties swiftly and with little publicity. The second incident was even more outrageous and rose to the Supreme Court. The issue surrounded production and distribution of extreme fetish films known as "crush videos." Chief Justice Roberts explained, "Such videos feature the intentional torture and killing of helpless animals, including cats, dogs, monkeys, mice, and hamsters. . . . Crush videos often depict women slowly crushing animals to death with their bare feet or while wearing high heeled shoes, sometimes while talking to the animals in a kind of dominatrix patter over [t]he cries and squeals of the animals, [who are] obviously in great pain. Apparently these depictions appeal to persons with a very specific sexual fetish who find them sexually arousing or otherwise exciting."[21] The Supreme Court granted certiorari to determine whether depictions of animal cruelty are categorically unprotected by the First Amendment in *United States v. Stevens*.

Writing for an 8–1 majority (Alito dissenting), Chief Justice Roberts viewed the issue from a historical perspective. "The prohibition of animal cruelty itself has a long history in American law, starting with the early settlement of the Colonies . . . ('No man shall exercise any Tirranny or Crueltie towards any bruite Creature which are usuallie kept for man's use'). But we are unaware of any similar tradition excluding depictions of animal cruelty from the freedom of speech codified in the First Amendment."[22] The state drew analogies between *Stevens* and *Ferber*: that animal cruelty, like child pornography, is so heinous a crime that depictions should be excluded from constitutional protections.

This strategy failed. The Court saw *Ferber* as a special exception based on policy and "cannot be taken as establishing a freewheeling authority to declare new categories of speech outside the scope of the First Amendment."[23] Defendant Robert J. Stevens was a video producer who specialized in pitbull-fighting films. He claimed to have not participated in the dogfights but merely videotaped the events: he would not have been guilty of the underlying crime of animal cruelty but only of producing depictions of the event. Under the Court's reasoning, the filmmaker was able to prevail on his free speech claims.

Justice Alito stood as the lone dissenter, arguing for the constitutionality of a law that established a criminal penalty for anyone who knowingly creates, sells, or possesses a depiction of animal cruelty if done for commercial gain.[24] Alito drew on the policies underlying *Ferber*, namely the protection of innocents, the elimination of a distribution network for such materials, and the fact that the harm caused by the criminal acts depicted greatly outweighed any value. Hence, Alito reasoned, the regulation at issue in *Stevens*, if properly interpreted, could be applied to crush videos and dogfighting films without criminalizing hunting films or scientific studies.

After the Court declined to carve out a new exception for animal cruelty, the federal government responded by enacting the Animal Crush Video Prohibition Act of 2010.[25]

Hate speech has also posed a challenge for free speech advocates: should expression that is calculated to harm and aims to hurt be protected? In the United Kingdom the Public Order Act of 1986 criminalized expression that was threatening or abusive and intended to stir up racial hatred.[26] France's hate speech legislation derives from the Press Law of 1881, section 24. Similarly, Australia, Canada, Denmark, Germany, India, the Netherlands, New Zealand, and South Africa are among the many nations that have prohibited hate speech.[27] In the United States hate speech falls within constitutionally protected guarantees of the First Amendment.[28]

While hate speech is protected, certain films have drawn fire for perceived messages of prejudice. When Martin Scorsese's *The Last Temptation of Christ* (1988) was released, protesters surrounded playhouses—over five hundred people assembled outside New York's Ziegfeld Theater.[29] In a throwback to earlier decades, Florida's Escambia County banned the film, but district court judge Roger Vinson enjoined the ban. Vinson commented that such censorship "was unconstitutional and that red flags should run up whenever government tried to violate the rights of citizens."[30]

Jewish groups expressed anger over Mel Gibson's *The Passion of the Christ* (2004), particularly the characterization of Jewish high priest Caiaphas. Much of this reaction was based on the director's outspoken anti-Semitic personal views. Other than making headlines during a news cycle, little action resulted.[31]

Christians objected to *The Last Temptation* and Jews criticized *The Passion*, but it was the international community of Islam that had the most incendiary reaction when they objected to a featurette entitled *Innocence of Muslims* (2012).

After a September 11, 2012, attack on the Libyan consulate, the U.S. State Department inaccurately cited an amateur video as a possible cause. *Innocence of Muslims* was a crudely made fourteen-minute-long video posted to YouTube in July 2012. With the most amateur production values, an absurd script, and wince-worthy acting, the video was ignored until it became a convenient scapegoat. It is likely that the featurette was *intended* as hate speech: Mohammad is presented as lascivious, aggressively warlike, and buffoonishly comic. The filmmaker, Coptic Christian Mark Basseley Youssef, a.k.a. Nakoula Basseley Nakoula, posed as an Israeli-American; in interviews he claimed Jewish donors had funded the video. This may have been a strategic effort to pin the film's anti-Islam sentiments on Jews, playing two Copt enemies—Jews and Muslims—off against each other in a region all too easy to ignite. The fact that the film was produced in Los Angeles and initially distributed on YouTube, an American company, served to reinforce the view of a direct attack on Islam. Clips of *Innocence of Muslims* were rebroadcast on the Egyptian Al-Nas television station and quickly became a magnet for disinformation.

Innocence of Muslims would become a historical footnote after the swirl of controversy and an extended news cycle. But the short video contributed an interesting sideshow to film-legal history. After appearing in *Innocence*, Cindy Lee Garcia received death threats. She brought suit to cease distribution of the video. In *Garcia v. Google, Inc.* the Ninth Circuit ruled in her favor with a novel theory that the actress had a protectable interest in her performance. Chief Judge Alex Kozinski viewed the balance of equities in Garcia's favor: the producer misrepresented the content of the film, no employment contract had been signed, and the threats were credible. *Innocence* was banned; YouTube and Google were ordered to cease distributing the video. Youssef's hate-instilled speech was curtailed under an innovative theory of copyright infringement. Google pushed for a rehearing, and the Ninth Court reconvened en banc. This time the eleven-judge panel announced on May 18, 2015, that Google had the right to post the *Innocence* video. The takedown order had been in error. Wrote Judge Margaret McKeown, "In this case, a heartfelt plea for personal protection is juxtaposed with the limits of copyright law and fundamental principles of free speech. The appeal teaches a simple lesson—a weak copyright claim cannot justify censorship in the guise of authorship."[32]

Innocence of Muslims was a special situation, but it also raises the issue of whether there *should* be state regulations on hate speech in the United States. Regulations on hate speech would bring America into alignment with other democracies that do ban such speech.

Despite the ugly effects of hate speech, extreme violence, and animal cruelty, it would be inconsistent with the ideals of the First Amendment to ban such communications. The dogfight promoter may be prosecuted but not the dogfight filmmaker. The price of broad First Amendment rights is tolerance of ignorant, offensive, and aggressive remarks.

19

THE POLITICS OF PROFANITY

———

As technology made distribution of seamy materials easier, sexually explicit content once relegated to backrooms, adult bookstores, and stag parties became accessible to wider audiences. Within a brief period of time explicit, once-illicit motion pictures became tolerated and even common. The availability of adult materials pushed the First Amendment to its limit and revealed the politics of profanity.

As mainstream audiences discovered blue movies, moral guardians found renewed motivation. The revived reform movement was politically charged, pitting proregulation believers against First Amendment advocates. Political regimes either went after smut or turned a blind eye as obscenity infiltrated everyday life in America.

The emergence of the pornography industry in America can be dated to the early 1970s. The earliest aboveground theatrical exhibition of adult films unspooled in *Mona: The Virgin Nymph* (1970) and *Boys in the Sand* (1971). X-rated entertainment gained ground with the one, two, three punches *Deep Throat* (1972), *Behind the Green Door* (1972), and *The Devil in Miss Jones* (1973). This taboo triumvirate was hailed—or reviled—as the "porno chic."

Another turning point occurred with Jim Buckley's *Debbie Does Dallas* (1978). *Debbie* was wildly popular, featuring Bambi Woods, a girl-next-door type, in the recognizable Dallas Cowboys cheerleader uniform.[1] The film was an important historical marker, both serving as the end point of the porno chic era and signaling hardcore's ascendance in home media.

Debbie Does Dallas was one of the first adult films to become widely available on video, meeting with phenomenal success in the new medium. The title was named "most popular adult product" by the Video Software Dealers Association for several years running—a perennial favorite that has been called one of the highest-grossing pornographic films of all time by the *New York Times*.[2] Although it won awards and made money on home video, *Debbie* met resistance in the theatrical market. The film was banned as obscenity on theater screens in Alabama, Florida, and Texas.[3]

As the porn industry penetrated the mainstream consumer home video marketplace, a counterbalancing force gathered strength on the side of state regulation. The federal government's initial attempt to justify more stringent regulations was stymied by its own study. Released in September 1970, the report of the Commission on Obscenity and Pornography delivered unanticipated results, finding that "the availability of explicit sexual materials is . . . not one of the important influences on sexual morality."[4] President Nixon distanced himself, announcing on October 24, 1970, "I have evaluated that report and categorically reject its morally bankrupt conclusions and major recommendations. So long as I am in the White House, there will be no relaxation of the national effort to control and eliminate smut from our national life. . . . The Commission on Pornography and Obscenity [sic] has performed a disservice, and I totally reject its report."[5]

The pendulum swung away from Nixon's socially conservative stance as Carter took office in 1977. Obscenity prosecutions found less favor. Two representative cases came down in the Texas Court of Criminal Appeals in 1980: *Berg v. State* and *Keller v. State*. These cases, which dealt with the distribution of allegedly obscene films theatrically and via home video, were setbacks for the state.

In *Berg* a theater owner was convicted for commercially exhibiting obscene materials.[6] Berg had programmed a double feature at the Trail Drive-In that included a film entitled *Deviates in Love* (1979). The jury found the film obscene and assessed punishment at 180 days in the county jail and a fine of $1,000. Berg appealed. At issue was the measure of contemporary community standards. A witness for the defense proffered evidence of comparable materials purchased in the Dallas–Fort Worth area to demonstrate contemporary community standards. The trial court excluded the ten items from evidence, reasoning that "such materials were not purchased close enough in time or distance to the event."[7] The decision was overturned on appeal; it was a reversible error to exclude such evidence. Judge Samuel Houston Clinton Jr. concluded, "An average jury could have reasonably found the State's case significantly less persuasive had these exhibits been admitted."[8]

Five months later Texas considered *Keller v. State*. Once again the cause of action was the commercial distribution of obscenity, but here the material at issue was the sale of a Swedish erotica home video entitled *Oversexed Secretary* (1979). Keller was convicted, sentenced to thirty days in the county jail, and fined $500. At trial, defense attempted to introduce evidence that *Deep Throat* had been playing theatrically in Houston continuously for four years, selling over 350,000 tickets. The evidence was excluded. Once again the decision was reversed. Judge Wendell A. Odom opined, "The statistical evidence of community patronage of the movie *Deep Throat* was offered as circumstantial evidence of contemporary community standards. Widespread attendance indicates community acceptance. We find such evidence was legally relevant to the issue."[9] Statistical evidence concerning the number of people patronizing *Deep Throat* in nearby Houston was probative of community standards and should not have been excluded.

By 1980 pornography had moved toward the mainstream, even in socially conservative Southern states like Texas. Cities tolerated and many viewers patronized films such as *Deep Throat* at theaters and watched dirty videotapes in their homes. Carter's term drew to a close, and the pendulum swung once again as Reagan took office in 1981.

Under President Reagan the home video revolution reached new heights. The medium witnessed massive growth in all areas, but adult titles in particular flew off the shelves. As emphasis shifted away from theatrically released adult films, the number of sexually explicit videotapes skyrocketed from 400 new releases in 1983 to 1,600 in 1985. Revenues from the sales of X-rated titles nearly doubled from $225 million in 1983 to $425 million in 1986.[10] These statistics moved the regime to take action. One month into his second term, Reagan commissioned the Attorney General's Report on Pornography, or as it became familiarly known, the Meese Report.

Released in 1986, the Meese Report's findings were diametrically opposed to those of the Commission on Obscenity and Pornography sixteen years earlier. The Meese Report found that erotic materials had a negative effect on individuals and communities and were a significant cause of crime, delinquency, sexual deviance, and emotional disturbance. Pornographic materials, the report stated, could have an accessory role in child abuse, violence against women, and familial breakdown. Finally, the report also made a connection between organized crime and the porn industry—a claim far less tenuous than the others. The report recommended intensified enforcement of existing regulations.

The Department of Justice looked for a case to reinforce the Meese Report's findings. In 1987 federal prosecutors brought suit against the owners and an employee of a chain of adult entertainment stores in *United States v. Pryba*.[11] The Prybas' Virginia-based franchise sold books and videos as well as offered peep booths. The jury found several videotapes obscene, including *She-Male Confidential: Bizarre Encounter 9* (1985), *The Girls of the A-Team* (1985), *Wet Shots* (1981), and *The Punishment of Anne* (1975).

Three years earlier, in 1984, obscenity had been added to the schedule of underlying crimes on which a federal prosecution under the Racketeer Influenced and Corrupt Organizations Act (RICO) could be based. *Pryba* was the first case brought under RICO in which the racketeering activity charges were based entirely on obscenity crimes.[12] The defendants were found guilty and sentenced to time ranging from ten years' imprisonment to three years' probation.[13] The Fourth Circuit upheld the convictions and the Prybas appealed. The Bush administration urged the Supreme Court to deny certiorari, which they did.[14] Justice White wrote a rare dissent to the denial of certiorari.[15] The most controversial aspect of the *Pryba* case was the penalty meted out to the corporate entity: all assets—including inventory, bank accounts, automobiles, and office furniture—were seized.[16] In their appeal the Prybas claimed that such forfeiture of a businesses engaged in constitutionally protected activities (i.e., the distribution of materials not found to be obscene) amounted to a prior restraint of speech. While the obscene materials could be proscribed, the Prybas argued that the extreme penalty offended the principles of the First Amendment as a de facto ban on further communications. The Supreme Court did not agree.

As the legal battle continued on the issue of obscenity projected on theater screens and distributed via videotape, a new medium was emerging: the Internet. By 1993 Netscape introduced a user-friendly web browser that enabled the technology to reach a wide audience. The first generation of web entrepreneurs launched visionary services, but the real prime movers were pornographers.

While she was probably not the first to post naughty pictures online, Danni Ashe, a former stripper and softcore video performer, put a comely face on Internet porn. Ashe began posting images on Usenet bulletin boards in 1994; within a year she launched a website called Danni's Hard Drive. The *Wall Street Journal* profiled Ashe, detailing how her move to cyberspace had raised her earnings from $1,500 to $15,000 a month. Within two years her site boasted over seventeen thousand members bringing in over $2 million in revenue.[17]

Despite the publicized cyberporn phenomenon and a handful of forward-thinking companies, most commercial interests struggled for traction on the web. In 1996—in an opinion that is difficult to comprehend today—Pennsylvania Judge Dolores Korman Sloviter wrote, "The Internet is not exclusively, or even primarily, a means of commercial communication. Many commercial entities maintain web sites to inform potential consumers about their goods and services, or to solicit purchases, but many other[s] exist solely for dissemination of non-commercial information."[18] That situation would change.

By 1998 the advent of secured servers allowed for online credit-card billing.[19] With new technology and a system for secured transactions in place, dirty words and filthy pictures could reach an ever-growing home-computing audience that had naughty curiosities, voracious appetites, and valid credit cards.

The Clinton regime allowed the Internet to develop. Inheriting forty-two federal obscenity prosecutions from the Reagan and Bush administrations, Clinton shifted priorities. By 1997 only six prosecutions of obscenity remained on the docket.[20] Porn helped fuel an economic boom. Smut producers were important innovators on the web, creating content as well as systems to bill, secure, and track payments online. The Clinton administration's laissez-faire attitude encouraged growth in the new medium. While obscenity prosecutions slowed, the Department of Justice did address concerns caused by the content, the quantity, and the accessibility of porn on the newly connected World Wide Web.

The response from Congress, embodied in Title V of the Telecommunications Act of 1996, was controversial from inception. The Communications Decency Act (CDA) was intended as a regulation analogous to the FCC's oversight of broadcasters. On February 8, 1996, immediately after the president signed the CDA into law, twenty plaintiffs filed suit to challenge the statute. A week later Pennsylvania district court judge Ronald L. Buckwalter entered a temporary restraining order against enforcement of the CDA.[21] Attorney General Janet Reno appealed the decision up to the Supreme Court. In *Reno v. ACLU* the first ruling on the Internet was handed down in a unanimous decision.

The Supreme Court struck down the government's attempt to regulate the web. At issue were two provisions intended to protect minors from indecent communications. Writing for the Court, Justice Stevens agreed with Buckwalter's conclusion that the statute's prohibitions of indecent and offensive communications "were so vague that criminal enforcement of either section would violate the fundamental constitutional principle of simple fairness and the specific protections of the First and Fifth Amendments."[22]

The government's argument relied on *Ginsburg*, *Pacifica*, and *Playtime Theatres*. In *Ginsburg*, the Court upheld the constitutionality of a New York statute that prohibited selling material to minors that would be considered obscene to them even if not obscene to adults (e.g., "nudie magazines"). *Pacifica*, the George Carlin "Filthy Words" case, maintained the state's authority to regulate broadcast media based on accessibility to young audiences. In *Playtime Theatres*, a zoning ordinance that blocked adult theaters from residential neighborhoods was upheld. Taken together, the state's argument was that the CDA was merely cyber-zoning on the Internet to protect minors from harmful, offensive, or age-inappropriate materials.

The attorney general also raised a new argument: "The Government asserts that—in addition to its interest in protecting children—its equally significant interest in fostering the growth of the Internet provides an independent basis for upholding the constitutionality of the CDA. . . . [T]he unregulated availability of indecent and patently offensive material on the Internet is driving countless citizens away from the medium because of the risk of exposing themselves or their children to harmful material." This was one step too far; Stevens continued, "We find this argument singularly unpersuasive."[23] The concern that the CDA would abridge protective speech carried the day. In striking down the Internet regulation, the Court dealt a blow to the DOJ's war on obscenity.

The war on obscenity continued as the government rebounded to defend the Child Pornography Prevention Act of 1996 (CPPA). The CPPA addressed virtual child pornography by prohibiting any sexually explicit depiction that "appears to be" of a minor or that is distributed or advertised in such a manner as to "convey the impression" that the depiction portrays a minor. The state's argument prevailed in the First, Fourth, Fifth, and Eleventh Circuits, covering wide swaths of the country, but suffered a setback when the influential Ninth found the law overbroad.[24] Judge Donald W. Molloy wrote, "We hold that the First Amendment prohibits Congress from enacting a statute that makes criminal the generation of images of fictitious children engaged in imaginary but explicit sexual conduct."[25] Based on this jurisdictional split the Supreme Court granted certiorari.

The war on obscenity had been deprioritized during the Clinton years and hindered by *Reno v. ACLU* and *Free Speech Coalition v. Reno*. However, when George W. Bush took office in 2001 the fight against filth took on a renewed urgency.

The second Bush regime promised a return to the aggressive enforcement of obscenity laws. Attorney General John Ashcroft resumed the battle to uphold the CPPA's ban on virtual child pornography. Justice Kennedy delivered the 6–3 opinion, finding the CPPA "cover[ed] materials beyond the categories recognized in *Ferber* and *Miller*, and the reasons the Government offers in support of limiting the freedom of speech have no justification in our precedents or in the law of the First Amendment. The provision abridges the freedom to engage in a substantial amount of lawful speech. For this reason, it is overbroad and unconstitutional."[26]

Ashcroft was undeterred. A month after *Ashcroft v. Free Speech Coalition* was decided on April 16, 2002, *Ashcroft v. ACLU* came down. The *ACLU* case took on the Child Online Protection Act (COPA), which regulated online communications that were potentially harmful to minors based on contemporary community standards. The Eastern District Court of Pennsylvania declared COPA overbroad and issued an injunction. The government appealed. The Third Circuit affirmed. The government appealed again. At last the state found the result they wanted. In an 8–1 opinion delivered by Justice Thomas, the Court held that COPA's reliance on community standards to identify material harmful to minors did not by itself render the statute overbroad for First Amendment purposes.[27] The case was remanded on other matters.

Justice Stevens was the lone dissenter. Five years earlier he had voted with the majority in *Reno v. ACLU*, but in *Ashcroft v. ACLU* he saw far-ranging issues with localized limits. He reasoned, "In its original form, the community standard provided a shield for communications that are offensive only to the least tolerant members of society. . . . In the context of the Internet, however, community standards become a sword, rather than a shield. If a prurient appeal is offensive in a puritan village, it may be a crime to post it on the World Wide Web."[28]

Back in the Third Circuit the injunction was upheld against COPA.[29] The ACLU demonstrated that the law was not narrowly tailored and restricted protected speech. On a return to the Supreme Court in 2004, the circuit court's ruling was narrowly upheld.[30]

Suffering setbacks with legislation, the George W. Bush regime pursued a policy of vigorously prosecuting producers and distributors of pornography. In 2005 Attorney General Alberto Gonzales established the Obscenity Prosecution Task Force. The official press release stated, "The Task Force will be dedicated to the investigation and prosecution of the distributors of hardcore pornography that meets the test for obscenity. . . . The Justice Department is committed to respecting and protecting the First Amendment rights of all individuals. However, the welfare of America's families and children demands that we enforce the laws on the books."[31]

The task force's initial targets were Joe Francis and Extreme Associates, respectively. Francis had gained infamy with his Spring Break softcore sexploitation video series *Girls Gone Wild*. At issue were several titles produced during 2002–2003, including *Ultimate Spring Break*, *Girls Gone Wild on Campus Uncensored*, *Totally Exposed Uncensored and Beyond*, and *Girls Gone Wild: College Girls Exposed/Sexy Sorority Sweethearts*. Francis and his production company were charged with failure to maintain age identification records. On September 12, 2006, Francis pled guilty; he was fined $500,000, and his production entities were fined $1.6 million.[32] The DOJ claimed a renewed victory in its battle against obscenity. Francis's troubles escalated with a myriad of civil suits that hounded him for years, concluding with *Plaintiff B v. Francis* (2011).[33]

Extreme Associates was the husband and wife team of Robert Zicari a.k.a. Rob Black and Janet Romano, a.k.a. Lizzie Borden. Extreme produced a series of hardcore videos that often featured rough sex and erotic humiliation; at issue were several titles, including *Extreme Teen 24* (2002), *Ass Clowns 3* (2002), and *Forced Entry* (2002). Zicari and Romano were charged with violating federal obscenity law and distributing allegedly obscene content via mail and Internet.[34] In *United States v. Extreme Associates, Inc.* the Pennsylvania district court handed down a verdict in favor of Extreme. Applying a strict scrutiny analysis, Judge Gary L. Lancaster found "that the federal obscenity statutes burden an individual's fundamental right to possess, read, observe, and think about what he chooses in the privacy of his own home by completely banning the distribution of obscene materials."[35]

On appeal, the Third Circuit reversed. Judge D. Brooks Smith wrote, "We are satisfied that the Supreme Court has decided that federal statutes regulating the distribution of obscenity do not violate any constitutional right to privacy."[36] Extreme appealed to the Supreme Court, but certiorari was denied. On March 11, 2009, Zicari and Romano pled guilty and were each sentenced to a year in prison.[37]

The task force next targeted Danilo Simoes Croce, a Brazilian national operating out of Florida. Simoes Croce offered allegedly obscene videos for sale that depicted defecation, urination, and vomiting in conjunction with sex acts, as in *Toilet Man 6* and *Scat Pleasures*. He was charged with using the mail for delivery of obscene materials and pled guilty on June 7, 2007.[38] He was fined $100,000 and forfeited all equipment and materials connected with his U.S. business operations, including copies of the films and Internet domain names.[39]

In 2004 Loren Jay Adams became the focus of a federal obscenity investigation. Adams, based in Indianapolis, unknowingly met with a government agent and offered fetish and bestiality DVDs, including a video entitled *Anal Doggie and Horse*. Adams was found guilty in September 2008. An appeal to the Fourth Circuit affirmed the holding.[40]

The task force already boasted a string of victories when federal prosecutors set their sights on a high-profile smut producer who worked under the moniker Max Hardcore.[41] Hardcore was the porn persona of Paul Little. A columnist frequently writing on the adult industry commented that Max Hardcore's movies "focused on the systematic degradation of his female costar of the moment who was not infrequently dressed up to resemble a child: wearing pigtails, discovered on a playground, sucking on a lollipop."[42] In another report, Hardcore's films were characterized as displaying rough, forced, and physically and verbally abusive sexual intercourse. Even Larry Flynt saw Hardcore's videos as "not within the norm. . . . That's somebody who's got some kind of deep-seated hatred toward women."[43] Little was indicted in May 2007 and charged with ten counts of violating Title 18, Section 1461, of the U.S. Code. The complaint named several titles, including *Max Hardcore Extreme Number 20, Pure Max 19: Euro Edition, Golden Guzzlers 7: Euro Edition*, and *Fists of Fury: Euro Edition*, which appeared on DVD as well as in electronically transmitted streams and downloads.[44] Little was scheduled for hearing in Florida, not far from where Francis and Simoes Croce had been tried.[45]

Following a seven-week trial, Little was convicted in June 2008 of transporting obscene matter by use of an interactive computer service. Judge Susan C. Bucklew handed down the sentence: three years and ten months in federal prison. His company was fined $75,000.

To arrive at this verdict the jury applied the three steps prescribed in *Miller*. Two irregularities in the Max Hardcore case deserve mention. First, in May 2008 a juror asked Judge Bucklew if it was possible to be shown clips in lieu of the full motion pictures at issue. The judge initially ruled that full movies must be shown, since *Miller* required works to be considered as a whole. But after forty minutes of viewing graphic, intense, and abusive pornography, Bucklew revised her ruling.[46] It is possible that this decision—not playing the material as a whole—violated the spirit of *Miller*.

The second irregularity concerned the elusive measure of contemporary community standards. In *United States v. Little*, the court defined the community as the Middle District of Florida, where the servers that hosted Little's websites were located and where federal investigators had opted for the DVDs they purchased to be sent. But the region had full Internet access to a broad range of adult materials. The disconnect between regional and worldwide standards had been raised in *Reno v. ACLU* and again in *Ashcroft v. ACLU*. Echoing Justice Brennan's original comment, the influential Ninth Circuit provided guidance, writing, "To avoid the need to examine the serious First Amendment problem that would otherwise exist, we construe obscenity . . . as defined by reference to a national community standard when disseminated via the Internet."[47] The Eleventh Circuit was not persuaded.

In *United States v. Little*, an unpublished per curiam opinion, the court affirmed both the reliance on local community standards as well as the clips serving to properly present the materials "as a whole."[48] Little served thirty-one months and was released in July 2011.

The pendulum of pornography was swinging once again. When President Barack Obama took office in 2009, partisan eyes monitored how his administration would handle obscenity prosecution. The answer arrived in an action pending since 2008; Obama's DOJ had inherited its first obscenity prosecution.

Barry Goldman was a Miami-based producer doing business under the names Torture Portal and Masters of Pain. As his entities might indicate, he specialized in S&M videos featuring scenes of extreme and explicit bondage and erotic discipline. The Bush-era Justice Department had unsealed their indictment in the socially conservative venue of Montana, charging Goldman with three counts of using U.S. mail to deliver allegedly obscene DVDs, which included *Torture of Porn Star Girl*, *Pregnant and Willing*, and *Defiant Crista Submits*.[49] Six months into Obama's term came a sign that may have alarmed anti-obscenity pundits. In July 2009 the DOJ moved the case to the more socially progressive venue of New Jersey, signaling to some that the new administration was stepping back from aggressive prosecution of obscenity.[50] But no change of venue could save Goldman. By July 2010 he reached a plea deal and quietly disappeared under the radar. The Goldman victory was not even announced in a DOJ press release; this was a far cry from the Obscenity Prosecution Task Force's chest-thumping during the Bush era.

The task force had seen better days. In 2007 the unit began investigating adult filmmaker John Stagliano. Stagliano had launched his career in 1983. By the end of the decade his signature "gonzo pornography," low-budget, amateurish POV-style scenes, proved to be hugely popular and lucrative. Unlike Max Hardcore, Stagliano was an adult industry insider, a celebrated entrepreneur, and one of the most successful porn filmmakers of the 1990s, consistently lauded at the Adult Video News (AVN) Awards. His *Fashionistas* (2002) was named Best Adult Film in 2003 and adapted into a Las Vegas stage show that ran from 2004–2008 at the Rio Hotel and Casino—evidence of Stagliano's crossover appeal to mainstream audiences.

By 2008 Stagliano had become an outspoken voice in the porn industry. At the AVN Awards that year he lampooned government censors who were "coming for them all."[51] Perhaps this was the trigger. Within three months U.S. prosecutors indicted him in federal court in the District of Columbia.[52]

At issue were several DVDs that FBI agents had obtained from Stagliano's Evil Angel website. Titles included *Milk Nymphos* (2007) and *Storm Squirters 2: Target Practice* (2007). Despite the lactation and enema-themed entertainments, the government was unable to make their case. In a stunning turn of events considering the task force's track record, Judge Richard J. Leon found the evidence "woefully insufficient to link defendants to the production and distribution of two DVD videos at the heart of the case."[53] The vindicated pornographer commented, "This is bad for my autobiography. . . . I was hoping for a better fight than they put on."[54]

A single obscenity case remained on the docket.[55] In January 2007 the FBI raided the offices of Stolen Car Films in Los Angeles. Among the materials discovered were three videos entitled *Gang Bang Horse: Pony Sex Game*, *Mako's First Time Scat*, and *Hollywood Scat Amateurs 7*. Ira Isaacs was charged with importing and distributing obscene materials. Isaacs's niche content, which included bestiality and scatological imagery, was not commercially available, being distributed only via an underground network. Isaacs positioned himself as a "shock artist," claiming his films were not pornographic "because there is nothing erotic about scat movies."[56]

Even with this extreme content, the task force's days of slam-dunk convictions were over. The saga of *United States v. Isaacs* saw two mistrials before concluding with a guilty verdict in April 2012. On January 16, 2013, Isaacs was

John Stagliano in production. Courtesy of Evil Angel.

sentenced to forty-eight months. The shock artist appeared unremorseful, stating, "I feel like I just won the Academy Award. If an artist can offend so many people that he has to go to prison to protect society, that's really saying something. . . . Most shock artists dream of this kind of attention, without the prison part."[57]

Despite the guilty verdict, it was a battle of attrition. Attorney General Eric Holder shuttered the Obscenity Prosecution Task Force in 2011, folding the unit into the Child Exploitation and Obscenity Section. The move angered antipornography groups and prompted criticism of Obama as soft on porn. *Isaacs* was the last adult obscenity case pending in the federal court system, signaling an end to the aggressive enforcement of obscenity that had been revitalized under Bush.[58]

The pendulum still swings. The underlying question is reconsidered by each new regime: does the First Amendment—*should* the First Amendment—protect the production, distribution, and exploitation of such extreme sexually explicit materials as have emerged? The politics of profanity continue to vie for control of American culture and the hearts, minds, eyes, and wallets of an ever-changing audience.

CONCLUSION

———

Dirty Words & Filthy Pictures: Film and the First Amendment chronicles the century-long balance between free expression and government regulation of content. Despite the Founding Fathers' broad grant of rights for free speech, practical circumstances and social pressures led authorities to set limits. Over time those limits shifted, evolved, constricted, loosened, and tightened again. In the landmark *Joseph Burstyn, Inc. v. Wilson*, Justice Frankfurter reflected on this dynamic relationship between freedom and control: "The Constitution, we cannot recall too often, is an organism, not merely a literary composition."[1]

In the beginning, the seemingly innocent on-screen smooch that John C. Rice planted on May Irwin in *The Kiss* ignited a controversy. Moral authorities feared the worst, foreseeing the cinema as the ruin of the social structure they knew. Film regulation commissions responded along with city and state agencies, and multiple overlapping mechanisms were set in place to monitor and approve the content of motion pictures.

By 1915, as *The Birth of a Nation* barnstormed across the country, the Supreme Court handed down an influential ruling. The Court declared that motion pictures did not fall within the protections of constitutional guarantees. The *Mutual v. Ohio* decision positioned movies as entertainment like the circus or carnival sideshows. But unlike the other diversions, film was problematic because of its perceived capacity for evil. The silver screen had a hypnotic allure that required oversight. *Mutual* empowered state censors and municipal regulators. Filmmakers were forced to develop creative solutions. Government regulations pushed moviemakers to create a cinematic language that allowed controversial subjects to be dealt with in a coded and elliptical style.

This highly regulated environment governed Hollywood's Golden Age. Then in 1952 the High Court changed its opinion on motion pictures. From the halls of justice a precedent was shattered. Five decades after the first hand-cranked Kinetoscopes packed nickelodeon parlors, film was repositioned as creative expression—an art form and a mode of communication worthy of First Amendment protections. The *New York Times* hailed the decision: "*The Miracle* Happens; The Supreme Court Proclaims Freedom of the Screen."[2]

Film's newfound freedom was not celebrated in all corners. Moral authorities were still wary of the effects that uncensored and unregulated cinema could have on society, particularly on impressionable audiences, such as children, women, and the uneducated. After the *Miracle* decision, moviemakers—what one judge called the "carpetbaggers of filth" and "merchants of obscenity"—had the upper hand.[3] The cinema's hard-won freedoms soon expanded to the breaking point—seen in the short-lived porno chic of the 1970s, when hardcore pornography played on mainstream movie screens. After reaching the point of anything goes, interpretations of the First Amendment contracted. Since 2004 more filmmakers have been investigated, tried, and convicted for the content of their films than in the fifty years prior.

The medium of motion pictures was originally seen as an arcade amusement, an attractive nuisance with the dangerous ability to corrupt audiences. A century later it is clear that the movies are a powerful means of communication, an art form, and a profitable industry. But the movies mean more. Motion pictures have influenced fundamental personal freedoms in America. Filmmakers have played an important role in expanding the legal concept of free speech under the First Amendment. The questions posed over the years by civic regulators remain relevant: Does film content affect behavior? How can objectionable material be controlled without diminishing or chilling free expression?

The story of cinema and censorship continues. The balance between regulation and freedom remains fluid. Lawmakers, filmmakers, and the courts maintain an uneasy equilibrium. As members of the creative community, it is in the nature of filmmakers to push boundaries, create controversy, and provoke thought. At the opposite extreme, it is the duty of the authorities to maintain the welfare of the community and preserve the status quo. Film-makers are in the business of selling tickets, but the history of film and film's interaction with the law exposes a vital part of our nation's ideals, under-standings, and inner life. Through the lens of film-legal history we can shed light on how constitutional principles have evolved.

Dirty words and filthy pictures can be silly and gratuitous, rude and offen-sive—but they can also contain the seeds of change.

NOTES

▬▬▬▬

Endnote Abbreviations

NYT New York Times
MPW Moving Picture World

INTRODUCTION

1. "Sacramento's City Censor Board Has Accepted the Verdict of Chicago's Municipal Regulators," *MPW*, March 14, 1914, 1404; and "Censorship Customs," *NYT*, July 21, 1929. For censorship commissions, see "Local and State Censorship of Movies Has All but Vanished," *Nashua Telegraph*, June 21, 1967, and various announcements appearing in *MPW*, 1915–1916.
2. "Birth of Buffalo Banned in Film," *Spokane Daily Chronicle*, August 10, 1954; and "State Censor Modifies 'Ancient Precedent' and Approves Calf Birth Scene in Movie," *NYT*, August 13, 1954.
3. Stanley Frank, "Headaches of a Movie Censor," *Saturday Evening Post*, September 27, 1947, 20.
4. Lester Velie, "You Can't See That Movie," *Collier's*, May 6, 1950, 11.
5. Frank Shyong, "Maker of Porn Films Gets 4 Years in Prison in Federal Obscenity Case," *Los Angeles Times*, January 16, 2013.

CHAPTER 1
Boxing, Porn, and the Beginnings of Movie Censorship

1. "Home-Made Comic Plays," *NYT*, September 17, 1895. Incidentally, *The Kiss* was not the first promotional film—John C. Rice had appeared in an earlier ad-film: "W. D. Mann, who is to manage [William] Hoey and [John C.] Rice in 'The Flams' next season, has conceived a new idea for advertising his show. Edison's kineto-scope and phonograph are to be used for a reproduction of the chief specular and vocal features of the farce." "Theatrical Gossip," *NYT*, June 21, 1894.

2. "Notes," *Chap-Book* 5 (July 15, 1896): 240.

3. Charles Musser, *The Emergence of Cinema: The American Screen to 1907* (Berkeley: University of California Press, 1994), 68; Musser, *Edison Motion Pictures, 1890–1900: An Annotated Filmography* (Washington, DC: Smithsonian Institution Press, 1997), 325; and Stephen Herbert and Luke McKernan, eds., *Who's Who of Victorian Cinema: A Worldwide Survey* (London: British Film Institute, 1996).

4. "The Exposition," *Washington Gazette*, November 14, 1895; also Charles A. Kennedy, "When Cairo Met Main Street: Little Egypt, Salome Dancers, and the World's Fairs of 1893 and 1904," in *Music and Culture in America, 1861–1918*, ed. Michael Saffle and James R. Heintze (New York: Garland, 1998), 271–298; and Dave Thompson, *Black and White and Blue: Adult Cinema from the Victorian Age to the VCR* (Toronto: ECW, 2007), 19–20.

5. Terry Ramsaye, *A Million and One Nights: A History of the Motion Picture* (New York: Simon and Schuster, 1926), 256.

6. Herbert and McKernan, *Who's Who of Victorian Cinema*.

7. John Baxter, *Carnal Knowledge: Baxter's Concise Encyclopedia of Modern Sex* (New York: Harper Perennial, 2009), 69–70; and Alex Duval Smith, "Tremendous Amount of Prudishness Over Porn Says Journalist," *Salina Journal*, November 13, 1996.

8. People v. Doris, 43 N.Y.S. 571 (App. Div. 1897), in Austin Abbott and Benjamin Vaughan Abbott, *Abbott's Cyclopedic Digest of All the Decisions of All the Courts of New York from the Earliest Time to the Year 1900*, vol. 10 (New York: Baker, Voorhis and John B. West, 1902), 422.

9. "Six Rounds," *Kansas City Daily Gazette*, June 17, 1894; also "Fought for Edison," *San Francisco Chronicle*, June 16, 1894; and Ramsaye, *A Million and One Nights*, 150.

10. "Knocked Out by Corbett," *Brooklyn Daily Eagle*, September 8, 1894; "Corbett Fights Six Rounds," *Philadelphia Times*, September 8, 1894.

11. Musser, *Emergence of Cinema*, 84n6; and Barak Y. Orbach, "Prizefighting and the Birth of Movie Censorship," *Yale Journal of Law and the Humanities* 21 (October 2009): 259.

12. "Pugilist Corbett May Be Indicted," *NYT*, September 9, 1894.

13. "Pantopticon Rivals the Kinetoscope," *NYT*, April 22, 1895; "Screen the Greatest," *NYT*, December 31, 1922.

14. "Watching a Bull Fight," *Brooklyn Daily Eagle*, June 8, 1896.

15. "Con Riordan's Last Bout," *NYT*, November 18, 1894.

16. People v. Fitzsimmons, 34 N.Y.S. 1102, 1107 (Ct. Sess. 1895).

17. "Fitzsimmons Is Willing to Pick Up His Share of the Kinetoscope Money," *Atlanta Constitution*, December 19, 1894; "Fitzsimmons Talks," *Hartford Courant*, December 26, 1894; "Lanky Bob Objects," *Los Angeles Times*, December 27, 1894; "Offer for the Championship Fight," *Idaho Daily Statesman*, October 28, 1894; "The Corbett-Fitz 'Go'," *Kansas City Star*, December 25, 1894; "The Wizard's Glass," *Los Angeles Times*, December 29, 1894.

18. "Pugilistic Fizzle Ended," *NYT*, November 3, 1895.

19. "May Fight in Mexico," *NYT*, October 4, 1895.

20. "To Fight in Carson City," *Brooklyn Daily Eagle*, January 13, 1897.

21. "May Fight in Nevada," *Brooklyn Daily Eagle*, January 27, 1897.

22. Despite the widely publicized results, gambling was still prevalent: "Last night while the audience was watching the Corbett-Fitzsimmons pictures . . . a well dressed man sitting in the second tier suddenly jumped up in his seat and shouted wildly 'Jim will lick him. I have got money that says he will.'" "Two Maniacs Arrested," *NYT*, June 17, 1897.

23. An Act to Prohibit Prizefighting and Pugilism and Fights Between Men and Animals, 54th Cong., vol. 29, § 5, (1896).

24. An Act to Prohibit Prize Fighting, S. 1187, 54th Cong. (1897).

25. Me. Rev. Stat. ch. 125, § 17 (1903).

26. Robert G. Rodriguez, *The Regulation of Boxing: A History and Comparative Analysis of Policies Among American States* (Jefferson, NC: McFarland, 2009).

27. "Corbett-Fitzsimmons Fight," *New York World*, May 12, 1897.

CHAPTER 2
The Rise of Salacious Cinema

1. "To Prohibit Indecent Pictures," *NYT*, February 28, 1900; "War on Indecent Pictures," *NYT*, August 5, 1900; and "Comstock Raids Picture Machines," *NYT*, July 25, 1901.

2. "Thaw Murders Stanford White," *NYT*, June 26, 1906.

3. "Thaw Trial Begins," *NYT*, January 24, 1907; and "Evelyn Thaw Tells Her Story," *NYT*, February 8, 1907.

4. "Thaw Murders Stanford White," *NYT*, June 26, 1906.

5. "Notes on the Coming Week at the Playhouses," *NYT*, October 21, 1906.

6. "Thaw's Plea is Unwritten Law," *NYT*, April 10, 1907.

7. "Thaw Mistrial," *NYT*, April 13, 1907.

8. "Gayety Burlesque," *Indianapolis News*, April 5, 1907.

9. "America," *MPW*, July 6, 1907, 280.

10. "Trade Notes," *MPW*, March 30, 1907, 57.

11. "Houston Authorities Object to Picture of Thaw-White Tragedy," *MPW*, April 20, 1907, 102.

12. "Trade Notes," *MPW*, April 27, 1907, 119.

13. *MPW*, May 25, 1907, 180.

14. "A More Rigid Censorship," *Chicago Tribune*, February 22, 1909; also "Nickel Theaters Crime Breeders," *Chicago Tribune*, April 13, 1907.

15. "Cities Fight Films Allowed," *Chicago Inter Ocean*, July 21, 1910; also "Censorship to Govern Motion Pictures," *Chicago Inter Ocean*, February 17, 1909; and "Chief Shippey Will Be Censor of Films if Aldermen Pass Proposed Order," *Chicago Inter Ocean*, June 25, 1907.

16. "Thaw Insane When He Shot," *NYT*, February 13, 1907; "Thaw Back in State Asylum," *NYT*, August 19, 1909; "Thaw to Try Again for His Release," *NYT*, September 15, 1911; "Escapes from Matteawan," *NYT*, July 26, 1914.

17. "Newspaper Comment on Thaw Escape," *Pittsburgh Press*, August 8, 1913; and "Thaw Dangerous Says Dr. Flint," *NYT*, August 18, 1913.

18. "Written on the Screen," *NYT*, December 1, 1918.

CHAPTER 3
State Regulations Emerge

1. "Cities Fight Films Allowed," *Chicago Inter Ocean*, July 31, 1910.

2. Ellis Paxson Oberholtzer, *The Morals of the Movie* (Philadelphia: Penn Publishing Company, 1922), 115.

3. "Funkhouser As Morals Guardian," *Chicago Tribune*, March 21, 1913.

4. Jas. S. McQuade, "Letter from Chicago," *MPW*, October 18, 1913, 249.

5. "Chicago Censorship Under Fire," *MPW*, November 7, 1914, 772.

6. "Pruning the Movies," *MPW*, December 26, 1914, 1886.

7. M. L. C. Funkhouser, "The Pro and Con of Police Censorship," *Photoplay* 7, no. 4 (March 1915): 66–68.

8. "Dance Pictures Barred in Chicago," *MPW*, November 8, 1913, 598.

9. "Freak Dances Behold in Moving Pictures," *Chicago Tribune*, October 23, 1913.

10. "Steffen Moves to Curb Power of Funkhouser," *Chicago Tribune*, September 25, 1917.

11. "Nude Statue on Art Institute Steps Must Go," *Chicago Tribune*, April 16, 1918; also "Art Head Balks at Interning Nude Farmer," *Chicago Tribune*, April 17, 1918; and [No Headline], *NYT*, April 29, 1918, 11.

12. "Major Funkhouser Out," *Variety*, May 30, 1918, 37.

13. "Alderman to Kill Blue Law Rule," *NYT*, December 10, 1907; also "The Rise of the Moving Picture," *Coffeyville Daily Journal*, December 21, 1911.

14. "The Closing of Nickelodeons in New York City," *MPW*, March 16, 1907.

15. "Police Get Orders to Enforce Blue Law," *NYT*, December 6, 1907.

16. "Sunday Recovers Much of Its Color," *NYT*, December 30, 1907; also "Picture Shows to Test Blue Law," *NYT*, December 7, 1907; and "New Move on Blue Sunday," *Brooklyn Daily Eagle*, December 28, 1907.

17. "Picture Shows All Put Out of Business," *Brooklyn Daily Eagle*, December 25, 1908; also "Moving Picture Shows May Resume in Gotham," *Daily Industrial News*, December 29, 1908.

18. "Moving Picture Cases Up Today," *NYT*, December 29, 1908.

19. "Observations by Our Man About Town," *MPW*, November 13, 1909, 679.

20. William Fox Amusement Co. v. McClellan, 114 N.Y.S. 594 (App. Div. 1909).

21. "New York Exhibitors Endorse Gaynor," *MPW*, October 30, 1909, 608.

22. "Censorship for Moving Picture Shows in N.Y.," *Charlotte News*, April 24, 1909.

23. "Binder Gives Details," *MPW*, October 31, 1914, 631.

24. "Observations by Our Man About Town," *MPW*, April 16, 1910, 594.

25. "Censors Destroyed Evil Pictures," *NYT*, May 14, 1911.

26. "National Board of Censorship of Motion Pictures," *MPW*, October 16, 1909, 524.

27. "Exhibitor's News," *MPW*, December 12, 1914, 1562.

28. "Say Motion Picture Censorship is Lax," *NYT*, November 8, 1911.

29. "Discuss Film Censorship," *Brooklyn Daily Eagle*, March 24, 1917.

30. "Urges One Control of Picture Shows," *NYT*, March 23, 1911.

31. "Dr. Crafts States the Case for a Federal Board of Censorship," *NYT*, May 19, 1914; and "Writing Censor Bill," *MPW*, November 20, 1915, 1517.

32. "Film Censorship Hearings Begin," *NYT*, January 14, 1916; and "Some Movie Producers for U.S. Censorship," *Atlanta Constitution*, January 30, 1916.

33. S. 4941, H.R. 14895, revised as S. 2204, H.R. 456; "Await Funkhouser Verdict," *Chicago Daily Tribune*, July 11, 1914; "Urges U.S. Movie Censors," *Washington Post*, October 3, 1915; and "Smith-Hughes Bill Radically Changed," *MPW*, May 20, 1916, 1319.

34. "A Great Historic Document," *MPW*, June 3, 1916, 1319.

35. Frequently running advertisement in *MPW*, beginning January 1, 1916.

36. *MPW*, January 15, 1916, 391.

37. *MPW*, October 19, 1907, 524.

38. Johnny D. Boggs, *Jesse James and the Movies* (Jefferson, NC: McFarland, 2007), 23.

39. "News Briefs," *MPW*, October 28, 1911, 298.

40. "Clash Over Troops in *Night Riders* Raid," *NYT*, May 17, 1911, 5.

41. An Ordinance to Prohibit the Exhibition of Obscene and Immoral Pictures, Chicago Municipal Code, § 1.

42. Block v. City of Chicago, 87 N.E. 1011, 1013 (Ill. 1909).

43. *Id.* at 1016.

44. *Id.*

45. *Id.* at 1013.

46. State v. Morris, 76 Atl. 479 (Del. 1910).

47. "Folks Film Bill Vetoed By Mayor," *NYT*, January 1, 1913.
48. "Observations by Our Man About Town," *MPW*, January 11, 1913, 148; also W. Stephen Bush, "Mayor Gaynor on Censorship," and "Mayor Gaynor's Veto," containing the full text of his letter to the Aldermen, *MPW*, January 11, 1913.
49. "Blames Canon Chase for 'Movie' Horror," *NYT*, February 3, 1913.
50. 4 Pa. Cons. Stat. Ann. § 6.4.
51. "Gov. Brunbaugh Recalls Tener Appointments," *Scranton Republican*, May 18, 1915.
52. Ellis P. Oberholtzer, "What Are the 'Movies' Making of Our Children?," *World's Work* 41 (January 1921): 249–263.
53. 4 Pa. Cons. Stat. Ann. § 30.
54. Mutual Film Corp. v. Industrial Commission of Ohio, 236 U.S. 230, 239 (1915).
55. Mutual Film Corp. v. Hodges, 236 U.S. 248, 257 (1915).
56. MPPC v. Independent Moving Pictures Co., 200 F. 411 (2d Cir. 1912); United States v. MPPC, 225 F. 800 (E.D. Pa. 1915); United States v. MPPC, 243 U.S. 502 (1917).
57. Weber v. Freed, 239 U.S. 325, 328 (1915).
58. "Cinema: Boxers Triumph," *Time*, July 15, 1940.
59. *Weber*, 239 U.S. at 329.
60. William M. Flynn, "Fight Film Appeal Lost," *MPW*, February 12, 1916, 986.
61. Jason S. Martinko, *The XXX Filmography, 1968–1988* (Jefferson, NC: McFarland, 2013); and Eva Christina, *The Book of Kink: Sex Beyond the Missionary* (New York: Penguin, 2011).

CHAPTER 4
Mutual and the Capacity for Evil

1. The Supreme Court definitively ended the Edison Trust's stranglehold on the film industry in MPPC v. Universal Film Manufacturing Co., 243 U.S. 502 (1917).
2. Mutual Film Corp. v. Industrial Commission of Ohio, 236 U.S. 230, 237 (1915).
3. Formal newsreel films began with Pathé's *Animated Gazette* in 1910. In the United States, the *Pathé Weekly* began in 1911, followed the next year by *Mutual Weekly*, *Gaumont Animated Weekly*, and *Universal's Animated Weekly*. See Raymond Fielding, *The American Newsreel: a Complete History, 1911–1967* (Jefferson, NC: McFarland, 2006); and Roger Smither and Wolfgang Klaue, eds., *Newsreels in Film Archives: A Survey Based on the FIAF Newsreel Symposium* (Madison, NJ: Fairleigh Dickinson University Press, 1996).
4. "Triangle Film Formed," *NYT*, July 21, 1915.
5. *Mutual*, 236 U.S. at 232.
6. *Id.*
7. *Id.* at 234.
8. *Id.* at 239.

9. Gibbons v. Ogden, 22 U.S. 1 (1824).

10. *Mutual*, 236 U.S. at 240.

11. *Id.* at 242.

12. *Id.* at 243.

13. *Id.*, emphasis added.

14. *Id.* at 244.

15. Mutual Film Corp. v. Hodges, 236 U.S. 248, 258 (1915).

16. *Id.* at 256.

17. *Id.* at 258.

18. *Id.*

19. Buffalo Branch, Mutual Film Corp. v. Breitinger, 95 A. 433, 434 (Pa. 1915).

20. *Id.*

21. *Id.* at 439.

22. *Id.* at 440.

23. Mutual Film Corp. v. City of Chicago, 224 F. 101, 139 (7th Cir. 1915).

24. Richard Able, *The Ciné Goes to Town: French Cinema, 1896–1914* (Berkeley: University of California Press, 1994), 23.

25. Pathé Exchange v. Cobb, 195 N.Y.S. 661, 664 (App. Div. 1922), *aff'd*, 236 N.Y. 539 (1923).

26. *Id.* at 665.

27. *Id.*

28. *Id.* at 667.

29. Hughes Tool Co. v. Fielding, 73 N.Y.S.2d 98, 101 (App. Div. 1947).

30. A selection of newsreels can be viewed at http://www.britishpathe.com/pages/newsreels.

31. "Fifth Largest Industry," *Cincinnati Enquirer*, January 10, 1915.

32. "Agency History for Board of Censors," Maryland State Archives Guide to Government Records, accessed December 28, 2014, http://guide.mdsa.net/history.cfm?ID=SH72.

33. "Bills to Regulate Movies, Boxing and Wrestling Signed," *Brooklyn Daily Eagle*, May 14, 1921.

34. *Pathé Exchange*, 195 N.Y.S. at 663.

35. William Sheafe Chase, *Catechism on Motion Pictures in Inter-State Commerce* (Albany, NY: New York Civic League, 1922), 39.

36. "Thomas Dixon Scores Virginia Censorship," *Danville Virginia Bee*, March 18, 1922.

37. "Film Censor Bill Passed," *Boston Daily Globe*, May 11, 1915; "Movie Men Form a Board of Trade," *NYT*, September 15, 1915; "Crime and the Movies," *Charleston Daily Mail*, December 15, 1920; "State Legislature," *Minnesota Princeton Union*, January 20, 1921; "Amended Movie Bill Passed," *Mountaineer-Courier*, March 17, 1920; "News of the Week," *Marble Rock Journal*, May 5, 1921; "Resolution Calls

for Picture Censorship Bill," *Joplin Globe*, March 19, 1921; memorandum, January 1, 1924, MPPDA Digital Archive, record no. 3262, accessed December 28, 2014, http://mppda.flinders.edu.au/records/3262.

38. Ellis P. Oberholtzer, *The Morals of the Movie* (Philadelphia: Penn Publishing, 1922), 117; "Censorship Board for Movies Wins," *Atlanta Constitution*, July 21, 1920; "Film Censorship Board Will Not Be Abolished," *San Francisco Chronicle*, May 5, 1916; "Provide for City Censors," *Tacoma Times*, January 10, 1917; "Trade Body Asked to Help," *MPW*, October 14, 1916, 282.

39. "Modification in Censorship," *Arkansas City Daily Traveler*, April 26, 1915.

40. "Oppose Legal Censorship," *NYT*, September 22, 1916.

CHAPTER 5
War, Nudity, and Birth Control

1. G. W. Bitzer, "Filming My First War: 1898," in *Billy Bitzer: His Story* (New York: Farrar, Straus and Giroux, 1973).

2. Anthony Slide, *The Big V: A History of the Vitagraph Company* (Lanham, MD: Scarecrow Press, 1978).

3. W. K. L. Dickson, *The Biograph in Battle: Its Story in the South African War* (Madison, NJ: Fairleigh Dickinson University Press, 1995).

4. Life Photo Film Corp. v. Bell, 154 N.Y.S. 763, 764 (App. Div. 1915).

5. *Id.*

6. *Id.* at 764–765.

7. Fox Film Corp. v. City of Chicago, 247 F. 231, 233 (N.D. Ill. 1917), aff'd, 251 F. 883 (7th Cir. 1917). Also see "Judge Straightens Out Mr. Funkhouser," *MPW*, September 15, 1917, 1665; "Judge Altschuler Says Funkhouser Had No Authority to Hold Up *The Spy*," *MPW*, September 22, 1917; and "Censor 34, December Funkhouser Loses *The Spy* Case," *MPW*, March 30, 1918, 1831.

8. *Fox Film*, 247 F. at 232.

9. City of Chicago v. Fox Film Corp., 251 F. 883, 884 (7th Cir. 1918).

10. *Id.* at 885.

11. "Crashing Through for Convention Hall," *MPW*, October 12, 1918, 259.

12. "The Screen," *NYT*, January 5, 1920.

13. "Negroes Object to Film: Say *Birth of a Nation* Characterizes Race Improperly," *NYT*, March 7, 1915.

14. "Epoch Co. Appeals, Supreme Court to Be Asked to Set Aside Censor Decision," *MPW*, May 13, 1916, 336; "*Nation* Film Suit Again," *MPW*, July 22, 1916, 753; "Kansas Board Recalls *The Birth of a Nation*," *MPW*, June 2, 1917, 1488; "*Nation* Film Arrests in Des Moines, Ia.," *MPW*, May 27, 1916, 717; and "*Nation* Film at the Atlanta," *MPW*, December 11, 1915, 307.

15. "Negroes Object to Film," *MPW*, March 7, 1915, 13; and "Conference on Moving Picture," *MPW*, April 2, 1915, 13.
16. "Negroes Mob Photoplay," *MPW*, April 18, 1915, 15.
17. "*Birth of a Nation* Stirs Twin Cities," *Eau Claire Wisconsin Leader*, November 7, 1915.
18. Bainbridge v. City of Minneapolis, 154 N.W. 964, 965 (Minn. 1915).
19. *Id*. at 966.
20. *Id*.
21. Bainbridge v. City of Minneapolis, 242 U.S. 353 (1916).
22. "*Birth of a Nation* Back to Twin Cities," *Bismarck Tribune*, December 14, 1915.
23. Joseph Henabery, *Before, In and After Hollywood*, ed. Anthony Slide (Lanham, MD: Scarecrow Press, 1997), 83.
24. United States v. Motion Picture Film "The Spirit of '76," 252 F. 946, 946–947 (S.D. Cal. 1917).
25. "Revive *Spirit of '76*, Film Barred in 1917," *NYT*, July 14, 1921.
26. "*Spirit of '76 Movie Granted Chicago Permit*," *Chicago Daily Tribune*, May 13, 1917; and "*Spirit of '76* Movie Fails to Move Its Critics," *Chicago Daily Tribune*, May 16, 1917.
27. Jas. S. McQuade, "Chicago News Letter," *MPW*, May 26, 1917, 1291.
28. *Spirit of '76*, 252 F. at 947.
29. *Id*. at 948.
30. *Id*.
31. *Id*.
32. *Id*. at 949.
33. Goldstein v. United States, 258 F. 908, 909 (9th Cir. 1919).
34. "The Screen," *NYT*, July 19, 1921; and "Revive *Spirit of '76*, Film Barred in 1917" *NYT*, July 14, 1921.
35. Anthony Slide, *Robert Goldstein and* The Spirit of '76, (New York: Scarecrow Press, 1993), xxiii; and "The Unluckiest Man in Movie History," Slate, June 13, 2000, http://www.slate.com/articles/news_and_politics/chatterbox/2000/06/the _unluckiest_man_in_movie_history.html.
36. "*Purity* at the Liberty," *MPW*, August 5, 1916, 917; "Many Mutuals Promised," *MPW*, September 2, 1916, 1552; "*Purity* a Tremendous Success," *MPW*, Sept. 30, 1916, 2150.
37. Louis Reeves Harrison, "*Purity*," *MPW*, July 29, 1916, 804.
38. "Arcadia," *Reading Times*, January 10, 1917.
39. M. A. Malanney, "Arrested for Showing *Purity*" *MPW*, February 17, 1916, 501; "*Purity* Banned By Censor," *MPW*, October, 27, 1917, 570.
40. Alice Rogers Hager, "Movies Reflect Our Moods," *NYT*, April 22, 1934.
41. "At the Theaters," *Topeka Daily Capital*, January 22, 1916; and "Theda Bara May Pass Up Topeka," *Topeka Daily Capital*, May 19, 1916.
42. "Is National Censor Board Growing Careless?," *MPW*, February 27, 1915, 1318; and "*Cleopatra* to Put Forty Shows," *MPW*, December 29, 1917, 1974.

43. "Ivan Abramson, Master Craftsman," *MPW*, March 4, 1916, 1454.
44. Ivan Film Productions v. Bell, 167 N.Y.S. 123, 123 (App. Div. 1917).
45. *Id.*
46. *Id.* at 124.
47. *Id.*
48. Message Photoplay Co. v. Bell, 167 N.Y.S. 129, 130 (App. Div. 1917).
49. *Id.*
50. *Id.* at 131.
51. *Message Photoplay*, 167 N.Y.S. at 132.
52. *Id.* at 134.
53. Message Photo-Play Co. v. Bell, 166 N.Y.S. 338, 344 (App. Div. 1917).
54. Griswold v. Connecticut, 381 U.S. 479 (1965).
55. "Lois Weber Talks Shop," *MPW*, May 27, 1916, 655.
56. "Reviews of Current Productions," *MPW*, November 24, 1917, 1184–1185.
57. "Wells to Open Lyric," *Atlanta Constitution*, February 21, 1915.
58. "Portland, Maine Bans *Hypocrites*," *MPW*, October 30, 1915, 994; "*Hypocrites* Sensation All Over Country," *MPW*, May 1, 1915, 732; "In Jacksonville," *MPW*, August 21, 1915, 1346; "Chips from Steel City," *MPW*, July 31, 1915, 847; "*Hypocrites* in Nashville," *MPW*, September 25, 1915, 2208; "*Hypocrites* Comes Back to Louisville," *MPW*, October 2, 1915, 105; "Atlanta Notes," *MPW*, June 5, 1915, 1951; "In the Southwest," *MPW*, May 8, 1915, 941; "Other San Francisco Notes," *MPW*, April 3, 1915, 92; "California Briefs," *MPW*, May 29, 1915, 1457; "Doings at Los Angeles," *MPW*, April 10, 1915, 221.
59. "Lewis Makes War on Film," *MPW*, June 18, 1916, 57.
60. "Lois Weber Feature to Play Broadway," *MPW*, May 19, 1917, 1146.
61. Universal Film Mfg. Co. v. Bell, 167 N.Y.S. 124, 128 (App. Div. 1917).
62. *Id.* at 125.
63. *Id.* at 128.
64. *Id.* at 127.
65. *Id.* at 128.
66. "Ask Wilson to Stop War Film Change," *NYT*, April 29, 1918.
67. "Written on the Screen," *NYT*, June 2, 1918.

CHAPTER 6: Self-Regulation Reemerges

1. "Will Hays to Quit Cabinet for Films," *NYT*, January 15, 1922.
2. "Movie Men Also Form National Union of All Picture Interests," *Chicago Daily Tribune*, July 15, 1916.
3. "Picture Show Producers Resolve to Keep Screen Clean and Wholesome," *Galveston Daily News*, March 7, 1921; "Organize to Fight Film Censor," *NYT*, January 15, 1917; and "Producers Agree to Reform Films," *NYT*, March 15, 1912.

4. "Industry Will Be Its Own Censor," *MPW*, May 10, 1919, 797; and editorial in ibid.

5. "Will Hays to Quit Cabinet for Films," *NYT*, January 15, 1922.

6. "Hays Outlines His Plans for Movies," *NYT*, April 16, 1922.

7. "Clara Hamon Freed by Murder Jury," *NYT*, March 18, 1921.

8. Weathers v. Cobb, 197 N.Y.S. 956 (App. Div. 1922).

9. "Teapot Tempests in Hollywood," *NYT*, May 8, 1932.

10. Resolution, June 29, 1927, MPPDA Digital Archive, record no. 365, accessed December 28, 2014, http://mppda.flinders.edu.au/records/365.

11. "A Code to Maintain Social and Community Values in the Production of Silent, Synchronized, and Talking Motion Pictures," March 31, 1930, MPPDA Digital Archive, record no. 1255, accessed December 28, 2014, http://mppda.flinders.edu.au/records/1255.

CHAPTER 7
Midnight Movies and Sanctioned Cinema

1. J. M. Shellman, "Trade News of the Week in Baltimore," *MPW*, October 27, 1917, 574.

2. "The Screen," *NYT*, December 22, 1918; "Revokes Theater License," *NYT*, June 5, 1920; "The Screen," *NYT*, June 30, 1919; "*The Solitary Sin* Draws Many People," *Iowa City Press-Citizen*, March 31, 1919; "Claire Adams Stars in End of World," *Evening Review*, September 22, 1919; and "A Film Controversy," *NYT*, May 18, 1919.

3. Public Welfare Pictures Corp. v. Lord, 230 N.Y.S. 137, 138 (App. Div. 1928).

4. Devin Orgeron, Marsha Orgeron, and Dan Streible, eds., *Learning with the Lights Off: Educational Film in the United States* (Oxford: Oxford University Press, 2011), 321.

5. Public Welfare Pictures Corp. v. Brennan, 134 Atl. 868 (N.J. 1926).

6. *Public Welfare Pictures*, 230 N.Y.S. at 138–139; and "State Censorship of Films Upheld," *NYT*, June 23, 1928.

7. "Film Censors Powerless," *NYT*, July 10, 1928.

8. Brooks v. City of Birmingham, 32 F.2d 274, 274–275 (N.D. Ala. 1929).

9. *Id.* at 275.

10. "Censors Ban Film on Russian Revolt," *NYT*, May 26, 1928.

11. "Passion Play Faces Novel Police Move," *NYT*, April 24, 1929.

12. "Tobacco Chewing Movie Is Banned," *Ogden Standard-Examiner*, January 13, 1928.

13. Dan Thomas, "In Hollywood," *Ogden Standard-Examiner*, September 14, 1928.

14. United Artists Corp. v. Thompson, 339 Ill. 595, 598 (1930).

15. *Id.* at 602.

CHAPTER 8
Sound Enters the Debate

1. Mutual Film Corp. v. Industrial Commission of Ohio, 236 U.S. 230, 232 (1915).
2. Edison's Kinetoscope had a public premiere in 1910; see "New York Applauds the Talking Pictures," *NYT*, February 18, 1913; and "Motion Pictures Are Made to Talk," *NYT*, August 27, 1919.
3. Anthony Slide, *Early American Cinema* (Lanham, MD: Scarecrow Press, 1994), 160; also see "Men Move and Speak in New Pictures," *NYT*, May 11, 1912.
4. *In re* Fox Film Corp., 145 A. 514, 516 (Pa. 1929).
5. *Id.* at 516–517.
6. *In re* Vitagraph, Inc., 145 A. 518, 519 (Pa. 1929).
7. *Id.*

CHAPTER 9
Tension Increases between Free Speech and State Censorship

1. Schenck v. United States, 249 U.S. 47, 52 (1919).
2. Gitlow v. New York, 268 U.S. 652, 666 (1925); also see People v. Gitlow, 183 N.Y.S. 846 (App. Div. 1920); People v. Gitlow, 195 App. Div. 783 (N.Y. App. Div. 1921); People v. Gitlow, 136 N.E. 317 (N.Y. 1922).
3. Near v. Minnesota *ex rel.* Olsen, 283 U.S. 697, 738 (1931).
4. *Id.*
5. "Film Magazines Merge," *NYT*, December 15, 1930.
6. See stenographic transcript of a meeting between Lord, Quigley, and Hays, February 10, 1930, MPPDA Digital Archive, record no. 679, accessed January 12, 2015, http://mppda.flinders.edu.au/records/671.
7. In September 1932 Col. Joy left the MPPDA to become an executive and scenario editor at Fox and later the studio's director of public relations; "Col. Jason S. Joy," MPPDA Digital Archive, record no. 297, accessed January 12, 2015, http://mppda.flinders.edu.au/people/297.
8. "Dracula," *Corsicana Daily Sun*, April 18, 1931.
9. Robert E. Sherwood, "The Moving Picture Album," *St. Petersburg Times*, April 10, 1932.
10. "Hays Talks to Studio Men," *NYT*, July 12, 1934.
11. "Censor is Named for Film Clean Up," *NYT*, July 7, 1934.
12. "Hollywood Cleans House," *NYT*, July 15, 1934.
13. "Movies Improving Catholics Report," *NYT*, October 13, 1934.
14. Douglas W. Churchill, "Hollywood Discovers That Virtue Pays," *NYT*, January 20, 1935.

15. "NRA Will Function in Four Divisions," *NYT*, October 26, 1933; and "Rosenblatt Heads NRA Compliance," *NYT*, November 20, 1934.

16. "Movie Trade Gets Code Ultimatum," *NYT*, August 9, 1933.

17. Letter, January 27, 1934, MPPDA Digital Archive, record no. 2344, accessed December 30, 2014, http://mppda.flinders.edu.au/records/2344.

18. Thomas Doherty, *Hollywood's Censor: Joseph I. Breen and the Production Code Administration* (New York: Columbia University Press, 2007), 70.

CHAPTER 10
Threats from Abroad and Domestic Disturbances

1. "Conboy Seeks Ban on Film as Obscene," *NYT*, March 6, 1935.

2. "Though Rich Husband Spent Large Sums Trying to Suppress Hedy Keisler's Film She Finally Lands in Hollywood Anyway," *Morning Herald*, October 30, 1937.

3. Tariff Act of 1930, 19 U.S.C. § 305.

4. "Film Shown in Court," *NYT*, June 26, 1935.

5. United States v. Two Tin Boxes, 79 F.2d 1017 (2nd Cir. 1935).

6. Eureka Productions v. Lehman, 17 F. Supp. 259, 260 (S.D.N.Y. 1936).

7. *Id.* at 261.

8. Eureka Productions, Inc. v. Byrne, 300 N.Y.S. 218, 221 (App. Div. 1937); also see "News of the Screen," *NYT*, December 30, 1936; and "Court Backs Ban on *Ecstasy*," *NYT*, October 28, 1937.

9. "Ban on *Ecstasy* Is Upheld," *NYT*, September 28, 1939.

10. "Certificate of Censorship Not Approved," accessed December 30, 2014, http://explorepahistory.com/displayimage.php?imgId=1-2-DC9.

11. *Mayer v. Byrne*, 10 N.Y.S.2d 794, 795 (1939).

12. *Id.* at 795.

13. *Id.*

14. Thomas M. Pryor, "Hal Roach Plays at Railroading," *NYT*, October 6, 1940; and Bosley Crowther, "*Whirlpool* French Film Is Presented at the Opening of Art Theatre," *NYT*, October 8, 1940.

15. Distinguished Films v. Stoddard, 68 N.Y.S.2d 737, 738 (App. Div. 1947).

16. *Id.*

17. "Lines from a Paris Watch Tower," *NYT*, November 11, 1934.

18. *Distinguished Films*, 68 N.Y.S.2d at 739.

19. "Seven Little Foys Dance with Eddie," *NYT*, July 16, 1912; "Vaudeville Gossip," *Winnipeg Tribune*, April 6, 1918; "Another Foy," *Capital Times*, April 14, 1922; and "Irving Foy, Last of the Seven Little Foys, Dies at 94," *NYT*, April 26, 2003.

20. B. R. Crisler, "Kinema Kaleidoscope," *NYT*, December 10, 1939; and "Bryan Foy, Vaudevillian and Film Producer, 80, Dies," *NYT*, April 22, 1977.

21. "Race Degeneration Seen For America," *NYT*, June 21, 1932; also "Miscellaneous Brief Reviews," *NYT*, June 17, 1934; and Waldemar Kaempffert, "The Problem of Sterilization," *NYT*, November 29, 1936.
22. Buck v. Bell, 274 U.S. 200, 208 (1927).
23. Foy Productions, Ltd. v. Graves, 3 N.Y.S.2d 573, 574 (App. Div. 1938).
24. *Id.*
25. *Id.* at 576.
26. *Id.* at 578–579.
27. "Thomas Ricketts, Pioneer of Movies," *NYT*, January 21, 1939; also "Al Christie," *NYT*, April 15, 1951; and "David Horsley, One Time Film Producer and Owner of Animal Circus," *NYT*, February 24, 1933.
28. "Al Christie an Independent Producer," *MPW*, September 9, 1916, 1680.
29. "Police Ban Picture Showing Baby Birth," *Bakersfield Californian*, April 7, 1938; "Controversy Over Film To Be Taken to Court," *Coshocton Tribune*, May 15, 1938; "Several Motion Pictures Endorsed, *Birth of a Baby* Showing Disapproved," *Moberly Monitor-Index*, November 12, 1938; and "Two New England Cities Place Ban on *Birth of a Baby*," *Warren Times Mirror*, April 7, 1938.
30. American Committee on Maternal Welfare v. Mangan, 14 N.Y.S.2d 39, 39 (App. Div. 1939); "Immoral or Educational?" *NYT*, March 17, 1938.
31. *American Committee on Maternal Welfare*, 14 N.Y.S.2d at 40.
32. *Id.*
33. *Id.*
34. *Id.* at 42.
35. American Committee on Maternal Welfare v. City of Cincinnati, 5 Ohio Supp. 425 (C.P. 1938); City of Lynchburg v. Dominion Theatres, Inc., 175 Va. 35 (1940).
36. "*Birth of Baby* is Shown at Studio," *Prescott Arizona Evening Courier*, February 14, 1939; "Birth of a Baby Life-Publicized Film To Show Here," *Eugene Register-Guard*, July 31, 1938; "Full-Length Film *Birth of Baby* Passed by Churches, Health Bodies," *Montreal Gazette*, January 22, 1948; "Granada Showing *Birth of a Baby*," *Spokane Daily Chronicle*, August 9, 1938.
37. "Partial Victory for Film," *NYT*, July 12, 1939.
38. "Stage Permit for Woman Is Denied," *Ogden Standard-Examiner*, August 22, 1933.
39. See advertisement in *Lubbock Avalanche-Journal*, January 21, 1934, 7.
40. Letter from John B. Lewis to Lester Thompson, March 23, 1934, MPPDA Digital Archive, record no. 969, accessed December 30, 2014, http://mppda.flinders.edu.au/records/969.
41. "Regents Bar Two Films," *NYT*, June 21, 1938; "Regents Ban Films on Narcotics," *NYT*, June 26, 1938.
42. "*This Nude World* Midnight Show at Hippodrome Friday," *Daily Independent*, February 14, 1934.

CHAPTER 11
Outlaws and Miracles

1. Quoted in Gerald R. Butters, *Banned in Kansas: Motion Picture Censorship, 1915–1966* (Columbia: University of Missouri Press, 2007), 232–233; Thomas Doherty, *Hollywood's Censor: Joseph I. Breen and the Production Code Administration* (New York: Columbia University Press, 2007), 254; Leonard J. Leff and Jerold L. Simmons, *The Dame in the Kimono: Hollywood, Censorship, and the Production Code* (Lexington: University Press of Kentucky, 2001), 115–116; Alan Gevinson, *Within Our Gates: Ethnicity in American Feature Films, 1911–1960* (Berkeley: University of California Press, 1997), 750.

2. "Ban on *The Outlaw* Upheld By Court," *Frederick Maryland News*, September 20, 1947.

3. Cy Rice, "Lots of Lawing Looms Over *The Outlaw* Ban," *Milwaukee Sentinel*, March 8, 1947; "Court Upholds Ban on Hughes *Outlaw*," *Spokane Chronicle*, October 24, 1946; "Censors Veto *The Outlaw*," *Spokane Chronicle*, December 10, 1946; "Offer to General Denied By Hughes," *Free-Lance Star*, November 11, 1947.

4. "*The Outlaw* is Banned," *NYT*, September 9, 1946.

5. Hughes Tool Co. v. Motion Picture Association of America, 66 F. Supp. 1006, 1010–1011 (S.D.N.Y. 1946).

6. *Id.* at 1009.

7. *Id.*

8. United States v. Paramount Pictures, Inc., 334 U.S. 131 (1948).

9. *Hughes Tool Co.*, 66 F. Supp. at 1011.

10. *Id.*

11. *Id.* at 1014.

12. Hughes Tool Co. v. Fielding, 73 N.Y.S.2d 98 (App. Div. 1947).

13. *Duel in the Sun* was banned in Memphis, with Binford commenting, "It is a barbaric symphony of passion and hatred. It is mental and physical putrefaction. It is stark murder! It is stark horror! It is stark depravity! . . . God help America!"; Lester Velie, "You Can't See That Movie," *Colliers Magazine*, May 6, 1950, 12.

14. "Hughes Leads Producers," *NYT*, September 20, 1946.

15. "All Time Domestic Champs," *Variety*, January 6, 1960; and Michael Levitas, "A Man Apart," *New York Times Book Review*, July 10, 1966; and Gevinson, *Within Our Gates*, 751.

16. Thomas v. Collins, 323 U.S. 516 (1945).

17. Hannegan v. Esquire, 327 U.S. 146 (1946).

18. Pennekamp v. Florida, 328 U.S. 331, 347 (1946).

19. United States v. Paramount Pictures, 334 U.S. 131, 166 (1948).

20. "Film Censors Ban *Scarlet Street*," *NYT*, January 5, 1946; and "Film Cuts Will Lift *Scarlet Street* Ban," *NYT*, January 11, 1946; also see Bosley Crowther, "Censors

Again," *NYT*, January 13, 1946; Buck Herzog, "Along Amusement Row," Milwaukee Sentinel, January 15, 1946; "Is It Legal?" *NYT*, January 20, 1946; "*Scarlet Street* Gets Censor's OK," *NYT*, January 25, 1946; "Atlanta Bans Picture," *NYT*, February 4, 1946; "Ban on *Scarlet Street* Upheld," *NYT*, February 15, 1946.

21. "*Lost Boundaries* Faces Atlanta Ban," *NYT*, August 21, 1949.

22. "*Lost Boundaries* T-V Show To Defy Bans in South," *Berkshire Eagle*, August 22, 1949.

23. "2 Cities Stab Pic on Race Problem," *Pittsburgh Courier*, August 27, 1949.

24. RD-DR Corp. v. Smith, 89 F. Supp 596, 597 (N.D. Ga. 1950).

25. RD-DR Corp. v. Smith, 183 F.2d 562, 565 (5th Cir. 1950).

26. RD-DR Corp. v. Smith, 71 Sup. Ct. 80 (1950), *cert. denied*, with Justice Douglas dissenting.

27. "*Pinky* Paves Way in Atlanta Opening," *Brooklyn Daily Eagle*, November 18, 1949.

28. "Negroes Permitted to Sit in Entire Balcony First Time," *Pittsburgh Courier*, November 26, 1949; and "*Pinky* Takes Dixie," *Pittsburgh Courier*, December 10, 1949.

29. See *Variety*, January 4, 1950, 59.

30. "Texas Theater Chain to Ban *Stromboli* and *Pinky*," *Lubbock Morning Avalanche*, February 11, 1950.

31. "Flashes from the Silver Screen," *NYT*, September 27, 1931; and David Kehr, "It's Spanky and Gang," *NYT*, November 10, 2008.

32. United Artists Corp. v. Censors of Memphis, 225 S.W.2d 550, 551–552 (Tenn. 1949).

33. "Producer Challenges Memphis Censors to Ban *Southerner*," *Berkshire Eagle* August 8, 1945; "*Brewster's Millions* Is Barred in Memphis," *NYT*, April 7, 1945; S. L. Kahn, "Memphis Censor Goes on a Spree," *NYT*, May 4, 1947; "Memphis Bans *Verdoux*," *NYT*, June 11, 1947; Lester Velie, "You Can't See That Movie," *Colliers Magazine*, May 6, 1950, 11; and Laura Nickas, "Lloyd T. Binford and the Memphis Board of Censors (1886–1956)," *The Tennessee Encyclopedia of History and Culture*, version 2.0, accessed January 1, 2015, http://tennesseeencyclopedia.net/entry.php?rec=1558.

34. *United Artists*, 225 S.W.2d at 553.

35. *Id.* at 554.

36. Gelling v. State, 247 S.W.2d 95, 96 (Tex. Crim. App. 1952).

37. Thomas M. Pryor, "Front Runner in Foreign Film Sweepstakes," *NYT*, December 3, 1950; and "Brief Obituaries for Strike Period," *NYT*, December 9, 1953.

38. Ezra Goodman, "Notes for a Geography of Morals," *NYT*, July 10, 1938.

39. "Movie Association Bans *Bicycle Thief* Because of 2 Scenes," *Chicago Daily Tribune*, March 2, 1950; and "Won't Cut *Bicycle Thief*," *NYT*, March 2, 1950.

40. Bosley Crowther, "The Screen in Review; *Ways of Love*," *NYT*, December 13, 1950; and "*Ways of Love*, a Film Trilogy Presented at the Paris Theater," *Brooklyn Daily Eagle*, December 13, 1950.

41. Joseph Burstyn, Inc. v. Wilson, 343 U.S. 495, 509 (1952).

42. *Id.*

43. "1950 Awards," New York Film Critics Circle, accessed January 1, 2015, http://www .nyfcc.com/awards/?awardyear=1950.

44. Richard H. Parke, "Rossellini Film is Halted by the City; the *Miracle* Held Blasphe-mous," *NYT*, December 24, 1950; "*Miracle* Banned Throughout City," *NYT*, Decem-ber 25, 1950; "Spellman urges *Miracle* Boycott," *NYT*, January 8, 1951; and "*Miracle* Picketed by 1,000 Catholics," *NYT*, January 15, 1951.

45. Thomas F. Brady, "Jackson Explains," *NYT*, April 23, 1950; Gladwin Hill, "Filmland Breathes Easier," *NYT*, April 30, 1950; and Thomas F. Brady, "Hollywood Relaxes," *NYT*, May 7, 1950.

46. "Memphis Censors Ban *Stromboli*," *Mason City Globe-Gazette*, February 4, 1950.

47. *Burstyn*, 343 U.S. at 508.

48. *Id.* at 513 n.18.

49. Glenn Fowler, "Ephraim London, 78, a Lawyer Who Fought Censorship, Is Dead," *NYT*, June 14, 1990.

50. *In re* Joseph Burstyn, Inc. v. Wilson, 303 N.Y. 242, 255 (App. Div. 1951).

51. *Id.* at 256.

52. *Id.* at 261.

53. *Id.*

54. *Id.* at 263–264.

55. *Id.* at 255–257, emphasis added.

56. *Id.* at 269.

57. *Id.* at 272.

58. *Id.* at 275.

59. *Id.* at 268.

60. *Id.* at 275–276.

61. *Burstyn*, 343 U.S. at 501.

62. *Id.* at 497.

63. *Id.* at 504.

64. *Id.* at 506.

65. *Id.* at 502.

66. *Id.* at 507.

67. Gelling v. Texas, 343 U.S. 960, 960 (1952).

68. ACLU v. City of Chicago, 3 Ill. 2d. 334, 335–336 (1954).

69. *Id.*

70. ACLU v. City of Chicago, 13 Ill. App. 2d. 278, 280 (1957).

71. *Id.* at 289.

72. *Id.* at 286.

CHAPTER 12
State Censorship Statutes on the Defense

1. *In re* Commercial Pictures Corp. v. Board of Regents, 305 N.Y. 336, 339 (1953).
2. *In re* Commercial Pictures Corp. v. Board of Regents, 280 A.D. 260, 261 (N.Y. App. Div. 1952).
3. "Appeals Court Backs Banning of *La Ronde*," *NYT*, May 29, 1953.
4. *In re Commercial Pictures*, 280 A.D. at 264.
5. Superior Films, Inc. v. Department of Education, 159 Ohio St. 315, 329 (1953).
6. *Id.* at 328.
7. *In re Commercial Pictures*, 305 N.Y. at 341–342.
8. *Superior Films*, 159 Ohio St. at 336.
9. *In re Commercial Pictures*, 305 N.Y. at 366.
10. "George Dixon's Washington Scene," *Anderson Herald*, January 12, 1954.
11. Superior Films v. Department of Education, 346 U.S. 587, 588 (1954).
12. *Id.* at 589.
13. RKO v. Department of Education, 162 Ohio St. 263, 277 (1954).
14. *Id.*
15. *Opinions of the Attorney General of Ohio for the Period from January 1, 1922 to January 8, 1923, Volume 1* (Springfield, OH: Kelly-Springfield Printing Company, 1922), 271.
16. Act Relative to the Examination and Licensing of Motion Picture Films to be Publically Exhibited and Displayed in This Commonwealth, Mass. Stat. ch. 428, § 3 (1921).
17. Brattle Films, Inc. v. Commissioner of Public Safety, 333 Mass. 58, 58 (1955).
18. *Id.* at 60–61.
19. Holmby Productions, Inc. v. Vaughn, 177 Kan. 728, 729 (1955).
20. Otto L. Guernsey Jr., "Chicago Seeing Controversial *Moon Is Blue*," *Toledo Blade*, June 28, 1953.
21. *Holmby Productions*, 177 Kan. at 730.
22. *Id.* at 731.
23. Holmby Productions, Inc. v. Vaughn, 350 U.S. 870 (1955).
24. "Cancels *Moon Is Blue*," *NYT*, August 4, 1953; "Jersey City Seizes *The Moon Is Blue*," *NYT*, October 15, 1953; and "Catholic Unit Lauds Film Censorship but Reports 4% Rise in Immoral Movies," *NYT*, November 26, 1953.
25. "A Free Screen," *Life*, February 8, 1954; William H. Brownell Jr., "Hollywood Resume," *NYT*, August 15, 1954; and *Variety*, October 28, 1953, quoted in Chris Fujiwara, *The World and Its Double: The Life and Work of Otto Preminger* (New York: Faber and Faber, 2008).
26. Md. Code Supp. ch. 201, art. 66A, § 6 (1955) as cited in United Artists v. Maryland State Board of Censors, 210 Md. 586, 589 (Md. App. 1956).
27. *United Artists*, 210 Md. at 590.

28. "Film Industry Bans Sinatra Drama," *Sydney Morning Herald*, December 9, 1955.

29. *United Artists*, 210 Md. at 593. Two years earlier New York State overruled the censors' ban on a narcotic-themed film entitled *Teenage Menace* (1952); see *In re* Broadway Angels, Inc. v. Wilson, 282 A.D. 643 (N.Y. 1953).

30. *United Artists*, 210 Md. at 593–594.

31. See *Variety*, September 14, 1955.

32. Parmelee v. United States, 113 F.2d 729, 733 (D.C. Cir. 1940).

33. "Regents Fix Ban on African Movie," *NYT*, March 29, 1951; also see William M. Blair, "Africa Film to Aid New York Museum," *NYT*, May 15, 1951.

34. "Confiscated Film Cleared in New Jersey," *NYT*, May 20, 1952; also see "Documentary Film Barred in Newark," *NYT*, May 10, 1952.

35. "Newark to Continue Fight on African Film," *NYT*, May 21, 1952; "Refusal to Ban Film Assailed in Newark," *NYT*, May 22, 1952; and "Banned Film Shown Privately," *NYT*, October 23, 1952.

36. Board of Censors v. Times Film Corp., 212 Md. 454, 458–459 (Md. Ct. App. 1957).

37. *Id.* at 459.

38. *Id.* at 457.

39. *Id.* at 462.

40. *In re* Excelsior Pictures Corp. v. Regents, 2 A.D.2d 941, 942 (N.Y. App. Div. 1956).

41. *Id.*

42. Commonwealth v. Moniz, 336 Mass. 178, 179 (1957).

43. *Moniz*, 336 Mass. 178.

44. Dickinson Operating Co. v. City of Kansas City, 317 S.W.2d 638 (Kan. Ct. App. 1958); "Film on Nudism Approved," *Corpus Christi Times*, January 22, 1957; "City Movie Ban Is Upheld," *Iola Register*, November 4, 1958.

45. Capitol Enterprises, Inc. v. City of Chicago, 260 F.2d 670, 672 (7th Cir. 1958).

46. "2 Movie Theaters Must Shut for Week," *NYT*, February 12, 1957; also see Library of Congress, National Film Registry press release, available at http://www.loc.gov/film/nfr2005.html.

47. "Forbes to Lecture at *Mom and Dad*," *Wilmington News-Journal*, October 9, 1945; and "*Mom and Dad* Excellent New Educational Film," *Daily Journal Gazette*, November 1, 1946.

48. "William Beaudine Directed Mary Pickford in Movies," *NYT*, March 19, 1970, 47; and Wendy L. Marshall, *William Beaudine: From Silents To Television* (Lanham, MD: Scarecrow Press, 2005).

49. Daniel Eagan, *America's Film Legacy: The Authoritative Guide to the Landmark Movies in the National Film Registry* (New York: Continuum, 2010), 381–382.

50. *In re* Capitol Enterprises, Inc. v. Board of Regents, 1 A.D.2d 990, 991 (N.Y. App. Div. 1956).

51. Regina v. Hicklin, 3 L.R. 360, 371 (Q.B. 1868).

52. Roth v. United States, 354 U.S. 476 (1957).

53. Georges Sadoul, *Dictionary of Film Makers* (Berkeley: University of California Press, 1972), 12.

54. "Claude Autant-Lara, 98, a Film Director," *NYT*, February 9, 2000.

55. Times Film Corp. v. City of Chicago, 244 F.2d 432, 436 (7th Cir. 1957).

56. *Id.* at 435–436.

57. *Capitol Enterprises*, 260 F.2d at 674.

58. *Id.*

59. *Id.* at 676.

60. Paramount Film Distributing Corp. v. City of Chicago, 172 F. Supp. 69, 72 (N.D. Ill. 1959).

61. Hallmark Productions, Inc. v. Carroll, 384 Pa. 348, 362 (1956).

62. *Id.* at 361.

63. *Id.* at 360.

64. *Id.*

65. *Id.* at 368–369.

66. "Obscene Movies Shown in Court as Testimony," *Hazleton Plain Speaker*, December 6, 1956, 18.

67. Commonwealth v. Blumenstein, 396 Pa. 417, 427 (1959).

68. *Id.* at 429.

69. *Id.* at 423.

70. Kingsley International Pictures Corp. v. Blanc, 396 Pa. 448, 461–462 (1959).

71. *Id.* at 466.

72. *Id.*

73. *Id.* at 472.

74. *In re* Kingsley International Pictures Corp. v. Regents, 4 N.Y.2d 349, 352–353 (App. Div. 1958).

75. *In re* Kingsley International Pictures Corp. v. Regents, 4 A.D.2d 348, 350 (N.Y. App. Div. 1957).

76. *Id.*

77. *In re Kingsley International Pictures*, 4 N.Y.2d at 365.

78. Kingsley International Pictures Corp. v. City of Providence, 166 F. Supp. 456, 458 (D.R.I. 1958); also see "Movie Suit Attacks Providence Censor," *NYT*, February 14, 1958, 19.

79. Kingsley International Pictures Corp. v. Regents, 360 U.S. 684, 688 (1959).

80. *Id.* at 698.

81. *Id.* at 690.

82. *Id.* at 702.

83. *Id.* at 691–692.

84. Grove Press, Inc. v. Christenberry, 276 F.2d 433, 434–435 (2nd Cir. 1960).

85. *Id.* at 439.

86. *In re* Excelsior Pictures Corp. v. Regents, 3 N.Y.2d 237, 242 (App. Div. 1956).

87. Excelsior Pictures Corp. v. City of Chicago, 182 F. Supp. 400, 405 (N.D. Ill. 1960).

88. "Edgar G. Ulmer, Movie Producer," *NYT*, October 2, 1972, 40; "Doris Wishman, B Film Director Dies," *NYT*, August 19, 2002; "David F. Friedman, Horror Pioneer, Dies at 87," *NYT*, February 15, 2011.

89. Ron Powers, "Big Bosoms and Square Jaws," *NYT*, July 24, 2005.

90. Douglas Martin, "Russ Meyer, 82, a Filmmaker of Classics in a Lusty Genre, Dies," *NYT*, September 23, 2004.

91. Murry Schumach, "Nudity Featured in Film Quickies," *NYT*, June 15, 1961.

92. State *ex rel.* Keating v. A Motion Picture Entitled "Vixen," 27 Ohio St. 2d 278, 280 (1971).

93. "Old Movie Taboos Eased in New Code For Film Industry," *NYT*, December 12, 1956.

94. Irving Rubine, "Boys Meet Ghouls, Make Money," *NYT*, March 16, 1958; Larry Glenn, "Hollywood B Hive," *NYT*, May 5, 1963; Aljean Harmetz, "The Dime-Store Way To Make Movies," *NYT*, August 4, 1974; Harmetz, "Samuel Z. Arkoff, Maker of Drive In Thrillers, Dies at 83," *NYT*, September 19, 2001; and "American International Pictures," Grindhouse Cinema Database, accessed January 5, 2015, http://www.grindhousedatabase.com/index.php/American_International_Pictures.

CHAPTER 13

Devil in the Details

1. Zenith International Film Corp. v. City of Chicago, 291 F.2d 785, 788 (7th Cir. 1961).

2. Times Film Corp. v. City of Chicago, 365 U.S. 43, 46–47 (1961).

3. *Id.* at 49.

4. *Id.* at 51.

5. *Id.* at 69–72.

6. *Id.* at 81.

7. *Zenith International Film*, 291 F.2d at 787.

8. *Id.* at 789.

9. *Id.* at 790.

10. Bosley Crowther, "The Screen in Review," *NYT*, November 9, 1954.

11. Freedman v. Maryland, 380 U.S. 51, 54–55 (1965).

12. *Id.* at 55, quoting United Artists Corp. v. Board of Censors, 210 Md. 586 (1956).

13. United States v. One Carton Positive Motion Picture Film, 247 F. Supp. 450, 456 (S.D.N.Y. 1965).

14. Drive In Theatres, Inc. v. Huskey, 305 F. Supp. 1232, 1235 (W.D.N.C 1969).

15. *Id.* at 61–62.

16. Trans-Lux Distributing Co. v. Board of Censors, 240 Md. 98, 100–101 (1965).

17. *Id.* at 105.

18. *Id.* at 107–109.

19. *Id.* at 111.

20. *Id.* at 112.

21. Howard Thompson, "Danish Film Ban To Be Appealed," *NYT*, May 9, 1963.

22. *In re* Trans-Lux Distributing Corp. v. Board of Regents, 14 N.Y.2d 88, 92–93 (App. Div. 1964).

23. *In re* Cambist Films, Inc. v. Board of Regents, 46 Misc. 2d 513, 515 (N.Y. 1965).

24. Cusack v. Teitel Film Corp., 38 Ill. 2d 53 (Ill. 1967).

25. *Teitel Film*, 38 Ill. 2d at 58.

26. Teitel Film Corp. v. Cusack, 390 U.S. 139 (1968).

27. Kansas *ex rel.* Londerholm v. Columbia Pictures Corp., 197 Kan. 448, 449 (1966).

28. *Id.* at 450.

29. *Id.* at 451–452.

30. "Judge Strikes Virginia Law on Censorship," *Fredericksburg Free Lance-Star*, April 20, 1965.

31. *Drive In Theatres*, 305 F. Supp. at 1233.

32. Drive In Theatres, Inc. v. Huskey, 435 F.2d 228, 229 (4th Cir. 1970).

33. Eve Productions, Inc. v. Shannon, 312 F. Supp. 26, 28 (E.D. Mo. 1970), *aff'd on appeal*, Eve Productions, Inc. v. Shannon, 439 F.2d 1073 (8th Cir. 1971).

34. Monica Theater v. Municipal Court, 9 Cal. App. 3d 1, 5 (Cal. Ct. App. 1970).

35. *Id.* at 7.

36. Quantity of Books v. Kansas, 378 U.S. 205 (1964).

37. State v. Eros Cinema, Inc., 264 So. 2d 615, 619 (La. 1972).

38. Lee Art Theatre v. Virginia, 392 U.S. 636, 636 (1968).

39. Rabe v. Washington, 405 U.S. 313, 314 (1972).

40. State v. Rabe, 79 Wn. 2d 254, 263 (Wa. 1971).

41. *Rabe*, 405 U.S. at 315–316.

42. Roaden v. Kentucky, 413 U.S. 496, 497 (1973).

43. *Id.* at 506.

CHAPTER 14
Dirty Words

1. Dunn v. Board of Censors, 240 Md. 249, 254 (Ct. App. 1965).

2. Jacobellis v. Ohio, 378 U.S. 184, 197 (1964).

3. Printed copy of 1930 production code, January 1, 1931, MPPDA Digital Archive, record no. 2254, accessed January 5, 2015, http://mppda.flinders.edu.au/records/2254.

4. Memorandum, January 11, 1939, MPPDA Digital Archive, record no. 1207, accessed January 15, 2015, http://mppda.flinders.edu.au/records/1207.

5. "Comedian Arrested," *Southern Illinoisian*, October 6, 1961; "Bruce Accused of Obscenity," *Bridgeport Post*, October 25, 1961; "Bruce Guilty of Obscenity," *Chicago Tribune*, March 1, 1963.

6. *In re* Connection Co. v. Regents, 17 A.D.2d 671, 671 (N.Y. App. Div. 1962), *aff'd, In re* Connection Co. v. Regents, 12 N.Y.2d 779 (Ct. App. 1962).

7. *In re Connection Co.*, 17 A.D.2d at 672.

8. Excerpt of Chief Justice Murtagh's trial-court opinion in *People v. Bruce* reprinted in a book authored by the prosecutor in the case; see Richard Kuh, *Foolish Figleaves? Pornography In——and Out of——Court* (New York: MacMillan, 1967), 184–186; also see Jack Roth, "Lenny Bruce Act Is Ruled Obscene," *NYT*, November 5, 1964.

9. Thomas Thompson, "Raw Dialogue Challenges All the Censors," *Life*, June 10, 1966.

10. FCC v. Fox Television Stations, Inc., 132 S. Ct. 2307 (2012).

11. FCC v. Pacifica Foundation, 438 U.S. 726, 731–732 (1978).

12. *Id.* at 745–746.

13. *Id.* at 747–748.

14. Ward v. Rock Against Racism, 491 U.S. 781, 791 (1989).

15. See MPAA ratings and history at http://www.mpaa.org/film-ratings/.

16. "Movie Censor Bill Halfway Through Legislature Today," *Amsterdam Evening Recorder*, March 22, 1962.

17. Michael Keating, "Regents Ask Right to Classify Movies on Suitability for Children," *Schenectady Gazette*, August 2, 1963.

18. Glen Levy, "Cinematic Cursing," *Time*, August 9, 2011.

19. *Fox Television Stations*, 132 S. Ct. at 2313.

20. *Id.* at 6.

21. *In re* Complaints Against Various Broadcast Licensees Regarding Their Airing of the "Golden Globe Awards" Program, 19 F.C.C. Rcd. 4975, 4976 n.4 (2004).

22. *Id.* at 4978.

23. Fox Television Stations, Inc. v. FCC, 489 F.3d 444 (2d Cir. 2007); Fox Television Stations, Inc. v. FCC, 613 F.3d 317 (2d Cir. 2010); ABC, Inc. v. FCC, 404 Fed. App'x. 530 (2d Cir. 2011).

24. *Fox Television Stations*, 489 F.3d at 449.

25. *In re* Industry Guidance on the Commission's Case Law Interpreting 18 U.S.C. § 1464 and Enforcement Policies regarding Broadcast Indecency, 16 F.C.C. Rcd. 7999, 8008–8009 (2001), as cited in Treasa Chidester, "What the #$%& Is Happening On Television? Indecency in Broadcasting," *CommLaw Conspectus* 13 (2004): 157.

26. FCC v. Fox Television Stations, Inc., 129 S. Ct. 1800, 1812 (2009).

27. *Fox Television Stations*, 132 S. Ct. at 2316.

28. *Id.* at 2320.

29. "Director Protests X Rating Given to Movie *Scarface*," *Sarasota Herald-Tribune*, November 5, 1983.
30. "*Wolf of Wall Street* Breaks F-Word Record," *Variety*, January 2, 2014.
31. Press release quoted in "Weinsteins Ready 'Fuck-less' PG-13 Version of *The King's Speech*," *Deadline*, March 24, 2011.
32. Lauren Effron and Jenna Millman, "*Bully* Film Rating Lowered to PG-13 After Public Pressure," *ABC News*, April 6, 2012.

CHAPTER 15
Filthy Pictures

1. Vernon Scott, "Decency Legion Gives Wilder Film 'C' Grade," *San Bernardino County Sun*, December 14, 1964.
2. Bosley Crowther, "Moral Brinksmanship," *NYT*, December 13, 1964; and A. H. Weiler, "*Kiss Me, Stupid*," *NYT*, December 23, 1964.
3. A. H. Weiler, "Board Gives Seal to *Pawnbroker*," *NYT*, March 29, 1965.
4. Roth v. United States, 354 U.S. 476, 482–483 (1957).
5. Commonwealth v. Sharpless, 2 Serg. & Rawle 91 (Pa. 1815).
6. Orison Swett Marden, *The Consolidated Encyclopedic Library, Vol. 2* (New York: Emerson Press, 1902), 513.
7. Regina v. Hicklin, 3 L.R. 360, 371 (Q.B. 1868).
8. United States v. One Book entitled Ulysses By James Joyce, 72 F.2d 705 (2d Cir. 1934); Grove Press, Inc. v. Christenberry, 276 F.2d 433 (2d Cir. 1960) (*Lady Chatterley's Lover*); Grove Press, Inc. v. Gerstein, 378 U.S. 577 (1964) (*Tropic of Cancer*).
9. *Roth*, 354 U.S. at 488–489.
10. Capitol Enterprises, Inc. v. City of Chicago, 260 F.2d 670, 674–675 (7th Cir. 1958).
11. Excelsior Pictures Corp. v. City of Chicago, 182 F. Supp. 400, 405 (N.D. Ill. 1960).
12. Fanfare Films, Inc. v. Motion Picture Censor Board, 234 Md. 10, 12 (Ct. App. 1964).
13. *Id.*
14. "Distributor of French Film Appeals State Regents' Ban," *NYT*, June 3, 1964.
15. *In re* Metzger v. Couper, 21 A.D.2d 920, 920 (N.Y. App. Div. 1964).
16. An interesting comparison is seen with *Jacobellis* and State v. Warth, 173 Ohio St. 15 (1962), since the material involved in both cases was the motion picture *Les amants*. The difference between the two actions was the statute invoked. Jacobellis was indicted, tried, and convicted for violation of § 2905.34: "No person shall *knowingly* sell, lend, give away, exhibit, or offer to sell, lend, give away, or exhibit, or publish or offer to publish or have in his possession or under his control an obscene . . . motion picture film." Warth was indicted for violation of § 2905.342, which criminalized *mere possession* of an obscene motion picture. Warth prevailed due to the constitutional infirmity of § 2905.342, which omitted the crucial element of scienter or knowledge of the obscenity of the materials at issue.

17. State v. Jacobellis, 115 Ohio App. 226, 230 (Ohio Ct. App. 1961).

18. State v. Jacobellis, 173 Ohio St. 22, 28 (1962).

19. Jacobellis v. Ohio, 378 U.S. 184, 187 (1964).

20. *Id.* at 193.

21. *Id.* at 197.

22. *Id.*

23. *Id.* at 197–198.

24. *Id.* at 203–204.

25. Md. Ann. Code Art. 66A § 19 (1965).

26. Dunn v. Board of Censors, 240 Md. 249, 257 (1965).

27. Memoirs v. Massachusetts, 383 U.S. 413, 445–446 (1966).

28. John Cleland, *Fanny Hill, or Memoirs of a Woman of Pleasure*, part X, second letter (Paris: Isadore Liseux, 1888), 309.

29. *Memoirs*, 383 U.S. at 415.

30. *Id.* at 419.

31. *Id.* at 433.

32. *Id.* at 454.

33. *Id.* at 441.

34. *Id.* at 458.

35. *Id.* at 455.

36. Douglas Martin, "Vilgot Sjöman, Filmmaker Without Taboos, Dies at 81," *NYT*, April 11, 2008.

37. United States v. One Carton Positive Motion Picture Film, 367 F.2d 889, 892–893 (2d Cir. 1966).

38. United States v. One Carton Positive Motion Picture Film, 247 F. Supp. 450, 465 (S.D.N.Y. 1965).

39. *Id.* at 375.

40. *Id.*

41. *One Carton Positive*, 367 F.2d at 896.

42. *Id.* at 897.

43. *Id.* at 905.

44. Judith Crist, "Sex Yes, Mediocrity No," *New York*, March 17, 1969, 54; and Bosley Crowther, "Screen: Swedish Enigma," *NYT*, February 20, 1967.

45. Lordi v. UA New Jersey Theatres, Inc., 108 N.J. Super. 19, 22 (1969).

46. Richard Schickel, "It Hides Nothing But the Heart," *Life*, March 21, 1969, 14.

47. United States v. A Motion Picture Film Entitled "I Am Curious—Yellow," 404 F.2d 196, 203 (2d Cir. 1968).

48. *Grove Press*, 276 F.2d 433; *Grove Press*, 378 U.S. 577; Attorney General v. A Book Named "Naked Lunch," 351 Mass. 298 (1966).

49. Barney Rosset interviewed by Ken Jordan, "The Art of Publishing No. 2," *Paris Review*, no. 145 (Winter 1997): 145.

50. Judith Crist, "Sex Yes, Mediocrity No," *New York*, March 17, 1969, 54.

51. Vincent Canby, "Screen: *I Am Curious (Yellow)*," *NYT*, March 11, 1969.

52. Andrew Sarris, "Films in Focus," *Village Voice*, January 15, 1970.

53. Roger Ebert, "*I Am Curious (Yellow)*," *Chicago Sun-Times*, September 23, 1969.

54. Richard Schickel, "It Hides Nothing But the Heart," *Life*, March 21, 1969, 14.

55. Alex Thien, "Curious? Well, It's Pornography," *Milwaukee Sentinel*, November 21, 1970.

56. Cooper v. Bailey, 257 So. 2d 332 (Ala. 1972); Grove Press, Inc. v. Bailey, 318 F. Supp 244 (N.D. Ala. 1970); NGC Theatre Corp. v. Mummert, 107 Ariz. 484 (1971); Evans Theatre Corp. v. Slaton, 227 Ga. 337 (1971); Grove Press, Inc. v. Maryland State Board of Censors, 401 U.S. 480 (1971); Byrne v. Karalexis, 401 U.S. 216 (1971); Lordi v. UA New Jersey Theatres, Inc., 108 N.J. Super. 19 (1969); Grove Press, Inc. v. Corrigan, 21 Ohio Misc. 185 (Ohio Ct. Com. Pl 1969).

57. Bob Thomas, "Morals of City Hard to Protect," *Sarasota Journal*, January 14, 1970.

58. "Catholic Group Condemns *I Am Curious (Yellow)*," *NYT*, March 22, 1969.

59. United States v. A Motion Picture Film Entitled "I Am Curious—Yellow," 404 F.2d 196, 198 (2d Cir. 1968).

60. *UA New Jersey Theatres*, 108 N.J. Super. at 22–23.

61. *I Am Curious—Yellow*, 404 F.2d at 198 n.2.

62. *Id.* at 199.

63. *Id.* at 199–200.

64. *Id.* at 203.

65. Wagonheim v. State, 255 Md. 297, 307 (1969).

66. *Id.* at 323.

67. *Evans Theatre*, 227 Ga. at 380.

68. *NGC Theatre*, 107 Ariz. at 489.

69. *Grove Press*, 21 Ohio Misc. 185.

70. *Grove Press*, 318 F. Supp. at 249.

71. *UA New Jersey Theatres*, 108 N.J. Super. at 31.

72. *Id.* at 25.

73. "Judge Backs Film Seizure," *Newport Daily News*, June 7, 1969.

74. *Karalexis*, 401 U.S. at 219.

75. Younger v. Harris, 401 U.S. 37 (1971); Samuels v. Mackell, 401 U.S. 66 (1961).

76. William O. Douglas, "Review of Points of Rebellion," *Sociological Quarterly* 12, no. 3 (Summer 1971): 410.

77. *Grove Press*, 401 U.S. 480.

78. Barney Rosset, "The Art of Publishing No. 2," *Paris Review*, no. 145 (Winter 1997).

79. Landau v. Fording, 245 Cal. App. 2d 820, 825 (Cal. Ct. App. 1966).

80. *Id.* at 822.

81. *Id.* at 826–830.

82. *Landau*, 245 Cal. App. 2d at 827.

83. Landau v. Fording, 388 U.S. 467 (1967).
84. Rob Craig, *Ed Wood, Mad Genius: A Critical Study of the Films* (Jefferson, NC: McFarland, 2009), 295.
85. Hewitt v. Board of Censors, 254 Md. 179, 186 (1969).
86. Richard P. Krafsur, ed., *American Film Institute Catalog of Motion Pictures: 1970*, vol. 2 (Berkeley: University of California Press, 1997), 788.
87. *Hewitt*, 254 Md. at 196.
88. *Id.* at 184.
89. Notable examples of "Nazi sexploitation" include *Ilsa, the She Wolf of the S.S.* (1975) as well as Frost's own *Black Gestapo* (1975), *Salon Kitty* (1976), *S.S. Experiment Love Camp* (1976), *Love Camp 27* (1977), *Fraulein Devil* (1977), *La Bestia in Calore* or *S.S. Hell Camp* (1977), *S.S. Girls* (1977), *Private House of the S.S.* (1977), and *The Gestapo's Last Orgy* (1977). For mainstream audiences, *The Night Porter* (1974) addressed a similar theme.
90. Hewitt v. Board of Censors, 256 Md. 358, 362 (1970).
91. *Id.* at 364.
92. United States v. A Motion Picture Film "Pattern of Evil," 304 F. Supp 197, 202 (S.D.N.Y. 1969).
93. *Id.* Contemporaneous with the *Pattern of Evil* case, the Georgia Supreme Court commented on how plot may play into the obscenity analysis. Reviewing the state's action against a putatively obscene film entitled *Sandra—The Making of a Woman* (1970), the Georgia court found the film's de minimis plot coupled with explicit depiction of sexual congress was sufficient to constitute probable cause that the picture was obscene. "The film was viewed by the trial judge, who found that sexual conduct was graphically demonstrated in the close up camera shots and scenes of *Sandra*, while completely nude, having sexual intercourse with nude men on numerous occasions throughout the entire film, and the cunnilingal act of Phil on Sandra, and Sandra masturbating. This, the court said gave it probable cause to believe that the picture film . . . is obscene as a matter of fact and as a matter of law. . . . Although the film has a plot and it does contain some non-sexual footage, the plot obviously is nothing but a contrivance to link together the various sexual experiences." Metro Theatre v. Slaton, 228 Ga. 102, 104 (1971).
94. People v. Bloss, 18 Mich. App. 410, 416 (1969).
95. Vincent Canby, "*I, a Woman* A Hit Despite Its Origin," *NYT*, August 10, 1967.
96. Metzger v. Pearcy, 393 F.2d 202 (7th Cir. 1968).
97. Duggan v. Guild Theatre, Inc., 436 Pa. 191, 199–200 (1969).
98. *Id.* at 201–202.
99. "Anything Goes," *Newsweek*, November 13, 1967.
100. "Production Code Approved only 87 U.S. Films in '62," *NYT*, January 10, 1963; Robert Windeler, "As Nation's Standards Change, So Do Movies," *NYT*, October 8, 1968.

CHAPTER 16

The Porno Chic

1. Lars Bo Langsted, Peter Garde, and Vagn Greve, *Criminal Law in Denmark* (Netherlands: Kluwer Law International, 2011), 37.

2. For history and filmography, see Lasse Braun's official website at http://www.lasse-braun.com.

3. The film shown in San Francisco entitled *Animal Lover* (1971) was directed by Alex de Renzy and incorporated clips from *A Summer Day July 1970*. See Paul Kern Lee, "Smut Films Last Straw to Some San Franciscans," *Eugene Register-Guard*, May 23, 1971.

4. Vincent Canby, "Have You Tried The Danish Blue?," *NYT*, June 21, 1970.

5. United States v. Strand Art Theatre Corp., 325 F. Supp. 256 (W.D. Mo. 1970); and Movies, Inc. v. Conlisk, 345 F. Supp. 780 (N.D. Ill. 1971).

6. United States v. 35mm Motion Picture Film Entitled "Language of Love," 432 F.2d 705, 711 (2d Cir. 1970).

7. *Id.* at 711–712.

8. John Heidenry, *What Wild Ecstasy: The Rise and Fall of the Sexual Revolution* (New York: Simon & Schuster, 1997), 74.

9. William Pade, "King of Smut Faces Spotlight," *Pittsburgh Press*, December 9, 1978; "Reuben Sturman Makes Smut Lucrative," *Pittsburgh Post-Gazette*, January 2, 1979; "Reputed Porn King Convicted of Fraud," *Pittsburgh Press*, November 17, 1989; "Porn Figure Gets 10 Years on Taxes," *Pittsburgh Press*, February 13, 1990; "Porn Figure Sturman Dies in Prison at 73," *Las Vegas Sun*, October 29, 1997.

10. Interview with retired FBI agent Roger Young, accessed January 7, 2015, http://www.catholicnewsagency.com/resources/life-and-family/pornography/.

11. United States v. Sturman, 679 F.2d 840 (11th Cir. 1982).

12. United States v. Kraig, 99 F.3d 1361 (6th Cir. 1996), citing United States v. Sturman, 951 F.2d 1466 (6th Cir. 1991), *cert. denied*, 504 U.S. 985 (1992).

13. "Porn Figure Sturman Dies in Prison at 73," *Las Vegas Sun*, October 29, 1997.

14. United States v. Sturman, 49 F.3d 1275 (7th Cir. 1995); also Greg Hernandez, "Porn Kingpin Who Escaped Prison Arrested," *Los Angeles Times*, February 10, 1993.

15. Redrup v. New York, 386 U.S. 767, 770 (1967).

16. I.M. Amusement Corp. v. Ohio, 389 U.S. 573, 573 (1968).

17. Stanley v. Georgia, 394 U.S. 557, 568 (1969).

18. State *ex rel.* Keating v. A Motion Picture Film Entitled "Vixen," 27 Ohio St. 2d 278, 281 (Ohio 1971); and "Court Rules Florida's Obscenity Law Unconstitutional," *Daytona Morning Journal*, July 23, 1970.

19. For Florida, see "After Five Weeks, Shut Down *Vixen*," *Variety*, October 29, 1969; for Ohio, "*Vixen* Obscene, Judge Leis Rules," *Cincinnati Enquirer*, November 18, 1969; for Georgia, "Nab *Vixen* Print and 18-year-Old House Mgr. in Macon Porno

Protest," *Variety*, January 22, 1969; for Illinois, Bill Acton, "Jury Rules *Vixen* Obscene," *Danville Commercial-News*, April 16, 1970; "Michigan Drops Its Charge of Obscenity Against *Vixen*," *Daily Variety*, May 15, 1969; for North Carolina, "Criminal Obscenity Dangles; Nabbed Duo of Prints Returned," *Variety*, June 4, 1969; for Utah, "Not Guilty *Vixen* Verdict," *Hollywood Reporter*, June 11, 1970; for Wisconsin, James Gahagan, "Sue to Keep Milwaukee from Censoring *Vixen*," *Daily Variety* September 9, 1959.

20. Meyer v. Austin, 319 F. Supp. 457 (Fla. 1970).

21. *Vixen*, 27 Ohio St. 2d at 293.

22. Davis E. James, *The Most Typical Avant-Garde: History and Geography of Minor Cinemas in Los Angeles* (Los Angeles: University of California Press, 2005), 375; also see William Paul, "New York's New Porn: Holding Our Own," *Village Voice*, May 20, 1971, 67; and "Cinema of Sex Made Them Rich," *Kansas City Star*, February 6, 1972.

23. See *Variety*, February 2, 1972.

24. Ed Halter, "Return to Paradise," *Village Voice*, June 18, 2002.

25. For *Boys in the Sand*, see Wakefield Poole, *Dirty Poole: A Sensual Memoir* (New Jersey: Lethe Press, 2011), 139–159; for *Bible*, see ibid., 181–197.

26. Claim was substantiated in author's conversations with Robert Evans.

27. Emmett George Price, Tammy L. Kernodle, and Horace J. Maxile Jr., eds., *Encyclopedia of African American Music, Volume 3* (Santa Barbara, CA: Gerwood, 2011), 341.

28. Miller v. California, 413 U.S. 15, 37 (1973).

29. *Id.* at 24.

30. *Id.* at 40–41.

31. Paris Adult Theatre I v. Slaton, 413 U.S. 49, 52 (1973).

32. Slaton v. Paris Adult Theatre, 228 Ga. 343, 347 (1971).

33. Slaton v. Paris Adult Theatre, 231 Ga. 312, 318 (1973).

34. *Paris Adult Theatre I*, 413 U.S. at 69.

35. United States v. Orito, 413 U.S. 139, 142 (1973).

36. United States v. 12 200-Ft. Reels of Film, 413 U.S. 123, 128 (1973).

37. *Vixen*, 35 Ohio St. 2d at 219–220.

38. Warren Weaver Jr., "Nixon Repudiates Obscenity Report as Morally Void," *NYT*, October 25, 1970.

39. Report of the Commission on Obscenity and Pornography (Washington, DC: U.S. Government Printing Office, 1970), 544.

40. *Paris Adult Theatre I*, 413 U.S. at 61.

41. See http://www.the-numbers.com/movies/1970/Beyond-the-Valley-of-the-Dolls; and http://www.ericagavin.com/the-films-2/beyond-the-valley-of-the-dolls/.

42. "Review *Deep Throat*," *Variety*, December 31, 1971; and Robert Berkvist, ". . . And What about the Peeps?," *NYT*, December 9, 1973.

43. Ralph Blumethal, "Hard-core Grows Fashionable—and Very Profitable," *New York Times Magazine*, January 21, 1973, 28.

44. Nicholas Gage, "Organized Crime Reaps Huge Profits From Dealing in Pornographic Films," *NYT*, October 12, 1975; and Clark Mollenhoff, "Other Mobsters Resented Columbo Heat," *Des Moines Register*, July 11, 1971.

45. People v. Mature Enterprises, Inc., 73 Misc. 2d 749, 752 (N.Y. 1973); *id*. at 764; and *id*. at 765.

46. *Id*. at 750.

47. Coleman v. Wilson, 123 N.J. Super. 310, 319–320 (1973).

48. United States v. One Reel of Film, 360 F. Supp. 1067, 1072 (D. Ma. 1973).

49. *Wilson*, 123 N.J. Super. at 320.

50. *Mature Enterprises*, 73 Misc. 2d at 752.

51. *One Reel of Film*, 360 F. Supp. at 1068–1069.

52. Gage, "Organized Crime Reaps Huge Profits from Dealing in Pornographic Films," *NYT*.

53. United States v. Thetford, 676 F.2d 170 (5th Cir. 1982).

54. *Id*.; Jon Lewis, *Hollywood v. Hard Core: How the Struggle Over Censorship Saved the Modern Film Industry* (New York: New York University Press, 2002), 210; Ralph Blumenthal, "Is This the Start of the Porno Chic?," *Lakeland Ledger*, January 21, 1973; Jody W. Pennington, *The History of Sex in American Film* (Westport, CT: Praeger, 2007), 56; David A. Cook, *Lost Illusions: American Cinema in the Shadow of Watergate and Vietnam, 1970–1979* (Berkeley: University of California Press, 2000), 275; Carolyn Bronstein, *Battling Pornography: The American Feminist Anti-Pornography Movement, 1976–1986* (New York: Cambridge University Press, 2011), 63; Linda Lovelace and Mike McGrady, *Out of Bondage* (Secaucus, NJ: Lyle Stuart, 1986), 143; Jami Bernard, *The X List: The National Society of Film Critics' Guide to the Movies That Turn Us On* (Cambridge, MA: Da Capo, 2005), 78.

55. "*Deep Throat*, Disputed Sex Film, Opens Near Princeton," *NYT*, September 28, 1972.

56. City of Sioux Falls v. Mini-Kota Art Theatres, Inc., 247 N.W.2d 676, 678–679 (S.D. 1976).

57. Redlich v. Capri Cinema, 43 A.D.2d 27, 28 (N.Y. App. Div. 1973).

58. *Id*. at 28–29.

59. United States v. Marks, 520 F.2d 913, 918–919 (6th Cir. 1975).

60. State v. Aiuppa, 298 So. 2d 391, 403 (Fla. 1974).

61. Addison Verrill, "No Jury, 10 Day 'Throat' Case," *Variety*, November 11, 1976, 80.

62. United States v. Various Articles of Obscene Merchandise, 565 F. Supp. 7, 8 (S.D.N.Y. 1982).

63. United States v. Various Articles of Obscene Merchandise, 709 F.2d 132, 136–137 (2d Cir. 1983).

64. Jonathan Coopersmith, "Pornography, Technology and Progress," *Icon* 4 (1998): 105, quoting Merrill Lynch, "The Home Video Market: Times of Turbulence and Transition," January 6, 1986.

65. As prices remained inflated, videotape technology drastically decreased production and distribution costs and increased the speed with which a production could be shot, edited, and marketed. Together these factors created a wildly lucrative business model.

66. "X-Rated Movies Still Major Factor in the Video Market," *NYT*, January 21, 1982.

67. Stephen Advokat, "Small Screen Begins to Dominate," *St. Petersburg Evening Independent*, December 26, 1985.

68. State *ex rel.* Wayne County Prosecutor v. Diversified Theatrical Corp., 396 Mich. 244, 246 (1976).

69. Universal Amusement Co. v. Vance, 404 F. Supp. 33, 48 (S.D. Tex. 1975).

70. Art Theatre Guild, Inc. v. Parrish, 503 F.2d 133 (6th Cir. 1974).

71. Legs McNeil, Jennifer Osborne, and Peter Pavia, *The Other Hollywood* (New York: Harper Collins, 2005), 183.

72. Alan M. Dershowitz, *The Best Defense* (New York: Vintage Books, 1983), 159.

73. *Marks*, 520 F.2d at 917.

74. Tom Goldstein, "Notables Aid Convicted *Deep Throat* Star," *NYT*, June 29, 1976.

75. Julia M. Klein, "Law Professor Will Present Appeal Of *Deep Throat* Obscenity Conviction," *Harvard Crimson*, June 16, 1976.

76. Dershowitz, *Best Defense*, 169.

77. Marks v. United States, 430 U.S. 188, 196 (1977).

78. Matt Schudel, "Marilyn Chambers, 56, *Green Door* Star, Found Dead in Her California Home," *Washington Post*, April 14, 2009.

79. Douglas Martin, "Jim Mitchell, 63, Filmmaker, Is Dead," *NYT*, July 19, 2007.

80. Arthur Bell, "The Whole Town's Talking About the *Jones* Girl," *Village Voice*, May 10, 1973, 91.

81. Martin, "Jim Mitchell Is Dead."

82. Susan Sward, "Porn King Jim Mitchell Walks Out of Prison Today," *San Francisco Chronicle*, October 3, 1997.

83. Roger Ebert, "The Devil in Miss Jones," *Chicago Sun-Times*, June 13, 1973.

84. Peter Krämer, *The New Hollywood: From Bonnie And Clyde to Star Wars* (London: Wallflower, 2005), 50.

85. Roger Ebert, "Interview with Deep Throat Director Gerard Damiano," *Chicago Sun-Times*, July 26, 1974.

86. Penthouse sought a declaratory judgment that *Caligula* was not obscene under Georgia's obscenity statute; see Penthouse Intern v. McAuliffe, 702 F.2d 925 (11th Cir. 1983).

CHAPTER 17

Just Not Here

1. United States v. One Reel of 35mm Color Motion Picture Film Entitled "Sinder-ella," 369 F. Supp. 1082, 1083 (E.D.N.Y. 1972).

2. United States v. One Reel of 35mm Color Motion Picture Film Entitled "Sinder-ella," 491 F.2d 956 (2d Cir. 1974).

3. Vincent Canby, "Screen: Andy Warhol's *Blue Movie*," *NYT*, July 22, 1969; J. J. Mur-phy, *The Black Hole of the Camera: The Films of Andy Warhol* (Berkeley: University of California Press, 2012), 223–224.

4. "New Warhol Movie Is Seized By Police," *NYT*, August 2, 1969.

5. Morris Kaplan, "3-Judge Panel Here Declares Warhol's *Blue Movie* Obscene," *NYT*, September 19, 1969.

6. People v. Heller, 29 N.Y.2d 319, 323 (App. Div. 1971).

7. Heller v. New York, 413 U.S. 483 (1973).

8. People v. Heller, 33 N.Y.2d 314, 232 (App. Div. 1973).

9. Jenkins v. Georgia, 418 U.S. 153, 158–159 (1974).

10. *Id.* at 161.

11. "Court Accepts Case On Screen Nudity," *Palm Beach Post*, October 16, 1974.

12. Erznoznik v. City of Jacksonville, 422 U.S. 205, 206 (1975).

13. *Id.* at 213.

14. *Id.* at 217–218.

15. Box office data for *The Stewardesses*, The Numbers, accessed January 7, 2015, http://www.the-numbers.com/movies/Stewardesses-The#tab=box-office.

16. State v. Gulf States Theatres, Inc., 270 So. 2d 547, 550 (La. 1972).

17. Shalini Dore, "3D Pioneer Chris Condon Dies," *Variety*, December 10, 2010; Ray Zone, *3-D Revolution: The History of Modern Stereoscopic Cinema* (Lexington: Univer-sity of Kentucky Press, 2012); and "The Annotated Biography of Chris J. Condon," accessed January 7, 2015, http://3d.hollywoodfilmsinternational.com/CHRIS-CONDON-BIO-v2.html.

18. Louisiana Abatement of Public Nuisances Statute, La. R.S. 13:4711 *et seq.* as cited in Gulf States Theatres, Inc. v. Richardson, 287 So. 2d 480, 551 (La. 1973).

19. *Gulf States Theatres*, 270 So. 2d at 552.

20. *Id.* at 559–560.

21. *Gulf States Theatres*, 287 So. 2d at 484.

22. *Id.* at 487.

23. *Id.* at 496.

24. Alabama Red Light Abatement Act, § 6-5-140 (1975) as cited in Trans-Lux Corp. v. State *ex rel.* Sweeton, 366 So. 2d 710, 713 (Ala. 1979).

25. *Id.* at 714.

26. *Id.* at 714, citing State *ex rel.* Ewing v. "Without a Stitch," 28 Ohio App. 2d 107 (Ohio Ct. App. 1971), *aff'd,* 37 Ohio St. 2d 95 (Ohio 1974), *cert. denied.* The precise statutory language at issue was a ban on "motion pictures." A question arose as to whether the infringement caused by motion pictures should be interpreted as the exhibition of multiple photoplays (e.g., a series of films), or whether motion pictures may be construed as the frames on a filmstrip (such that a single motion picture may be regulated). The Ohio court opted for the latter approach and was affirmed on appeal in state court in *Without a Stitch,* 37 Ohio St. 2d at 97–98, and in federal court in Grove Press, Inc. v. Flask, 326 F. Supp. 574 (N.D. Ohio 1970).

27. Detroit city ordinance no. 742-G § 32.0007 as cited in American Mini Theatres, Inc. v. Gribbs, 518 F.2d 1014, 1015 (6th Cir. 1975).

28. Young v. American Mini Theatres, Inc., 427 U.S. 50, 52 (1976).

29. Nortown Theatre, Inc. v. Gribbs, 373 F. Supp. 363 (E.D. Mich. 1974); and *American Mini Theatres,* 518 F.2d 1014.

30. Entertainment Concepts, Inc., III v. Maciejewski, 631 F.2d 497, 503 (7th Cir. 1980).

31. *American Mini Theatres,* 427 U.S. at 62–63.

32. City of Renton ordinance no. 3626 as cited in City of Renton v. Playtime Theatres, Inc., 475 U.S. 41, 44 (1986).

33. *Id.* at 47.

34. *Id.* at 48.

35. Natco Theatres, Inc. v. Ratner, 463 F. Supp. 1124, 1133 (S.D.N.Y. 1979).

36. *Entertainment Concepts III,* 631 F.2d at 504.

37. Alexander v. City of Minneapolis, 531 F. Supp. 1162 (D. Minn. 1982).

38. 15192 Thirteen Mile Road, Inc. v. City of Warren, 626 F. Supp. 803, 827 (E.D. Mich. 1985).

39. Pringle v. City of Covina, 115 Cal. App. 3d 151, 160 (Cal. Ct. App. 1981).

40. *Id.* at 162.

41. *Id.* at 163.

42. See Albuquerque, New Mexico, Revised Ordinances, ch. 14, art. XVI, § 14-16-1-5(B) (2009, amended 2011).

43. City of Albuquerque v. Pangaea Cinema LLC, 284 P.3d 1090, 1101 (N.M. Ct. App. 2012).

44. Michael Williams, "Pornotopia Festival Zoning Difficulties Good for Families," *Albuquerque Examiner,* October 25, 2010.

45. *Pangaea Cinema,* 284 P.3d at 1105.

46. State v. Pangaea Cinema LLC, 310 P.3d 604 (N.M. 2013), citing Tollis Inc. v. San Bernardino County, 827 F.2d 1329 (9th Cir. 1987), and People v. Superior Court (Lucero), 774 P.2d 769 (Cal. 1989).

47. *Id.* at ¶ 25.

CHAPTER 18
Is Censorship Necessary?

1. Mutual Film Corp. v. Industrial Commission of Ohio, 236 U.S. 230, 244 (1915).

2. Joseph Burstyn, Inc. v. Wilson, 343 U.S. 495, 501–502 (1952).

3. Miller v. California, 413 U.S. 15, 23 (1973).

4. Hamling v. United States, 418 U.S. 87, 105–106 (1974).

5. Ward v. Illinois, 431 U.S. 767, 773–776 (1977).

6. Brockett v. Spokane Arcades, Inc., 472 U.S. 491 (1985); also see Spokane Arcades, Inc. v. Brockett, 631 F.2d 135 (9th Cir. 1980).

7. Pope v. Illinois, 481 U.S. 497, 500–501 (1987).

8. An Act for the Suppression of Trade in, and Circulation of, Obscene Literature and Articles of Immoral Use, 42nd Cong., (March 3, 1873).

9. Harold H. Martin, *Atlanta and Environs: A Chronicle of Its People and Events, 1940s-1970s, Volume III* (Athens: University of Georgia Press, 1987), 411.

10. Rose Bennett, "Censoring Job," *Free Lance-Star*, August 31, 1961.

11. Stanley Frank, "Headaches of a Movie Censor," *Saturday Evening Post*, September 27, 1947, 20.

12. "Rutherford Sheriff Damon Huskey Prepares to Hang Up His Badge," *Times-News*, November 22, 1986.

13. Karen Peterson, "Mary Avara, a Censor Who's Been Censored, Rates the New Freedom in Films PG—Pure Garbage," *People* 15, no. 19 (May 18, 1981); also see Jacques Kelly and Frederick N. Rasmussen, "Film Censor Mary Avara, 90, Dies," *Baltimore Sun*, August 10, 2000; and Rasmussen, "Mary Avara Scrubbed Those Dirty Movies," *Baltimore Sun*, April 12, 2009.

14. State v. Jacobellis, 173 Ohio St. 22, 24 (Ohio 1962).

15. Lordi v. UA New Jersey Theatres, Inc., 108 N.J. Super. 19, 24 (N.J. Super Ct. Ch. Div. 1969). *UA New Jersey Theatres* expands upon Justice Brennan's statement that the effect of an ordinance under review "is to reduce the adult population . . . to reading only what is fit for children." Butler v. Michigan, 352 U.S. 380, 383 (1957).

16. New York v. Ferber, 458 U.S. 747, 763 (1982).

17. Ashcroft v. Free Speech Coalition, 535 U.S. 234, 241 (2002).

18. *Id.* at 247–248.

19. Lawrence Scanlan, *Wild About Horses: Our Timeless Passion for the Horse* (Canada: Random House, 1962); and "8 Troubling Tales of Animal Abuse on Film Shoots," *The Week*, November 19, 2012.

20. David Sarno, "A Marine Apparently Throws a Puppy Off a Cliff, and a Virtual Lynch Mob Forms," *Los Angeles Times*, March 16, 2008; also Mike Mount, "Puppy-Throwing Marine is Removed from Corps," CNN.com, June 13, 2008, http://www.cnn.com/2008/US/06/12/marine.puppy/index.html.

21. United States v. Stevens, 130 S. Ct. 1577, 1583 (2010). For more information see http://www.stopcrush.org/.

22. *Id.* at 1585.

23. *Id.* at 1586.

24. 18 U.S.C. § 48(8)(a).

25. Bill Mears, "Obama Signs Law Banning 'Crush Videos' Depicting Animal Cruelty," CNN.com, December 10, 2010, http://www.cnn.com/2010/Politics/12/10/animal.cruelty/.

26. Public Order Act of 1986 § 18(1).

27. For Australia, see Racial Discrimination Act of 1975; for Canada, see §§ 318, 319, and 320 of the Canadian criminal code; for Denmark, see § 266B of the Danish penal code; in Germany, *Volksverhetzug* is prohibited by § 130 of Germany's criminal code; article 19(2) of the Indian constitution imposes reasonable restrictions on the freedom of speech in the interest of the security of the state, public order, decency, or morality; the Dutch penal code § 137 *et seq.* prohibits both insulting a group and inciting hatred, discrimination, or violence; New Zealand prohibits hate speech under § 61 of the Human Rights Act of 1993; South Africa's constitution specifically excludes hate speech from protections.

28. Michael W. McConnell, "You Can't Say That," *NYT*, June 22, 2012.

29. Aljean Harmetz, *"The Last Temptation of Christ* Opens to Protests but Good Sales," *NYT*, August 12, 1988.

30. "Judge Overturns Ban on Film," *NYT*, September 11, 1988.

31. Laurie Goodstein, "Months Before Debut, Movie on Death of Jesus Causes Stir," *NYT*, August 2, 2003.

32. Garcia v. Google, Inc., No. 12-57302 (9th Cir. 2015) at 7.

CHAPTER 19

The Politics of Profanity

1. Dallas Cowboys Cheerleaders, Inc. v. Pussycat Cinema, Ltd., 604 F.2d 200, 202 (2d Cir. 1979). *Debbie Does Dallas* was subject to a trademark infringement suit. The Second Circuit found that the Dallas Cowboys cheerleaders had a protectable interest in their identifiable outfits. Several years later the Second Circuit considered the film on the issue of obscenity and found that the picture was not patently offensive and therefore not obscene. See United States v. Various Articles of Obscene Merchandise, 709 F.2d 132 (2d Cir. 1983).

2. Jason Zinoman, "Debbie's Doing New York Now, But Rate Her PG," *NYT*, October 27, 2002.

3. *"Debbie Does Dallas* Confiscated," *Lakeland Ledger*, February 8, 1979; "Three Reputed Smut Kings Swept Up," *Reading Eagle*, February 15, 1980; John J. Gersuk, "Authorities Stop Debbie's X-Rated Show," *Palm Beach Post*, April 29, 1982.

4. *Presidential Report of the Commission on Obscenity and Pornography* (Washington, DC: U.S. Government Printing Office, 1970), 55.

5. "Text of Nixon's Statement Rejecting the Report of Obscenity Panel," *NYT*, October 25, 1970.

6. Texas Penal Code Title 9, Offenses Against Public Order and Decency, ch. 43, § 43.23: Obscenity.

7. Berg v. State, 599 S.W.2d 802, 804 (Tex. Crim. App. 1980).

8. *Id.* at 805.

9. Keller v. State, 606 S.W.2d 931, 933 (Tex. Crim. App. 1980).

10. Steven Prince, *A New Pot of Gold: Hollywood Under the Electronic Rainbow, 1980–1989* (Berkeley: University of California Press, 2000), 122–123.

11. United States v. Pryba, 674 F. Supp. 1518 (E.D. Va. 1987); and United States v. Pryba, 678 F. Supp. 1225 (E.D. Va. 1988).

12. "High Court Gets Tough on Obscenity Ruling," *Los Angeles Times*, October 15, 1990.

13. United States v. Pryba, 900 F.2d 748, 752 (4th Cir. 1990).

14. "High Court Gets Tough on Obscenity Ruling," *Los Angeles Times*, October 15, 1990.

15. United States v. Pryba, 498 U.S. 924 (1990).

16. *Pryba*, 900 F.2d at 752.

17. Thomas E. Weber, "As Other Internet Ventures Fail, Sex Sites Are Raking in Millions," *Wall Street Journal*, May 20, 1997.

18. ACLU v. Reno, 929 F. Supp. 824, 843 (E.D. Pa. 1996).

19. *Id.* at 846.

20. Mike McManus, "Clinton Not Living Up to His Pledge to Enforce Federal Obscenity Laws," *Sumter Item*, March 6, 1999; and Bob Peters, "President Clinton's Hardcore Pornography Legacy," Morality in Media, n.d., http://66.210.33.157/mim/full_article.php?article_no=171.

21. Reno v. ACLU, 521 U.S. 844, 861 (1997).

22. *Id.* at 862.

23. *Id.* at 885.

24. United States v. Hilton, 167 F.3d 61 (1st Cir. 1999); United States v. Acheson, 195 F.3d 645 (11th Cir. 1999); United States v. Mento, 231 F.3d 912 (4th Cir.); and United States v. Fox, 248 F.3d 394 (5th Cir. 2000).

25. Free Speech Coalition v. Reno, 198 F.3d 1083, 1086 (9th Cir. 1999).

26. Ashcroft v. Free Speech Coalition, 535 U.S. 234, 256 (2002).

27. *Id.* at 566.

28. *Id.* at 602–603.

29. Ashcroft v. ACLU, 322 F.3d 240 (3d Cir. 2003).

30. Ashcroft v. ACLU, 542 U.S. 656 (2004); also see final ruling in Mukasey v. ACLU, 129 S. Ct. 1032 (2009).

31. Department of Justice press release, "Obscenity Prosecution Task Force Established to Investigate, Prosecute Purveyors of Obscene Materials," May 5, 2005, http://www.justice.gov/archiva/opa/pr/2005/may/05_crm_242.htm.

32. Department of Justice press release, *"Girls Gone Wild* Company sentenced to Pay $1.6 Million in Fines in Sexual Exploitation Case," December 13, 2006, http://www.justice.gov/archive/opa/pr/2006/December/06_crt_831.htm; *"Girls Gone Wild* Producers Fined $2.1 Million," CNN.com, September 12, 2006; and "Meet Joe Francis: Legal Story," http://www.meetjoefrancis.com.

33. Plaintiff B v. Francis, 631 F.3d 1310 (11th Cir. 2011).

34. 18 U.S.C. § 1461, Mailing Obscene or Crime-Inciting Matter.

35. United States v. Extreme Associates, Inc., 352 F. Supp. 2d 578, 586 (W.D. Pa. 2005); Department of Justice press release, "Justice Department to Appeal District Court Ruling Dismissing Charges in the Extreme Associates Case," February 16, 2005, http://www.justice.gov/archive/opa/pr/2005/February/05_crm_066.htm.

36. United States v. Extreme Associates, Inc., 431 F.3d 150, 161 (3d Cir. 2005).

37. Paula Reed Ward, "Porn Producer, Wife Get 1-Year Jail Terms," *Pittsburgh Post-Gazette*, July 2, 2009.

38. United States v. Croce, U.S. District Court, Middle District of Florida (Orlando), plea agreement, June 6, 2007, case no. 6:06-cr-182-Orl-31DAB, http://www.justice.gov/criminal/pr/2007/06-07-07dcroce-plea-agree.pdf. Simoes Croce's *2 Girls 1 Cup* went viral on the web in 2007 and attained a degree of recognition and notoriety uncommon for scat films. Many users posted "reaction films" to YouTube in which unwitting subjects are shown the trailer as the camera focuses on the viewers' faces to record their intense reactions, usually of disgust and disbelief.

39. Department of Justice press release, "Foreign Operator of Obscene Web Sites Pleads Guilty to Obscenity Charges," June 7, 2007, http://www.justice.gov/archive/opa/pr/2006/September/06_crm_599.htm; "Feds Give *Toilet Man 6* Two Hands Up," September 7, 2007, http://www.thesmokinggun.com/documents/crime/feds-give-toilet-man-6-two-hands; and Jeffrey C. Billman, "Filth or Free Speech?," *Orlando Weekly*, September 28, 2006.

40. United States v. Adams, unpublished opinion no. 08-5261 (4th Cir. 2009), http://www.ca4.uscourts.gov/opinions/unpublished/085261.4.pdf; Department of Justice press release, "Federal Grand Jury Charges Indiana Man with Obscenity Violations," May 22, 2008, http://www.justice.gov/archive/opa/pr/2008/May/08-ag-456-html; Department of Justice press release, "Indianapolis Man Sentenced for Obscenity Violations," December 12, 2008, http://www.justice.gov/archive/opa/pr/2008/December/08-ag-1097.html; Adams v. State, 804 N.E.2d 1169 (Ind. Ct. App. 2004).

41. The Obscenity Task Force did suffer some setbacks after indicting Five Star Video in June 2006 in an Arizona district court for several films, including *Gag Factor 15*, *American Bukkake 13*, and *Filthy Things 6*, but charges were dropped by October 2007. See Department of Justice press release, "Federal Grand Jury Charges Arizona and California Companies and Their Owners With Obscenity Violations," June 1, 2006, http://www.justice.gov/archive/opa/pr/2006/June/06_crm_343.html.

42. Susannah Breslin, "Adult Director Max Hardcore Released from Prison," *Forbes*, September 21, 2011, http://www.forbes.com/sites/susannahbreslin/2011/07/21/adult-director-max-hardcore-released-from-prison-2/.

43. Robert D. Richards and Clay Calvert, "The 2008 Federal Obscenity Conviction of Paul Little and What It Reveals About Obscenity Law and Prosecutions," *Vanderbilt Journal of Entertainment and Technology Law* 11, no. 3 (2009): 583; Kevin Graham, "Jurors in Tampa to Decide; What is Obscene?," *Tampa Bay Times*, May 27, 2008.

44. United States v. Little, case no. 8-07-cr-170-T-24 MSS (M.D. Fla. 2008).

45. Department of Justice press release, "Producer Paul Little Indicted on Obscenity Charges," May 31, 2007.

46. Kevin Graham, "Juror Asks to View Less Porn in Court," *Tampa Bay Times*, May 29, 2008. Jurors still viewed a substantial amount of pornography: "8½ hours of extreme pornography [played] on a giant screen in court. At times, [the jurors] winced as an adult film producer who calls himself Max Hardcore performed in scenes that included urinating, vomiting and violently dominating women." Kevin Graham, "Jurors Convict Adult Film Producer," *Tampa Bay Times*, June 5, 2008.

47. United States v. Kilbride, 584 F.3d 1240 (9th Cir. 2009), citing Justice Breyer's concurring opinion in Ashcroft v. ACLU, 535 U.S. at 590.

48. United States v. Little, 365 Fed. App'x 159 (11th Cir. 2010).

49. Department of Justice press release, "Federal Grand Jury Charges Florida Man with Obscenity Violations," September 16, 2008, http://www.justice.gov/criminal/pr/2008/09/09-16-08.

50. Josh Gerstein, "Porn Prosecution Fuels Debate," *Politico*, July 31, 2009, http://www.politico.com/news/stories/0709/25622.html.

51. Richard Bowitz, "Obscenity Undefined," *Las Vegas Weekly*, July 14, 2008; Robert D. Richards and Clay Calvert, "The 2008 Federal Obscenity Conviction of Paul Little," *Vanderbilt Journal of Entertainment and Technology Law* 11, no. 3 (2009).

52. Indictment, United States v. Stagliano, no. 08-093 (D.D.C. 2008); "John Stagliano, Evil Angel Indicted on Federal Obscenity Charges," *AVN*, April 8, 2008, http://business.avn.com/articles/video/John-Stagliano-Evil-Angel-Indicted-on-Federal-Obscenity-Charges-52034.html; United States v. Stagliano, 693 F. Supp. 2d 25 (D.D.C. 2010); United States v. Stagliano, 729 F. Supp. 2d 215 (D.D.C. 2010).

53. Spencer S. Hsu, "U.S. District Judge Drops Porn Charges Against Video Producer John A. Stagliano," *Washington Post*, July 17, 2010.

54. Ashby Jones, "Stagliano,'" *Wall Street Journal* Law Blog, July 19, 2010, http://blogs.wsj.com/law/2010/07/19/stagliano-dismissal-of-obscenity-case-bad-for-my-autobiography/.

55. Excluding child pornography prosecutions.

56. Steven Mikulan, "Shit Happened," *LA Weekly*, June 10, 2008.

57. Megan Griffo, "Ira Isaacs, Defecation Porn Shock Artist, Sentenced 4 Years In Prison," *Huffington Post*, January 17, 2013, http://www.huffingtonpost.com/2013

/01/17/ira-issacs-defecation-por_n_2495505.html; Dennis Romero, "Ira Isaacs," *LA Weekly*, January 16, 2013; "Adult Film Producer Convicted in Obscenity Trial," *Daily News*, April 27, 2012; and Department of Justice press release, "Ira Isaacs Sentenced to 48 Months in Prison in Los Angeles Adult Obscenity Case," January 16, 2013. Isaacs also commented on the irony of his conviction: while *Hollywood Scat Amateur* 7 used simulated feces, his other productions employed authentic feces. See Steven Mikulan, "Shit Happened," *LA Weekly*, June 10, 2008.

58. Josh Gerstein, "Eric Holder Accused of Neglecting Porn Fight," *Politico*, April 16, 2011, http://www.politico.com/news/stories/0411/53314.html; and Josh Gerstein, "X-Rated Video Maker Gets 4-year Prison Term," *Politico*, January 17, 2013, http://www.politico.com/blogs/under-the-radar/2013/01/xrated-video-maker-gets-year-prison-term-154463.html.

CONCLUSION

1. Joseph Burstyn, Inc. v. Wilson, 343 U.S. 495, 518 (1952).
2. Bosley Crowther, "*The Miracle* Happens," *NYT*, June 1, 1952.
3. Kingsley International Pictures Corp. v. Blanc, 396 Pa. 448, 472 (1959).

SELECTED BIBLIOGRAPHY

Balio, Tino. *Grand Design: Hollywood as a Modern Business Enterprise, 1930–1939.* Berkeley: University of California Press, 1996.

Bowser, Eileen. *The Transformation of Cinema, 1907–1915.* Berkeley: University of California Press, 1994.

Butters, Gerald R. *Banned in Kansas: Motion Picture Censorship, 1915–1966.* Columbia: University of Missouri Press, 2007.

Cook, David A. *Lost Illusions: American Cinema in the Shadow of Watergate and Vietnam, 1970–1979.* Berkeley: University of California Press, 2002.

Crafton, Donald. *The Talkies: American Cinema's Transition to Sound, 1926–1931.* Berkeley: University of California Press, 1999.

Doherty, Thomas. *Joseph I. Breen and the Production Code Administration.* New York: Columbia University Press, 2009.

Herbert, Stephen, and Luke McKernan, eds. *Who's Who of Victorian Cinema: A Worldwide Survey.* London: British Film Institute, 1996.

Jowett, Garth S. "'A Capacity for Evil': The 1915 Supreme Court *Mutual* Decision." In *Controlling Hollywood: Censorship and Regulation in the Studio Era,* ed. Matthew Bernstein, 16–41. London: Athlone, 1999.

Koszarski, Richard. *An Evening's Entertainment: The Age of the Silent Feature Picture, 1915–1928.* Berkeley: University of California Press, 1994.

Leff, Leonard J., and Jerold L. Simmons. *The Dame in the Kimono: Hollywood, Censorship, and the Production Code.* Lexington: University Press of Kentucky, 2001.

Lev, Peter. *The Fifties: Transforming the Screen, 1950–1959.* Berkeley: University of California Press, 2006.

Lewis, Jon. *Hollywood v. Hard Core: How the Struggle over Censorship Saved the Modern Film Industry.* New York: New York University Press, 2000.

Miller, Frank. *Censoring Hollywood: Sex, Sin, and Violence on Screen.* New York: Turner, 1994.

Musser, Charles. *Edison Motion Pictures, 1890–1900: An Annotated Filmography.* Washington, DC: Smithsonian Institution Press, 1997.

———. *The Emergence of Cinema: The American Screen to 1907.* Berkeley: University of California Press, 1994.

Oberholtzer, Ellis Paxson. *The Morals of the Movies.* Philadelphia: Penn Publishing, 1922.

Orbach, Barak Y. "Prizefighting and the Birth of Movie Censorship." *Yale Journal of Law and the Humanities* 21 (October 2009): 251–304.

Phillips, Kendall R. *Controversial Cinema: The Films That Outraged America.* Westport, CT: Praeger, 2008.

Prince, Stephen. *A New Pot of Gold: Hollywood under the Electronic Rainbow, 1980–1989.* Berkeley: University of California Press, 2002.

Ramsaye, Terry. *A Million and One Nights: A History of the Motion Picture.* New York: Simon and Schuster, 1926.

Schaefer, Eric. *"Bold! Daring! Shocking! True!": A History of Exploitation Films, 1919–1959.* Durham, NC: Duke University Press, 1999.

Slide, Anthony. *The Big V: A History of the Vitagraph Company.* Lanham, MD: Scarecrow, 1978.

———. *Robert Goldstein and "The Spirit of '76."* New York: Scarecrow, 1993.

Walsh, Frank. *Sin and Censorship: The Catholic Church and the Motion Picture Industry.* New Haven, CT: Yale University Press, 1996.

Wertheimer, John. "The Mutual Film Reviewed: The Movies, Censorship and Free Speech in Progressive America." *American Journal of Legal History* 37, no. 2 (April 1993): 158–189.

Wittern-Keller, Laura. *Freedom of the Screen: Legal Challenges to State Film Censorship, 1915–1981.* Lexington: University Press of Kentucky, 2008.

INDEX

15192 Thirteen Mile Road, Inc. v. Warren (1985), 285–286
Opening of Misty Beethoven, The, 281
Ordeal, The, 57, 58
Orito, United States v. (1973), 252, 253, 254
Otsep, Fyodor, 102
Outlaw, The, 117–120, 121, 122, 134, 148, 297

Pace that Kills, The, 111, 113
Pacifica Foundation, FCC v. (1978), 203–205, 207–208, 209, 308
Pangaea Cinema, Albuquerque v. (2012), 287, 289
Paramount Film Distributing Corp. v. Chicago (1959), 163–164
Paramount Pictures, 40, 67, 84, 160, 164
Paramount Pictures, Inc., United States v. (1948), 120, 135
Paris Adult Theatre I v. Slaton (1973), 252, 253, 254, 255
Parmelee v. United States (1940), 153
Parrish, Larry, 265–266, 267, 268
Pathé, 11, 19, 26, 40, 51–53
Pathé Exchange v. Cobb (1922), 51–53, 135
PCA. *See* Production Code Administration (PCA)
Pennekamp v. Florida (1946), 122
Pennsylvania, 34–35, 36, 47–50, 87–88, 100, 164–170, 183, 296
Penthouse Intern v. McAuliffe (1983), 349n86
People's Institute, 28–29
Peraino, Louis "Butchie," 257, 260, 271
Persson, Essy, 240, 241
Pickford, Mary, 76, 77–78
Pinky, 125–126, 127, 130, 139, 140
Pirou, Eugène, 10–11
Plan 9 from Outer Space, 191, 235
Playtime Theatres, Inc., Renton v. (1986), 284, 286, 289, 308
political speech, 65, 74–76, 90, 106, 120
Poole, Wakefield, 250, 251
Pope v. Illinois (1987), 296

pornography, 232, 243–244, 274, 310, 312, 355n38; child, 297–298, 299; cyber, 306–307; early, 10–12, 38–39; and federal government, 255–256, 271, 305–306, 315; hardcore, 239, 244, 249, 251, 264, 271, 281, 312, 317; and home video, 264–265, 272, 303–305, 349n65; and mainstream audiences, 249–250, 256, 268, 272, 303, 305, 317; and porno chic, 257, 264, 270, 281, 284, 303, 304, 317; possession of, 243, 247, 253, 254, 264, 310
Poverty Row, 111, 160, 164
Powell, Lewis F., 252, 284
Preminger, Otto, 150, 151, 152, 153, 178, 189, 210
Pringle v. Covina (1981), 287
prior restraint, 92, 150, 172, 186, 193, 283, 306
prizefighting, 12–18, 24, 36, 321n22
production code. *See* self-regulation
Production Code Administration (PCA), 80, 95–97, 114, 117–119, 122–123, 152, 178, 201, 294
profanity, 201–209, 308
Pruning the Movies, 25
Pryba, United States v. (1990), 306
Purity, 65, 66

Quigley, Martin, 93, 94, 96

Rabe v. Washington (1972), 194–196, 197
Ramrodder, The, 190, 192
ratings, 205–206, 208–209, 248, 286
RD-DR Corp. v. Smith (1950), 124–125, 135
Reagan, Ronald, 305, 307
Redrup v. New York (1967), 247, 253, 264, 265
Reed, Stanley Forman, 140
Reems, Harry, 257, 260, 266, 267, 268, 270
Rehnquist, William, 252, 277, 284, 295
Remous, 100–101, 103, 131
Renoir, Jean, 101, 129, 131, 161
Reno v. ACLU (1997), 307–308, 309, 312

Revenge at Daybreak, 185–186
Rhode Island, 54, 172
Rice, John C., 7, 8, 316, 320n1
RKO Pictures, 50–51, 53, 96, 123, 148
Roach, Hal, 110, 126, 128
Roaden v. Kentucky (1973), 194, 196–197
Road to Ruin, The, 83
Roberts, John G., 299
Rossellini, Roberto, 131, 132, 139, 140, 147, 294
Rosset, Barney, 174, 225, 227, 230, 232
Roth-Memoirs obscenity test, 228–229, 233–236, 239, 241, 248, 254, 268
Roth v. United States (1957), 160–161, 174–175, 177, 179, 184, 203, 212–213, 216–217, 219
Russell, Jane, 117–118, 119, 122, 147, 148

sacrilege, 135, 139–140, 147, 152, 172, 277
Sanford, Edward Terry, 91–92
Sanger, Margaret, 71–72, 73, 74, 76
Saturn Film Company, 37, 38
Scalia, Antonin, 207, 208
Scarlet Street, 123
Schenck v. United States (1919), 90–91, 92
self-regulation, 9, 54–55, 77–80, 93–96, 100, 177, 201–203, 242, 294; and film ratings, 205–206, 208–209. *See also* Production Code Administration
Selig Polyscope Company, 18, 31, 40
Sennett, Mack, 42, 43
Seventh Commandment, The, 111, 112
Sex Lure, The, 70–71
"*She Shoulda Said 'No'!,*" 159, 164–166
Shientag, Bernard Lloyd, 120, 122
Shientag, Florence Perlow, 144–145
Shurlock, Geoffrey, 177
Simoes Croce, Danilo, 310, 311, 355n38
Sinderella, 273–274
Sjöman, Vilgot, 222, 223, 224, 225, 235
Sloviter, Dolores Korman, 307
Smell of Honey, A Swallow of Brine, A, 194, 195

Smith, Charles Sprague, 28, 29
Smith, Christine, 124, 126, 130, 296–297
Smith, D. Brooks, 310
social issues films, 56, 71–76, 97, 123–126, 128–130, 153
Some Like it Hot, 178, 210
Son of Sinbad, 147, 148, 149
sound technology, 50, 51, 86–89, 104
Spanish Earth, The, 183
Spellman, Francis, 132, 134
Spelvin, Georgina, 270
Spirit of '76, The, 59, 61–65, 90
Spokane Arcades, Inc., Brockett v. (1985), 295–296
Spy, The, 58
Stagliano, John, 313, 314
Stanley v. Georgia (1969), 247, 253, 254, 255, 264, 265
St. Cyr, Lili, 148
Stevens, John Paul, 204, 283, 284, 308
Stevens, United States v. (2010), 299–300
Stewardesses, The, 278–279, 280, 281
Stewart, Potter, 173, 201, 217, 234, 252
Stranger Knocks, A, 187–188, 189, 213, 214, 218
Studio Relations Committee, 79, 80, 93, 94, 95
Sturman, Reuben, 246, 249, 257
Summers, Frank W., 279, 280, 281
Superior Films, Inc. v. Department of Education (1954), 144, 146, 147, 277
Supervixens, 253, 255
Supreme Court. *See specific cases and justices*
Syskonbädd 1782, 224–225

Tariff Act of 1930, 100, 227, 274
Taylor, Elizabeth, 203, 241–242, 250
Teitel Film Corp. v. Cusack (1968), 189, 190, 191
television, 53, 181, 206–208
10 Days in a Nudist Camp, 83, 175
Texas, 126, 130, 261, 265, 304–305